A Scholar's Odyssey

A Scholar's Odyssey

FERENC A. VÁLI

Edited by KARL W. RYAVEC

Iowa State University Press / Ames

© 1990 Iowa State University Press, Ames, Iowa 50010
All rights reserved
Manufactured in the United States of America
⊗ This book is printed on acid-free paper.

First edition, 1990

Library of Congress Cataloging-in-Publication Data

Váli, Ferenc A. (Ferenc Albert), 1905–1984
    A scholar's odyssey / Ferenc A. Váli : edited by Karl W. Ryavec. – 1st ed.
    p. cm.
    Bibliography: p.
    Includes index.
    ISBN 0–8138–1533–9
    1. Váli, Ferenc A. (Ferenc Albert), 1905–1984. 2. World War, 1939–1945–Hungary. 3. Hungary–Officials and employees–Bibliography. 4. Scholars–United States–Biography. I. Ryavec, Karl W. II. Title.
DB950.V35 1990
943.905′2′092–dc20
[B]   89–15339

CONTENTS

FOREWORD

These memoirs by a decent Central European whose life spanned both the age of decency and then of tyranny enrich our understanding of a region which most Americans know little and which is geopolitically of vital importance.

Ferenc Váli was a great humanist, an impressive scholar, and a very good human being.

Zbigniew Brzezinski

EDITOR'S PREFACE

THE details surrounding the origins of this book are not known to me. I learned from Ferenc Váli shortly before his death in 1984 that he had written his memoirs, and he requested that I see the work published. I felt honored by this request and agreed readily.

Ferenc Váli survived war, a wrenching change in Hungarian society, brutal interrogation, bleak imprisonment, revolution and its failure, and having to leave his homeland and begin a new profession in a different country. He was one of the persons who has truly impressed me. I admired him for his powerful intellect, his deep knowledge of history and politics, and also his warm personality and helpful manner, qualities undiminished by his difficult experiences under Communism. As a senior colleague in Soviet and East European studies at the University of Massachusetts at Amherst, he and I had many discussions over the years from which I learned a great deal about Central Europe and international politics.

These memoirs will be of particular interest to scholars of the Second World War, students of the politics and history of East Central Europe, particularly Hungary, and to those interested in the early phases of Communist rule.

I am deeply grateful for the kind assistance and encouragement of Rose Váli in preparing these memoirs for publication. We at the University of Massachusetts are also grateful to her for her generous bequest in Ferenc's memory to facilitate graduate studies in political science.

I am particularly appreciative of the meticulous copyediting of Richard C. Miller, the impressive help given me in clarifying several points by Joyce Merriam, Richard Teller, Larry Feldman, and other librarians of the University of Massachusetts, and the friendly assistance of Director Richard R. Kinney and Managing Editor Bill Silag of Iowa State University Press. I appreciate, too, the helpful assistance of Meg Worcester and Doris Holden in preparing the final manuscript.

Amherst, Massachusetts   KARL W. RYAVEC
August 1988

INTRODUCTION

BY the middle of 1975 I had completed writing a manuscript on the politics of the Indian Ocean region and thus had concluded a project that had kept me busy for several years. At about that time I reached the age for mandatory retirement from my university. All this impressed me as an end to one cycle and the stimulus for a new beginning.

For years my wife and some close friends who knew about my antecedents had encouraged me to write an autobiography. I had hesitated and procrastinated because I preferred to give priority to my various research projects. But now, with a new and last chapter of my life opening, I decided, in the words of Benjamin Franklin, to do "the next thing most like living one's life again," namely, to prepare a personal account of my life.

This memoir is intended to be both a documentary of our times and a contribution to contemporary history. I hope my readers will meet me as I attempt to show myself—in all sincerity. I hope too that my words at the very least vindicate Henryk Sienkiewicz when he wrote: "A man who leaves memoirs, whether well or badly written, provided they be sincere, renders a service to future psychologists and writers."

My readers will note that I never held a top job in government service, although I was given a number of highly delicate and responsible assignments. Yet my story may be a top story—more interesting, more venturesome and dramatic, more characteristic of our epoch than the life stories of many top personages.

My endeavor to provide a truthful account compelled me to present what I believe to be accurate descriptions and characterizations of the persons who play a role in this book. I regret if thereby I had to step on some toes or hurt some sensibilities. Without my proceeding in a candid manner, my narrative would have been historically slanted or insincere.

There are no fictional characters in this story and, with few exceptions, all names are genuine. Again, the story would cease to be documentary and historical without such a procedure. I did use initials or change the initials of various nonhistorical personages in a few instances, but only in order to protect their safety or privacy.

The rise and fall of my fortunes convinced me of the essential transitoriness of human existence. Whether on top of the wave or deep underneath, I never doubted that there would be change — for the better or for the worse. Somehow I always felt that things were the best they could be under the circumstances. Still, I am not a fatalist; I believe that one's success depends on — in addition to good fortune, health, and providence — one's diligence, perseverance, and talent.

If you would not be forgotten,
As soon as you are dead and rotten,
Either write things worth reading,
Or do things worth the writing.

Benjamin Franklin

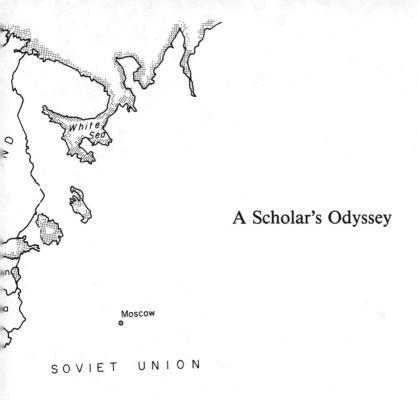

A Scholar's Odyssey

I

Mission to Turkey

The whole history of the world is summed up in the fact that
when nations are strong they are not always just, and when
they wish to be just they are often no longer strong.

Winston Churchill

JOURNEY TO ISTANBUL

The train was rattling noisily and for a long time I was unable to fall
asleep. I was lying in a compartment of Mitropa, the German sleeping
car company, which even in the midst of World War II was running cars
between Berlin and Sofia. The date was February 10, 1943.

After the hectic weeks that preceded my departure from Budapest,
this was the first time I felt relaxed enough to think over the significance
of my journey and of the task that lay ahead. I recalled that this was a
trip I had almost undertaken two years before—a trip I had to give up
almost at the last minute. In December 1940, before Hungary became
involved in the war, I had been one of those designated to go to Great
Britain or the United States on a confidential diplomatic assignment.

As I lay half-asleep I remembered how in the fall of 1940 I met
Count Paul Teleki, the prime minister of Hungary. It was a few months
after the collapse of France. In a few cautious words he expressed his
fear that, Germany being paramount on the Continent, Hungary was
likely to be pressed into the war. France's defeat had upset the balance,
and now Nazi Germany had an almost free hand in southeast Europe.
Hungary was being squeezed between the German and Soviet giants. Not

unlike Czechoslovakia in World War I, Hungary should have had a skeleton government in the Anglo-Saxon countries, which could be recognized as her legitimate representative should she become a victim of Nazi domination. Teleki, who had known me from the Boy Scout movement (he was a chief scout of Hungary) and as a young man with good English contacts, invited me to get in touch with Domokos Szent-Iványi, head of the information section in the prime ministry, a cover name for the agency that dealt with Teleki's Grand Design, to reestablish Hungarian independence with British support.

Thereafter, I became a frequent visitor to the small baroque palace in the Castle district of Buda, where Szent-Iványi had his office. I was instructed to prepare for my top secret trip. Since all countries west of Hungary were controlled by the Germans, the route to reach Britain and America led across the Balkans to Greece or Turkey, thence to Egypt, and from there across the Mediterranean to the Atlantic.

At the end of 1940 and during the first half of 1941 the British Legation still operated in Budapest, as did that of the United States. Hungary was still neutral although under much pressure from Germany. At the British mission I was soon introduced to Basil Davidson, officially a correspondent for Reuters; he handled confidential contacts on behalf of the British and especially those with anti-Nazi circles in Hungary. He was also in touch with the Szent-Iványi agency and, when he heard of my assignment, promised his help and encouraged me to accept it.

Teleki's Grand Design was to be implemented gradually. I was told to be ready but the date of my departure was to be set later. However, black clouds began to gather in southeast Europe. When visiting the Hungarian parts of Transylvania on a lecture tour, I saw trainloads of German soldiers on their way to Rumania. How was I going to reach my destination when the door across the Balkans was closed? The crisis in Yugoslavia burst by late March 1941. The pro-German cabinet was overthrown by a military coup and General Simović became prime minister. Hitler's reaction was to be swift.

I urged Szent-Iványi to let me go but he could not get the green light from Teleki. It was at that time that Tibor Eckhardt, leader of the opposition Smallholder party, left for the United States. He was part of the Grand Design.

In the early morning hours of April 3 I was telephoned and told that Prime Minister Teleki had committed suicide the night before. He had opposed allowing passage through Hungary to German troops on their way to attack Yugoslavia; since resistance was impossible (the chief of the General Staff already had arranged matters with the Germans), he thus wished to clear his name before history.[1]

Later that day all of Budapest witnessed German motorized columns passing along the embankment of the Danube from north to south. I saw Szent-Iványi but he no longer felt authorized to act without consulting the next prime minister.

Two days later Basil Davidson came to my apartment. "I am leaving. Taking the night train to Belgrade. This is probably the last train. Are you ready to join me? Others will also join now or in a day or so." He mentioned a few names, among them that of György Páloczi-Horváth, a well-known leftist journalist.

I was very tempted to go. But it looked unlikely, with Teleki's death, that I would obtain a military exit permit (required since the beginning of the war). I was also determined not to leave without official authorization. As long as Hungary was not "taken over" by Hitler, as long as our top people sympathized and even cooperated within the limits of reason with the West, I felt reluctant to become a free-lance political agent, one totally dependent on the British or some other power. I had not given up hope of embarking on my mission in a legal manner.

Basil informed me that his new assignment was centered in Istanbul, Turkey. We agreed to remain in contact; I gave him the name of a friend in Istanbul who could pass information. He left, and I did not see him again until sixteen years later in London.

In the early morning hours of April 6, 1941, the Germans bombed Belgrade, invaded Yugoslavia from all sides, and attacked Greece. Within a few weeks both countries were defeated and their territory occupied by the Nazi forces. For some time I entertained the fear that Turkey's turn would be next. But by May it was an open secret in diplomatic circles in Budapest that Hitler's army was concentrating along the extensive Soviet border between the Baltic and the Black seas.

László Bárdossy succeeded Teleki as prime minister, and Szent-Iványi was transferred back into the Ministry of Foreign Affairs. I had known Bárdossy since the early 1930s when he occupied the post of counselor at the Hungarian Legation in London and I was a graduate

---

1. Stephen D. Kertesz, *Between Russia and the West: Hungary and the Illusions of Peacemaking, 1945–1947* (Notre Dame, Ind.: University of Notre Dame Press, 1984), pp. 110–1.

student in England on a state scholarship. I asked Szent-Iványi whether I should not raise the question of my departure with Bárdossy himself, but he strongly discouraged me from doing so. When I had known him previously, he was definitely an Anglophile, but now he was diametrically opposed to any anti- German move.

I was spending my weekend at Lake Balaton when on Sunday morning, June 21, the radio announced the German invasion of the Soviet Union. Bárdossy was induced to declare war on Moscow. The British diplomatic and consular missions already had left Budapest after the attack on Yugoslavia, in which Hungary participated to recover territory lost at the end of World War I. Now London presented an ultimatum and, having received no satisfactory answer, declared war on Hungary.

In December 1941, following the German declaration of war on the United States after Pearl Harbor, Hungary foolishly followed suit. Budapest wit then invented the following scene between President Roosevelt and Secretary of State Cordell Hull:

> HULL: I am sorry to announce, Mr. President, that Hungary has declared war on us.
> ROOSEVELT: Hungary? What kind of country is it?
> HULL: It is a kingdom.
> ROOSEVELT: Who is the king?
> HULL: They have no king.
> ROOSEVELT: A kingdom without a king! Who is the head of state?
> HULL: Admiral Horthy.
> ROOSEVELT: Admiral? Now, after Pearl Harbor, we have another navy on our neck!
> HULL: No, Mr. President. Hungary has no navy, not even a seacoast.
> ROOSEVELT: Strange! What do they want from us? Territorial claims, perhaps?
> HULL: No, sir. They want territory from Rumania.
> ROOSEVELT: Did they declare war also on Rumania?
> HULL: No, Mr. President. Rumania is their ally.*

* * *

---

*A shorter, later version of this story appears in *The Ciano Diaries* for May 11, 1942, as a "little story which is going the rounds at Budapest." See *The Ciano Diaries,* ed. Hugh Gibson (Garden City, N.Y.: Doubleday, 1946), 484. —ED.

I was awakened when the train stopped at the frontier station, on the border of the Nazi-created Independent State of Croatia. I overheard the discussion of the Hungarian customs and passport officers with the German sleeping-car conductor, who showed the travel documents of his passengers to the officials. The main topic seemed to be the passenger in the neighboring compartment who carried fifty thousand dollars, duly registered in his passport. Finally, the customs officer said, "I am going to see these fifty thousand dollars. I have never seen so much money in my life."

The officials did not care to see me, and soon the train moved on and we entered Croatia. I fell asleep again. It was already daylight when I woke up and looked out between the window curtains. The train proceeded slowly and had just passed a provincial station; at the other end of the station three men were hanging from a tree—evidently partisans executed in the murderous feuding between Croatians and Serbs. At about noontime the train, moving cautiously, crossed the bridge over the Sava River and entered the ruins of the Belgrade station. We were told that this would be a stop of several hours.

Before arriving in the Yugoslav capital, I had opened the door of my compartment and asked the conductor for some coffee. My neighbor, the person with the fifty thousand dollars, walked up and down the corridor. He was a tall young man with an Oriental appearance: dark skin, strong aquiline nose, and gracious movements. We soon entered into conversation in German, the lingua franca on the train; he told me that he came from Berlin and was on his way to Istanbul. He gave his name as Melek Manzur Quashquai, and mentioned that he was Iranian. I was surprised. "Wasn't Iran compelled to declare war on Germany when occupied by the British and the Russians?" He smiled enigmatically. "Oh, the Germans have nothing against me; on the contrary."

To get a meal, we went to the Kommandatura, the German military command, for ration coupons. Quashquai and I climbed up the Kalemegdan, Belgrade's castle hill. The city was in a desperate state—it seemed every house was either damaged or destroyed and hardly anybody was in the streets. We were given coupons and directed to a restaurant filled with German military and civilian personnel.

The journey to Sofia was uneventful, although I had been warned that railroads were frequently blown up at night. I had earlier arranged to spend two days in the Bulgarian capital before proceeding to Turkey. My new acquaintance, Mr. Quashquai, continued his journey and I was to meet him again in Istanbul. Professor Géza Fehér, the Hungarian cultural attaché, waited on the platform for me and took me to the hotel Bulgarie.

The purpose of my stopover in Sofia was to obtain some preliminary information concerning neighboring Turkey and the circumstances under which I would operate in Istanbul. I had known Fehér and also knew that he was frequently a visitor to Turkey. He was an orientalist who had written on the Turkic origin of the Bulgarians. He had also conducted excavations and discovered the gigantic relief of Krum Khan, a ninth-century leader of the Turks, hewn in stone in the Balkan Mountains. This had made him something of a nationally renowned scholar.

During my conversations with Fehér I was careful not to reveal the main purpose of my journey (his talkative nature was well known to me). I told him the official reason, namely, that I had been invited to lecture at Istanbul University. He was aggressively hostile to Nazi Germany and bitterly complained of the German domination of all Bulgarian matters. He provided valuable information on the life of the cosmopolitan and diplomatic elite in Istanbul and Ankara, pointing out among other things the attitudes of the Hungarian diplomatic personnel in the legation in Ankara and the consulate general in Istanbul. He was a great talker and for hours he gossiped, told anecdotes, and provided useful details that prevented me from making major faux pas in my delicate assignment.

Fehér also informed me that the Park Hotel in Istanbul was frequented mainly by German and other Axis visitors, whereas the Pera Palace was used by British and other Allied nationals. Therefore, I decided to stay in the old Tokatliyan Hotel, which was neutral and located on the crowded Istiklal Caddesi, the main street in the Pera district.

I left Sofia on the evening of February 13, 1943, traveling again in a sleeping car. Because of the wartime conditions, the journey from Sofia to Istanbul, which ordinarily took one day, now required two nights. The first night was spent traveling from the Bulgarian capital to the frontier. Lying in my berth as I approached my destination, Turkey, I instinctively recalled further antecedents of my journey.

During Bárdossy's premiership, Teleki's Grand Design remained dormant. The prime minister seemed convinced that, Hungary being squeezed between the Germans and the Russians, he had to choose between two evils—Nazi and Soviet domination. His preference was the

former. He considered British or American influence geographically unrealistic; these forces were too distant to be able to save Hungary;
further, he believed that neither London nor Washington would be willing to assist Hungary, which they had allowed to be dismembered after
World War I.

In March 1942, however, Bárdossy was replaced by Miklos Kállay.
The new prime minister, a longtime politician, was no expert on foreign
policy. However, unlike Bárdossy, he was ready to listen to the Western-
oriented political elite, including leading officials of the Hungarian Foreign Ministry, who were all convinced that eventually Hitler would be
defeated. But because of German proximity, the participation of the
Hungarian army in the campaign against Russia, and the manifold and
intensive contacts that developed between Hungarian and German
authorities, especially those of the military, he knew that he had to
proceed with the utmost caution. Many Hungarian leaders and members
of the officers corps were Germanophiles and were much impressed by
the achievements of the Nazi war machine. And there were Nazi-inspired
and Nazi-supported elements such as the Arrow Cross and other
Hungarian fascists.

After the dissolution of Teleki's Information Section, the delicate
questions of Western orientation and contacts were handled by the Press
and Information Section of the Ministry of Foreign Affairs and its ambitious head, Antal Ullein-Reviczky. I never had close relations with him,
but through a friend, György Baross, the editor of the journal *Hungarian Foreign Affairs,* I managed to establish contact. In the summer of
1942 Ullein-Reviczky, who must have been familiar with the Teleki project, let me know that my mission would be considered in due time; it was
yet premature.

The decision to approach the Western powers was prompted by the
landing of American and British forces in North Africa in November
1942 and also by the impending German disaster at Stalingrad. In December 1942 word came from Ullein-Reviczky that Prime Minister Kállay had agreed to my mission.

During the preceding one and a half years, I had renewed my personal contacts with the British in Istanbul through the intermediary Professor Andreas Schwarz. A well-known scholar of Roman law born in
Hungary and a professor in German universities, he had had to leave
Germany after Hitler's takeover and had accepted an invitation to join

the newly expanded Istanbul University. Turkey's man of genius, Kemal Atatürk, attracted many refugee scholars, who helped to strengthen his country's system of higher education.

Cemil Bilsel, the rector of Istanbul University and a professor of international law, happened to be another acquaintance of mine. We met in Copenhagen in 1938 at a conference of the League of Nations Union. We sat side by side on a committee dealing with questions of international law, and I think he liked the presentation I made. For the next five days we frequently exchanged ideas and remained in correspondence thereafter. Upon my request, he sent me an invitation to come and deliver a series of lectures at his university.

I went to see Ullein-Reviczky in his office on Christmas Eve, 1942. He instructed me to depart as a scholar to lecture in Turkey; I would be traveling on an ordinary passport and was to obtain my travel papers without attracting undue attention. He would see to it that the military exit permit would be issued. While talking to me, he was tense; a radio was set at high volume. Evidently, he was not certain whether his office was bugged.

In January 1943 I went through the intricate formalities of obtaining my passport and other permits, among them a visa for Turkey, a neutral country. Ullein-Reviczky promised to send a *note verbale* to the Turkish Legation; I was to talk to the minister and to nobody else. I called on Ruşen Eşref Ünaydin, a poet and diplomat, in the palace of the Turkish Legation, which after March 1944 was to provide asylum for Hungarian prime minister Kállay. The Turkish envoy was tactful enough not to ask about the purpose of my visit (he must have been told by Ullein-Reviczky) and, after a courteous conversation, gave orders to issue the visa.

On February 8 I saw the press chief for the last time. The radio was playing again, perhaps even louder. Almost whispering, Ullein-Reviczky made me memorize a message to be passed on to the British and American governments through their representatives in Turkey. I still remember the five points:

1. The Hungarian government does not wish to fight British or American forces.

2. The Hungarian government does not, in fact, consider itself to be at war with these governments because Hungary should be regarded as under German constraint.

3. When British or American forces reach the territory of Hungary, the Hungarian government does not intend to put up any resistance against them.

4. Moreover, the Hungarian government hereby directly invites the British and American governments to dispatch their forces into Hungary.

5. The Hungarian government asks these Allied governments for information of what should be done in order to implement the previously mentioned plans.

Upon my question, Ullein-Reviczky emphasized that this message came from Prime Minister Kállay directly.

I memorized the message again and again. It was somewhat unusual that the Hungarian government felt it desirable to entrust such an offer to be forwarded by an individual with no formal authorization. Hungarian diplomatic missions existed in such neutral countries as Sweden, Switzerland, and Portugal (not to speak of Turkey) side by side with Allied diplomatic representatives. Why were these channels of communication not used to pass on the message? Subsequently, I realized that Kállay wanted to use intermediaries whose actions could be easily repudiated. Upon the advice of the Foreign Ministry staff, he may have thought that contacts by Hungarian diplomats could be more easily detected by the German espionage system in view of their infiltration of Hungarian civilian and military circles.

And why did the choice fall on Turkey? Ullein-Reviczky had spent some years as consul general in Istanbul. His wife was the daughter of a retired British consular official whose residence was in that city. The summer before he spent his holiday with his in-laws and must have made contacts in preparation for the present move. I concluded from some of his remarks that I was not to be the only harbinger of this message.

Ullein-Reviczky instructed me that in the event my contacts with Budapest were severed, I should continue to cooperate with the Allied authorities until the conclusion of the war for the good of Hungary. We agreed on several means of communication, including one which was to pass through a top official of the Hungarian Revision League, an organization that strove for a revision of the boundaries established by the Treaty of Trianon after the end of World War I. I was also to be generously provided with financial means. Just before my departure Ullein-

Reviczky murmured in an even softer whisper, "If necessary to save the country, you may repudiate Regent Horthy."*

* * *

At noontime the train reached Svilengrad, the Bulgarian frontier station. This was also the external limit of German control. Bulgarian passport and customs officials were accompanied by German agents, evidently members of the Gestapo, in civilian clothes. I was warned against them by Fehér. In the silent presence of the Bulgarian officials, the Gestapo asked the questions: "Where are you going? Why? Do you carry letters or other papers?"

I answered in a faultless German that apparently impressed the Gestapo agents. As to letters, I carried an open letter from a Hungarian lady to her Turkish friend, written in German. I showed the Gestapo man the letter, which he immediately took away, promising that it would be sent by mail. It never arrived. After a thorough search of my luggage, the agents withdrew. A few months later I remembered this scene when a retired Hungarian diplomat went through the same examination and refused to be questioned by Germans "on Bulgarian territory." He carried a diplomatic passport and the Gestapo let him pass. Of course, his journey was entirely innocuous; he could risk a scandal, I could not.

After we had been waiting for hours, the train began to move. We had to cross the Pithion (Rodhopi) quadrangle. First, we entered German-occupied Greek territory, where German soldiers stepped through the doors of the cars. The train then pulled into Edirne Station, which was Turkish territory and where Turkish policemen boarded. Later, before the bridge across the Maritsa River, the train stopped for a moment and the German soldiers jumped off. Crossing the bridge, to my great relief we finally reached Turkish territory, Uzunköprü Station.

Smiling Turkish police and customs officers carried out the examinations. Here the language of communication was French. The station and surrounding area were teeming with officers and soldiers. One could see that Turkey was mobilized and that a considerable portion of her armed forces was concentrated between the border and Istanbul.

---

*Miklos von Nagybanya Horthy, 1868–1957, commander in chief of the Austro-Hungarian fleet in World War I, later led a nationalist Hungarian army and served as regent of a kingless Hungary from 1920 to 1945, but left day-to-day government to his premiers in a conservative, but not openly fascist, political system. — ED.

appeal the decision to the Permanent Court of International Justice at The Hague. At this point the Hungarian state had to step in to protect the rights of the university; László Gajzágo, an eminent international legal scholar and state commissioner for international arbitral affairs, acted as chief representative, while I functioned as representative of the university and adviser to the government representative.

From October to the end of December 1933 the World Court held oral proceedings in the case. The president of the court at that time was Ambassador Adatci, a Japanese, while the American judge on the panel of fifteen judges was Frank B. Kellogg, the former secretary of state. The pleadings dragged on week after week. Gajzágo was a voluminous speaker; he spoke in French and his words were translated into English. By the end of November his rejoinder had lasted more than two weeks and no end was in sight. He explained the status of the university since its foundation to the present day, a narrative interlocked with the history of Hungary and the constitutional intricacies of the Austro-Hungarian monarchy. At the beginning of the third week he gave a slight hint that soon he would end his address. There arose a spurt of movement among the otherwise stiffly sitting fifteen judges; Frank Kellogg, seventy-seven years old, awoke from his slumber because of the commotion (he did not speak French and only listened to the English translation) and looked at his neighbor, the Polish judge Count Rostworowski, who quite audibly told him, "Finish!"

On December 18 the court pronounced its elaborate and long judgment: with only the Czechoslovak judge dissenting, it affirmed the decision of the Czechoslovak-Hungarian mixed arbitral tribunal. The successful conclusion of the judicial phase of this international lawsuit in which I was fortunate enough to have played a leading role brought me both material and academic rewards. I was hardly twenty-nine years old and was already sought by many on questions of international law. In the meantime, my dissertation was published in England; I had earlier written another book, which was brought out by a publisher in Vienna. In 1934 the University of Budapest, conservative in making appointments, conferred on me despite my youthful age the title and rank of docent (a kind of professorial lecturer), the stepping-stone to a professorial appointment.

The World Court's judgment in the university case did not settle the dispute. The judgment declared the seizure of the properties illegal, but a return of these estates to the management of the university was desirable neither for the Czechoslovak authorities nor for the university. Long negotiations followed between the government in Prague, the authorities in Bratislava, and the university. For about two years I shuttled between these cities. Finally, in 1935 an agreement was reached and the Czechoslovak government paid compensation, which enabled the university to purchase an estate in Hungary.

Following these events and until the outbreak of World War II, I maintained an international legal practice while also teaching at the university. I was often on the road — or, rather, on the rail — between Budapest and Paris, London, The Hague, Vienna, Berlin, and Rome. I also attended international conferences, such as the one in Copenhagen where I met the future rector of Istanbul University, Cemil Bilsel.

ESTABLISHING CONTACTS

Hardly had I entered my room in the Tokatliyan Hotel when the phone rang and Prof. Andreas Schwarz asked me to visit him at his home in Bebek, a suburb of Istanbul on the shore of the Bosporus. To avoid attention — I observed that my taxi was followed by a car from the station to the hotel — I chose to travel by streetcar. Then totally ignorant of the Turkish language, I managed with some difficulty to descend by cable car from Pera Hill and in Galata, the harbor district, to catch a streetcar to Bebek. Later I found out that the car that followed me was from the Turkish police, who wanted to ascertain that I really settled in the hotel. I shortly gained much respect for the police, who were discreet but eager to know everything about foreigners in wartime. They only interfered when the security interests of Turkey were affected.

At Bebek I received a most cordial welcome. The professor, aware of my desire to contact the British, cabled his acquaintance at the mission. He was told that somebody knowledgeable about Hungarian affairs was on the way from Cairo to Istanbul. I was to meet this person at Professor Schwarz's apartment two days later.

During the next day I paid several visits, first to the Hungarian consul general, János Mihalkovits, whom I had known when he was assigned to the Agency for Mixed Arbitral Tribunals when I represented cases before these international courts. Mihalkovits had been appointed counselor to the Hungarian Legation in Moscow when diplomatic relations were resumed in 1940 between Hungary and the Soviet Union. When the Germans attacked Russia and Hungary broke off relations, members of the Hungarian mission were first interned and then allowed to leave. Mihalkovits thus lost all his personal belongings; his present appointment in Turkey gave him an opportunity to make up for his losses. He was a jovial, sincere person and a genuine bureaucrat. But under my instructions I was not supposed to say anything to him, although he was no friend of the Nazis and may have guessed the reason for my coming to Turkey.

I also went to see Father János Vendel, a Jesuit priest and the Roman Catholic pastor of the Hungarian colony in Istanbul. He invited me to attend a dinner at the Hungarian Club that evening in honor of Prof. Albert Szent-Györgyi, a Nobel Prize winner who taught biochemistry at the University of Szeged in Hungary and was on a short visit to Turkey. At the dinner party I was introduced to several Hungarian dignitaries.

On February 17 I went again to Professor Schwarz's place. After some delays the person from the British mission arrived. Professor Schwarz introduced him as George Howard, a Hungarian Canadian. However, I recognized him as György Páloczi-Horváth, who had left Hungary at the time of Teleki's suicide. I did not show that I recognized him until we were left alone.

Páloczy-Horvath thanked me for not having revealed his identity. Since he had entered wartime British service, it was impractical to use his cumbersome Hungarian name and so he became George Howard. He used a British service passport under this name and said it would be harmful if his real identity were to become known. In Cairo he had seen Basil Davidson, who sent greetings to me. Páloczi-Horváth was informed, probably through Basil, about my abortive assignment under Teleki.

I told him that I had a message from the Hungarian Foreign Ministry to the British and United States governments, and that the message should be passed to an authorized representative of the British mission. Páloczi- Horváth said that he fully understood my reluctance to give him the message and promised to arrange the necessary meeting. We both agreed that it would be unwise for me to go to the former British Embassy building, as carefully watched as it was by German agents. (The British Embassy had been transferred to Ankara, but the huge edifice that had housed it in Istanbul was still referred to as the British Embassy.

During the war not only the offices of the consul general but also those of the commercial and naval attachés as well as special wartime agencies were located there.)

On February 19, in the home of a consular official, I met Maj. Leslie Harrop. It would have been naive for me to expect to be confronted with the British ambassador or counselor of the embassy, or even a secretary of the embassy. After all, I had no written credentials nor even a written message. All I could expect at this juncture was to be trusted and that the message should reach the addressee, the Foreign Office in London.

I told Harrop about my assignment and also about my invitation to lecture at the university. Then I imparted to him the official message of the Hungarian government. Asked how this was entrusted to me, I gave a detailed account of who invited me to forward this message and under what circumstances.

Harrop wrote down the text of the message and made further notes. He said he would pass on his report to his superiors in Turkey and it would be promptly cabled to London. He thought the message would also be passed on to Washington and possibly to Moscow. Until a reply was received, he would not comment on anything I had told him, at least not officially. What he said now expressed his personal views.

He suggested that for the time being I should remain in Turkey, which was my intention. He also thought it useful that I should remain in contact with him and his associates and promised to introduce me to others. All this could be done in a manner that would remain confidential and would not interfere with my official and unofficial contacts with Hungarians. He asked me whether I had an opportunity to forward classified messages to Hungary. I answered that I was told that instructions to this effect would be sent to the consulate in Istanbul and that I also possessed a code, which, however, might not be convenient to pass long texts.

Harrop remarked that, in the case that "substantive talks" were to be conducted, Hungary would be required to send to Turkey a "plenipotentiary." I knew, as he did, that János Vörnle, the Hungarian minister in Ankara, and his military attaché, Kálmán Bartalis, were unsuitable because of their pro-Nazi attitude. Besides, it was also known that Vörnle cooperated with Franz Papen, the German ambassador, and hurried to him even in matters of the smallest detail. The talk I had with Harrop was pleasant and, although I was closely questioned by him, he did not appear to doubt what I was telling him. I could not expect anything more or better at the moment.

During the next days I met several times with Páloczi-Horváth, who told me the story of his odyssey. He left Budapest two days before the German attack on Yugoslavia (one day after Davidson had left) and joined the British mission in Belgrade. Together with the mission he fled before the advancing Germans until they reached Hercegnovi on the Gulf of Cattaro. A British seaplane picked them up and took them first to Greece and later to Egypt. Since 1941 he had been working with the British, interviewing Hungarians in Iran (after the occupation by the British of part of that country), Syria, and South Africa. Several times he had come to Istanbul, where he could meet Hungarians and obtain information from them.

Harrop soon invited me to his apartment for dinner, where I met several of his colleagues. Eventually the identity of the organization to which Harrop, Páloczi-Horváth, and others belonged was disclosed to me. It was the Special Operations Executive (SOE), a wartime organization created by the pragmatic British to suit the special requirements of World War II. The SOE was a confidential arm of the government, connected mainly with the Foreign Office but also with the military and with various agencies. Its members were to cooperate with individuals in the Resistance, get others to join, and maintain confidential contacts with persons who could be helpful in ending the war successfully. The main task of the SOE was not intelligence; its activity was essentially political but could be useful to the military as well. Its members were persons who knew the country or countries with which they were dealing. Harrop had lived for many years in Rumania, where he was in charge of a British-owned plant, and also had visited Hungary quite frequently. The SOE also enlisted political refugees, such as Páloczi-Horváth.

My postprandial discussions with these British officials often centered around the crucial question of how Hungary could extricate herself from the tight grasp of Germany and defect from the Axis. This could only be done— without exposing Hungary to outright German occupation—when the fighting front reached Hungarian territory. But in that case, as it was put to me, it was indispensable to establish contacts with the Hungarian General Staff. I was asked whether the Hungarian Government would have control over its armed forces, should the latter be required to oppose the Germans. I could only answer that although

many, perhaps even the majority, of the Hungarian officers were mes-
merized by Hitler's military achievements, evidence of Germany's
forthcoming defeat might change the situation.

In this context I had to raise the question of Hungary's borders. The
popularity of Germany among many Hungarians was due to the fact
that it was with German help that Hungary was able to recover some of
the territory she had lost after World War I, a loss that was widely
considered utterly unjust. Could at least self-determination for Hungary
after the war be promised? I asked. But the British officials, though
familiar with the problem, would not enter into this delicate area. They
continued to say that eventually all would depend on what every nation
now subjected to German control contributed toward the victory of the
Allies. The Poles, Yugoslavs, and Greeks, for example, had made great
sacrifices for the cause; Hungary, however, had lost fifty thousand men
before Voronezh in fighting against the Russians, that is, against the
interest of the Allies, and thus appeared reluctant to incur the risk of
helping them. I replied that Hungary's entry into the war against the
Allies was in fact only against the Russians and was a story different
from that of the Poles, Yugoslavs, or Greeks. The Poles had collaborated with the Germans against Czechoslovakia before they were attacked by them. Likewise, Yugoslavia and Greece had suffered aggression; Hungary thus far had not. Joining the Germans against the Soviets
was, of course, a mistake, but I wondered how this could have been
avoided.

It was clear, however, that the Hungarian view of the boundary
problems was highly unrealistic. Although my British interlocutors were
neither authorized nor competent to express opinions on this subject,
their responses must have reflected the views of their superiors or must
have been expressions of widely held judgments. The Hungarian hope
that the territorial gains of 1938–40 could be preserved in a postwar
world seemed rather vain. The Allies appeared to be determined to support Czechoslovakia and Yugoslavia, the victims of Nazi aggression, in
their demands for territorial restitution. Only the Transylvanian question
seemed to remain open, because of Rumania's participation, together
with Hungary's, in the war against the Soviet Union. Self-determination,
annexation of Hungarian-inhabited areas after the end of the previous
world war, and promises of the Atlantic Charter were of no interest.
Rather, the fate of East Central Europe seemed to hinge on the attitude

of Moscow or the success of the Soviet army and on the military situation at the end of hostilities.

(It must be remembered that in February 1943 the Germans still held positions deep in Russia, their offensive strength as yet unbroken. The decisive tank battle of Kursk, which ended German offensive mobility in the east, took place only in July 1943. British and American forces had not yet set foot on the European continent; they would soon, however, establish control over all of North Africa.)

My contacts with the British familiarized me with some of the methods of their wartime political military mechanism. The SOE allowed for an unusual flexibility in dealing with the restive populations under Nazi control, quisling governments, and governments unhappy to have sided with the Germans. There was also proof of unparalleled internal flexibility: successful collaboration between the SOE, the official diplomatic staff, and the military.

In the course of these conversations, I became aware that messages, identical or similar to the one I bore, had been forwarded to British and American agencies in neutral capitals, such as Stockholm and Lisbon. I also realized that Andrew Frey, a journalist who had come to Turkey approximately at the same time as I did, had contacted the British in Istanbul, evidently with the same message.[2]

While this multiplication of approaches did serve to confirm the authenticity and credibility of the move, this limited advantage was largely outweighed by the probability of leaks. The success of a conspiratorial abandonment of German ties depended on utmost secrecy. Historically, Hungarians were not famous for masterminding and carrying out successful conspiracies, nor did their extrovert and often talkative character support the secretiveness here necessary. Despite the political oppression they had suffered, they were basically an imperial nation, ruling over peoples other than their own. Other oppressed nations, such

---

2. Various published accounts of Hungary's peace feelers mention Frey as the emissary to Istanbul. See Stephen D. Kertesz, *Diplomacy in a Whirlpool: Hungary Between Nazi Germany and the Soviet Union* (Notre Dame, Ind.: University of Notre Dame Press, 1953), p. 67; Miklos Kállay, *Hungarian Premier* (New York: Oxford University Press, 1954), pp. 302–5; and C. A. Macartney, *October Fifteen: A History of Modern Hungary, 1929–45* (Edinburgh: University of Edinburgh Press, 1956–57), vol. 2, pp. 122–23. At the time when these books were written, I was still in prison in Hungary (from 1951 to 1956), and any reference to my activity might have been harmful to my person, whereas Frey, outside Hungary, was in a position to tell his version of the story.

as the Czechs, the Serbs, and the Irish, were good conspirators; Hungarians were not.

I soon felt the need to report back to Budapest about my contacts and impressions. Mihalkovits, the consul general, had not received instructions to allow me the "right to the bag," that is, the diplomatic pouch. He was willing to forward my letters to officials of the Foreign Ministry provided they were unsealed. This, of course, I was unwilling to do.

Ferenc Csiki, the commercial attaché, had left for Budapest. I guessed that he might have been ready to accommodate me because he maintained confidential contacts with the British. In his absence I decided to approach Péter Bruckner, the assistant commercial attaché and Csiki's son-in-law. Péter did not refuse me outright, but he did have some misgivings. About a year before, the British-born wife of the then Hungarian consul in Istanbul had carried letters to Budapest, which were intercepted and found highly incriminating. She was tried by a military court and eventually given a life sentence. Her husband had to resign from the foreign service.

I told Bruckner that my letter would be addressed to Ullein-Reviczky. This convinced him, and he made only one condition: that I pay a courtesy visit to Colonel Bartalis, the military attaché. Evidently Bruckner did not wish that Bartalis should reproach him that I had not visited him while calling on Bruckner. There must have been somebody in the commercial attaché's office who reported to Bartalis. Bruckner also suggested that I deposit with the consul general, for appearance's sake, another open letter addressed to Ullein-Reviczky. I was ready to comply with these suggestions.

I went immediately to see the colonel in his office. The military attaché resided not in Ankara but in Istanbul. Thus it was clear that the main task of Bartalis was not the maintenance of contacts with the Turkish military but the collection of information, which was more abundant in Istanbul than in the Ankara, the interior capital of Turkey, where the assistant military attaché of Hungary resided. Bartalis, as it was widely known, in imitation of German Nazi tactics in Turkey, maintained a spy network directed mainly at supporting the German war effort. He also kept a close watch on members of the Hungarian colony in Istanbul. Some of Bartalis's professional informers were well-known figures in the city. They could be seen in nightclubs, restaurants, hotel lobbies, even entrances of apartment houses. I noticed that I was frequently followed by an individual by the name of Kovács, a pharmacist's assistant who had worked for the Germans in Baghdad until the anti-British coup in Iraq in 1941. In Istanbul he joined the ranks of Bartalis's informers and in Hungarian circles he gained the sobriquet Kovács of Baghdad.

Bartalis received me at once. He seemed to be very interested in talking with me but he maintained a cool reserve. I told him about my invitation to lecture at the university and declared that I was intent upon improving Hungarian-Turkish relations in the field of academic exchanges and cooperation. It was quite clear that he did not believe what I was saying. He began to talk about the Turkish police, how well informed they were when defending Turkish interests—tolerant, yet ruthless. Was this to warn me or to frighten me? At the end of our conversation Bartalis asked me to visit him again and to tell him about my problems, plans, and experiences. This conversation took place on March 1, 1943. I was not to step into his office again until August 1944, when our meeting would be more dramatic.

On March 6 I was at least able to establish contact with the American side. Through the British I was informed that Walter Birge, the American vice-consul, would call on me without special announcement in my hotel room.

The United States had no organization similar to the SOE. Their more recently created intelligence agency, the Office of Strategic Services (OSS) was not yet fully operative in early 1943, at least not in Turkey. But the United States Consulate General in Istanbul had been expanded since the American entry into the war and now included a number of political vice-consuls to whom the various enemy countries were assigned.

Birge arrived at the agreed time. Without much preliminary talk he asked me about the purpose of my journey to Turkey. He had only recently arrived and admitted to having little knowledge of Hungarian matters. I promised to provide him with the information he needed and also told him about myself (he already had been fully informed in this regard by the British). Thereafter I frequently met Walter in his home. As long as my status was confidential, I did not wish to visit the American Consulate General for the same reasons that I avoided visiting the British Embassy. Walter proved to be an interesting conversationalist and was ready to listen when I reported to him on Hungary's internal and external problems.

In early March I also visited Cemil Bilsel, the rector of Istanbul University, in the central building on Beyazid Hill, which in Ottoman times used to be the pompous Ministry of War. Bilsel was an experienced, wise man and a good administrator; he maintained excellent relations with the numerous foreign professors. I met many of the excellent people among the refugees from Germany. In addition to Prof. Andreas Schwarz, I should mention Prof. Ernst Reuter, who became mayor of Berlin after the end of the war, Prof. Alexander Rüstow, a famous sociologist, and Clemens Holzmeister, a well-known architect.

Bilsel received me courteously, offering me a ceremonial cup of Turkish coffee, and confirmed that I was welcome to give a series of public lectures. He proposed to schedule them for the months of April and May. He suggested that before speaking to the students I should go to Ankara and make some official visits there. He must have guessed that I had other reasons for coming to Turkey but was too discreet even to hint at the possibility.

On March 5 Harrop phoned me asking for an interview. He then read to me the text of the reply that had arrived from London: "The British government will undertake no negotiations with the present Hungarian government or with any possible Hungarian government, so long as Hungarian troops are outside the frontiers of Hungary."* He added that the reply contained some further comments and, since his office was not quite certain whether these were also to be conveyed verbatim to me, he wished to paraphrase them in his own words. London appeared to express some considerable impatience with the Hungarian attitude, which considered it feasible to enter into negotiations without previously complying with the above demand. London also wished to note that the British declaration of war against Hungary was prompted by the participation of Hungarian forces in the war against the Soviet Union, an ally of Great Britain. The Hungarian forces sent in 1942 against Moscow (or the remnants of them, as Harrop caustically remarked) still had not been recalled. Hungary's present endeavors appeared to be "attempts at reinsurance" in the event that the Nazis lost the war, and London was unlikely to honor such attempts.

Harrop commented that contacts between Great Britain and Hungary should be continued in the hope that these demands would be met. Upon my query whether the meaning of the words "outside the

---

*This suggests SOE was not concerned about tapped telephones. —ED.

frontiers of Hungary" related only to Russia or they included territories recovered by Hungary in 1938 (southern Slovakia), 1939 (Ruthenia), and 1940 (northern Transylvania), Harrop stated that reference was being made only to Hungarian forces on Soviet territory. However, insofar as there were Hungarian troops in Serbia, they should also be withdrawn. I assured him that the German request of Hungary to participate in the occupation of Serbia had been rejected. He also strongly urged that since all the primary questions to be discussed — if to be discussed at all — were of a military nature, the dispatch of two Hungarian staff officers should be seriously considered.

The official reply was curt and brusque, but Harrop's comments were more conciliatory and encouraging. Within an hour I wrote my report and submitted it in a sealed envelope to Péter Bruckner. A diplomatic courier was just about to leave for Budapest. This courier must have crossed paths with his counterparts, for another courier arrived in Istanbul four days later, on March 9. He brought letters to me and a report by Polish refugees in Hungary to their government in London. Attached to it was an introductory letter for me addressed to the Polish military attaché in Ankara, whom I was enjoined to visit.

Perhaps even more important than these writings was the courier himself. He was László Veress, an official of the Press Bureau of the Foreign Ministry. Soon I heard from the British that he was trying to contact them. Two days later he left for Ankara to deliver the rest of the pouch. I followed him on March 12.

TO ANKARA

The purpose of my first visit to the Turkish capital was twofold. I wished to meet members of the Hungarian Legation and to contact the Poles, but I did not wish to call on János Vörnle, the Hungarian minister, who was fanatically pro-German. Fortunately, Vörnle was at that time back in Hungary and so I did not commit any violation of the code of courtesy by avoiding him.

At the Hungarian Legation two secretaries, Ödön Gáspár and Tamás Márffy-Mantuano, were well known to me. Gáspár had attended the International Law Seminar at the University of Budapest where I occasionally substituted for Professor Gajzágo. Márffy-Mantuano had been one year behind me in high school. I had also worked together with his late father, who had been Hungarian minister at Rome, in a lawsuit before the mixed arbitral tribunal. I also had met briefly the counselor of the legation in Ankara, Baron Heribert Thierry, when he was assigned to the Hungarian Legation at the Vatican.

All these acquaintances already knew I was in Turkey. I was certain they suspected the reason for my coming to that country; they all gave me a most cordial welcome. Márffy-Mantuano invited me for dinner on the day of my arrival. Gáspár, who was a more recent appointee, entertained me the next day in the Karpiç Restaurant. Two days later I was Thierry's guest for luncheon. All of us refrained tactfully from talking high politics; instead, I spoke of my forthcoming lecture in Istanbul and my hosts discussed Turkey and Ankara.

An extra advantage of my visit to Ankara was the opportunity for a long and fruitful talk with Lászlo Veress. Now I was able to tell him in detail of my contacts with the British and the Americans. He seemed surprised to learn that I was informed of his confidential conversations with British representatives in Istanbul. I knew also that Veress used Frey to establish contacts with the journalist Páloczi-Horváth and that he had seen Maj. William Morgan, a British officer. I had the impression that Veress's boss, Ullein-Reviczky, had failed to inform him of my mission — a foreboding of what was to come next.

However, I was able to create a climate of mutual trust with Veress and we quite openly discussed the nature of our contacts. We both agreed that it appeared preferable to deal with the British themselves rather than with Páloczi-Horváth. The latter's role was evidently resented in Budapest, where he was considered to be an extreme leftist and even suspected of being a Communist or a Soviet agent. I could only tell Veress that Páloczi-Horváth was highly thought of by the British I had met, and I assured him that in my activities and reports I would not let myself be influenced by Páloczi-Horváth's personal views.

On the third day of my stay in Ankara I went to meet the Polish military attaché. The pretty Polish Embassy building was located, as were most of the foreign missions, along the road leading to Çankaya Hill, where Atatürk had his house and where later the palace of the Turkish president was constructed. Without any prior announcement I walked to that wing of the mansion where the office of the military attaché was indicated in French. I was ushered into the presence of Col.

Marian Zimnal. The Polish Embassy represented the government-in-exile of Poland in London. At that time the Soviet Union had not yet set up its own Polish government in Lublin, but the Poles were highly suspicious of what Moscow might be planning for their future.

Colonel Zimnal welcomed me with the routine cordiality of a man accustomed to dealing with confidential assignments and operations. After having read the letter written by my Polish friend in Budapest, he became more genuinely friendly. Characteristically, he immediately offered me a drink (he seemed to have been well stocked with Scotch whiskey and English gin), then another, and so forth. I believe this was his method to make his guest talkative and he certainly succeeded, except that I refrained from telling him anything about the real purpose of my coming to Turkey. Instead, I told him about the Poles I knew in Budapest. Zimnal was familiar with the hospitality Hungary had offered to the Polish refugees in 1939 who were squeezed between the advancing German and Soviet armies but managed to cross the Carpathian Mountains into Hungary. I mentioned several names of those who were or had been in Hungary; most of those of military age had slipped out of Hungary and joined the Allies in France and, after France's fall, in Britain.

Noticing my reticence to talk about my assignment, Colonel Zimnal asked me whether I would like to see his boss, the ambassador. I replied that he had just preempted my own request. We arranged for him to call me at my hotel.

Late in the afternoon I got a phone call informing me that Ambassador Michael Sokolnicki would receive me next morning. Sokolnicki was a former professor of history at the University of Cracow. His appointment as ambassador to Turkey preceded the outbreak of World War II. Because of the recall of other heads of diplomatic missions, Sokolnicki advanced in seniority; as the senior ambassador in the Turkish capital he became the dean of the diplomatic corps there. His seniority, however, was not accepted by the Axis diplomats nor by the Soviet ambassador.

The diplomatic corps itself was fragmented into three groups following the outbreak of the war: Allied diplomats, Axis diplomats, and the neutrals. Members of the two first groups could not be invited to the same function, whereas the neutral diplomats could be with either of the former. On New Year's Day or on the Turkish national holiday (October

29) two separate receptions with the Turkish president had to be arranged for the two hostile groups; the neutrals were divided between the two.

Subsequently, I was advised that Ambassador Sokolnicki, before inviting me, had called on the counselor for political affairs of the British Embassy and inquired about me. The counselor, familiar with my conversations in Istanbul, evidently gave a favorable report, because Sokolnicki spoke quite openly as soon as I was introduced to him in his study.

The ambassador mentioned first that he had pleasant memories of Hungary, a country he visited for the first time in 1916 on behalf of General (later Marshal) Piłsudski. At that time he had conversations with Count Mihaly Karolyi, the opposition leader. Sokolnicki expressed a polite regret that the Polish and Hungarian nations should officially find themselves in opposing camps. He remarked that he had never met the present Hungarian envoy, János Vörnle, but before the war had developed a deep friendship with his predecessor, Máriássy. The Polish ambassador did not fail to make a few sarcastic remarks concerning the relationship between Vörnle and German ambassador Papen, who made unfavorable comments concerning Vörnle's intelligence.

Asked about the purpose of my visit to Turkey, I told him the essentials of my mission. He point-blank inquired: Does Hungary wish to secede from the side of Germany and, if so, how? His second question referred to the territorial arrangements to be expected after the war. In reply, I could only express a hope that the secession would be successfully achieved, but I refrained from quoting the text of the message of which I was the bearer.

Sokolnicki explained at some length why, in his view, the volte-face of Hungary and the exact date of such a move would be of great importance. For the Poles, he said, this was more than a simple military question. Poland's as well as Hungary's future existence might depend on it. While along the German- Russian front a colossal life-and-death struggle was continuing, another gigantic front on the European continent was being prepared by the Americans and the British. An immense concentration of men and material was taking place along the African shore of the Mediterranean. Where and when the invasion of the continent was to occur he could not tell, but he was certain that the Balkan Peninsula would play an important role in future military operations. The landing of these Anglo-American forces on the European continent would finally determine the outcome of the war. It would be at that moment — when the Allies established their foothold on the Balkans — that Hungary would have to choose whether she wished to rid herself of the fatal consequences of her pro-German status. "Il faut prendre la décision," he repeated several times.

It was during this conversation with Ambassador Sokolnicki that I caught a first glimpse of the project attributed to British prime minister Winston Churchill to invade the "soft underbelly" of Europe somewhere along the Balkan Peninsula and move the Allied forces north in the general direction of Hungary, Czechoslovakia, and Poland. This would not only deny these valuable territories to the Germans but would also forestall the Soviet descent into the heart of Europe.

The ambassador went on to explain Poland's huge stake in this venture. "We have, as is well known, our territorial problem with Moscow." The Kremlin should not be tempted by having its forces occupy excessive areas of Central Europe. No government likes to give up territory conquered at the price of human sacrifice. An advance of American and British forces would prevent a crisis between the opponents of Hitler rather than create one. It was thus essential and in the interest of future world peace that these forces move faster in the northern and eastern directions than the Soviet advance in the western direction. According to Sokolnicki, the position of these competing frontal advances at the end of hostilities after the inevitable collapse of Germany would determine the fate of "intermediate Europe," that part of the continent that lies between the German and Russian colossi. It would, in particular, determine the future of both Poland and Hungary. The destiny of these two countries was inextricably linked. Sokolnicki added that the Polish army now assembled in the Middle East was closely interested in the plans Hungary had, for the road from the Balkans to Poland leads across Hungary.

Speaking of the territorial problem, I remarked that Hungary hoped to keep the overwhelmingly Hungarian-inhabited areas after the end of the war. The ambassador mentioned that he had talked to many Czech leaders who were rather disinterested in the southern borders of Slovakia. This was, however, not the official view of the Czechoslovak government-in-exile in London.

I asked Sokolnicki whether there was any substance in the reports recently published in the Western press on a plan for a Polish-Czechoslovak federation. My host replied that with this concept the Polish government wished to express a desire that European peace be maintained with the cooperation of the smaller nations of East Central Europe. Hungary should also have a place in this combination of smaller powers.

When, inevitably, the question of Transylvania came up in our conversation, Sokolnicki suggested that both Hungary and Rumania should endeavor to find a satisfactory solution. In his view Iuliu Maniu (the Rumanian opposition leader) was the man of the future in Rumania. An agreement should be sought with him. I remarked this would not be an easy thing since Maniu was himself a Transylvanian Rumanian. Now the former professor of history revealed himself when Sokolnicki delivered a discourse on the historic destiny of "cultural border areas" to bring together rather than to separate the nations involved in their composition. Perhaps, he added, Transylvania could be made a territory of joint sovereignty, an idea which I found unrealistic.

A restrained optimism was evident in the ambassador's presentation when he delivered his *tour d'horizon* of the political and military situation relevant for both Hungary and Poland. This was especially noticeable when he disclosed the march-order toward the north, vague as it was, of the Polish army in the Middle East. It was known that the members of the Polish army, evacuated with some difficulty from the Soviet Union and reinforced by escapees from Rumania and Hungary, were concentrated in Syria, where they received up-to-date equipment from the British. Colonel Zimnal, in one of the conversations I had with him during subsequent visits to Ankara, mentioned that he was terribly impressed by these well-trained and well-equipped troops and that they were ready and eager for action. (Zimnal himself had seen action when he served with the Polish contingent that defended for five months against the Germans and Italians at Tobruk.) Although I could not share this optimism, I still felt elated when I returned to Istanbul on March 17.

INTRIGUE

Immediately upon my return to the shores of the Bosporus, two unpleasant pieces of news were awaiting me. The first concerned my lecture at the university, which I expected to deliver in late March. On March 18 Turkish newspapers, including the French-language daily *La*

Turquie, published a report from London summarizing a speech made by the president of the Czechoslovak government-in-exile, Edvard Beneš. Therein Beneš wished to draw attention to the fact that the Hungarian government was attempting to contact the Allies and had, for that purpose, sent two professors to Turkey. Only one name was mentioned, a certain Ikziki, evidently a distortion by the Turkish press. The Turkish papers simultaneously published an official denial by the Hungarian government. As it happened, and not for the first time, it was the denial that probably prompted the publication of this news item.

The Hungarian response, however, added that two Hungarian professors— Albert Szent-Györgyi, a biophysicist and Nobel Prize winner, and Gyula Mészáros, a professor of Turkic languages—visited Turkey for professional reasons. The Hungarian report also stated that Szent-Györgyi, upon the invitation of Istanbul University, had given a lecture.

Most likely Ullein-Reviczky approved these travels. As to Mészáros, it was known that he cherished extreme rightist and, therefore, pro-Nazi views; in the early 1920s he had been involved in the ill-famed affair of the counterfeiting of French francs by Hungarian irredentist adventurers and had taken refuge in Turkey before being permitted to return to Hungary. Why such a person was allowed to go to Turkey at such a delicate moment appeared incomprehensible to me. But many incomprehensible events occurred during those days.

I was told by the British that Professor Szent-Györgyi had sought contacts with Allied missions. It was almost common knowledge in diplomatic circles in Istanbul that he had blundered into Gestapo agents posing as Americans and that he had presented himself to them as a representative of the Hungarian Independence Front, an anti-German organization. He also met genuine British representatives as well as Páloczi-Horváth, who told him he was a Canadian journalist of Hungarian extraction.

The first unpleasantness in connection with these developments struck me when I visited Rector Bilsel concerning the date of my public lecture. "The Minister of Education has reproached me," he said, "for having allegedly 'invited' Szent-Györgyi. I never did. When he was here, he offered to give a talk to members of the Faculty of Medicine, an offer gladly accepted by his friends. I have to travel to Ankara to explain matters. I feel now that I must obtain clear permission from the minister to allow your public lecture. We are living in a delicate atmosphere; everything has political implications." It was clear that the rector was much displeased with the Hungarian report according to which Szent-Györgyi had been "invited" to lecture. The postponement of my own lecture was most unwelcome; I wished to legitimize my stay in Turkey with it.

The second unpleasant surprise was a coded message from Budapest, which invited me to leave Turkey for Cairo or London or else to return to Hungary. In the latter case the Foreign Ministry "guaranteed" that I would be neither prosecuted nor inconvenienced for my activity in Turkey. No reason for my recall was given. However, the date of the message was March 17, the same as the date of the Hungarian denial of the Beneš accusations.

The dispatch of so many persons not only to Turkey but also to other neutral countries to establish contacts with the Allies was a major blunder. But the fact that I was one of those to be recalled, after my discreet activities and initial success, made me rightly assume that an intrigue was going on behind my back. It was easy to detect that it was Andrew Frey who perpetrated this deed.

I refrained from reacting and began discussing the matter with my British and American contacts. I raised the question whether I should go to Cairo or London. The British, however, immediately let it be known that they considered my moving to these centers to be of little value for them and also for Hungary compared to my usefulness in Turkey.

On April 13 the Hungarian courier brought me another message from Ullein-Reviczky, again in the nature of an ultimatum. According to this missive, I should by all means leave Turkey before May 1; otherwise, he would be forced to use reprisals. The reason given was that my stay in Turkey had caused too much of a sensation.

This was untrue. I had acted most discreetly, never showing myself in the company of "enemy aliens"; furthermore, I had a valid reason to be there: I had been invited to lecture at the university. Even after Ullein-Reviczky's ultimatum I was determined not to leave Turkey. After all, it was the foreign press chief himself who had whispered to me before my departure in Budapest that I should pursue my mission even if there were a "change" in Hungary, that I should even, if necessary, turn against Horthy.

Accordingly, I wrote Ullein-Reviczky a long letter explaining why I could not return to Budapest. His promise of immunity was simply ridiculous in the face of the danger from the Germans. Had I returned, the Gestapo certainly would have arrested me on March 19, 1944, when the Germans occupied Hungary. I have since realized that I was blacklisted with the pro-Nazi Hungarian military intelligence. I also pointed out the impossibility of leaving for Cairo or London when the British preferred that I remain in Turkey.

However, I was aware that Ullein-Reviczky could render my sojourn in Turkey rather difficult. In Ankara, Vörnle was just waiting for an opportunity to jump at a person like myself. He could have told the Turkish authorities that my passport had been declared invalid or some other story. If my contacts with Budapest had been broken off, my usefulness in working for the cause of Hungary would have been greatly diminished.

To counteract the intrigue, I now accepted the offer made to me by the British, who were ready to contribute their weight in this matter. As mentioned earlier, Ferenc Csiki, the commercial attaché, maintained discreet contacts with the Allied representatives in Istanbul. Furthermore, he was an important person because the commercial ties with Turkey were of great importance to Hungary as a source of raw materials. Csiki was on good terms with Ullein-Reviczky, so it was arranged that Major Morgan should meet Csiki on April 27 at the apartment of the Greek consul, Mr. Caloyanni, a friend of both of them. Morgan very strongly urged Csiki to convey to the Hungarian Foreign Ministry that my recall orders were considered an unfriendly gesture. He also emphasized that my presence was of considerable significance for further confidential contacts between Budapest and London. Csiki immediately sent off the message to Budapest.

The result of the British intervention in my favor was spectacular. On May 3 I received a cable telling me to postpone my journey (I had no intention of leaving anyhow). The courier who arrived two days later brought me another message from Ullein-Reviczky with instructions to stay in Turkey and continue my activity. There was no further explanation and no apology. Since Ullein-Reviczky's wife was the daughter of a former British consul general in Istanbul, he was rather sensitive to British reactions to his doings. But there had taken place another development, of which we were unaware at that time.

On April 16, 1943, Regent Horthy traveled to Schloss Klessheim near the city of Salzburg upon the invitation of Hitler. The Hungarian leaders wished to use this opportunity to press the Germans for the withdrawal of the remaining Hungarian units from Russia (partly remnants of the destroyed Second Hungarian Army, partly occupation forces). But Hitler adamantly refused and asked for more intensive Hungarian participation in the forthcoming campaign against the Soviets. He also asked for the removal of Prime Minister Kállay, reproached the Hungarians for their lenient attitude toward the Jews, and, finally, accused Horthy of having sent representatives to Turkey to conspire with the Allies. He mentioned three names: Andrew Frey, Gyula Mészáros, and Albert Szent-Györgyi. My name was not mentioned.[3]

It seems well established that another reason for Ullein-Reviczky's about-face was that whereas the other emissaries (as far as they were emissaries) did attract the attention of the Germans, I did not. A word about these "emissaries." Weeks earlier Szent-Györgyi had returned to Hungary, and Mészáros was not one to act as an intermediary with the Allies. On the other hand, Frey did maintain contacts with the British, but his activities soon proved abortive, mostly because of his personal inadequacies in the face of the task before him.

Frey, a foreign correspondent for the liberal Budapest daily *Magyar Nemzet,* gained some reputation in the late 1930s with his reporting. He developed an inflated ego that rendered it difficult for him to make real friends but easy to make many enemies. From the first days of his contacts with the British in Istanbul he had almost exclusively done business with Páloczy-Horváth, with whom he could hardly see eye to eye in most matters. Frey was greatly handicapped in his limited contacts with the British in Turkey by a poor knowledge of the English language. He came to Istanbul in the monomaniacal belief that he and he alone would be the architect of Hungary's jump-off from the Axis, a task for which he had neither the means nor the capability. In pursuit of this self-created illusion, he fanatically wished to eliminate any rival or competitor. In early March he flatly refused my offer to collaborate with him.

Páloczy-Horváth was a problem I was able to handle. At that time he was an obsessed radical who hated the Hungarian sociopolitical system identified with Admiral Horthy, the Hungarian regent. But he was unable to realize the difficulties of the Hungarian government amidst German-Nazi pressures, as well as the fact that the so-called Horthy regime, however objectionable it may have been, was far from totalitar-

---

3. See Horthy's letter of May 7, 1943, to Hitler in *The Confidential Papers of Admiral Horthy,* edited and introduced by Miklos Szinai and Lászlo Szücs (Budapest: Corvina Press, 1965), pp. 248–55. In this letter the regent gave detailed answers to the accusations of the Führer. He denied any knowledge of the allegedly harmful contacts of these persons.

ian. Rather, it was a continuation of the semifeudal, paternalistic regime inherited from the Habsburg monarchy with a limited ballot and an influential aristocracy and gentry, a class of big landholders. Until the German occupation in March 1944 Hungary remained alone among her neighbors as a bastion of conservative and moderately authoritarian leanings, with a multiparty system and a relatively independent press — an island in a Fascist-Nazi sea.

The task with which I was concerned was not one of internal politics. It was a foreign policy issue: how to extricate Hungary from the German embrace, how to help destroy Hitler's rule without an undue price being paid by Hungary. Of course, many who wanted to promote the defeat of Germany hoped that after the end of the war a genuinely democratic regime and, along with it, much-needed social reforms would be introduced in Hungary. But in 1943, in the throes of the Nazi menace, it would have been preposterous to demand social or political change at a time when the Germans were almost daily demanding from the Kállay government and from Horthy that they "solve the Jewish question," disband the Social Democratic party, and eliminate all anti-Nazi elements from leading government and academic positions. Evidently, foreign and military policy had to be considered not only as the primary but as the exclusive determinant over everything else.

I let Páloczy-Horváth's objurgations against Hungarian domestic attitudes pass by my ears and continued to concentrate on pragmatic and practical points in my conversations. In spite of his demagogic outbursts I received help from him in my talks with members of the British mission. It is incorrect to consider his activity as highly destructive, as it appears from the memoirs of Kállay (inspired by one-sided reporting from Frey). He was neither in the pay of the Soviets nor a card-carrying Communist at that time, although he did join the Communist Party after the end of the war.[4]

With his overweening attitude and lack of diplomatic skill, Frey had more and more clashed not only with Páloczy-Horváth but also with other members of the British mission. He was suspected of having changed the wording of messages and of having withheld material intended for the SOE. After the middle of 1943 he was hardly ever consulted. When his intrigue to have me recalled misfired, he used other

---

4. See George Páloczi-Horváth, *The Undefeated* (London: Secker & Warburg, 1959), chapters 10–12.

tactics and went as far as to refer in open press reports to my person and mission, employing easily recognizable forms of disguise. In the August 15, 1943, issue of *Magyar Nemzet* he wrote from Istanbul a concocted story of an Afghan lawyer who had come to Turkey with a message (acquired unlawfully) and with the purpose of mediating peace. Since the allusion was obvious from this and other references and since it could be feared that German intelligence would try to ascertain what was behind the story, this article was more than an indiscretion—it was a betrayal of Hungary's approaches to the Allies. Indeed, shortly thereafter the political counselor of the German Embassy in Ankara, a certain Kleiber, protested against my presence in Turkey to Vörnle. The Hungarian minister passed on the protest to Budapest, but this time the Hungarian Foreign Ministry replied that while they were unable and unwilling to interfere with my private activities, the ministry would be glad to furnish the German Embassy with a list of German citizens in neutral countries who have contact with alien enemies.

After this article the British and Americans reduced their relations with Frey to a minimum. His dialogues with Páloczi-Horváth ended in a physical encounter. Two years later Frey was forcefully removed from the premises of the British Embassy in Istanbul.

As a result of Hitler's accusations the Hungarian Government seemed to have discontinued or at least slowed down its advances to the Allies. For some time Budapest considered the possibility of dropping the Turkish channel of communications altogether. The Hungarian forces could not be withdrawn from Russia; the outcome of the fighting between the Germans and the Russians may have appeared inconclusive to Budapest; and in April 1943 the battle for Tunisia was still in full swing. It was in late April and early May that I exchanged letters with Basil Davidson, who had now entered military service somewhere in the Middle East. Since these letters are so characteristic of the polemics of these days, I prefer to quote them without abridgment:

M.E.F. Apr. 20, 1943

My dear Vali,

   I came through Cairo the other day on a sketchy leave and saw P. H. [Páloczi-Horváth] who told me you'd at last managed to get down to Istanbul. Good for you: and my congratulations! I tried it for a long time, but old Schwarz wouldn't really take the plunge and the Hungarians hadn't yet got cold enough feet. They seem to be seeing the red light now—at last. I hope it isn't too late.

Nowadays I don't know anything in the political world. My life—for nearly a year now—has settled with one long and weary (but rather happy, in a contrarious way) conflict with sand and sun and good tangible things you can see and fight and understand. Believe me, it's a good life. The people are good. They know what they want. Honest straightforward chaps. Nobody could ever hope to get them down. The 8th Army is about the finest fighting machine that ever existed: and one day the whole world will know it. The Italians, of course, aren't serious: the Germans—as we have seen them—have been very good. But they haven't any longer (if they ever had) that certain tension of morale which keeps troops on the move. We think they're flopping badly. You'll see.

I'm writing for old time's sake. I'd like to see you again after the war. And because P. H. tells me you people think you're doing fine I'd like to put you right on that. As I say, I'm writing without the book. I don't any longer know what's happening in the political world. And, personally, I don't much care. But I was treated kindly by a handful of people, including your good self when I was in Hungary: and I do think you had a bad treat and a rotten deal at the end of the last war. You didn't deserve it. What happened to you then, though, is nothing to what is going to happen this time. And this time, in my opinion and in the opinion of us all, you will deserve every inch of it. Do you know how ordinary Englishmen think about Hungary? It's very simple and you ought to know. I was lecturing about it to some of the men in my company the other day. Their opinions may not seem important to you: but they are for they mirror, in our democratic army, the opinions of postwar England. They think of Hungary as an unknown country full of traitors and thieves; and they consider that the more strongly Hungary is treated by the United Nations the better it will be for the mental and physical health of Europe. Look at the record. You helped to dismember Czechoslovakia; you gave Germany all she asked in 1939/40 (nobody believes your stories of passive economic resistance—they are in any case so undramatic, so unreal, so far away); you threw away all vestige of moral decency when you attacked the Yugoslavs (who are still fighting); snivelled about the dangers of German occupation; you went to war with Russia like the most almighty bloody fools you are, and on the silliest pretext I've ever heard. And now, if what P. H. tells me is true—you actually think Hungary has some credit left. Well, *I* can understand it because I know a few elementary things about Hungarians; and I even know a few Hungarians who have risked more than a few whispered words against the Germans. But nobody of importance in the United Nations will understand it. Take that for certain. You can't behave like Germany's closest ally for three years (for *that,* and nothing less, is your reputation) and expect to be treated any differently from the way we are going to treat Germany. Not one man of importance will raise a voice for Hungary—as things stand at present. Personally, I think you'd do better yourself to go home and live quietly and hope to survive. Words are no good. We've had enough words from Hitler, Horthy, and Co. If we could we'd bomb hell out of Budapest. Later on we shall be able to, and then you'll see how high your credit stands. Why should you expect anything else? This war may not have touched you much—yet; but it has touched us. My mother lives in a town in England which the Germans have bombed about 219 times (I know that because my godfather is in charge of air defense services and he told me when I was home in 1941). That's nothing exceptional. Millions of other families have had the same experience. Why should you—who have done nothing in the last three years but prate about the dangers of German occupation, and so have given the Axis all and more than they could have wanted—expect to be treated differently from the Germans? And look at your newspapers. P. H. showed me a few. Disgusting.

Don't ask me to tell you what should be done. I haven't an idea. And it's not my business any more. Only remember *this* from an old friend: that Hungary stands now to be dealt with incomparably *more* harshly than in 1918. Don't say I didn't warn you!

Finally, don't run away with the idea that I've grown anti-Hungarian and that's why I write like this. I haven't: and you shouldn't allow yourself to be led astray by petty suspicions like that. Look the facts in the face. Then we shall have at least one friend in Hungary.

Sincerely, and with good wishes

Basil Davidson Capt.

Istanbul, May 12th, 1943

My dear Basil,

Thank you for your long and interesting letter. When I came down here, at last, I had hoped to see you here. In compensation, I heard a lot of you from your friends here, and now I have your letter which I greatly value.

My life in Budapest during the last years after you left that city were [*sic*] rather uneventful in comparison to what you, or P. H., have gone through. Still it was not uninteresting. I was quite busy and, in a small way, did what I could—writing articles, and pepping up the spirit of people I used to meet. Of course, I gathered from various telegrams what you were doing to help me out, and I did my little bit in various quarters. If it hadn't been for the sudden death of Teleki, I would have gone long ago. So I had to wait, getting promises to this effect again and again. At last, in January it was decided that I should go, and here I have been for three months, and do not regret it and never shall.

It was nice of you to write me all you are thinking of Hungary in the present crisis. I'd agree with much of what you said although I don't like it. But while I accept the facts which are true, I can't agree with your conclusions. I don't believe they are just, equitable, or well-balanced. And, at any rate, they are still premature.

So I won't argue with what you wrote about the behavior of our Government, and that of many of our people. You are right, it was and is disgusting, preposterous, and shameful. Nevertheless, in my view your arguments, based on these facts and others, as well as your final conclusions, are wrong.

Firstly, I don't believe in the principle of collective responsibility. Those who are the culprits should be punished but the innocents should not. Collective responsibility is a barbarous vestige, a thing employed by Nazis or other terrorist regimes. It's unjust, indecent, and cruel. One doesn't punish nations, one punishes culprits. I know, you will gainsay: why, and the thousands and thousands slain in the war, they were innocent, too! Yes, they were innocent. But you can't make good the wrongs which have been committed by doing other wrongs. That is one of the principles on which I can't agree with you.

Further, there is something in the criminal law of all civilized nations termed proportionate punishments and also what are called "extenuating circumstances." Now, don't tell me this is legal nonsense. It is not, it is essential and elementary justice. You can't sentence a child to death for petty larceny, if you rightly condemn a man for murder. It would be unjust, as unjust as condemning an innocent person. You admit yourself that Hungary received a rotten deal after World War I. And it was never made good. Here there is an important "extenuating circumstance" which you have to take into account if you wish to administer justice. If you wish Hungary to be treated even more harshly than in the last war, well, how are you going to treat Germany which started the whole bloody nonsense; or what are you going to do with Rumania which benefited from the Treaty of Trianon, was your ally and still betrayed you, a thing which we never did. If you are to treat Hungary more harshly than after the last war, what are you going to do with Rumania? Exterminate her population or rape her womenfolk, or else, what some of your compatriots suggest even now, to reward her by returning to her all of Transylvania which was taken away from Hungary in the same rotten deal of Trianon. And may I ask you what, in the past twenty years or so did England do to help Hungary which would justify a demand for reciprocal cooperation?

Well, one should have some sense of proportion, if not one of justice. Or will you again spare the real warmonger, Germany, and hit the weaklings or cowards which were compelled to follow her warpath? That's fine justice when the little fellows are hanged and the big ones are allowed to escape!

From all that you said I presume you want to do justice. That's why I speak of justice myself. Because, if you only want to carry out vengeance, well, that's another matter. Thus I can't follow your argument when you say that Budapest should be and will be bombed because England was being bombed by the Germans. If you were to say that Budapest should be bombed because of military necessity, to destroy industries which work for the Germans, or communication centers used against the Allies, I would regret it but still understand and not utter a word of protest. But when you write that Budapest is to be bombed because the *Germans* bombed England, that's an inference beyond me.

And, in fine, I believe your conclusions are still premature. The stage is not yet ready for a judgment. Perhaps some more extenuating circumstances will accrue, many things may still happen. The jury may still acquit. The "judges" will have to be not only just men but also wise men, with a foresight that was lacking in Trianon. Perhaps they will not again make a mess of Central Europe, a hotbed for dangerous insects, and an allurement for voracious tyrants.

The case seems still worth defending. And even if it would look quite hopeless, one has to defend it out of decency. And so I shall stay, and not go home as you advised me. Complacency is, in these days, more than a crime. And so is despair. I won't know either of them.

I have not misunderstood your letter. I see that you still care for my country, you say so yourself; otherwise, you wouldn't have taken the trouble to write such a long letter. Thus, I trust you will consider all I have just said in an open mind, in the way we discussed matters on the Corso or in the Carlton in Budapest.

Certainly I hope to see you during the war or after it is over. We might perhaps meet one of these days and follow up this conversation. In the meantime, I wish you the best of luck, good hunting, and good health.

                                        Very sincerely yours,
                                            Ferenc Váli

After the developments that have taken place in the last thirty years, it seems almost ironic to peruse these letters. Basil Davidson's arraignment of Hungary was hardly justified. It was certainly not Hungary that was responsible for allowing Hitler to rearm Germany. It was the

Munich Agreement, not Hungary, that dismembered Czechoslovakia; nor did Hungary participate in the attack on Poland (which sparked World War II), as did the Soviet Union. Basil completely ignored the threat of Soviet occupation, which Hungarians (except, of course, the Jewish part of the population) feared more than an occupation by the Germans. He warned that Hungary would be treated as harshly as Germany. In later years many Hungarians, smarting under Stalinist terrorism, would have much preferred to have been treated as the people of West Germany.

I saw, of course, the wartime pro-Soviet sentiment in the United States and Great Britain; therefore, I refrained from speaking of the Soviet issue in my letter. But for Poles, Rumanians, Bulgarians, and Hungarians, this was the number one problem. Caught between the devil and the deep blue sea — Germans and Russians — these nations ardently hoped for occupation by the Americans and British — a vain hope, as it proved later.

In the lull of waiting for new initiatives from Budapest, it appeared useful to meet some of the criticism broadcast by the BBC and other Western radio and press organs charging Hungarians with passivity. While the Allies fight, the Hungarians do nothing — so went the broadcasts. They should turn against their regime and force it to oppose Germany. Any such move would have resulted, of course, in an earlier German occupation with no advantage to the Allies. On the contrary, Hungary would have been fully integrated into the German war machine, and the Hungarian Jews would have been completely exterminated.

This unrealistic and harmful campaign could perhaps be stopped or at least diminished if the situation could be explained by a recognized representative of the pro-Allied opposition movement in Hungary. The idea originated between Páloczi-Horváth and myself. The person we considered a reliable spokesman for the opposition, then known as the Independence Front, was Prof. Gyula Szekfü, a historian and an advocate of the underdogs — the peasants and the workers.

Father Vendel, pastor of the Hungarian colony in Istanbul, had been Szekfü's student. Without revealing the real reason, I persuaded him to collect signatures from among the members of the Hungarian colony and to invite the professor to deliver a lecture in Turkey. I also wrote Szekfü a letter, which was passed on to him through the diplomatic pouch. Shortly, Professor Szekfü replied that he would be ready to come to Turkey provided he obtained the necessary travel permit, exit permit, and passport. Because of subsequent developments, his visit had to be postponed until spring 1944, when it could no longer be carried out.

At the beginning of April a humorous incident focused some attention on myself, without immediate political implications, however. Hungarian consul general Mihalkovits wished to invite me and others for dinner. He wrote the names of his guests on a piece of paper and gave it to the Turkish telephonist to issue invitations for dinner on the following Thursday. On the top of the list was my name, Váli, which in Turkish means governor. The telephonist found it natural that the consul general planned to invite Lütfi Kirdar, the all-powerful governor of Istanbul province, and so she called the governor's office and then connected the governor with Mihalkovits. The latter began talking in Hungarian (thinking that he was talking to me); on the other end of the line the response came in Turkish (which the consul general did not speak). Mihalkovits finally replaced the receiver. A few minutes later the governor called back and the telephone operator assured him, "Yes, Your Excellency, the consul general wishes to talk to you. He wants to invite you for dinner." When the connection again was made between the two, the scene was repeated; Mihalkovits shouted in despair, "Have you forgotten your Hungarian?"

When, eventually, the error was discovered, Mihalkovits drove to the governor's palace, apologized — and invited him for dinner. The story later circulated among members of the diplomatic and consular corps, and I was jokingly referred to as the "vali of Budapest," as opposed to the vali of Istanbul. However, the governor, whom I had the pleasure of meeting at the dinner, remembered me throughout my stay in Turkey. The good-natured Mihalkovits was, unfortunately, recalled soon after that incident.

On May 20 I traveled again to Ankara. The principal reason for my journey was to introduce the new assistant military attaché of Hungary, Capt. Károly Bálintitt, to the Poles. Budapest had the good sense to appoint a staff captain who was ready to take up contacts with the Allies as deputy to Colonel Bartalis. I met him while he was passing through Istanbul to his new post (the assistant military attaché resided in Ankara) and we agreed that I would arrange a meeting for him with Colonel Zimnal. In Ankara I took Bálintitt to the Polish Embassy, where we were received by Zimnal with the usual hospitality. The libations on that occasion were not strange to the youthful and gregarious Bálintitt.

While in Ankara I also made my first contact with representatives of the Free French, an acquaintance that later proved highly productive. Before returning to Istanbul on May 23, I received word from Rector Bilsel that the minister of education had approved my lectures. The first was scheduled for June 1.

PUBLIC LECTURE

The public lecture I was to deliver in French on June 1 was to be translated, sentence by sentence, into Turkish. At that time the foreign faculty members lectured either in French or in German and thus students were accustomed to translated deliveries. My translator, a graduate assistant by the name of Mahmut Belik, visited me a few days before the lecture and we discussed the text. When I met him again some twenty years later, Mahmut Belik had become the professor of international law, the chair once held by Cemil Bilsel.

On May 30 the successor to Consul General Mihalkovits arrived in Istanbul. Dezsö Ujváry had served in the Political Section of the Ministry of Foreign Affairs in Budapest. His assignment demonstrated an increased interest in Istanbul on the part of the Hungarian government. I had never met Ujváry before. All I knew about him was that earlier he had strongly supported the German orientation of Hungary. He had publicly condemned those who opposed such a policy, including Hungarian diplomats who defected in protest. However, now I received instructions from Budapest inviting me to cooperate fully with him.

Soon after Ujváry's arrival I informed him of my contacts with the British and the Americans as well as with the Poles. Upon his request I arranged discreet meetings between him and William Morgan and also Walter Birge. He insisted on attending my lecture, which gave him an opportunity to meet with the university rector and some members of the Faculty of Law.

In addition to the students, who almost filled the large hall, an array of guests attended my lecture: Vice-Consul Birge with the dragoman of the American Consulate; several members of the British mission; Allied, Turkish, and German journalists; the Greek consul Caloyanni; and

Colonel Bartalis, who must have been eager to report to Budapest what I was saying.

The title of my lecture was "Justice and Force," concepts of basic importance both in international law and international politics. The central theme focused on the classical formula of Pascal: "Justice without force is impotent; force without justice is tyrannic. Therefore, justice is tyrannic. Therefore, justice and force have to be merged so that who is just should be strong and the strong should be just." While I thus referred in rather esoteric language to the causes of the current conflict, I emphasized the desire not only that the war be won by those who seek justice but also that peace be won by applying the demands of equity. I mentioned the rights and duties of neutrals and received a warm applause from the audience when I referred to the case of the Hungarian statesman Lajos Kossuth, who in 1849 sought refuge in Turkey. In closing remarks to my lecture Rector Bilsel returned to this event, emphasizing that the Ottoman Empire refused Kossuth's extradition even in the face of threats by Russia and Austria.

On June 5 a long summary of my lecture appeared in *La Turquie;* other newspapers gave shorter accounts of it. I had achieved what I wanted: a reason for my stay in Turkey.

For some time I had no word from Ullein-Reviczky. On June 15, 1943, Ujváry informed me that he had been relieved of his duties as foreign press chief and appointed minister to Stockholm. A few days later Budapest instructed me to report to a member of the Political Section in the Foreign Ministry, Aladár Szegedi-Maszák.

By now the British had become restless. Morgan told me on June 12 that if Budapest did not come forward with some reasonable proposals, London might wish to sever all contacts. On June 20 Ujváry left for Budapest to urge further action.

It should be recalled that on May 12, 1943, Tunis fell to the Allies, and the Germans and Italians in North Africa were either expelled or captured. On June 11 the island of Pantelleria was taken by the British in preparation for the invasion of Sicily on July 9 by American and British forces. The assault against the "soft underbelly" of the Axis had begun.

UNCONDITIONAL SURRENDER

At an April meeting with Horthy, Hitler made two serious accusations against Hungary: seeking secret contacts with the Allies and—no less an infraction of loyalty in the Führer's mind—refusing to carry out his policy of Jewish extermination. The anti-Semitic laws enacted in Hungary in 1938 and 1941 were harmless measures in comparison to the deportations and killings practiced in Germany against the Jews and followed in practically all the countries surrounding Hungary—Slovakia, Yugoslavia, Poland, and Rumania.* In contrast, Hungary had become a refuge for Jews from Germany, Austria, and other surrounding countries, whether or not under direct German occupation. The excesses committed by the police and the military against Jews in 1942 had been discontinued under orders from Prime Minister Kállay and condemned by the Hungarian government.

In May I was contacted, through the intermediary of the British, by Shimon Barlas, the representative in Turkey of the Jewish Agency of Palestine, which was to form the nucleus of the future Israeli government. In June, Barlas handed me a list of requests to be passed on to the Hungarian authorities. Arthur Whitall, the British consul, confirmed that these requests were fully supported by his government. The most important item on this list was a request for transit and exit permits for Polish and Slovak Jews, many of them children, whom the agency sought to rescue and transport to Palestine via Turkey. I passed on this aide-mémoire to Budapest and obtained an encouraging reply. Thus, the Hungarian representative of the Jewish Agency was allowed to function within the framework of the International Red Cross in Hungary. The Foreign Ministry also let it be known that Hungarian authorities would not prevent the departure of Jews provided that they could be disguised from the Germans on the route across the Balkans and that their entry into Turkey could be assured.

Until the occupation of Hungary by the Germans in March 1944 a slow but constant flow of Jewish emigrants trickled into Turkey on the way to their final destination, Palestine. Jewish children arrived in the company of Swedish, Swiss, Turkish, and other adults with all kinds of

---

*See Nicholas M. Nagy-Talavpra, *The Green Shirts and Others* (Stanford, Ca.: Hoover Institution Press, 1970), pp. 136, 147–9, and 171–2 for another view of the anti-Jewish laws.—ED.

travel papers. This exodus gave me utter satisfaction in my work. Even if it was not possible at that moment to achieve a breakthrough in the diplomatic negotiations, at least in the humanitarian field some limited results could be attained.

The successful Allied invasion of Sicily convinced the Hungarian government (or at least most of its members) of Italy's incapacity to defend herself. The belief in German invincibility began to dissipate, although many still hoped that a compromise peace might stave off a Soviet advance into Europe. The forthcoming loss of Italy placed an invasion of the Balkan Peninsula in the realm of possibilities. It was at that time that Budapest gossip recalled General Ludendorff's prediction of 1927 that the decisive battle of the next war would be fought in Hungary along the shores of Lake Balaton.

On July 25 I received news from Budapest: Prime Minister Kállay, who up to then was also in charge of foreign affairs, had handed over this portfolio to Jenö Ghyczy, secretary general of the Foreign Ministry (deputy foreign minister); simultaneously, Andor Szentmiklossy, head of the Political Section, was promoted to secretary general, and Aladár Szegedi-Maszák became head of the Political Section. István Bede became press director in the place of Ullein-Reviczky, who at long last was able to travel to his post as minister in Stockholm. This reshuffle, which placed persons of a definite anti-German tendency into key positions, forecast for me that some important steps might be forthcoming.

I congratulated Szegedi-Maszák on his appointment and he thanked me in a rather pessimistic letter:

> It is the irony of fate that both Bede, a twenty-year friend of mine, whose opinions I have shared throughout that period, and I are forced at the same time into key positions. Our new responsibilities are no joy to us, as we have to accept them before and not after the occurrence of events which we should like to happen. [This is a reference to the planned defection of Hungary from the German side.] I tried to evade promotion, but when I told the new Foreign Minister of my reluctance, he said: "Mitgefangen, mitgehangen." ["Captured together, be hanged together."] To this I could say nothing, as Ghyczy is a sick old man for whom it is a still greater sacrifice than for me.

Evidently the new leadership of the Foreign Ministry now went through an agonizing appraisal of what to do next. The dispatch of a

General Staff officer (which had been urged earlier by the British) was considered again. Szegedi-Maszák wrote me:

> I think that your friend [the General Staff officer] will arrive around August 20th. I do not say that this is 100 percent certain because lately there have been so many indiscretions on the other side that we are worried lest his arrival be used to denounce us to the Germans and to provoke a German occupation. Do you think it is in their interests to have our country occupied before we are able to do something for them? Please let me have your opinion. If there is only a slight risk of their wanting to denounce us, then I am prepared to take the responsibility, but if you think there is a great probability then I will not do so.
>
> The bombardment of Rome had a very bad effect on conservative circles. [On July 19, 1943, American bombers attacked railroad yards and the airport around Rome, causing heavy damage.] Bethlen & Co. [Count István Bethlen, prime minister of Hungary, 1921–31] are of the opinion that the Allies are doing their utmost to provoke the Germans into occupying further territories. This is of course nonsense. But, what I do not quite understand is how do the Allies imagine a Hungarian unconditional surrender? Would they drop their armistice commissions by parachute into captivity? And what about the invading army?

The questions that vexed the Budapest leaders and on which I was frequently asked advice involved the meaning of the Casablanca formula on unconditional surrender and the possibility of an invasion of the Balkans.* As to this unfortunate device of unconditional surrender, I always thought that as far as Hungary was concerned it was completely meaningless. There was no army in the neighborhood to which Hungary could surrender. Therefore, as a gesture—I thought—it should be freely given. In any case, unconditional surrender was unfeasible, as the Italian, Japanese, and even the German surrender demonstrated later; there were always "conditions."

About an invasion in the direction of Hungary I could only report that according to my Polish sources, this was being planned. Also, the

---

*The unconditional surrender doctrine, announced after the Churchill-Roosevelt meeting at Casablanca in January 1943, was the brainchild of Roosevelt's concern to head off any German-Soviet deal and to convince the Soviets of Western commitment to the war. However, both Stalin and the British government later criticized the idea. See Adam B. Ulam, *Expansion and Coexistence,* 2d ed. (New York: Praeger, 1974), pp. 338–9, and Charles E. Bohlen, *Witness to History* (New York: Norton, 1973), pp. 144 and 156–58.

interest the Allies had shown in Hungary's attitude appeared to be convincing proof. I already knew that at that time feelers for a surrender had been put out on behalf of Bulgaria and that the opposition in Rumania, led by Maniu, also maintained contacts with the Allies in Turkey.

After midnight of July 25 I heard over the radio the dramatic announcement of Mussolini's fall. By then the Allied forces had already set foot on the Italian mainland, and we all were full of expectations as to what was going to happen next.

It was midsummer and the Ankara diplomatic corps had descended, as usual, on the shores of the Bosporus. On July 30 I had dinner with my friend Ödön Gáspár in the Yolcu Salonu overlooking the harbor. The previous day the Istanbul papers had reported that Raffaele Guariglia, the Italian ambassador to Turkey, was offered and had accepted the post of minister of foreign affairs in the new Italian cabinet formed by Marshal Badoglio, who was instrumental in the unseating of Mussolini.

Gáspár complained of having been very busy the whole day. On the way to Rome Guariglia visited Vörnle, and the Hungarian minister immediately reported the conversation to Budapest in a long, coded cable. Sending the cable was the task of Gáspár, who hinted that it contained an important message from Guariglia to Hungarian prime minister Kállay.

We had some raki, the Turkish national drink, before our meal and drank wine with dinner. We discussed the political situation. What was going to happen in Italy? Would Badoglio ask for an Armistice? Gáspár was absolutely definite in his pronouncement: Badoglio *will* ask for an armistice. The way he said it left no doubt that this was the message of the new Italian foreign minister to the friendly Hungarian government. I once more asked Gáspár whether he was convinced that this was going to happen; with a wry smile he said yes. I called Walter Birge and Bill Morgan later that night and told them about my conversation with Gáspár. Birge told me later that Washington commended him on the news; his word was the first definite report of the impending surrender of Italy.

No Hungarian staff officer arrived. But on August 14 László Veress came with the official assignment to supervise the Hungarian exhibition at the Izmir Fair, which was to open on August 20. The impact of the events in Italy had, at last, given courage to the Hungarian leaders to make formal commitments to the Allies. Veress brought "full powers" to

Consul General Ujváry and was himself authorized to negotiate fully with the Allied side.

Hungary's offer of unconditional surrender was discussed first between Veress and members of the SOE mission in Istanbul; the Foreign Ministry in Budapest then gave its blessing to such an offer. Clearly, the matter was now ripe enough to be raised on the official diplomatic level. The highest-ranking British diplomat in Istanbul was John Cecil Sterndale-Bennett, who held the diplomatic rank of minister under the ambassador in Ankara. The document of surrender was handed to Sterndale-Bennett by Ujváry and Veress on August 17.

On September 9 the capitulation of Italy to the Allies was announced. On that day Veress was invited by the British ambassador, Sir Hughe Knatchbull-Hugessen, to his yacht, *Makook II,* which was cruising in the Sea of Marmara. A motor launch took the Hungarian representative to the yacht after nightfall. At about midnight the ambassador handed Veress the reply from London to the Hungarian surrender offer. For reasons of security (Veress was soon to return to Budapest) no signed document was given to Veress, but he was asked to copy it in the presence of the ambassador. Since these notes were later destroyed in the Hungarian Foreign Ministry in March 1944 when the Germans moved in, several texts of this British reply were later circulated, though with essentially the same meaning.[5] According to my notes, the Allied declaration ran as follows:

1. The Hungarian government is to confirm the declaration of August 17 concerning Hungary's capitulation and the acceptance of the conditions set by the Allies.

2. The surrender of Hungary will be kept secret. It will be made public by the Allies and the Hungarian government simultaneously at a time to be found suitable by both parties. At the express wish of the Hungarian side, this publication shall not take place before the Allies have reached the borders of Hungary.

3. Hungary is to reduce gradually her military cooperation with Germany, in particular by withdrawing her forces from Russia and by

5. Kállay, *Hungarian Premier,* pp. 373–74; Kertesz, *Diplomacy in a Whirlpool,* pp. 67–69; Macartney, *October 15,* pp. 185–86; Páloczi-Horváth, *The Undefeated,* pp. 111–14. A somewhat incorrect story of the surrender was reported in The *New York Times,* February 5, 1945.

assisting Allied aircraft flying across Hungary to reach German bases.

4. Hungary is to gradually discontinue her economic cooperation with Germany and refuse to participate in Germany's war production.

5. Hungary undertakes to resist a possible attempt by Germany to occupy her territory. For this end, the Hungarian Army Command is to be reorganized so as to render the army capable of cutting off its ties with the Germans and to attack them.

6. At a given date, Hungary is to place all her resources, her means of transportation, and her air bases at the disposal of the Allies in their pursuit of the war effort against the Germans.

7. An Allied military mission is to be dropped into Hungary at a suitable date to prepare the necessary steps for her surrender.

8. Regular radio contact will be established between the Allies and organs of the Hungarian government. The Allies are to be informed of German and Hungarian developments.

In accordance with this declaration, the Hungarian offer of surrender of August 17 was promptly confirmed by Andor Wodianer, the Hungarian minister in Lisbon, in a communication to Sir Ronald Campbell, the British ambassador there.

László Veress left Istanbul for Budapest on the night of September 10. He took with him, under diplomatic seal, two sets of shortwave transmitters to be operated from Budapest. Regular exchanges of messages between Budapest and the British Embassy building in Istanbul became possible.

Some complications arose when Kállay and his advisers objected against an unconditional surrender so that Wodianer confirmed an offer only of surrender. Indeed, it remained unclear whether this exchange of declarations was to be considered the armistice or only a preliminary instrument to be followed by a regular armistice or capitulation when Allied forces reached the frontier of Hungary. Even the word *Allies* remained ambiguous. In Budapest it was hoped that the Allies were the Americans and the British, whereas in fact the Russians also might have been included. My British colleagues were uncertain whether the Hungarian capitulation was discussed at the first Quebec Conference in August 1943, which was attended by President Roosevelt and Prime Minister Churchill. But it appears likely that Moscow was advised, although it preferred to ignore the entire event completely when Soviet forces moved into Hungary.

The "unconditional" surrender of August 17 was in fact conditional on the Allied forces reaching Hungary. It was on this hypothesis that the agreement was concluded. We in Istanbul and those few in Budapest who knew about this action watched the developments in Italy with greater attention than anybody else, it being expected that they were preliminary to the deployment of Anglo-American forces in the Balkans.

INVASION OF THE BALKANS?

When the news of the Italian surrender reached Istanbul, I, like other observers, was particularly eager to speculate as to its impact on the military situation and on the possibility of Hungary's defection from the Nazi camp. From the confidential correspondence I maintained with Budapest I gathered that the anti-German circles, including those in the Foreign Ministry, believed that with Italy's capitulation the entire peninsula would soon be occupied by Allied forces and that their approach to Hungary's borders would be within the realm of possibility. No clear notion existed of the Allied planning with regard to the Balkans; but this uncertainty increased rather than decreased expectations because, after the North African landing, secret plans and surprise moves were easily ascribed to the Allies. Winston Churchill's enigmatic pronouncement about assaults against the "soft underbelly" of the Axis encouraged these anticipations.

If one were to speculate on the causes of the eventual fiasco of Hungarian attempts to change sides, as promoted from Istanbul, the failure of the Allies to exploit Italy's surrender must rank as the most significant. The second reason, closely linked and consequential to the former, was the failure to convince Turkey to join the anti-German coalition. All these developments frustrated the hope that the German position in the Balkans would become untenable with the loss of Italy and with certain military-political moves, especially along the Balkan coastline of the Adriatic Sea and in the Aegean Sea. As it happened, the Germans managed to preserve their rule over the Italian peninsula until the arrival of the Soviet forces in late summer and early fall 1944.

Unfortunately, the events of September and October 1943 proved disappointing. The Anglo-American forces did not land in central Italy and the Germans gained control over the entire country except for its southern tip. The advancing armies of the Allies were eventually stopped well below Rome and hopes that they might reach northern Italy and move along the northern Adriatic into the Ljubljana gap or land along the Yugoslav coast were soon dissipated.

The Germans succeeded in disarming or neutralizing Italian troops in the Balkans, including those on the Greek islands of the Aegean. A daring attempt by the British to capture the Dodecanese Islands and Rhodes proved to be abortive; the forces that temporarily held Leros, Kos, and Samos had to be evacuated with much loss of life. These latter events just a few miles off the Turkish coast exercised a devastating effect on Turkey's attitude toward the Allies. The failure provided evidence of the relative weakness of Germany's enemies in the eastern Mediterranean and of the still formidable German strength in that theater of the war.

Although these disappointing occurrences cast a shadow over the recently concluded secret agreement, progress was nevertheless achieved in its execution as far as circumstances permitted. The months following the conclusion of this agreement were the most active of my stay in Turkey. The shortwave stations Veress took to Budapest began daily operation. These exchanges occurred between the Ministry of Foreign Affairs in Budapest and the British Embassy in Istanbul; naturally, I was not fully aware of their content. Nevertheless, from the British side some of these messages were conveyed to me, generally to question some of their points or to complain about the scarcity and nature of the material passed on. Some of the bulky material, as well as some messages Budapest wished me to know, continued to arrive via the diplomatic bag and passed through my hands. Ujváry also received some material intended to be forwarded to the British or Americans; he occasionally asked me to forward it to the addressees. Quite frequently members of the British mission met with Ujváry in my apartment and in my presence.

Ujváry left on September 28 for Budapest and only returned around October 10. He brought back the interesting news that Colonel Bartalis had been recalled and would be replaced by Col. Otto Hátszegi-Hatz. The new military attaché had been serving in this capacity in Sofia; he was thus also familiar with the Turkish scene. Hátszegi-Hatz, unlike Bartalis, was not considered pro-German. As soon as he settled down in Istanbul, he established contacts with the military representatives of Great Britain and the United States.

Ujváry also surprised me with the message, allegedly from Szegedi-Maszák, that henceforth I should place my reports to Budapest, which I intended for the diplomatic bag, into his hands in open envelopes (thus far I had given him sealed letters). Although I was convinced that this was conceived by Ujváry himself to pry into my reports, I did not object. I still kept open my other channel of communication via the diplomatic bag of the commercial attaché.

Besides forwarding papers and messages and reporting to Budapest while maintaining contact with the American, British, Polish, and other Allied missions, through my activity I became involved with several agencies other than the Jewish Agency. In the second half of 1943 the United States Office of Strategic Services began to extend its operations into Turkey. It was only established in 1942 and lacked the experience, traditions, and continuity of similar British organizations, such as the SOE. The resident representative of the OSS, whose cover was as correspondent for the *Chicago Daily News* (a genuine, not a sham, assignment), was Sam Brewer. I was able to provide him with some useful advice and suggestions.

Another much-valued contact I made was with Dr. Wolfgang Brettholz, the correspondent of the Swedish newspaper *Svenska Dagbladet*. Dr. Brettholz was a refugee from Prague. He had excellent sources of information and told me all he knew; he was much interested in Hungary, and I tried to satisfy his thirst for news but naturally could not always tell him a great deal. He was ready to support any anti-Nazi move. The technique we used was to place a news item — often a trial balloon — in *Svenska Dagbladet* and, with reference to this Swedish source, repeat it in the Turkish press, giving it a somewhat different emphasis or interpretation.

There were some individual problems that had to be handled as a result of the Hungarian-Allied cooperation, as was foreseen in the secret agreement. One was the question of Baroness Miske-Gerstenberger. She was born British and retained her citizenship when she married Jenö Miske-Gerstenberger, a Hungarian diplomat. In 1942 she was sentenced to life imprisonment by a Hungarian military court for having passed seditious letters to Socialist leaders in Hungary. She was now to be exchanged for a Hungarian citizen sentenced for espionage in London. This man, Jenö Wieser, happened to be a former classmate of mine. An aeronautical engineer, Wieser stayed on in England after the outbreak of the war and supplied classified material to the Hungarian military attaché in the period before the rupture of diplomatic relations between Great Britain and Hungary in 1941.

Turkey and Portugal volunteered to make the exchange possible. Wieser was taken by plane to Lisbon and the baroness arrived in Istanbul by train; each was handed over by a police escort to the neutral authorities of Portugal and Turkey, respectively. Then they were simultaneously released from custody and allowed to travel to their home countries.

Messages continued to be exchanged between Budapest and Istanbul, but there was discontent on both sides. The British complained that the information they were receiving was of no or only secondary value. Many of the direct questions they asked were answered evasively by the Hungarians. It appeared from these replies that the Foreign Ministry officials either were not informed of military secrets or else could not obtain them and were reluctant to admit their ignorance. The reason for this centered upon the split in the Hungarian leadership between the pro-German wing (most of the military) and the pro-Allied group. The contacts with the Allies as well as their questions had to be kept secret from all those who could not be trusted — and they were many. Those officials who maintained close contact with the German General Staff and who knew a great deal were almost exclusively untrustworthy. Nor did such officials trust the often strongly anti-Nazi Foreign Ministry employees.

On the other hand, Hungarian inquiries of the British that were of a political nature did not receive a substantive answer, if indeed they were answered at all. It happened that in response to such queries the Hungarian side was rebuked by the British for wishing "to create dissension between the Allies." Of course, some of these questions referred to postwar territorial settlements in which Czechoslovak, Yugoslav, and Rumanian interests clashed with those of Hungary. But the most pressing question related to the threat of a Soviet occupation of Hungary. It may have been that such questions lacked tactfulness or prudence (Budapest could not have expected London to admit that it had an interest in forestalling Soviet penetration into Central Europe); nevertheless, the British must have known that the raison d'être for the Hungarian promise of surrender was precisely to prevent or forestall such an event from happening.

An unconfessed ambivalence in this relationship was the cause of the malaise. Budapest was primarily interested in the preservation of Hungary's territorial status and in the prevention of both German and Russian occupation. The fundamental Allied goal was to defeat the Germans irrespective of what fate Hungary would suffer before or after such a defeat. The Allies were unwilling to promise anything in return for the sacrifice and risk taking it insistently demanded of Hungary except for the cryptic encouragement that the Hungarian people should "work their passage home."

I found this cliché rather distasteful. After all, Hungary was not responsible for the outbreak of the war. It was more than unrealistic—it was frivolous to expect that she should have resisted or turned against Germany when the Allies were as patently unable to protect her as they had proved in the cases of Poland, Yugoslavia, and Greece. British foreign minister Anthony Eden and others admitted several times that Hungary had received unfair treatment at the end of World War I, and nothing had been done to make up for that inequity. With the help of Italy and Germany, help which popular sentiment made it impossible to refuse, some of the lost and overwhelmingly Hungarian-inhabited areas were returned to Hungary. This should never have been construed as full participation on the side of Germany.

The primary reason for mistakes committed by Hungary, such as participation in the war against the Soviet Union, was the terrible pressure to which she was subjected by Germany because of her geopolitical position. Previously, Yugoslav intransigence had forced Hungary to cooperate with Hitler (the Hungarian prime minister paid with his life in protest against such action); otherwise, she would have shared Yugoslavia's fate, without having the good fortune of the Yugoslav mountains in which to organize a guerrilla campaign. The Hungarian people at large disliked Hitler and what he stood for; but it was not for Hungary to stand up against German might, which with their shortsightedness and gullibility the Allies helped to create. Great Britain and France tolerated German rearmament and by default were coresponsible for Hitler's early successes in the Rhineland, Austria, and Czechoslovakia. But it was not the first time in history that the great powers displayed a lack of sensitivity toward the needs and views of small nations who were desperately trying to maintain their independence and territorial integrity. I could hardly do anything to create better understanding between the British in Istanbul and London and the Hungarian leadership. All I could try was to smooth out misunderstandings and to make the secret agreement operable.

Despite the existing misapprehensions, the agreement proved useful to both parties. American and British aircraft overflying Hungary in the direction of German-occupied Austria remained unmolested. They could fly from southern Italian bases across Yugoslavia into Hungarian airspace and then drop their bombs on German targets. They were not fired on or attacked over Hungarian territory, a virtual sanctuary for them. In return they refrained from bombing Hungarian targets.

No arrangement was made for a long time concerning the dispatch of staff officers from Hungary to meet Allied personnel. After a long silence Budapest let it be known that for security reasons it could not risk sending staff officers into a neutral country; they could not remain undetected in the face of the German espionage system. Budapest now suggested that Allied officers travel to Hungary "with neutral passports." London and Washington turned this offer down. In late December, after London threatened to consider the surrender agreement void, Budapest gave its consent to receive British and American military missions to be parachuted into Hungarian territory.

After October 1943 I noticed that interest was flagging in the Allied approach toward Hungary. The existing channels of communication were not being fully exploited—at least this was my impression. The main reason for this slowdown was not mutual misapprehension. Instead, it revolved around the rather unhappy military developments in Italy and the dissension among the Allies in regard to planning, both of which created wavering and indecision.

At the end of November 1943 President Roosevelt and Prime Minister Churchill met in Cairo in preparation for the tripartite conference to be held with Stalin in Teheran. Generalissimo Chiang Kai-shek also attended the Cairo meeting (he was not to go to Teheran because the Soviet Union was not at war with Japan). As Churchill recorded in his memoirs,[6] Roosevelt promised the Chinese a sizable amphibious military operation across the Bay of Bengal against the Japanese, despite British objections. Tank landing craft required for similar operations in the Aegean and in other parts of the Mediterranean theater thus would not be available. Evidently, the American General Staff did not support the British prime minister's projects against the Germans in the Balkans; the question of priorities loomed large over Allied decision making.

Numan Menemencioğlu, the Turkish foreign minister, also came to the Cairo meeting, where the Americans and the British tried to impress upon him the usefulness of Turkey joining the Allied war effort. It seeped out from my various sources of information that the Turkish foreign minister asked primarily for air protection against expected Ger-

---

6. Winston Churchill, *Closing the Ring* (New York: Bantam, 1962), pp. 279–80.

man air attacks on Istanbul, Ankara, and Izmir in case Turkey did decide to participate in the war. He must have referred to the frailness of Allied air power in the eastern Mediterranean evident from the Allies' inability to hold on to Leros and Samos in the Aegean.

The Teheran Conference opened on November 28. I arrived in Ankara that morning and met Polish ambassador Sokolnicki and Colonel Zimnal on the following day. They told me with undisguised disappointment that the Polish army was being transferred from Syria to Italy. Allied diplomatic circles in Ankara were convinced that a decision would soon be taken about a landing in the Balkans and Turkey's entry into the war. However, the secretly pro-Allied Bulgarian minister, Nikola Balabanov, told me that Bulgaria would fight the Turks if they attempted to invade her, although she would not fight British, American, or Polish forces.

I returned to Istanbul on November 20, eagerly awaiting further developments. The Teheran Conference ended on December 1, and on December 4 a second meeting with Turkish leaders was held again in Cairo; this time Turkish president Ismet Inönü also participated. Turkey was enjoined to declare war on the Germans before February 15, 1944. British fighter squadrons would fly in and protect Turkish airfields as well as civilian targets. The first objective was the capture of the Greek islands in the Aegean Sea and the opening up for shipping of the route to Istanbul and to the Black Sea. I was told at that time that the Turks had made no decision at the conference; they would make their decision on the basis of the size and nature of military assistance that would be forthcoming from the Allies.

On the first day of January 1944 a British military mission headed by Air Marshal John Linnel came to Ankara and began talks with members of the Turkish General Staff. By the middle of January I was again in Ankara to pick up some news. My informants were pessimistic as to the outcome of these talks. The Turks received not more than a fraction of the military hardware promised to them by Churchill in January 1943 during his meeting with President Inönü at Adana. At that time assistance was offered by the Middle Eastern Forces (including the Polish army), which would have moved into Turkey as soon as she entered the war. It appeared well substantiated — knowing the Turkish penchant for realism — that this time Turkey would not rely on promises before breaking off relations with the Germans.

Hardly had I returned to Istanbul when an urgent appeal came from

Szegedi-Maszák in Budapest. The Foreign Ministry had obtained information that Turkey's entry into the war was just around the corner, and Szegedi-Maszák wanted to have my report on this. I immediately replied through the courier who departed for Budapest on January 29 that Turkey definitely would not open hostilities at that time and that Budapest should not reckon such a development. Indeed, a few days later the British military mission left Ankara without having reached an agreement.

Although Turkey was a neutral country and an ally, British attitudes toward her somewhat resembled those displayed toward Hungary. Later, when Turkish active belligerency was no longer called for, well-informed Turks complained that the Allies completely ignored the Turkish urge for self-preservation when they demanded Turkish participation in the war against Germany. At that time Americans were scarcely familiar with the precariousness of Turkey's geopolitical situation. Like the British, they were obsessed by their desire to see Nazi Germany destroyed and forgetful of the vital national interests of a country such as Turkey. Had Turkey lightheartedly entered the war, her European area together with the city of Istanbul likely would have been occupied by the Germans. Before that, Istanbul, with its fledgling industry, as well as other Turkish cities, would have been destroyed by the still powerful German Luftwaffe. But such sacrifice was still secondary in the thoughts of the Turkish leaders, who traditionally cast their eyes toward the colossus north of their borders, Russia.

The Turks believed that if they were invaded by the Germans, they would be forced to accept Russian assistance; this would mean Soviet forces would land on their Black Sea coast or move across the Caucasian border. Eventually, they would be "liberated" but they instinctively felt that the Russians would never pull out from the straits leading to the Mediterranean, so long an object of Russian covetousness, and would place Turkey under their control. Ankara foresaw what would happen to the East Central European nations, to the Poles, Hungarians, Czechs, and Slovaks, to the Rumanians and Bulgarians, once the Soviet forces set foot on their territories. Turkey would have been less able to free herself from the crushing Russian embrace than the countries of East Central Europe. The Turkish leaders well remembered how in 1939 and 1940, when Stalin was Hitler's ally, the Georgian tried with all his diplomatic finesse to persuade the German leader to abandon Turkey to the "sphere of influence" of the Soviet Union. Turkey was saved only by the priority given by Hitler to the invasion of Russia herself.

In January 1944 I very much hoped that Turkey's entry into the war would hasten the liberation of the Balkans and of Hungary from German control. But it appears certain now that Turkey's participation in the war, without adequate Anglo-American assistance, would not have helped Hungary. Instead, it might have compelled the Germans to extend their defense perimeter further and contributed to their downfall. Essentially, it would have benefited only Russia by allowing her to place Turkey and the Dardanelles under her control. In retrospect, the Western powers should be grateful to the wartime leaders of Turkey for having resisted pressures and temptations to turn against Germany in 1943 or early 1944. How less advantageous would the strategic position of NATO be in the eastern Mediterranean if Turkey (and probably Greece, as well) were a satellite of the Kremlin? In 1945 and 1946 Moscow tried to subdue Turkey again, an attempt that Ankara was able to thwart. A Turkey devastated by war would hardly have been as able to do so.

The secret agreement with Hungary and the Hungarian attempt to escape from the worst consequence of the war, namely, incorporation into the Soviet Communist orbit, failed. It did so mainly because of Anglo-American foundering in Italy, because of Hitler's unexpectedly stubborn insistence not to give up real estate, and, lastly, because of the relative weakness of the Allies in the eastern Mediterranean theater, which weighed heavily in persuading Turkey against entry into the war.

Churchill probably hoped that the Allies would capture Italy and reach the Alps shortly after the Italian surrender and then extend their pressure across the Adriatic by joining forces with the Yugoslav guerrillas. At the same time, the Aegean would be cleared of the Germans and Greece liberated. From Turkish airfields the airspace above the Balkan Peninsula could be controlled and from Turkey the Allied armies, reinforced by Turkish detachments, could threaten the relatively small ground forces of the Germans. The defection of Bulgaria and Rumania, contingent on an Allied advance into these countries, would finally force the Germans to give up the Balkans and to try to establish a front along the borders of Hungary. From Italy, American and British forces would move through the Ljubljana gap into the border area of Hungary and Austria. This would be the time for the implementation of the surrender agreement whereby Hungary would sever her ties with Germany and open up her territory to the Allied advance.

This was the hope to which the Hungarian anti-German leadership was clinging. But by February 1944 it became quite evident that British and American interest in Hungary was slackening. While observing this, I refrained from unduly discouraging Budapest. Already some of my predictions as to the inevitable return of territories regained between 1938 and 1940 to Czechoslovakia and Yugoslavia, possibly even to Rumania, was being taken amiss. Strangely enough, the initiative of sending Allied military missions to Hungary was taken up at a time when the ambitious Balkan Plan was already buried. I believe that these missions were to serve purely military purposes: to gather information behind the lines and perhaps to dissuade Hungarian army leaders from supporting the German cause. By this time many of these officers were already wavering in their faith in German invincibility.

However, the sword of Damocles, which Hitler hung above his reluctant ally Hungary, fell in March 1944 and extinguished the hopes that still existed in the hearts of many of us.

HITLER OCCUPIES HUNGARY

At the time of my arrival in Istanbul in February 1943 the German front in the east stretched from Leningrad to Taganrog at the northeastern tip of the Sea of Azov. In July the Germans were still able to mount a major offensive around Kursk, an event duly noted in Ankara. But by the end of 1943 the Germans had been pushed back two hundred fifty to three hundred miles on the central and southern sections of the front; Kharkov and Kiev were recaptured by the Russians and the front now reached the Black Sea east of Odessa. The Soviet winter offensive, which opened in January 1944, relieved besieged Leningrad; on the central section the Russian armies reached the pre-1939 Polish frontier and in the south they lined up along the border of Rumania in March. In April the Crimean Peninsula, originally left behind, was recaptured.

By March 1944 the Russians were menacingly close to the Carpathian Mountains, behind which lay Hungary. Although Hitler may not have been aware of the secret agreement of the previous September, he certainly knew of some of the contacts maintained with the Allies by Hungarian emissaries, including diplomats accredited to neutral governments. Hungarians often gave vent to their anti-German sentiment and their feeling that Germany already had lost the war. As the tide turned against Hitler, especially under the impact of the Italian capitulation, Hungarian press organs were allowed to behave in a less restrained fashion; in the Hungarian parliament anti-German voices were frequently raised, and the Foreign Ministry openly quarreled with the German Legation on such issues as the continued recognition of the Italian royal diplomatic mission.

The precedent of Italy's loss must have sounded a warning to Hitler. As long as the eastern front was hundreds of miles away from Hungary, a country surrounded by German forces and strongholds, there was no immediate danger of a Hungarian volte-face. By March 1944, however, the situation in this respect was growing critical: the Russian forces were within reach of the Hungarian border. Now Hitler was determined to forestall any Hungarian "treachery."

The government of Miklos Kállay also sensed that the critical hour was approaching. By February 1944 the various reports that reached Budapest rendered it probable that Anglo-American forces would not be able to enter Hungary before the arrival of the Russians. The leadership was resolved to hold Soviet forces along the strategic Carpathian Mountains. In the Hungarian imagination these mountains appeared like the Maginot line to the French. In the first year of World War I the Austro-Hungarian armies managed to defend this wooded, rugged mountain wall against the gigantic tsarist steamroller. This time, however, the master plan of defending the Carpathian line had a serious shortcoming: the southern section of the Transylvanian Carpathians belonged to Rumania.

The overly optimistic Hungarian prime minister and his entourage never believed in the reality of cooperation between the Anglo-Saxon powers and the Soviet Union. To hold back the Russians would be welcomed—so they thought—by Washington and London. Thus, Hungary could obtain a quasi-neutral status and preserve it until the German collapse. It even was naively assumed that the Germans would be pleased by such a development because it would shorten their front against the Soviets.

The major flaw in this scenario was that it was based on the possibility of reasonable negotiations with the Germans and did not take into account the utter irrationality of Hitler, who was determined to defend every inch of territory. Moreover, the geographically central location of Hungary was totally unsuited to the type of disengagement action that Finland, on the periphery, successfully performed in September 1944.

I learned from Budapest's questions and instructions that people there still lived with the illusion that Hungary would be able to retain the territorial gains she had made since 1938. During his visit to Moscow in December 1943 Czechoslovak president Beneš obtained Moscow's promise of all Slovakian territories lost in 1938. Beneš even intervened with Stalin in favor of Rumania for a restoration of the pre-1940 border with Hungary. However, Budapest insisted on believing that Beneš was unsuccessful and reproached me for my alleged defeatist views. It is never rewarding to play the role of Cassandra.

My gloomy picture came from discussing military potentialities with British and American experts in view of the impending German threat as well as Budapest's ambitious plans for stopping the Russian advance. The remnants of Hungary's Second Army were still hostages encapsulated within the German occupation troops in Russia and Poland. The Hungarian First Army, stationed in eastern Hungary and in the Hungarian part of Transylvania, was insufficiently equipped. No other substantial Hungarian forces existed. The Kállay government flirted with the idea of decreeing a general mobilization but procrastinated so as not to provoke the Germans; and Germany (after the desertion of Italy) was the only source for obtaining sophisticated modern weapons, tanks, aircraft, and antiaircraft gunnery.

In this deteriorating situation both London and Washington still pressed for the establishment of direct contacts between the military staffs. In February formal agreement was reached to drop a British and another American military mission by parachute into Hungary. Because of this arrangement, and to handle other matters that caused dissatisfaction on both sides, László Veress was sent once more to Istanbul, officially to carry the diplomatic bag. He arrived on Sunday, February 27, and on Tuesday I had a long talk with him in my apartment. The question of the British and American military mission was now settled; but one of Veress's principal assignments was to establish contacts with the Russians and to do so with the assistance of the British.

It was understandable that under the existing circumstances Budapest was eager to create a direct line of communication with Moscow. Evidently Kállay wished to raise the question of a neutral Hungary with the Russians. If this would be acceptable, the Kremlin might concentrate its forces in the area between the Carpathians and the Baltic, thus bypassing the Carpathian basin or at least Hungary. All this overlooked Moscow's ominous designs to establish itself in the entire area between and including the Balkans, the Adriatic Sea, and the Baltic Sea. Budapest asked that members of the British mission to be parachuted not carry out or instigate sabotage actions (not even against the Germans). This was agreed upon; such details as the place of descent were also discussed. However, some further matters were left to be determined through shortwave communications between the Hungarian capital and Istanbul.

In respect to contacts with Moscow, Veress's endeavors were unsuccessful. Advised by London, the British in Istanbul refused to be intermediaries for such a rapprochement. Veress was told that Turkey was not a suitable venue for such contacts because of Ankara's sensitivity. It was suggested to him that such contacts be established in one of the other neutral capitals; Stockholm, where Ullein-Reviczky was now stationed, was considered one possibility.

Veress had explained to his British contacts the enormous difficulties the Hungarian government had to face when preparing to leave the German alliance. He pleaded for understanding, as I did, by explaining the physical and psychological impediments. I raised before him the point of a possible German occupation of Hungary. Budapest still appeared to be optimistic and did not believe in the imminence of such a move. Veress, nevertheless, had promised the British to discuss the options: resistance and the flight of Horthy and Kállay to neutral territory or to that of the Allies. The emissary from Hungary left on March 5, 1944; I was not to see Veress again until after the end of the war and my return to Hungary.

By mid February Soviet forces approached Cernauti, the capital of the Bukovina region in Rumania, at the foothills of the Carpathians, thus endangering the last north-south railroad connection between Rumania and Poland. Hungarian forces would soon be in contact with the approaching Russian armies. It must have been this development that finally persuaded Hitler to act.

The American military mission was parachuted into Hungary's southwest corner (Csáktornya) on March 15. The British mission was to be dropped around March 20 on the estate of Count Michael Andrássy, a pro-Western aristocrat, at Szigetvár in southern Transdanubia; but it was not sent and thus was not captured by the Germans, as the American mission was.

On March 17 I gave another public lecture at Istanbul University. Before I left for my lecture, I received a phone call from Col. W. Harris-

Burland, the successor to Major Morgan (who was transferred to Italy), inviting me to see him in the evening. Páloczi-Horváth was also there. On the shortwave line a few hours before, Budapest had reported the visit of Admiral Horthy to Hitler and the concentration of German forces along the western borders of Hungary. The Hungarian Foreign Ministry let it be known that because of the critical situation it would, for the time being, discontinue the operation of the microwave stations. There was nothing to do except to wait.

On March 18 the Hungarian courier left for Budapest. I sent my usual report with him, which contained material certainly compromising in the eyes of the Germans if they were to capture it. I had considerable disquiet about it, but evidently my letters did not come into unauthorized hands.

It subsequently became known that Regent Horthy and Foreign Minister Ghyczy, after being admitted into the presence of the Führer, were subjected to his accusations and invectives. Horthy was instructed to dismiss Kállay and replace him with someone the Germans could trust. To ensure the required changes, Hitler informed them, Hungary would temporarily be occupied by German forces. Horthy threatened to resign but was told that if German occupation was refused, Hungary would be invaded by Slovak, Rumanian, and Croatian forces, assisted, of course, by the Germans. When Horthy further resisted, he was told that German armies were already on the way and could not be stopped. Finally, he consented, but his return to Budapest was delayed forty-eight hours.

During the night of March 18–19, 1944, the Germans crossed the Hungarian border; about eleven divisions were involved in the action. Budapest was occupied by German parachutists. On March 19, a Sunday, Hitler's usual day of aggression, Germans occupied ministries and police buildings in Budapest and the Gestapo began arresting those who had been blacklisted by the various German missions in Hungary. Had I been in Budapest, surely I would have been among those arrested.

Kállay and his cabinet resigned; the prime minister took refuge at the Turkish Legation. Members of the conspicuous anti-German group in the Foreign Ministry — Andor Szentmiklossy, Aladár Szegedi-Maszák, István Bede, and others — were also arrested and deported to concentration camps in Germany; Szentmiklossy died there.

Horthy was forced to appoint a pro-Nazi prime minister. He selected the Hungarian minister to Berlin, Döme Sztojay, who also took the portfolio of foreign minister. The new cabinet was formed by pro-German quislings.

The news of the German coup reached Istanbul in the morning of March 19. We still hoped that some of the Hungarian leaders would attempt an escape. Kállay's flight to the Turkish Legation and Horthy's apparent cooperation were a disappointment. However, on second thought I concluded that the regent's continued presence and activity was not harmful; on the contrary, it saved what still could be saved.

After having exchanged views with Hungarian envoys in other neutral countries, Consul General Ujváry refused to serve under the new administration. He left the consulate and settled down in a private apartment. He joined the Committee of Dissident Diplomats, which comprised diplomats accredited to Switzerland, Sweden, Portugal, and to some Latin American countries, who similarly rejected the new Hungarian government. Vörnle, the pro-German Hungarian minister in Ankara, and his staff continued to serve the new government.

For me the major consequence of the events in Hungary was that my official and many unofficial contacts with Budapest discontinued. My subsequent activities were to assist the Hungarian cause in an unofficial capacity and to participate in rescue operations of victims of Hitlerite vengeance and racial persecution. There was no longer any reason to disguise my activity; henceforth, I could visit the British missions or the American Consulate General in Istanbul and Allied missions in Ankara.

It was shortly before March 19 that Walter Birge, who had been transferred to Baghdad, introduced me to his successor, Christopher Squires. He was one of the new appointees to join the rapidly expanding foreign service of the United States. Accordingly, the new vice-consul for political affairs was only slightly familiar with East Central Europe. I brought Squires and Ujváry together and attempted to cooperate with the former, although this was not as easy as with his predecessor.

On April 3 I traveled with Ujváry to Ankara. His status as consul general was now uncertain. The Turkish government continued its relationship with the Sztojay government. Thus, Ujváry did not represent any government. He hoped to retain some of his privileges and to be given permission to remain in Turkey.

In Ankara I introduced Ujváry to Polish ambassador Sokolnicki, who, as I mentioned earlier, was the dean of the diplomatic corps in Turkey. He offered to intervene with the Turkish Foreign Ministry in favor of Ujváry. He finally was given permission to reside in Turkey and to retain certain signs of his former status: a diplomatic license plate on his car and a personal identification card, which exempted him from some police formalities.

I also met confidentially with some members of the Hungarian Legation, among them Thierry, Gáspár, and Bálintitt, who continued to serve under Vörnle but were ready to cooperate with me. For the first time I also visited with the chargé d'affairs of the provisional French government in Algiers, Jacques Tarbé de Saint-Hardouin, who later, after the liberation of France, became the ambassador of his country to Turkey. I had been in the past months in constant contact with the Istanbul representatives of the Free French movement and, upon their request, I asked for information concerning the status of French prisoners of war who escaped from Germany and found refuge in Hungary. Just a few days before March 19 I had received an exhaustive report from the Foreign Ministry in Budapest, a satisfactory one indeed: Hungary did not consider herself to be at war with France and, therefore, under The Hague Convention of 1907 only reserved her right to restrict the free movement of escaped prisoners of war. Of course, once the Germans entered Hungary they began hunting down these and other refugees and their fate became uncertain.

Back in Istanbul, on April 7, Csiki and Bruckner assured me of their continued friendship and assistance. They still operated the trade mission but did so with the approval of the British. Among those who needed rescuing was the Hungarian minister to Athens, Lászlo Velics. He had remained there when the Germans invaded Greece in 1941 and was allowed to function during the occupation. Velics maintained contacts with the Greek underground. After March 19, reluctant to serve under the pro-Nazi government, he managed to escape to Turkey with the help of Greek partisans. After an adventurous two-day voyage from island to island he arrived in the Turkish harbor of Çeşme, west of Izmir, a place where the SOE maintained contact with the partisans. I only spoke with Velics over the telephone; the British saw to it that, with the tacit understanding of Turkish police, he should be brought across the Syrian border. Velics spent the remaining years of the war in Cairo, and I saw him only when I returned to Hungary.

The fate of many friends who must have been targets of Nazi persecution in Hungary concerned me closely. Among them Laszlo Veress was foremost in my mind. For six weeks I heard nothing about his whereabouts. On May 19 Csiki told me that Veress was in Sofia and had called on the Turkish Legation there, where he and Csiki had a mutual friend. Thus we learned that Veress first hid in Budapest when the Germans arrived; he then managed to travel to Transylvania, where his uncle, Lt. Gen. Lajos Veress, was in command of an army corps. From Hungarian Transylvania, Veress succeeded in passing across Rumania into Bulgaria. He still had his diplomatic passport and sought entry into Turkey, but the Bulgarian-Turkish border was guarded by agents of the Gestapo and Veress had little chance to cross the border legally.

After consultation with the British, who obtained instructions from Italy, we advised Veress through a Turkish diplomat to travel to Belgrade and Zagreb, the capital of the Croatian puppet state, instead of Turkey. We rightly assumed that moving toward Germany would not be checked by the Gestapo. Veress was told to take up residence in a certain hotel in Zagreb, where he would be contacted by members of the Yugoslav partisan movement. He did exactly what he was advised to do. On June 11, the British informed me that Veress had safely arrived in Bari, Italy, where he was to spend the remainder of the war. Titoist guerrillas had guided him to one of their airfields, where he was flown on a British plane to Italy.

Col. Hátszegi-Hatz, who had replaced Bartalis as Hungarian military attaché in September, unfortunately happened to be in Budapest on March 19 and was immediately placed under house arrest. Eventually he was released, but he was told that his assignment to Turkey had ended and that Colonel Bartalis had been reappointed to Istanbul by the Sztojay government. Giving his word of honor to return, Hátszegi-Hatz was allowed to travel to Turkey for two days. He had the key to his safe and wanted to dispose of some incriminating material. On June 13 he arrived and came to see me.

I was informed by him that a resistance group, consisting of Hungarian officers and soldiers, was requesting help from the Allies. Its center of activity was in the Bakony forest southwest of Budapest. They asked for wireless sets, weapons, and shoes to be dropped by parachute between July 3 and July 8.

I hurried to the British to convey the message, at least one evidence that there was some open resistance against the Germans in Hungary. A few hours later I was able to assure my friend that the plane would be dispatched with the objects he had asked for. Unfortunately, I heard later from the British that the aircraft, having failed to spot the signals, returned to base with its cargo. And from Hátszegi-Hatz, via Csiki, came the news that an American plane dropped some material to the partisans that fell into German hands. The resistance group thereafter left the area and nothing was heard of it again.

Hátszegi-Hatz left Istanbul after his allotted two days. At the time of Regent Horthy's armistice announcement on October 15, 1944, in a dramatic move reported by the international press, he crossed the Soviet lines. When Budapest fell to the Russians, he became commander of the Hungarian garrison. Later, presumably because of his American and British connections, he was arrested by the NKVD (the Soviet secret police) and disappeared.

In May, Istanbul had an interesting visitor, Francis Deak. The Hungarian-born professor of law at Columbia University had entered the foreign service during the war and was assigned to the United States Embassy in Lisbon. His arrival there in 1943 raised a naive hope in Budapest that Washington was showing more interest in Hungary. As I mentioned earlier, the Hungarian diplomatic mission in Lisbon maintained contacts with the Allies. Deak and I had never met before, but as one international lawyer to another we knew about each other. He confirmed to me that in the American view any major military engagement in the Balkans would only dissipate Allied strength much needed for the formidable landing operation in France. However, Deak assured me that it was the determined intention of the American General Staff to oppose any permanent Soviet control over the region west of the Curzon line, which included the Danube basin and the Balkans.

A few weeks after Deak's departure, on June 6 at 9 A.M., the BBC broadcast the German report on the beginning of the invasion of France. At 11 A.M. we heard General Eisenhower's announcement. Thereafter, for hours every day I sat with American, British, and Hungarian friends listening to the news. But this pleasure was mixed with the deep anxiety we all felt for the Jewish population of Hungary, whose tragedy could not be prevented by the Allied success in faraway Normandy. There were consistent rumors about the wholesale deportation of Hungarian Jews to Auschwitz and the gas chambers.

THE JEWISH TRAGEDY

My passing of messages between the representative of the Jewish Agency in Palestine, Chaim Barlas, and the Hungarian Foreign Ministry came to an end with the German occupation of Hungary. I saw Barlas frequently. He somehow had reliable information of the arrival of Adolf Eichmann and his henchmen, Hermann Krumey and Otto Hunsche, in Hungary; he also knew of the collaboration of pro-Nazi Hungarian officials with the Germans to carry out their sinister plans.

On June 4 Barlas came to me and mentioned that a member of the Budapest Jewish Council, Joel Brand, had arrived in Istanbul equipped with a German passport and carrying a message about a deal that might save the lives of the one million Hungarian Jews. Barlas asked me to meet Brand, who was being kept in isolation in the Pera Palace Hotel. Similar requests reached me from the British and American consulates. I was to ascertain the reliability and authenticity of Brand's mission.

At 10 P.M. that same day I went to Brand's hotel room, number 94. A Turkish plainclothes policeman stood before the door, but he had instructions to let me in. I had a long, often very painful conversation with Brand, who seemed to be almost crushed under the weight of the message he professed to carry. He spoke a broken Hungarian, so we soon switched to German. He told me that he had been born in Transylvania (Bistrita) but had lived most of his life in Germany. However, he retained his Hungarian citizenship and left Germany when Hitler came to power. He worked for the Zionist organization as mediator between Central European Jewish communities and the Jewish Agency of Palestine. He denied being a leader but, as he put it, he wished to keep himself in the background as mediator. Most of the correspondence between Hungarian Jewish organizations and the Jewish Agency passed through his hands. As an interesting item he mentioned that he was also in touch with Hungarian military intelligence, who wished to be informed of his activities. He was rather reluctant to enlarge on these contacts but mentioned Colonel Hátszegi-Hatz; he hinted that money from the Jewish Agency reached him through the colonel and was used to support Jewish refugees in Hungary.

Brand referred to the fact that for years he had tried to rescue Polish Jews and that he had actually saved quite a number from the gas chambers by bribing members of the Gestapo. As soon as the Germans occupied Hungary, he established contacts with the Gestapo, as did the

Jewish leadership of Hungary. This was necessary because they soon
discovered that it was useless to discuss Jewish matters with the Hungarian authorities, who were merely tools of the Gestapo. Brand then
described to me in dramatic detail the measures taken against about
eight hundred thousand Jews outside Budapest. The instructions for
these measures were issued by the Budapest headquarters of the Gestapo, located in hotels on Svab Hill, primarily the Hotel Majestic. Attached to the Gestapo was a liaison office of the Hungarian political
police. Adolf Eichmann and Hermann Krumey were in supreme command.

Before Brand's departure from Budapest three hundred thousand
Jews in the northeast of Hungary had already been concentrated in
camps and twelve thousand were being "shipped" daily to Poland.* The
treatment of these internees varied from place to place but in many
camps it was utterly inhuman, worse than the treatment of Polish Jews.

About his mission, Brand explained that he was allowed to leave for
Turkey with the consent of the Gestapo in order to submit certain proposals.

"Why were you selected?" I asked.

"My humble person was chosen because I had negotiated previously
with the Germans. The Jewish Community of Hungary also agreed to
the choice because I belonged to none of the often rival sects, the Ortho-
dox, the Neologues, and the Zionists. Any more important person could
have represented only one section, whereas I enjoyed the confidence of
all."

Then he described his journey to Turkey:

"I was taken by Oberstandartenführer Krumey in his car to Vienna
where a German passport was handed to me."

"What can you tell me about your assignment?"

"The proposal was discussed between Kascher [another Zionist
leader], Eichmann, and myself. Eichmann told us the offer came directly
from Himmler. The Germans want ten thousand trucks, with spare
parts. In return they will allow the emigration of all Hungarian Jews.
With regard to the trucks, the Germans were ready to commit themselves
not to use them except on the eastern front against the Russians."

Brand further mentioned that the offer was known to some other
Jewish leaders in Hungary. But he added:

---

*As many as five hundred thousand Jews may have been seized. —ED.

"The offer is not known to the Hungarian government. The deal is to be concluded with the Germans alone."

I knew that Brand had come in the company of another Hungarian by the name of György, who was frequently to be seen in Istanbul and had the reputation of being a Jew working for the Gestapo.

"What is György's role in this affair?" I asked.

"Gross—that is his real name—was taken with me to Vienna. He traveled with a Hungarian service passport. He works for Hungarian counterintelligence and for the Gestapo. This time he was sent with me to Turkey in order to check on me. Gross is now frightened to return, but I cannot return without him. He has now thrown himself at the mercy of the British. As soon as I arrive in Palestine to submit the offer, I shall ask the British authorities to send Gross along with me to Vienna."

We also discussed general political conditions in German-occupied Hungary. He seemed to be well informed. Brand was rather confident in the success of his mission and I had no reason to discourage him, although I was skeptical as to its outcome. It was past midnight when I left his hotel room. Back in my apartment I immediately wrote a report on my conversation with Brand and my impressions and view of his mission.

I gave my report to Barlas and to the British and American consulates. I concluded that Brand was genuine and well intentioned. He ardently believed that through the message he carried and the acceptance of this offer the lives of Hungarian Jews could be saved. He wanted to help them, at any price, an endeavor which I found praiseworthy and understandable. However, I thought at the same time that he was rather naive and that he had misjudged the Germans. The real purpose behind the Nazi maneuver was to create discord between the Anglo-Saxon powers and the Russians. There may also have been some monetary interest behind the scheme, for Brand revealed that he had succeeded in bribing even high-ranking Gestapo officers.

A few days later Brand received permission to travel to Palestine, where he was interned for the rest of the war. Gross, alias György, alarmed by Brand's failure to return and fearing deportation by the Turks to Germany, implored the British for permission to go south. While crossing the Syrian border he was arrested by British military police.

During June the news concerning the deportation of Hungary's Jewish population gained prominence over other reports from the area.

Barlas was desperately trying to do something; he was in contact with the Roman Catholic apostolic administrator for Turkey, Monsignor Angelo Giuseppe Roncalli, who subsequently became Pope John XXIII. I also went to see Monsignor Roncalli on this matter, but I had no means of sending direct messages to Hungary. However, I suggested to Barlas that he approach Baron Thierry, the counselor of the Hungarian Legation in Ankara.

On June 10 I traveled with Barlas to Ankara to enlist the help of Baron Thierry. He met with us outside the Hungarian Legation, where the pro-German Vörnle still ruled. Later I met Thierry again while Barlas went to the British Embassy. The counselor told me that to his knowledge the Turkish government had already made friendly representations, based on humanitarian grounds, to the Hungarian Foreign Ministry in favor of the Jews. Having previously served at the Hungarian Legation to the Vatican (when I first met him in 1937), he thought that the papal nuncio in Budapest would also approach Regent Horthy directly in this matter. Of course, neither of us knew really to what extent Horthy was now a free agent. However, Thierry was ready to undertake a step on his own, without the knowledge of his boss, Vörnle. He would write to the new secretary general of the Hungarian Foreign Ministry Béla Arnothy-Jungerth, telling him of the dismay and horror created throughout the world by the deportation to extermination camps of hundreds of thousands of innocent victims. Since Prime Minister Sztojay was also the foreign minister, Arnothy-Jungerth was practically in charge of that branch of the administration. All these messages emphasized that despite the German occupation of Hungary, the cooperation of Hungarian authorities in these inhuman and criminal actions would be duly condemned by international public opinion.

Barlas expressed great satisfaction over the cooperation of Thierry. When back in Istanbul, I read President Roosevelt's protest note, passed on to Budapest via the Swiss Legation, which represented American interests in Hungary. Secretary of State Cordell Hull gave similar warnings. Brettholz told me that according to his reports from Stockholm, the king of Sweden wrote a personal letter to Horthy about this matter.

In early July the correspondent of the Hungarian Telegraph Agency in Ankara, Jozsef Zalan, who continued to serve Budapest and who invariably met Hungarian foreign service personnel traveling as couriers to Turkey, informed me that on June 20, at a session of the Council of Ministers, Arnothy-Jungerth gave a detailed report on the vehemently hostile reactions and avalanche of protests caused by the deportation of the Hungarian Jews. It was by now a tragic fact that all the Jewish population in the provinces had been deported to Poland and the gas chambers of Auschwitz. Barlas conveyed to me the ominous news that the Germans and their Hungarian accomplices were now preparing to round up the quarter of a million Jews in Budapest, among them many who had managed to escape from the provinces into the Hungarian capital. Because the Budapest police were considered unreliable to carry out the murderous design, gendarmerie units had entered the city.

On July 9 I traveled once more to Ankara, where Barlas was to follow me the next day. But this time Thierry had good news for both of us: Regent Horthy personally had ordered the gendarmerie out of Budapest and thus, for the time being, the danger was removed. The International Red Cross would now be allowed to look after Jewish refugees in Budapest, its representative in Ankara assured me.

There was other good news as well: Horthy's initiative showed that he had now recovered his freedom of action. He had emerged as a controlling power; Sztojay, as I was told, was prime minister in name only (to please the Germans) and was no longer in charge, certainly not of the Foreign Ministry. With the Allied advance in France and the further success of Soviet arms, only blind fanatics doubted that the Germans had lost the war. On the other hand, I found the Poles, Ambassador Sokolnicki and Colonel Zimnal, no longer optimistic. Poland was about to be completely overrun by the Russians, and there were no American or British forces anywhere in the neighborhood.

At that time I had become a member of the local branch of the International Rescue and Relief Committee. In June an American attorney by the name of Dennenberg came to Istanbul on behalf of the mother organization. The committee had some limited financial means to assist intellectuals who suffered persecution to escape from the Axis countries, or at least (and this was the more practical goal) to aid such refugees in Turkey. The chairman of our branch was Dr. Floyd H. Black, president of Istanbul's Robert College;[7] other members included professors Ernst Reuter (who later became mayor of Berlin), Alexander von Rustow, and Philip Schwartz, of the medical faculty. The committee met frequently, usually at Robert College, to discuss individual cases. We not

---

7. Dr. Black had been President of the American College in Sofia until Bulgaria came under German control.

only provided financial assistance to some unfortunates but also intervened on their behalf to obtain the visas and transportation necessary for their travel to countries where they could make a decent living.

In July a young English scholar working for the SOE visited Istanbul for a short time. He was Hugh Seton-Watson, a historian of Russia and Central Europe. He was well acquainted with Hungary and it was a pleasure to exchange ideas with him.

There was still another development, one less significant now than it would have been a year earlier. Following Allied pressure, Turkey severed diplomatic relations with Germany on August 2, 1944. There was no danger that she would do the same with Hungary; nevertheless, the British prepared papers for me that would have enabled me to go to Cairo. German nationals were interned in the Anatolian interior, except for those who were teaching in the universities.

Further developments in the situation in and around Hungary were expected to occur soon—for better or worse. Soviet advances were spectacular. By the end of July on the Ukrainian front Soviet forces entered Galicia, captured Lvov, and along a broad front reached the foothills of the Carpathians. On August 22 the long-expected offensive against Rumanian territory began.

Horthy evidently still wished to pursue the Kállay design to keep the Russians out and to establish nonbelligerent status for Hungary, but Soviet strength and the absence of Anglo-American forces in the vicinity rendered such expectations illusory. On the very day when the Russians opened their attack against Rumania, her well-prepared defection materialized. The entire German-Rumanian front from the Bukovina region to the Black Sea collapsed and Hungary became directly threatened from the southeast.

THE RUSSIAN INVASION OF HUNGARY

On the evening of August 23 I received a telephone call from the British mission informing me of Rumania's defection. The effect of this event on Hungary, as could be expected, was dramatic. On August 24 the ailing Sztojay was invited by Regent Horthy to resign; the regent then appointed as prime minister Gen. Géza Lakatos, a man in his confidence. As Thierry, who had come to Istanbul, told me a few days later,

Lakatos's instructions included the assignment "to restore Hungary's sovereignty" and to prepare for the withdrawal of Hungary from the war, as well as to end the persecution of the Jews. The Lakatos cabinet's foreign minister was another general, Gusztáv Hennyey. Gen. János Vörös—no pro-German—was named chief of the General Staff.

I rightly expected that the Lakatos government would be eager to take up contacts with the Allies. But almost all of those in the Foreign Ministry who knew of the contacts in Istanbul were no longer occupying their posts; they were either in German concentration camps, like Szegedi-Maszák, or had fled to safety, like Lászlo Veress. The British agreed with me that attention should be drawn to the formerly operative communication channel in Turkey. But how to inform Budapest promptly? I hoped that under the pressure of events Bartalis, the military attaché, would be willing to pass a message to Budapest through the telecommunication device we knew he had in his office.

Péter Bruckner, on my request, telephoned Bartalis and asked whether he would receive me. He immediately consented, and on August 24 I called on him for the second time. I handed over to him a short text addressed to the Foreign Ministry asking for the immediate resumption in Istanbul of the contacts between Hungary and the Allies, which had been interrupted by the events of March 19. Bartalis, after some hesitation, accepted the text, muttering something to the effect that he would do what I asked of him. He was evidently shaken by Rumania's capitulation; he asked no further questions. Because I did not trust him, I said nothing more and left.

Four days later he returned the paper through Bruckner. I thought that he had consulted Minister Vörnle and that the latter must have advised him not to do anything. However, I also heard that Vörnle himself cabled Budapest to suggest a move similar to Rumania's. (Papen, the German ambassador, was no longer present to dissuade him.)

All this I heard from Thierry, who had returned to Istanbul. On August 29 he sent the message Bartalis had refused to send. On September 4 Thierry obtained a reply from the Foreign Ministry, in which it was vaguely intimated that something would be done to approach the Allies. He also received an assurance that the persecution of Jews had been discontinued. I immediately passed on this information to Barlas.

Following the fall of Rumania, Soviet forces crossed the Danube into Bulgaria, which also surrendered. Géza Fehér, the Hungarian cultural attaché in Sofia, took refuge in Turkey. Unfortunately, my former schoolmate Endre Szöke, the military attaché, was taken prisoner by the Russians, who disregarded his diplomatic immunity. He was deported to Siberia. For many years there was no news of him and his family thought he was dead, but he was miraculously returned to Hungary in 1955 and set free in the spring of 1956.

News about Hungarian initiatives soon reached me. On August 28 the British passed on to me a report that the previous day the Hungarian military attaché in Lisbon had approached his British counterpart with the request that talks in regard to the withdrawal of Hungary from the war be reopened. The British reply was not yet available.

On September 11 Thierry received news from Budapest, again in response to the message sent from Istanbul, that armistice feelers in a country other than Turkey were being put out. Ferenc Csiki, who was caught in Hungary when the Russians moved into Bulgaria and was unable to return to Turkey, also sent a similar message through his Turkish diplomatic friends.

On September 27 the British informed me that Hungarian colonel-general Béla Náday had been flown from Hungary to a British military airfield in Italy. Náday appeared as Horthy's official representative to negotiate an armistice. But now the British and Americans advised Budapest through various channels to seek an armistice directly with the Russians. It was revealed to me that Moscow had become suspicious and had urged London not to recognize Náday as a plenipotentiary.

The silence that followed these futile initiatives indicated that the Hungarian government was now trying to develop contacts with the Soviet Union. Three emissaries of Horthy — Gen. S. H. Faragho, Domokos Szentivanyi (Teleki's confidant, with whom I was in touch in 1941), and Géza Teleki, the son of the former prime minister — crossed the front line in the last days of September and arrived in Moscow on September 30.

It was certainly timely by now that something be done because the military situation of Hungary was rapidly approaching hopelessness. For a few weeks in August and September 1944 the Hungarian armies were able to hold the line of the Carpathian Mountains against the Soviet onslaught. But with the capitulation of Rumania and her invasion by Soviet Forces, the strategic advantage of defending the crest of the Carpathian range along the eastern border of Transylvania was lost.

After the Rumanian surrender Budapest was confronted by the awkward dilemma of whether to attempt to occupy the Rumanian part of Transylvania (and thereby expose herself as an aggressor) or to give up the Kállay plan of defending the country against the Russians along the Carpathians in the east and the Transylvanian Alps in the south. Hesitation and the lack of available forces resulted in a halfhearted attempt to push toward the strategically more defensible Transylvanian border. But Soviet forces, helped by the Rumanians, were much faster. By early September they had already infiltrated the southern valleys of Transylvania, thereby turning the Hungarian defense line along the Carpathians. Three weeks later they managed to work themselves into the southeastern plain of Hungary proper. In early October the fighting shifted along a wide front into Hungarian territory, with Russian armor and infantry pushing the weaker Hungarian forces before them while the Carpathian defense line had to be abandoned.

On the evening of October 15, 1944, the long-awaited news was broadcast: Regent Horthy announced that an armistice had been concluded with the Soviet Union and invited Hungarian forces to stop fighting. But later that night, at 10:30 P.M., the Hungarian Nazi (Arrow Cross) leader Ferenc Szálasi declared that he had taken over from Horthy and that Hungary was to continue the struggle jointly with her German comrades in arms until final victory.

Thus, the Hungarians, unlike the Rumanians, failed in their attempt to defect from the side of Germany. The reasons were manifold. Rumanians were more accomplished conspirators and their king's authority over the army was uncontested. In Hungary betrayals and indiscretions caused the plan to become well known to the German command. After the humiliating way Hitler treated Horthy, the regent's authority was shattered even with the military. Hungary was also much more under German Nazi influence than Rumania, and geographically nearer to the German homeland. Essentially, however, Horthy's plan miscarried because of long hesitations and the blabbering or direct deceit of the persons involved.

The Germans were fully prepared and struck as soon as Horthy made his announcement. They removed the Lakatos government and installed Szálasi, their puppet, and his Arrow Cross minions. Horthy was arrested and taken to Germany. A period of chaos, destruction, and massacre followed. There was nothing one could do from Turkey but remain a distant observer.

All communication with Hungary ceased after October 15. Soviet forces crossed the Danube south of Budapest. The Germans were now taking over from the demoralized and wavering Hungarians. There was a pitched battle between the Germans and Russians around Lake Balaton (as Ludendorff had foreseen) and the Germans were pushed back. Just before Christmas the city of Budapest was surrounded by Soviet forces.

It was on Christmas Eve that the news arrived of the formation of a provisional Hungarian government in the Soviet-occupied city of Debrecen. This coalition government included the Communists and all "democratic" opposition parties: the Smallholders, the Social Democrats, and the Peasant party. The prime minister of this government was Gen. Béla Miklos, one of the few high-ranking officers who obeyed Horthy's cease-fire appeal and went over to the Russians. The foreign minister of the new government was János Gyöngyösi, a completely unknown provincial bookstore owner affiliated with the Smallholder party and hand-picked by the Russians because he spoke some Russian.

A few weeks later the new government dispatched a delegation to Moscow, which on January 20, 1945, concluded an armistice treaty with the Soviet Union, the United States, and Great Britain. The treaty made no reference to the unconditional surrender agreement of September 9, 1943.

Up to that point I had refrained from entering into contacts with Soviet representatives in Turkey, upon the advice of the British and the Americans. But in view of developments in Hungary, contacts with Soviet representatives could no longer be delayed. John Bennett, the British press attaché in Istanbul, had good relations with the Soviet consul general Ivanov (probably a pseudonym; it was rumored that Ivanov was an NKVD agent). Bennett introduced me to him. The Soviet official spoke a somewhat broken French and let me talk about my assignment to Turkey. I asked him whether his government would be willing to forward a report on my activity to the new foreign minister of the provisional government of Hungary. Ivanov replied that the answer to my request lay beyond his competency and that I should address myself in this matter to the Soviet Embassy in Ankara. Therefore on January 10, even before the signing of the armistice, I left for the Turkish capital.

I asked Tarbé de Saint-Hardouin, the accredited minister of the Free French provisional government in Algiers, for an introduction to the Soviet Embassy. He immediately called Soviet ambassador Vinogradov; it was agreed that I should meet a secretary of the Soviet Embassy by the name of Vasily Fedorovich Grubyakov in the Ankara Palace Hotel. The reason for this arrangement was probably to keep the Turkish police from observing my entry into the embassy building. I also think that the Soviets were uncertain what I was about to tell them.

Grubyakov, a young fair-haired Russian, arrived in the company of another embassy official who introduced himself as Valuyisk. Grubyakov spoke excellent French and, especially in the course of our later contacts, proved to be pleasant and relatively outspoken and even to understand humor. In this first meeting, however, our conversation was rather stiff, perhaps because a third person was present. I explained to them my mission to Turkey and my request to send an open letter, written in French, to the new Hungarian foreign minister through the Soviet Embassy. Grubyakov made notes and said that permission to forward such a letter must be given by Moscow. He promised to send me word through Consul General Ivanov in Istanbul.

Ten days after my return to Istanbul, on January 23, Ivanov telephoned me saying that Grubyakov was ready to receive my letter. My journey to Ankara was known to the British. I now asked them whether I could refer in my letter to the unconditional surrender agreed in Istanbul in 1943. Leslie Harrop informed me on January 30 that London's request was that no direct mention be made in my report of the 1943 agreement. I do not know why this agreement was to be glossed over. Was it not true, as I was told at the time of the agreement, that Moscow was informed of the action? Or was it simply that London, considering the agreement void, did not wish to remind Moscow or Budapest of this event, which had now been superseded by a new armistice agreement?

My letter to Hungarian foreign minister Gyöngyösi, a copy of which is still in my possession, was dated January 31. In it I described my activity and, in general terms, the attempts to enable Hungary to secede from the German alliance. I also reported that the government of Turkey considered diplomatic relations with Hungary broken and had closed the Hungarian Legation in Ankara as well as the consulate general in Istanbul. I imagined that all this information might be useful to a government that had lost contact with the previous administration. I also reported that the Hungarian colony in Turkey feared deportation because of the lack of diplomatic relations between Turkey and Hungary. I suggested that these relations be resumed. I also expressed a wish to return to Hungary as soon as transportation was available.

The next day I handed the letter to Grubyakov in Ankara, for which purpose I had been invited to visit the Soviet Embassy. I also saw Colonel Zimnal of the Polish Embassy, who expressed bad forebodings. On February 4 the Yalta Conference was to be opened with the participation of President Roosevelt, Prime Minister Churchill, and Marshal Stalin. It was feared that the Polish government-in-exile in London would be prevented from returning to Warsaw, which was now in Soviet hands. Moscow had severed diplomatic relations with this government and had installed one of its own making in the Polish capital.

My journey to Ankara gave rise to a serious altercation with Ujváry. On February 8 he came to my apartment. Evidently, he knew of my two visits to the Turkish capital but had no inkling of their purpose. Now he demanded that I should tell him what I was doing. He appeared very frustrated; after October 15 he had attempted a return to the consulate general, but the Turkish authorities had closed the building. Diplomatic relations with Hungary were discontinued because the Ankara government refused to recognize the Szálasi regime.

Grubyakov asked me not to reveal the fact that Soviet diplomatic channels were transmitting my report to Hungary. He was afraid that "other Hungarians" might embarrass the Soviet Embassy with similar requests. So I told Ujváry that I was not in a position to say anything about my doings in Ankara. This refusal brought his wrath upon me, which he continued to harbor even after his return to Budapest and may have been one of the causes of my subsequent misfortunes in Hungary.

After a prolonged siege Budapest was finally captured by the Red Army in early February 1945. First Pest, on the eastern bank of the Danube, then Buda, on the hilly western bank, fell to the besiegers. A few months later the provisional Hungarian government moved from Debrecen to the half-destroyed capital.

In early April 1945 the first travelers from Hungary arrived in Turkey as part of a trainload of Allied and neutral nationals, many of them ethnic Hungarians, whose evacuation from the devastated country, to which the Soviet military authorities gave their consent, had been pressed by their governments. Among these passengers was Angelo Rocca, the papal nuncio to Hungary, who, however, was forced to leave his post; the group also included British, Dutch, Norwegian, and Swiss citizens. I had the privilege of being received by the nuncio, who in sober words described German and Hungarian Nazi atrocities and the barbarities committed by the Soviet "liberators." A Hungarian-born Dutch couple were particularly helpful in giving a detailed description of their experiences. He was an engineer who spent many decades in the Dutch East Indies and retired to Holland; after the German occupation of that country the couple, possessing dual citizenship, moved to Hungary. They had not expected to have to pass through the tribulations of the Hungarian hell in 1944–45.

The great question for many in the world and for me personally was the Soviet enigma. What would be the Soviet conduct in the large region of East Central Europe and, in particular, in Hungary? Would the military occupation be replaced by a genuine popular and democratic regime? The outlook was somber. While the war against Germany was still in progress, an excuse for Soviet control was acceptable. But by May 8 Germany capitulated and there was no longer any fighting in Europe.

Another question was how the Western powers would behave. Would they acquiesce in the permanent extension of Soviet power into Central Europe, into areas that even in the heyday of tsarist Russia were never under Moscow's control? Would they accept the subjugation to Soviet Communist rule of peoples to whom they had promised liberation from Nazi tyranny and oppression? Bulgaria and Rumania already appeared to be ruled by a monocratic Communist Party. Poland was officially granted a coalition government, and elections were to be held soon. Czechoslovakia was governed by a coalition of political parties under an apparently democratic system. There still was more than a glimmer of hope for Hungary. There, despite Soviet excesses, a coalition government had been established, which, with Moscow's consent, was to arrange for popular elections in November 1945.

On July 12 I received a cable from Bucharest from Robert Hardi, a friend who, as it appeared, was now a high-ranking official in the Ministry of Commerce and, to my surprise, a member of the Communist Party. He had come to Rumania for trade negotiations and informed me that my mother was well and expecting to see me soon.

I had been spared the afflictions of those living in Hungary. I had worked against the German Nazis and thought I had nothing to fear. Moreover, there was now work to be done at home. I had no doubt in my mind that I had to return. But almost another year passed before I managed to obtain the travel documents for a journey across the Soviet-occupied countries of Bulgaria and Rumania back to Hungary.

END OF A MISSION

By early summer 1945 I was preparing to return to Hungary. Previously, in April, I delivered another public lecture at the university.
Cemil Bilsel was no longer the rector; he had retired the year before and
was elected a deputy to the National Assembly. In mid 1945 the Government appointed him a member of the Turkish delegation that was soon
to travel to San Francisco for the drafting and signing of the United
Nations Charter. Upon the urging of Allied leaders at the Yalta Conference, Turkey had declared war on Germany on February 23 — a purely
symbolic act, because the nearest German forces were in Hungary. But
this declaration enabled Turkey to participate in the creation of the
United Nations.

The new holder of the chair of international law at the university
had suggested in a faculty meeting that I be invited to join the university
permanently. However, I had to decline any such offer. Had I been prevented from returning to my homeland, I would have preferred to go to
England or the United States. I considered the position of Turkey pre-
carious. She had wisely refrained from engaging in hostilities against
Germany, but now it seemed likely that she would become subject to
increasing Soviet pressure. Moscow, having achieved a paramount position in East and Central Europe, would not miss an opportunity to have
its centuries-old dream fulfilled: to capture the Bosporus and the Dardanelles, thereby establishing a secure route to the Mediterranean Sea
and subjugating Turkey.

I took leave from the university but was to stay in Turkey for
another year. To travel legally back to Hungary required transit permits
from the Soviet occupation administration in Bulgaria and Rumania.
This was not easy to obtain and demanded utmost patience. I refused an
enticing plan to go to Western Europe and return via Germany with help
from the British or the Americans. This would have made me suspect
before the Russians and the Hungarian government.

However, 1945 was not an idle year. Thus far I had had little time
and opportunity to acquaint myself with Turkey and Turkish problems.
Now I found time to travel into the interior of Anatolia, not only to
Ankara, and to read extensively. All this proved extremely useful to me
when twenty-five years later, after a second prolonged stay, I wrote a
book on Turkish foreign policy.

I also continued to watch political developments in the Near East and Eastern Europe. But most of the American and British friends with whom I had such pleasant relations gradually departed. In March, Christopher Squires, who had been transferred to Budapest, introduced me to his successor as the American vice-consul, Mr. McVickers, a fresh product of the State Department. Instead of accepting a briefing from me, he avoided meeting me, evidently frightened of becoming "compromised." When, after my return to Hungary, I saw him once, he looked even more panicky. Barlas returned to Jerusalem, but I was occasionally consulted by the Istanbul representative of the Jewish Agency, Mr. Goldin. And I made new acquaintances, among them Colonel Babbitt, the American assistant military attaché.

I had interesting contacts as well with the Chinese consul general, Abdullah Ma. He was a member of a well-known Moslem Chinese family from Ningsia province, and he never used his full Chinese name. He represented the Chiang Kai-shek government, which in 1945 was still on the Chinese mainland. Evidently, he was assigned to Turkey because he was Moslem. Ma Hung-kuei, the governor of Ningsia, was his uncle. The consul general was fanatically anti-Communist. He was a pleasant companion who did not despise alcoholic drinks but ate no pork. He told me that even the Chinese emperors respected this abstinence by his family whenever a member was invited to court. Ma often tried to dissuade me from returning to Hungary, saying that the Communists would kill me.

When I first went to Turkey in 1943 my traveling companion on the train to Istanbul had been a young Iranian, Melek Manzur Quashquai. In Turkey I soon learned that the Quashquai were a powerful Turkic tribe in southwest Iran and my friend was a member of the ruling family. The Quashquai tribal leaders sympathized with the Germans and, when the British moved into Iran, Melek and his brother Hussein took refuge in Germany. Melek served in the German army on the Russian front. However, having refused to work for German intelligence, he left Germany. He had been on his way back to Turkey when I met him on the train. In Istanbul I was introduced to Hussein, but subsequently both brothers disappeared. By mid 1944 they strangely had turned up again. As I heard later, the brothers were caught by the British but exchanged for two British agents held by the Germans. In 1944 and 1945 I saw the brothers not infrequently; they even invited me to their apartment. Their stories about the life of their tribe and their own experiences were fascinating. They were not only interested in the welfare of their tribe but at the same time were enthusiastic about Iranian culture. In 1945 they bade me fare-well: the Shah had forgiven them and they were returning to Iran. Hus-sein was elected deputy to the Mejlis (the Iranian parliament) but later I heard they got into trouble again with the central government.

My endeavors to obtain Soviet travel documents were greatly facili-tated when my Ankara contact, Vasily Grubyakov, was appointed consul general in Istanbul. I was able to meet him occasionally and we even had meals together. He began to open up to me. He said he liked his job but wished that his wife and child were allowed to join him. He promised to intervene to secure my travel papers.

The constantly deteriorating relations between Ankara and Moscow prevented me from seeking out Grubyakov's company more often. In March 1945 the Soviet Union refused to renew its nonaggression treaty with Turkey. In June, Molotov demanded that Turkey cede two prov-inces in the east and a military base in the straits. In December the Soviet press published articles by two Soviet Georgian professors who claimed the historic right of Georgia to a considerable portion of the Turkish Black Sea coast. At the same time, rumors of Soviet troop concentra-tions on the Bulgarian and Caucasian borders of Turkey were wide-spread in Istanbul, a city—in contrast to the serene Ankara— prone to panic and to the jitters.

I was still in Istanbul when, in early June 1946, the United States battleship *Missouri,* on which the Japanese had formally surrendered nine months before, entered the Dardanelles and was received with jubi-lation in Istanbul. The pretext for this gesture was the return of the remains of the Turkish ambassador, who had died in Washington in 1945. But the real reason was to strengthen Turkish morale and to warn the Soviets that Turkey could count on American assistance. The rejoic-ing of the people and the hospitality shown to the crew of the ship were indescribable. My American friends gave me an opportunity to visit the battleship and to look at the commemorative disk on the place where General MacArthur stood when he received the Japanese surrender.

I was now in the happy possession of all the papers I needed for my return to Hungary. On June 15, 1946, three years and four months after my arrival in Turkey, I left by train from Istanbul's Sirkeci Station. When I had arrived in 1943, nobody had greeted me. Now, as was the custom in Istanbul and Ankara for departing diplomats, a large crowd of friends gathered to see me off. They included members of the Ameri-can and British missions and of the Hungarian colony, as well as Turkish friends. Hungarian friends asked me to take food and clothing for their relatives in Hungary, so I carried eight pieces of luggage with me.

I traveled in a sleeper compartment from Istanbul to Sofia. This time, along the short Greek section of track, instead of the Germans I saw units of the new Greek army in their British uniforms. At the Svilengrad Station, on the Bulgarian border, instead of the Gestapo man a Soviet NKVD officer examined my papers and searched my luggage. There was no Hungarian diplomatic or consular mission in Sofia, only representatives of the Hungarian State Steelworks and a steamship company. I was received by these two gentlemen upon my arrival in the Bulgarian capital and they were helpful in providing temporary lodgings in their office. Sofia still had the characteristics of an occupied city, with Soviet military personnel everywhere. Female traffic police directed the scant movement of cars. Streets were mostly deserted. "Everything goes into reparation payments," I was told.

On June 16 I boarded a sleeper compartment on the train from Sofia to Ruse, a Bulgarian port on the Danube opposite the Rumanian coast. I had to pay for two berths, otherwise I would not have had room for my luggage. The ferry service, which once carried railroad cars across the Danube, because of wartime events now carried trucks and pedestrians only. I hired two horse-drawn cabs at the Ruse station to carry me and my luggage to the ferry. Having acquired some knowledge of Turkish, I discovered that one could get around with this language in that part of Bulgaria. The coachmen helped me carry my bags on board the ferry. The captain had been in the United States as a temporary immigrant and spoke English.

The boat was slowly filling up with Soviet military vehicles and personnel. I was the only civilian except for the crew. My presence and, even more, my abundant baggage drew the attention of the Russians; many of them were uncomfortably staring at me and my bags with greedy eyes. When we were out on the Danube, two Russian soldiers came over and began a one-sided conversation. I shook my head as a sign that I did not understand them (I spoke no Russian at that time). Soon the skipper was brought over in order to translate. The Russians offered to take me and my luggage to Bucharest. I saw on the face of the Bulgarian that he hoped I would not accept the proposal, and I had no intention of doing so. To impress them, I said that I was in the diplomatic service and that the Hungarian Embassy was expecting me in Bucharest; they might even meet me at some station on the way to the

Rumanian capital and expected me to travel by rail.

In the meantime, one of the Russians began putting my bags on his truck. I went and returned the bags to where they had been before. I had a very unpleasant feeling when, in the middle of the Danube, the Russians behaved rather threateningly. Of course, had I accepted their offer, they would have robbed me of my belongings on the road to Bucharest, perhaps even killed me. Finally, with the captain of the boat anxiously watching, the Russians shrugged their shoulders, swore, and went away. I was much relieved when, reaching the Rumanian pier, they all boarded their vehicles and moved off the boat quickly.

I saw a Rumanian railroader on the pier. He spoke Turkish, being a Tatar from the Dobrudja. I gave him some Turkish cigarettes and explained to him what I wanted. He ran up to the station and a few minutes later an engine pulling a freight car rolled down to the pier. I placed my luggage on it and was transported quickly into the river station of Giurgiu.

Throughout this journey I handed out Turkish cigarettes — a great treasure at that time for all smokers. I gave away a number to the railroader, the engineer, and others who helped me into the train, which was already at the station. My ticket was brought to me and along with some drinks while I ate the food I had carried from Istanbul.

At last the train started, but soon it stopped at the city station of Giurgiu. There it was stormed by a horde of passengers, some of them climbing into the cars through the windows. Now I sat in a crowded compartment with no space for other people's luggage, all the racks being filled with my eight pieces. But my fellow passengers remained patient and friendly and were delighted when I offered a round of cigarettes.

After a journey of many hours the train rolled into the spacious station of Bucharest, where, to my great pleasure, I was received by the chancery director of the Hungarian mission. I had sent a cable to Bucharest from Sofia but was not certain whether it would engender any reaction. I soon found out that the head of the Hungarian diplomatic mission (full diplomatic relations were not yet established) was an old friend, Alex Nékám. His deputy was another friend, István Gyöngyösy (no relation to the foreign minister). Gyöngyösy was born in Oradea, a town ceded by Hungary to Rumania after World War I. He attended Rumanian schools before returning to Hungary and spoke perfect Rumanian. Another surprise was to find that Gyöngyösy had joined the

Communist Party. He revealed that before the Soviet takeover of Hungary he had worked for the Communist underground.

I spent two days in Bucharest staying at the Hungarian Legation building on Strada Cantacuzino. Both Nékám and Gyöngyösy gave me their evaluation of the political situation in Rumania. King Michael had become a mere figurehead and was unlikely to last much longer. He was glad to escape with his life. The non-Communist members of the cabinet were fellow travelers. The only reason why the dictatorship of the proletariat had not yet been declared was the weakness of the Communist Party, which at the time of the Russian entry did not number more than two thousand clandestine members. The real masters, however, were the Russians, who may have wished to incorporate Rumania into the Soviet Union as a member republic. In regard to Hungary, Nékám insisted that the situation was less gloomy than in Rumania and that there was a glimmer of hope she might escape Rumania's inevitable fate. Of course, Gyöngyösy was more cautious, although he refrained from any propagandistic discourse on that subject.

The last leg of my journey home from Turkey was to travel from Bucharest to Budapest. I again filled a sleeper compartment with my luggage. This time I was warned of bedbugs. Though I was bitten during the night, the expectation of arriving the next day in my homeland after a more than three years' absence made me forget all inconveniences.

The Bulgarian customs officers, upon my request, had sealed most pieces of my luggage when I entered Bulgaria. The seals were not removed when I came to the Rumanian border. After I had offered cigarettes to the passport and customs officers, they abandoned the inspection and rushed to the corner of the station building to light up.

The train then slowly moved across the border and soon entered Lököshaca, the Hungarian border station. Here I encountered some difficulties with the passport officer: while I had travel papers issued by the Soviet military administration to pass through Bulgaria and Rumania, I had no such document to enter Hungary. Moreover, my Hungarian passport had long since expired. But I was eventually able to relieve his conscience by pointing out that transit through Rumania could have meaning only if one were allowed to enter Hungary. Evidently, the passport officer's instructions were contradictory, and I succeeded in persuading him that he would not commit any violation of the rules, under the circumstances, by accepting my expired passport.

The more amiable customs inspector looked with amazement at my eight pieces of luggage, among them a huge sack full of food. I told him I was bringing food and clothing to relatives. Once more he looked over all the sealed bags and said, "There is something wrong if you want me to consider these pieces examined." I understood and quickly gave the remainder of my cigarettes to the inspector and the other frontier guards. "Welcome back to Hungary," they said. I was happy when the train started to move, but I also had some forebodings about the future.

II

The Hungarian Imbroglio

Two roads diverged in a wood, and I—
I took the one less traveled by,
And that has made all the difference.

Robert Frost

RETURN TO HUNGARY

Upon returning to Hungary in mid June 1946 after an absence of three and a half years, I felt like a quasi Rip van Winkle. The country had passed through the cruel devastations of war, the mass deportation and murder of Jews under the Gestapo and the Hungarian Nazis, the spoliations of the German occupiers, and the brutalities of the Red Army. It now had a republican and, as a haranguing press pointed out, a "democratic" form of government.

The physical vestiges of the war were still visible, but it was evident that enormous efforts had been made to remove the ruins of besieged Budapest and to restore the orderly appearance of the city. There was a dire shortage of housing; the apartment in which I had lived with my mother was half-destroyed by a bomb, and so I had to find accommodations elsewhere.

But the physical changes were far less significant than those in governmental and societal relations as well as in political and administrative personnel. The semiauthoritarian, semiparliamentarian Horthy regime of over twenty years, as well as the Arrow Cross dictatorship of the last months of the war, had been replaced by a coalition government of four political parties. But to a considerable extent, and especially in regard to ultimate decisions, this was a facade. Basically, the country was ruled under the so-called armistice regime of the Soviet Military Command and the strong influence of its minions, the Communist Party of Hungary under the leadership of Mátyás Rákosi.

Although the Armistice Commission consisted of representatives of all three victors—the Soviet Union, the United States, and Great Britain—the real power was wielded by the head of the commission, Marshal Voroshilov, and later by his successor, General Sviridov.*

Moscow generally disregarded the Yalta Agreement, in which it had pledged to allow free elections in the East Central European countries occupied by Soviet forces. Yet strangely enough, the elections held in Hungary in November 1945, more than six months before my return, were relatively free from interference. The balloting had produced results that reflected the mood of the nation but must have been a shock to Stalin.

Only "democratic" parties were permitted to participate in these elections. Under these restrictions the Smallholder Party (one of the opposition parties during the Horthy regime, which represented a centrist and anti-Communist line, obtained 59 percent of the vote, whereas the Communist Party, financed and supported by the Soviet occupation forces, obtained only 17 percent. The Social Democratic party, another former opposition party, also received 17 percent; the fourth "democratic" party, the National Peasant party, 5 percent. However, before the Soviet Military Command would allow the elections, all parties had to agree that the coalition regime, irrespective of the outcome, would continue and that the controlling post of minister of the interior (in charge of the security police) would remain assigned to a member of the Communist Party.

Public speakers, the press, and radio—especially the media under Communist or Socialist control—constantly reminded their readers and listeners that they were now living in a free country under a democratic regime. They attempted to distinguish the present rulers from the erst-

---

*The Allied Control Commission in Hungary was established by an armistice agreement signed in Moscow on January 20, 1945, between the governments of the United States, Great Britain, the Soviet Union, and the provisional government of Hungary. Its functions consisted of the regulation and control of the armistice terms. See U.S. Department of State, *Treaties and Other International Agreements of the United States of America, 1776-1919,* vol. 3, pp. 1002-4.—ED.

while undemocratic Horthy regime, which in a rather simplistic or ignorant manner they often referred to as having been fascist. This was one of the Soviet Communist gimmicks used to disorient people and to prevent them from differentiating between various gradations of authoritarian rule and to persuade them to think in terms of a dichotomous world of progressive (meaning Communist) and fascist.

However, more sophisticated or unbiased persons were all aware that it was a blatant misnomer to apply the term *democratic* to the Hungarian Communist Party, modeled as it was after the Soviet Communist Party. Many of my friends reacted to these tactics by using the word in an ironic or pejorative sense, that is, to mean undemocratic. People began to employ other political keywords antithetically. Reactionary meant to strive for genuine democracy; proletarian internationalism meant Soviet domination; nationalism came to describe an anti-Soviet attitude, whereas patriotism denoted love of the Soviet Union.

All these concepts were further obfuscated when Communist theoreticians and their fellow travelers introduced the distinction between "bourgeois democracy" and "people's democracy." The first was supposed to apply to the capitalist countries, where only the bourgeoisie enjoyed democratic equality, whereas the second was the real democracy of the people as a whole. This second term was turned upside down years later when, after the Communist takeover, Rákosi declared that people's democracy was the Hungarian equivalent of the Soviet dictatorship of the proletariat.

Still, it should be noted that from 1946 to 1948 the coalition regime led a paradoxical existence. Agonizing under increased Communist pressures and the threatening presence of the Soviet army, it was able to exercise a retarding influence before it finally collapsed and Hungary became a Soviet satellite.

Hungarians who had been induced or forced to leave their country during the Horthy years and who were now returning to their homeland were carefully screened. This procedure gave considerable power to the political police (which later became the security police), already under the strict control of the Communist Party. Thus, before doing anything else, I had to register with the police in order to obtain a certificate of residence. For this purpose one had to go to the local police station and obtain the signature of the political officer.

Those who had left Hungary before the Russian advance and who were now returning in great numbers, the so-called Westerners, were considered suspect and were examined carefully in case they were war criminals or Western spies. On the other hand, repatriates from the Soviet Union, the so-called Muscovites, were few in number and, when in possession of a Soviet travel document, were above suspicion.

When I showed my passport, the political officer's first question was, "Are you a Westerner?" Having arrived from Turkey, an unusual place, I replied, "No, I am a Southeasterner." But sensing that the man lacked a sense of humor, I quickly added, "I have returned from Turkey." "What were you doing there?" "I was a member of the resistance movement." (I had been instructed that *resistance movement* was the key name to apply to what I had been doing in Turkey.) The officer became more interested. "I have not heard that there was a resistance movement in Turkey." I truthfully explained, "I was sent there by the Foreign Ministry to work against the Germans." Now the political officer quickly pronounced his verdict, "You have to produce a paper from the Foreign Ministry to prove why you were in Turkey. Failing this, you will not be registered." Fortunately, one of the deputy foreign ministers, Pál Sebestyén, an old hand, knew about my mission and immediately issued the required paper.

In Hungary, as in postwar Germany, most of the adult citizens had to pass through a process of denazification, or "testimonialization," as it was called in the former Third Reich. In order to be allowed to reoccupy my former positions—my university post and membership in the Budapest bar—I had to pass through that screening.

The testimonialization committees, formed for various professions and trades, consisted of five members: four were delegated by each of the four political parties that participated in the coalition government; the fifth, the chairman, was a nonparty lawyer. Although the Communist Party member of the committee that examined me was trying to embarrass me by such questions as, "Why did you go to Turkey?" and "Have you not been a German agent?" the decision was prompt and unanimous. Thus, I became reinstated without much ado and was able to resume my teaching in the fall 1946 semester.

As in the testimonialization committees, all public offices were parceled out among the four political parties in proportion to their strength in the National Assembly. The prime minister was a member of the largest party, the Smallholders; the other ministries were apportioned among all four parties. When the minister was a Smallholder, at least one of the deputy ministers had to be a Communist or a Socialist; when he was a Communist, his deputy belonged to another party. Still, the party affiliation of the minister largely determined the party affiliation of most of the officials in that ministry. Thus, there were Smallholder, Communist, Socialist, and even Peasant Party ministries. As I mentioned earlier, the minister of the interior was a Communist, and so were most of the officials in his ministry, including the members of the security police. The Ministry of Trade was headed by a Social Democrat, so it was largely a Socialist ministry; and so on.

Under the interwar regime, as under the Austro-Hungarian monarchy, members of the civil service were not permitted to belong to any political party (except for the few top political appointees). But under this postwar system members of the civil service as well as those of the army or the police were all expected to belong to one of the recognized political parties. Many naive persons even believed that this was one of the requisites of a democratic system, and were much encouraged in this belief by the Communists. The Communists, the best organized and most strongly disciplined party, wanted the officials to be party members — their own if possible, or at least to be sympathizers.

I could have made a fast career, as some of my friends did, had I joined *any* political party after my return to Hungary. Suggestions — even open invitations — to this effect were made to me by leading members of all four parties. But I steadfastly refused then and later to join any of them. I did not approve of the party apportionment system among public officials; furthermore, none of the political parties was to my taste. Nearest to my philosophy was the Smallholder Party, but I soon sensed the internal weaknesses of this suddenly overexpanded party — the refuge of many former German sympathizers as well as of careerists and opportunists — and the prevalency in its ranks of secret Communist fellow travelers.

The core leadership of the Smallholder Party consisted of those who led it in opposition to the ruling party during the Horthy regime. These were mostly persons with strong democratic convictions. But now they were often outdistanced or submerged in the sea of newly professed party members, who often had no experience or convictions and stood ready to serve any winning team.

Although I was approached by the Communists as well as by the Socialists, I had no intention of joining any Marxist party and certainly not one owing allegiance to a Stalinist Soviet Union. The Social Democratic Party was already under strong pressure to join with the Communists and establish a joint workers' party. Two years later this merger was implemented and the union bore all the characteristics of a shotgun marriage.

In 1946 my refusal to join any political party was not helpful to me. When I met the Socialist István Ries, the Minister of Justice, he told me bluntly, "Whoever does not join one of the democratic parties must be a reactionary." Poor István Ries! In 1950 he was to suffer a cruel death at the hands of the Communist security police.

However, almost all of my friends had become party members. Most of them joined the Smallholder Party, which appeared to be the least risky undertaking. Others joined the Socialists, rationalizing their decision by explaining that this party would act like the British Labour Party. Strangely enough, a few had become Communists because this was the most leftist party or the party of the future or because they had been clandestine party members in the prewar years. The National Peasant Party, the weakest of all the other parties, was eager to expand. It included genuine peasants as well as those who were involved in raising the status of peasants in prewar Hungary (the so-called village explorers), but quite a number of intellectuals joined this party because it was considered progressive though not Marxist. It was this party that was to become the easy prey of Communist infiltrators and sympathizers.

Whether a party member or not, I was advised to contact members of the new foreign policy elite in the four parties. As a teacher of international politics and international law and a participant in secret anti-German negotiations during the war, I should—so I was told—meet with these new experts on foreign policy and thus avoid becoming known as a loner or as one who refuses to collaborate with the democratic system. I myself felt the necessity of doing so because I believed that my experiences in Turkey should be utilized by those who were now in charge of handling foreign policy issues, which included the preparation for the peace conference to be held in Paris and the conclusion of a peace treaty. Those who in the past had been directly or indirectly involved in advising or decision making on questions of international concern were now reduced to a bare minimum. Most of those with experience in such affairs had fled before the Soviet advance or, when at diplomatic posts abroad, failed to return. I did not quite realize at the time that for a Communist-influenced regime, reliability in the eyes of the Soviets was far more important than genuine expertise.

When visiting persons now in charge or dealing with various aspects of foreign and international affairs, I found many old acquaintances who had been catapulted by events or by their new party membership into positions of considerable responsibility. All this added to the bizarre picture I acquired of the new Hungary.

NEW PROFILES

Only a few old officials remained in the Ministry of Foreign Affairs, where I was a frequent visitor. The minister was János Gyöngyösi, and one of his deputies was the brilliant Pál Sebestyén, who was well known for his anti-Nazi attitude. He was the only top person who possessed experience. The other deputy minister was Elek Bolgár, a Communist who had spent twenty-six years in exile in the Soviet Union. His entire foreign policy experience rested upon the singular fact that he had been the diplomatic representative of the Béla Kun regime in Vienna for two months in 1919.*

The all-important political section of the ministry was headed by a Communist Party member, György Heltai, who had been a student in the Faculty of Law and Political Science and had attended the international law seminar under Professor Gajzágo and myself. Lászlo Veress, who returned from Italy after the end of the war, was in charge of the Anglo-American desk. He had a difficult time, as he was suspected of being a British agent. In 1947 he was relieved of this post and sent to Germany to work for the agency in charge of the recovery of displaced Hungarian property.

Shortly after my return to Budapest I called on Foreign Minister Gyöngyösi and found him listless and suspicious. I assumed he must have received my report from Turkey, yet he hardly commented on it. He may have been warned against me by the Soviets. He was vague and noncommittal on any question I raised, being incompetent to assess

---

*The Communist government led by Béla Kun (1885–1937) existed for nine months in 1919 until it was deposed by Rumanian troops. He died in the Soviet Union during Stalin's Great Purge. —ED.

pertinent points. His inexperience and unexpected accession to his post caused him to be overly cautious and in awe of everybody. On the other hand, György Heltai gave me a friendly welcome.

After thus having interviewed members of the Smallholder and Communist foreign policy elite, I went to see the chairman of the Social Democratic foreign affairs committee, Zoltán Horváth, a former journalist. Horváth was interested in Turkey. After my short analysis of Turkish internal politics, he asked, "They are fascists, are they not?" "That depends on your definition of fascism," I replied cautiously. "According to my definition they certainly are not." The next time I met Horváth both of us were political prisoners.

The foreign policy expert from the National Peasant Party I was to meet was a former schoolmate, who after the war ran a weekly political journal. His name was Iván Boldizsár. He asked me for an article on the United Nations, which I promptly delivered. Boldizsár later confided to me that he was reproached by the Communists for having published it. In my paper I predicted that the Security Council would become inoperative unless there was harmony between its five permanent members. At that time (late 1946) Moscow was already generous in invoking its veto.

Boldizsár's story is a characteristic chronicle of his time. In his schooldays he bore the family name Betlen, which, when embarking on a career in journalism, he changed to Boldizsár. He told me then that he did not wish to give the impression that he was in any way related (which he was not) to Count Bethlen, the prime minister of Hungary between 1921 and 1931. In fact, it was a different relationship that he was eager to conceal during the Horthy regime. He happened to be a nephew of Oscar Betlen, who had played an important role during the first Communist regime of Béla Kun in 1919 and who was waiting in Moscow to stage a comeback. In 1945 Uncle Oscar did return and, as a prominent Muscovite, became the editor in chief of *Szabad Nép,* the Hungarian *Pravda,* and the éminence grise of Mátyás Rákosi. He continued to maintain direct contact with the Soviet leaders and probably with the Soviet security police. However, his nephew (was there an understanding between the two?) did not join the Communist Party but rather the National Peasant Party. Iván soon was regarded as the chief prototype of a fellow traveler.

Iván Boldizsár was not the only one among my friends who was catapulted into an astounding if not unusual career. Revolutions invariably toss up a number of individuals who otherwise might have remained in the twilight. Some of these careers were deserved, others not. Often, independent of merit, the truism that what goes up must come down proved to be accurate for many of these careerists. To those I have already mentioned let me add two more names.

Robert Hardi had worked before and during World War II in his father's modest office running an import-export business, mostly dealing in chemicals. In 1945, now a member of the Communist Party, he became the head of the foreign trade section of the Ministry of Commerce. He seemed to turn into a different person. No more an affable, friendly interlocutor, he now was a stiff, reserved partner in conversation, with a suspicious look, who spoke in clichés rather than spontaneous phrases. "Things have changed," he lectured me. "The world has become polarized. You either join the progressive division of mankind or you remain a reactionary, a stick-in-the-mud conservative." I soon realized that all this was partly an explanation of why he had joined the Communist Party and partly a cautious attempt to get me to join the Party as well. At subsequent meetings he became quite outspoken in this proposal and acted as though he were addressing a popular meeting. At the same time, however, he offered to assist me should there be a need.

When speaking of changed personalities, I have to mention my accidental meeting with György Páloczi-Horváth. He returned to Budapest from England in the spring of 1947. I met him in the street and, in view of our close collaboration in Turkey, I expected a warm greeting. Instead, he displayed a distant and awkward demeanor. He told me that he now had formally entered the Communist Party. In contrast to the way he appeared in Istanbul — a leftist liberal with socialistic leanings — he now acted and spoke as a person fully committed to Soviet Communism who blindly obeyed the commands of his party. He revealed to me only that he was working in the editorial offices of *Szabad Nép*.

The other profile I wish to present is of Nicholas Nyárádi, a close friend since high school. I had last seen him before my departure for Turkey, but since then he had achieved an unexpected promotion. Nyárádi was handsome and intelligent, with a receptive mind and the gift of gab. Otherwise, he abhorred strenuous work, including desk work, and preferred to devote himself to the amenities of human existence — the "good life." He could afford to do so because he inherited from his father the attorneyship of a leading bank in Budapest. There, as in his subsequent career, he was most skillful in picking the brains of others. When I had known him previously, he avoided any public service or any pursuits outside his office and his leisure activities. He was far from being endowed with boldness and, not taking any risks, he passed unscathed through the dangers of the German and the Russian occupations. It was a surprise to me when I found after my return that Nyárádi not only had joined the Smallholder Party but also had become state commissioner for displaced property with the rank of undersecretary in the Ministry of Finance. This job was particularly suited to his talents and character, for he spoke foreign languages and had traveled widely.

As a consequence of the war, the German occupation of Hungary, and the subsequent Soviet invasion, billions of dollars' worth of Hungarian property had been removed from Hungary to Germany. This property included the gold reserve of the Hungarian National Bank, entire factories, railroad equipment, cattle, horses, and anything movable. All this eventually fell into the hands of the Allied armies when they occupied Germany and Austria. In principle, the Americans, the British, and the French were ready to return this displaced property (except for what could be considered war booty), a policy later endorsed in the peace treaty with Hungary.

The new Hungarian leaders, as mentioned before, lacked access to persons with international experience and linguistic ability. Nyárádi was able to fill this lacuna and enter public office for the first time in his life. He thereby could represent the government in negotiations while leaving serious paperwork and study to others. Nyárádi and his wife were often abroad on official trips. They invited me to live in their spacious apartment until I could obtain an apartment for myself and my mother. They did so not only to be helpful to me but also for reasons of safety: my presence would prevent other persons or families deprived of housing from applying to the authorities for accommodation in the Nyárádi home, one that was too large for two persons under the existing regulations. Even someone in such a position as Nyárádi was not safe from interference by, say, a Communist district housing commissar.

I lived for several months in this apartment. This sojourn was very useful to me at a time when it was difficult to obtain housing. It also provided me with the invaluable opportunity to meet my future wife, Rose. In February 1947 Mrs. Nyárádi invited some of her friends for an afternoon coffee while her husband was abroad. She asked me to attend. It was late when I returned to the apartment and the party had already settled down into several groups. I knew all the couples present but immediately spotted a young lady who seemed to be without a partner. I sat down next to her and we had a hearty conversation.

In addition to her good looks, I found her elegant and tasteful dress remarkable and attractive. She seemed to be interested in my stay in Turkey and, without caring much for the other guests, I spent almost all the time talking with her. When she was about to leave, I helped her into her overcoat fitted with Persian lamb. We both expressed the hope that we might meet again.

During the following months we spoke several times over the telephone. I had asked her to call me late at night because I spent little time in my friend's apartment, eating supper at my mother's place in the early evening and only returning thereafter. But I was reluctant to allow the development of a real attachment. I felt so utterly insecure: I had no reliable income (my university salary was minimal) and not even an apartment of my own. I did not feel that I had any solid status in this new society. Eventually, by mid 1947 an event happened that precluded or, rather, rendered dangerous a continued and closer relationship with Rose. I shall recall this development later; it confirmed to me how unsettled, transitory, and hazardous existence was in the Hungarian imbroglio.

The duality of this world—the old drifting toward the new, totally Sovietized community—was felt everywhere. I encountered it at every step. Not that I deeply deplored the loss of the old; it was rather the distastefulness of this new one that I found revolting. This trend was nowhere more apparent than in the university, where I gradually felt more and more alienated.

In fall 1946 I attended the inaugural convocation at the beginning of the academic year. The initial outward formalities followed the pattern to which I had been accustomed. The Academic Senate, consisting of the rector, the prorector (the rector of the previous academic year), and the deans and prodeans of the four historic faculties, presided over the assembly of faculty and students. Before the opening of the ceremony members of the Senate and other faculty members gathered in the lobby. I gained the impression that senior faculty members were largely ignored by the new ones—strange faces, many of them wearing the Communist Party badge on their lapels. The deans of the Faculty of Theology, in their soutanes and purple cinctures, looked forlorn in the crowd. Soon they and their faculty and students would be ousted from the university.

A large group surrounded George Lukács, the famous Communist philosopher, who rejoined the faculty in 1945 after an absence of twenty-five years, which he spent partly in Germany and partly, after the rise of Hitler, in the Soviet Union. He had been people's commissar for education in the short-lived first Communist regime in Hungary in 1919. A friend of mine, a member of the Faculty of Philosophy, introduced me to Lukács, who, however, seemed little interested in me. He continued his discourse, attentively listened to by his admirers, many of them his critics during the past twenty-five years and, therefore, an even more faithful audience now. Lukács had just returned from a short visit to Switzerland, where he had attended a Marxist conference. "As you know," he explained, "the Swiss are most reactionary." "Fascists!" shouted a portly sycophant, whom I recognized as an erstwhile admirer of Nazi Germany.

I turned away in disgust and sought solace in the company of my senior colleague, Professor Lászlo Gajzágo, who occupied the chair of international law. He was a world-renowned authority in his field, who had pleaded on behalf of the Hungarian government before the World Court at The Hague and was a member of the prestigious Institute of International Law. Prior to 1918 Gajzágo served in the Austro-Hungarian diplomatic corps, in particular in the embassy at Constantinople, a most sensitive post in those years. After the dissolution of the monarchy he was absorbed by the Hungarian foreign service. He represented Hungary before the League of Nations and acted as the principal legal and political adviser to his government on many delicate issues. Upon his retirement from the foreign service he was appointed to the chair of international law at the University of Budapest. When I returned from Turkey, he supported my promotion to professor extraordinary. I assumed that he wished me to succeed him in the chair of international law after his retirement.

In 1946 Professor Gajzágo was in his mid sixties and his health had suffered, as had that of many others, from the deprivations during and after the siege of Budapest. The house where he lived was burned down by the Russians in retaliation for a shot alleged to have been fired from it. All the inhabitants were gunned down except Gajzágo, who barely escaped with his life. Due to his extraordinary knowledge of languages, which included Russian, he was able to explain that he was absent when the event occurred.

He lost all his belongings in the fire, including his valuable library, the loss he deplored most. He was reduced to a meager existence in sharp contrast with his erstwhile luxurious diplomatic life. However, he stoically accepted his misfortune. But his entire lifestyle, manners, and erudition hardly fitted into the new environment. He had served under Emperor-King Francis Joseph, and now was obliged to teach in a university that was gradually being transformed into a Marxist-Leninist institution of Soviet-inspired learning. I could hardly foresee how he could survive much longer in this environment, a forecast that also applied to myself, although I was more than twenty years younger than Gajzágo and felt better able to resist pressures and to survive.

In the spring of 1947 it appeared that "democratic" Hungary was to become completely subservient to Soviet Communist forces. The competing forces — the Smallholder leadership, backed up by the overwhelming majority of the population as shown in the popular elections, and the small Communist Party — were unequal opponents in this struggle. The Soviet military presence tilted the balance in favor of the Communists. The ultimate question was whether Moscow was willing and determined to intervene in order to impose the minority Communists upon a reluctant country.

Three decades later I watched the developments in Portugal with considerable alarm. There another minority Communist Party endeavored to take over the government of that country with the help of fellow travelers, intimidation of all kinds, and infiltration into the armed forces. But eventually that attempt failed. In view of the lack of geographic contiguity and the absence of its forces on Portuguese soil, Moscow was able to provide only financial and "moral" support, and the democratic forces could rally against the Communists. I became more convinced than ever that in postwar Hungary the Communists, despite their superior tactics and discipline, would not have been able to sweep away all other parties had it not been for the direct and indirect pressure and intervention by the Soviet military and security forces present in the country.

The Hungarian security police (both the Military-Political Section of the Ministry of Defense and the political police of the Ministry of the Interior) had come under exclusive Communist and Soviet control. In early 1947 it began to "discover" antidemocratic and anti-Russian conspiracies. Under this pretext mass arrests were carried out. People of all kinds — mostly former luminaries, both military and civilian, but also workers and peasants — were arrested. They confessed under duress to having conspired to overthrow the existing regime. The Hungarian Community, an allegedly conspiratorial organization, figured prominently as the main target of these accusations. In January 1947 the leaders of this group, among them Gen. Lajos Veress, were taken into custody. Soon the press reported that many deputies who belonged to the Smallholder Party were also involved in this affair. A move was under way to disrupt, weaken, and eventually destroy the majority party in the National Assembly.

Deputies of the National Assembly enjoyed immunity from arrest by the Hungarian police. They could be lawfully apprehended only if their immunity was lifted by the Assembly itself. To forestall an open rift with other coalition partners and under pressure from the Soviet military commander, the Smallholder leaders consented to the removal of this immunity from a number of their deputies, who were accused of being members of an antidemocratic (rather than anti-Soviet) conspiracy. The Assembly so voted and these deputies were promptly arrested by the Hungarian security police. The same device was applied several times thereafter. Rákosi extolled the method as his salami tactic: the majority party, like a salami, was sliced up into manageable pieces. New names were added to those involved in the alleged conspiracy, and more deputies disappeared into the dungeons of the police. Some of those whose names were mentioned in the Communist press fled abroad to avoid arrest.

The crucial confrontation occurred when the Minister of the Interior, the Communist leader László Rajk, demanded the arrest of the popular secretary general of the Smallholder Party, Béla Kovács. Here the Assembly refused to waive his immunity. Kovács was forthwith arrested by the Soviet security police, which was not bound to respect his immunity, and charged with conspiracy against the occupation forces.

Finally, the ax struck at the highest level of the Smallholder Party. While vacationing in Switzerland, Prime Minister Ferenc Nagy was warned over the telephone by Rákosi that the Russians were planning to arrest him as soon as he returned to Hungary. He did not return; instead, he resigned from his position in return for permission for his young son to leave the country. The exchange of the letter of resignation and the child took place on the Austrian-Swiss border. The new prime minister, Lajos Dinnyés, also from the ranks of the decimated Smallholder Party, was an early fellow traveler of the Communists.

Other Smallholder leaders, among them Father Béla Varga, the speaker of the National Assembly, soon fled the country to escape Communist and Soviet persecution. Most of the Hungarian diplomats abroad, among them Aladár Szegedy-Maszák, the ambassador to Washington, and Paul de Auer, the ambassador to Paris, refused to serve the new government.

These Hungarian events, of course, were not isolated incidents on the world scene: the Cold War had intensified and Moscow had begun to consolidate further its hold over East Central Europe. But the rising opposition in the United States to Soviet violations of the Yalta Agreement, the American endeavor to stabilize and normalize the western part of Europe with the Marshall Plan, the struggle for the control of Germany—all these could be considered as favorable signs. Hopes were set on the coming into force of the peace treaty, which would end the armistice regime and the occupation of Hungary by Soviet forces. It was therefore expected that within a year or so these forces would be withdrawn from Hungary, thus removing the possibility of continued direct Soviet interference.

I felt that since I had been abroad during the years of the German terror and the Soviet invasion, it was my duty to stay in Hungary and strive for a better future for my homeland. For other reasons, personal and sentimental, I felt inclined to stay on as long as my safety was not endangered. However, an urge to be helpful to my country as well as financial need persuaded me to accept public assignments in my field of specialization.

FOREIGN ASSIGNMENTS

Six months after my return from Turkey I was compelled to accept an assignment concerning the foreign relations of Hungary. Since I was not a full professor, my university salary was completely insufficient to provide a living. I was permitted to practice law, but private practice in my field, international law, had dried up as a result of the nationalization of major enterprises and the elimination of private fortunes. On the other hand, there was a lack of specialists in international trade, which was now carried on by various branches of the government and by state-owned corporations.

My first public assignment was entrusted to me by my friend Nicholas Nyárádi, the state commissioner for displaced property. He had achieved considerable success with the United States military government in Germany; the gold of the Hungarian National Bank and a great many industrial assets had been returned to Hungary during 1946. In March 1947 he was appointed Minister of Finance; he was untainted by any connection with the Hungarian Community and was acceptable to Rákosi.

Nyárádi faced considerable difficulty in one particular case, namely, that of the Hungarian studhorses shipped by the American army to the United States. With the approach of Soviet forces in 1944, the studhorses were removed — as were most other Hungarian movable assets — first to Austria and then to Germany. When American units reached Donauwörth in northern Bavaria, they captured the horses, which were still guarded and attended by their Hungarian staff. Later in 1945 the horses were transported to the United States; in 1946 Hungary claimed them as displaced property.

I was asked by Nyárádi to work out a memorandum that would prove that the horses should be returned. The legal question to which I sought the answer was whether under international law these horses should be considered war booty (military equipment or arms) or displaced property to be restituted. In order to set out all the relevant facts and legal issues, I arranged a conference where I interviewed members of the staff who had accompanied the studhorses to Germany and had witnessed their capture by the Americans. We invited representatives of the American Legation to these interviews, and a secretary attended the sessions in the company of an interpreter. I assume that the legation reported favorably concerning this claim. My memorandum was presented to the American minister, who forwarded it to Washington. The Department of State supported the return of the horses to Hungary, and their shipment was already being prepared when this move was frustrated by an action of a Senate subcommittee.

The subcommittee, headed by Sen. Wayne Morse of Oregon, himself a great lover of horses, produced a report that recommended against the return of these stallions and mares. To my amazement the report absolutely ignored the essential issue, namely, whether the United States was under a legal obligation to restitute the horses. Rather, it dwelt at length on their good quality and their significance for the Hungarian army in case of war. The report assumed that in the next war there would be Hungarian cavalry and horse-drawn artillery pieces, the employment of which would be inconsistent with the strategic interests of the United

States. This was almost a repetition of the wartime joke of the Hungarian navy threatening the United States. Now it was the cavalry. But this time it was no joke—it was spelled out in a Senate report.

I was not yet fully familiar with the role of the Congress and of congressional committees in the conduct of U.S. foreign relations. Not that the restitution of these horses would have made any difference to political developments in Hungary or to relations between Hungary and the United States, which gradually deteriorated as the Communist takeover materialized and Hungary fell into the Soviet orbit. Nor would these horses, if returned, have contributed effectively to the strengthening of the Hungarian armed forces, which soon were mechanized along the Soviet model. However, Hungarian farmers, who still relied on draft animals, were thus deprived of first-rate horses.

But what struck me most was the complete lack of understanding displayed by a responsible congressional body in regard to the foreign policy pursued by the Department of State. After all, Hungary at that juncture was not yet a Communist country, and official American policy wished to demonstrate the goodwill and friendliness of that great democracy toward Hungary, which was then on the threshold of choosing between East and West. It was disheartening to observe how international law and the rights of a small nation were disregarded in this report, which was not only one-sided but also myopic and preposterous in its meaning.

Since the conclusion of the Armistice Treaty of January 20, 1945, Hungary, at an enormous sacrifice, had been paying reparations in kind to the Soviet Union. Soviet authorities had also taken possession of all German property in Hungary. But now Moscow demanded other German "assets." At the end of the war Hungarian corporations and the Hungarian state owed a considerable sum of German marks to a defeated Germany on account of arms delivered by the Germans. On the other hand, Germany owed much more to Hungary for food and mineral products, which Hungary had shipped to its wartime ally. The balance, therefore, was clearly in favor of Hungary. But the rather arbitrary Soviet interpretation of assets included the Hungarian claims vis-à-vis Germany, irrespective of Germany's much greater liability toward Hungary. Shortly after the signing of the peace treaty on February 10, 1947, Moscow presented the Hungarian government with a bill representing its claim to German assets at the astronomical figure of over four hundred million dollars.

Shortly after his appointment as minister of finance, Nyárádi was invited to lead a delegation to Moscow to negotiate the question of these and other Soviet financial claims. The natural thing would have been for Deputy Prime Minister Ernö Gerö, who was in overall charge of economic questions, to lead this delegation. But Gerö was a Communist, the second in command under Rákosi, and it was the habit of Communists that difficult questions to be discussed with Moscow should be entrusted to members of other parties in the coalition cabinet.

Nyárádi asked me to join his delegation to Moscow. I accepted. He submitted the list of participants to General Sviridov, the Soviet head of the Armistice Commission. Sviridov immediately struck my name from the list. "Why do you need this man?" he asked. Nyárádi explained that he needed an international law expert because some legal questions were involved in the negotiations. Sviridov replied, "The function of the Hungarian delegation will not be to discuss anything on legal grounds. It will have to agree and sign."

Nyárádi declined to head the delegation under these circumstances. Prime Minister Nagy then talked with Sviridov, who simply denied what he had told Nyárádi. Nevertheless, he refused to issue a visa to me. Nyárádi and the delegation left without me. This event alerted me to the fact that I was not a persona grata to the Soviets.

Soon I received yet another ominous signal. In late spring 1947 I was at last able to obtain an apartment and, with my mother, moved into a new place in the center of the city near the university. One afternoon, when I returned home, the janitor met me in the doorway. "A very attractive young lady was here and inquired about you. She must have a crush on you. She said she will return."

An hour later my visitor arrived. She certainly had the looks of an enchantress with her blond hair, blue eyes, and slender body. She introduced herself as Lia Gántay, wife of a Hungarian officer who had disappeared at the Russian front; she had no idea whether he was still alive. She explained that the purpose of her visit was to gain legal advice; she was to inherit from a relative who lived in Slovakia, and there were various legal complications she wished to clarify. When I asked who recommended me to her, she mentioned a former student of mine. Since I had many in the past, and the name was not uncommon, I could not immediately determine whether the reference was real or not. I promised that I would examine her questions and seek information from the Foreign Ministry and from the Czechoslovak mission in Budapest.

A week later she telephoned and came again. I gave her some of the information she wanted; for other answers I had to write to Prague. She became a frequent visitor, and I also met her in several coffeehouses. Later I invited her for dinner to a restaurant. I found her company entertaining and became attracted to her.

After a few months, being always on the alert myself, I noted she had begun asking probing questions about my activities. By then our relations had grown intimate. I became more and more convinced that somebody must have sent her to me. Eventually she admitted that this had been the case, but by that time she said that she had been authorized to reveal her mission. She was working for the Military-Political Section, an arm of the Ministry of Defense, which was also in charge of counter-espionage. Lia now revealed that because of the alleged or genuine involvement of her husband with the Germans, she was unable to get a job. On the other hand, she was constantly pressured and finally compelled to serve the counterespionage agency. I never found out whether, as she assured me, she was really infatuated with me or whether she was only playing a role.

It was later in 1947 when Lia asked me to meet with her boss, who was a former Horthyist counterintelligence officer. There might have been several reasons for him to serve "democratic" Hungary: he may have been slighted or have participated in the anti-Nazi resistance, or his ambitions may have led him to seek advancement under the new regime. Lia begged me to see him and I thought that it would be unwise to refuse her request.

Maj. Géza Mátray was a middle-sized and middle-aged military type with excellent manners and an endearing demeanor. He hinted that the present regime was ready to use his talents and experience in the field of counterintelligence. He made disparaging remarks about his superiors and complained that he was surrounded by idiots and that he had great difficulty in penetrating Western diplomatic missions, which he was expected to do. He more than hinted that in certain circles I was highly suspect, since I had been in touch with Western intelligence agents in Turkey. He advised me to cooperate with him rather than with anybody else. He would never ask me to say or do anything against my will.

I told him all about my work and about my assignments abroad (while in contact with Mátray I undertook several journeys, which I shall recall later) so as to enable him to write reports. By late 1947 the Military-Political Section had merged with the political police, which was to become the State Security Section of the Ministry of the Interior, known by its Hungarian initials as the AVO. But by then Mátray had disappeared. Later on Lia told me he had fled abroad in early 1948, but he may also have been arrested. During our contacts I felt that he held a certain protective hand over me, and for this reason I was sorry to lose him.

My meetings with Lia became less frequent. In the first half of 1948 she often sought to see me, although I warned her that I was busy, and I spent many weeks abroad. Finally, we agreed — she somewhat reluctantly — that it would be better if we would not meet anymore. I advised her to marry and convinced her that I, whom she was expected to spy upon, was not the proper person.

During our time together Lia frequently showed signs of jealousy. This liaison barred me from continuing my deepening friendship with Rose. Although I enjoyed Lia's company, I was afraid of her and was aware that she could endanger me as well as Rose had she discovered this relationship. I thought it prudent to avoid any contact with Rose, whom I did not meet or speak to for over a year. Only some months after Lia had completely vanished from my sight did I dare to see Rose again.

In September 1947 I left Hungary for the first time since my return from Turkey, and once again it was to Turkey I traveled, if only for two weeks. Hungary was seeking to reestablish its economic ties abroad. To earn hard currency through exports was considered vital, because indispensable raw materials could be purchased only with dollars and Hungarian missions abroad could be maintained only with such funds. The Soviet and other East European trade connections were barren in this respect; they did not produce hard currency.

It was remembered in Hungary that trade with Turkey during wartime (except for the very end of the war) was very profitable. Turkey had been a market for Hungary's electrical appliances and agricultural machinery. Having had experience with Turkey, I was asked by the Hungarian National Bank and the Ministry of Finance to undertake exploratory talks in Turkey that could lead to the resumption and expansion of commercial ties.

On September 23 I left Budapest for Istanbul by train. The journey was slowed by the disruption of direct rail traffic on the short Greek section owing to the Greek civil war. Because of guerrilla activity, the Turkish railroads refused to operate in the so-called Pithion quadrangle. From Svilengrad I had to travel by bus to the Turkish border, where — in an open field—we had to change to a Turkish bus, which took us to Babaeski, where we rejoined the train for Istanbul.

The short stay in Istanbul provided me with an opportunity to meet with many of the friends I had made during the three years I had spent in Turkey. I also visited Chinese consul general Ma, who was amazed to see me still alive despite his predictions to the contrary. I ran across Soviet consul general Grubyakov in one of the restaurants, who remarked with a sarcastic smile, "So, you were able to penetrate the Iron Curtain." Otherwise, my mission was of little avail. The Turks were highly fearful of Soviet designs and already considered Hungary to be a Soviet province. As always, the Turks were very pragmatic and were thinking in black-and-white terms.

I hardly had returned again from Turkey when the Ministry of Commerce required my services as a troubleshooter. This time it was Robert Hardi, head of the section for foreign trade, who recommended me to Undersecretary Sándor Barcza, a Social Democrat, to disentangle a fouled-up situation between Hungary and Switzerland.

In 1946 Hungary, in search of hard currency, offered to ship Switzerland thirty-five thousand tons of crude oil from its modest oil fields. An agreement was signed between MASZOVOL (the Hungarian-Soviet Joint Oil Corporation) and a Swiss oil import firm. Delivery was due before the winter of 1946–47 set in, but no deliveries took place because the Soviet side of the company preferred to deliver the available oil elsewhere. That winter was a particularly hard one; the Swiss firm was obliged to supply heating oil to its customers and had to obtain it with great difficulty and at a much higher price from other sources. Among the further difficulties of obtaining replacement oil (at a time when the economic conditions in Western Europe were far from stabilized) was the problem of shipment to Switzerland. The Rhine had frozen over, and tankers from Rotterdam were unable to reach Basel. Instead, the oil had to be transshipped by rail, an expensive alternative.

Under Swiss law the claimant was able to have twenty Hungarian MASZOVOL tank cars attached by court order while in transit across the Swiss rail network. The Swiss firm claimed one million Swiss francs compensation. A number of evidently incompetent and mendacious emissaries were dispatched by MASZOVOL and the Ministry of Commerce to Bern. They either returned without any results or else made promises that were never fulfilled. The Hungarian economy needed the tank cars, and it looked as if the impending lawsuit was already lost. In addition to all this, in early 1948, in retaliation against the breach of the agreement (the Hungarian government had guaranteed the implementation of the contract), the Swiss Department of Trade stopped all deliveries of goods to Hungary.

Amid this bungled and inauspicious situation I was directed to go to Switzerland and negotiate an equitable settlement with my Swiss counterparts. An able director of the Hungarian National Bank, Elemér Jármay, was to join in the talks. Arriving in Bern on February 12, 1948, I was received— rightly, I must say—with utmost distrust. After having talked to ignorant and deceitful agents of both the Hungarian government and the Hungarian-Soviet Joint Oil Company, they were surprised to meet with somebody who not only spoke a civilized German but was also able to discuss the issues of the case with competence and frankness.

Jármay and I admitted that mistakes had been committed and that these had to be made good. At the same time, I argued, the Hungarian side should not be made responsible for more than its share of responsibility. We soon realized that the Swiss oil importers were still interested in the delivery of the Hungarian oil and, if agreement could be reached on compensation, would be ready to pay the present world market price of oil—a price higher than the original agreement stipulated. Such a pattern of compromise could extricate Hungary from this painful situation without having to pay the excessive indemnity demanded by the Swiss.

The negotiations lasted for over six weeks. Once, I had to return to Budapest in order to obtain approval from the complicated governmental party machinery for the continuation and completion of the talks according to my plan. Socialist and Communist Party interests were at stake (the merger of the two parties would only take place in May 1948), as well as Soviet interests. Eventually, approval was obtained.

Certain technical questions also had to be handled concerning the quality of the heating oil to be delivered. I asked that an oil expert from MASZOVOL be sent to Bern. A young man by the name of Leo Konduktorov came. He spoke a halting Hungarian, which I had to translate into German during the negotiations. Konduktorov was from Carpatho-Ruthenia, a territory of mixed Hungarian and Ukrainian population. His family emigrated to the Soviet Union, where he was brought up as a Soviet citizen. Now he had returned to Hungary and was serving the Hungarian-Soviet Joint Oil Company. He was in the limelight eight years later when, during the Hungarian Revolution in 1956, he appeared before the Security Council of the United Nations as a representative of Hungary under the name of Peter Kos and was immediately denounced and recalled by the revolutionary prime minister Imre Nagy. After the collapse of the Revolution, he continued to serve in the Hungarian diplomatic service and acted for some time as Hungarian ambassador in India.

While in Bern I was in permanent contact with the Hungarian Legation. The principal figure in this diplomatic mission was not the minister (a member of the Smallholder Party) but the Communist secretary Jozsef Száll. The trade attaché, János Nyerges, was also a Communist; he received his instructions from Hardi and supported my endeavors. Száll, with whom I was able to establish a working relationship, revealed to me that he was informing the Soviet ambassador daily of the developments in our negotiations. I was careful to keep Száll informed because he was also reporting to the Budapest headquarters of the Hungarian Communist Party.

On March 25, 1948, I finally returned to Budapest with the draft agreement. With Jármay's help I succeeded in having the indemnity reduced to three hundred thousand Swiss francs. However, the much higher price set for the thirty-five thousand tons of oil to be delivered came to about the same amount as the compensation paid. The implementation of the agreement followed shortly: on the day when the check was handed to the member of the Swiss Legation in Budapest, the sequestration of the Hungarian tank cars was lifted. I had gained the confidence of my Swiss interlocutors to the extent that the Trade Department in Bern instructed the legation to follow my suggestions should divergencies appear in the interpretation of the agreement.

Until the settlement of the conflict Switzerland had suspended all commercial activities with Hungary; now these activities were resumed. The successful completion of these talks had greatly increased my reputation. Undersecretary Barcza personally came to congratulate me. When I next met him, five years later, we both were in prison.

It was Nyárádi's turn to offer me a permanent position in the Ministry of Finance. The peace treaty had come into force on September 15, 1947, and various legal questions had to be handled: the foreign claims for compensation arising out of war damages, nationalization issues, reparations to be paid, and a number of Hungarian counterclaims. Nyárádi was eager to have these questions included in the competency of his own ministry and not the Foreign Ministry, since he already handled the issue of displaced property. Because I needed the regular income and because I believed that my activity could counter Communist inroads into these affairs, I accepted. I was to become, in fact, a kind of international legal adviser to the ministry with the official rank of counselor.

MINISTERIAL COUNSELOR

In April 1948, at the time of my appointment as counselor in the Ministry of Finance, the Cold War, centered mostly around the vexed German question, reached the boiling point. Developments in Hungary contributed to a deterioration of American-Hungarian relations and Budapest was slowly coming to be regarded in Washington as a forlorn post. The swallowing up of the Social Democratic party by the Communists and the subservience of the remaining political parties (including the rump Smallholder Party) to Soviet and Communist demands were the writing on the wall portending a Soviet-model totalitarian regime.

In May 1948 Gen. Lucius Clay, the American commander in chief in Germany, stopped all further repatriation of displaced Hungarian property. The apparent reason for this measure was an incident at the Hungarian-Austrian frontier station of Hegyeshalom, where members of the United States armed forces—soldiers who accompanied a group of repatriates—were mistreated. The American commander demanded a formal apology from the Hungarian government.

While the international horizon was dark, my activity in the ministry began under more auspicious circumstances. Most of my coworkers in the section where foreign financial questions were handled were old-time civil servants— specialists in their field and not political nominees—and were somewhat known to me. They were only too happy to welcome a new colleague who was a nonparty man and who specialized in international law. István Vásárhelyi, the undersecretary for foreign financial operations, was also an old hand.

First, I had to grapple with that article of the peace treaty that provided for the payment of wartime damages to the Allies or their nationals. Such claims already flooded the ministry from the United States, Great Britain, France, Belgium, the Netherlands, and others. We wished to propose a quasi-arbitral procedure to determine the validity of claims and to assess the amounts to be paid. The ministry had already informed the interested foreign missions in Budapest and also the legations of neutral countries, such as Sweden and Switzerland, that I would handle these questions. The responsible members of the diplomatic corps soon contacted me.

A number of claims relating to wartime damages were submitted by Swiss and Swedish firms, supported by their governments. Since these countries were not ex-enemy states and therefore were not signatories to the peace treaty, their claims were to be decided on the basis of general international law. I drafted the diplomatic notes on this issue, which were sent by the Foreign Ministry (whose economic section was then headed by my friend István Gyöngyösy, whom I met in Bucharest on my way home from Istanbul in 1946) to Switzerland and Sweden and also to some other neutral countries that presented claims. In these notes I contended that war damages, caused by Allied bombing or by combat situations (never was I allowed to mention Soviet spoliations or destructions), were acts of state that the Hungarian government was unable to prevent and could not, therefore, be held responsible for. Eventually, this legal argument was accepted by the interested governments.

In fact, much of the damage done to foreign as well as Hungarian property was due to the destruction—often deliberate arson—committed by members of the Soviet armed forces. It was the policy of the Foreign Ministry and other Hungarian departments never even to hint at the Soviet actions responsible for all the devastation in Hungary. We, of course, did refer to the acts of the German military in removing property to the West. For such actions Hungary could not assume financial liability. Through these diplomatic notes and endless conversations with members of the foreign missions I was able to clarify many doubtful points and restrict the scope of Hungarian responsibility.

While my work in the ministry absorbed most of my time, I had little leisure to see my friends. But in May 1948 I certainly found time to participate in a reunion with my schoolmates from the Budapest High School of the Piarist Teaching Order, where we had graduated twenty-five years earlier.* We met in the school and were received by the head of the Hungarian province of the religious order, Father Sándor Sik, a well-known writer and poet. It was a crucial moment for the Catholic and

---

*Vali would later attend yearly reunions in New York City of the graduates of this school.—ED.

Protestant churches in Hungary. The government had taken the first step, to be followed by more drastic ones, to reduce and remove the influence of the churches. The teaching of religion, up to now an obligatory subject in elementary and secondary schools, was now to be made optional.

Nicholas Nyárádi and I had been schoolmates. He was present at the reception where in his welcoming address Father Sik strongly criticized the government for what he called an atheistic policy. Nyárádi looked rather nervous; he told me later that he considered Sik's words, uttered in the presence of a member of the government, highly tactless.

In the evening our class (only a few were absent or had died or disappeared in the past years) gathered for dinner in a restaurant. The majority, if not all, of our classmates were strongly hostile to Communism. Soon Nyárádi became a target of verbal attacks by some of our more vocal colleagues. One reproached him for having supported the nationalization of banks (with the considerable industrial interests they controlled), an action that fell directly under the jurisdiction of the Ministry of Finance. Nyárádi's rather lame excuse was that he happened to be in Moscow when nationalization was decreed. But some lawyer friends reminded him that ministerial responsibility extends to acts carried out by others under the name of the minister. He should have resigned if anything so important happened during his absence. Some of our colleagues then suggested that he should have remained abroad (it was well known that he returned from Moscow via Stockholm); others reminded him that he used to be the attorney for one of the banks that had been nationalized.

Nyárádi remained silent. His main concern, as he admitted to me, was the return of displaced property by the Americans. He believed — rightly or wrongly — that his position as a minister depended solely on the continued flow of returning displaced goods. He thought he was indispensable even to the Communists in this matter. It was therefore of vital interest to him to reach out to the Americans and persuade them to change their attitude.

There was also some displaced Hungarian property in the Soviet zone of Germany. In order to urge its return, but actually to find a pretext to contact General Clay, Nyárádi decided to go to Berlin in July 1948. I was to accompany him. The time chosen for this journey was not the most appropriate. West Berlin had been under Soviet blockade since the end of June. The airlift initiated by the United States and its allies was just beginning. From Budapest one could not fly to East Berlin (except via Moscow); a train journey via Prague would have taken several days. But Nyárádi managed to secure from the Ministry of Transportation one of the cherished diesel-engine rail coaches equipped with sleeping berths and a kitchen.

Our party left on July 10. Nyárádi was afraid that because of the strained situation in Berlin he might be caught in an armed confrontation between the Russians and the Western powers. However, the appointment in East Berlin could not be postponed.

On the morning of July 11 our motorcoach reached the Czechoslovak-German border. On the East German side we were examined by Soviet security officers. They had been informed of our arrival, and the captain in charge wished to see the minister personally. I conducted him to the compartment where Nyárádi sat, and he began welcoming him in Russian. But Nyárádi, despite his prolonged stay in Moscow, did not know any Russian; whereupon the captain exclaimed, "Vengerskii ministr ne govorit po-russki?" ("The Hungarian minister does not speak Russian?").

Before our departure from the frontier station at Bodenbach, a director of the East German railroads climbed up next to our Hungarian engineer. It was customary that a local railroader accompany the engineer to explain signals, but it was unusual that a director should come to assist. Soon we invited him to join our table and he ate voraciously of the white rolls, butter, and marmalade we had in abundance. Later he joined us for luncheon and stuffed himself with porkchops and chocolate cake. Before we arrived at the Anhalter Bahnhof in East Berlin, Nyárádi gave him the rest of the chocolate cake for his family.

In East Berlin we were lodged at the Intourist Hotel, which was run by the Russians. Here there was plenty to eat and drink, including caviar and vodka, but only for American dollars. East Berlin itself was in ruins — drab and miserable. People moved like shadows through the deserted streets.

On the following day, July 12, I left for West Berlin in a rented taxicab. The Berlin Wall did not yet exist, and there was no official control between the Soviet and American sectors of the city. My car was soon followed by an American military vehicle. We drove to the headquarters of the American army in the palace of Hermann Göring's former Air Ministry. Curiously, it had escaped destruction during the war.

The previous night I had helped Nyárádi draft a letter addressed to

General Clay in which he explained the reason why he had come to Berlin and asked for an interview with the general. I had also informed Selden Chapin, the American minister in Budapest, of our trip so that our presence in Berlin would not be a surprise. I handed the letter to a secretary—a tall, energetic young woman—who asked me to sit down and wait. It was more than an hour before she returned with a response: "General Clay is expecting Dr. Nyárádi tomorrow at eleven o'clock."

I returned to East Berlin, again followed by an American military escort to the zonal border. While crossing West Berlin I could hear the constant drone of aircraft—units of the airlift—over the city. Nyárádi was overjoyed that General Clay would receive him. He had just returned from a conversation in the Soviet military headquarters, where he was given only promises.

On July 13 we set out for West Berlin. When we entered the office of General Clay, the secretary with whom I had talked the day before jumped to her feet and approached us, saying, "The general is very sorry but he is unable to see you because of his official duties. You are to see instead Mr. Murphy." She conducted us to a room where Ambassador Robert Murphy, Clay's political adviser, awaited us.

Nyárádi was very disturbed and concealed his embarrassment with some difficulty. He had planned to extend to General Clay his personal regret for the Hegyeshalom incident (he had not obtained authorization to express regret on behalf of the Hungarian government) and had hoped to induce him to lift the embargo on Hungarian displaced property. As it happened now, he sat silent and morose while I did most of the talking.

Robert Murphy had many questions to ask: our plans to begin conversations concerning the American war damage claims, the intentions of the Hungarian government to settle other grievances, and the status of American-owned oil companies in Hungary. He appeared to be well informed and talked tactfully, never inquiring about internal conditions in Hungary. He seemed to be fully aware of the precariousness of the position in which Nyárádi and I found ourselves. As to the displaced Hungarian property, Murphy could only promise that he would report to General Clay what we had to say on this matter; any decision would be made known to us via diplomatic channels. He also remarked that conditions in and around Berlin were so tense that he did not think General Clay would have time (he was frequently shuttling between Berlin and Frankfurt) to consider these questions immediately.

With this we left and returned to the Intourist Hotel. Nyárádi made me promise not to tell anybody at home that he was unable to see Clay. I never knew what he reported to Rákosi, but for the next several months he seemed to be more confident. Indeed, he had reason to be hopeful: hardly were we back in Budapest when the American minister, Selden Chapin, suggested in a conversation with Rákosi that negotiations should be conducted on the various complaints from the American side. Rákosi agreed. Forthwith, Nyárádi appointed me to conduct these talks, assisted by an official of the Ministry of Foreign Affairs—István Gyöngyösy. A disciplined Communist Party member, he could display a certain flexibility, and I considered his participation a guarantee that his party meant business.

Negotiations with the American side began on July 23, 1948, and we agreed to hold two sessions weekly. On behalf of the American Legation Counselor (Deputy Head) William P. Cochran and a secretary, Lewis Revey, an ethnic Hungarian, were always present. The talks were held in English, but Gyöngyösy, who understood but did not speak English, expressed himself in Hungarian. Either I or sometimes Revey, who spoke excellent Hungarian, translated. At the opening session Gyöngyösy invited the Americans to "tell us where the shoe pinches" so that, if possible, redress could be made.

The talks were conducted in a friendly atmosphere and all the points raised by Cochran, as well as some raised by us, were thoroughly discussed. Eventually, we agreed on all points: various measures were to be introduced to help avoid further difficulties and to eliminate causes of trouble. The negotiations ended on August 17, and we promised to submit the draft agreement to the Hungarian government for final approval. Thus, by the end of August one could look forward with some optimism to the time when relations with the United States would be improved and the repatriation of displaced property would be resumed.

During the summer the diplomatic situation had changed somewhat. The Berlin blockade appeared to have been defeated by the airlift, at least until winter. The most important event with relevance to Hungary was the expulsion of the Yugoslav Communist Party from the Cominform, the Soviet-led fraternity of Communist parties, and the condemnation of Tito as a heretic to the Communist creed. This announcement at the very end of June 1948 generated some slight hope by demonstrating that it was still possible to oppose Moscow. The event also compromised in the eyes of some believers the alleged infallibility of the Communist Party: how was it possible that Tito was first exalted and now reviled?

Another significant development many connected with the excommunication of Tito was the demotion of Lászlo Rajk, the Hungarian minister of the interior, to the less important post of minister of foreign affairs. Rajk had masterminded the disruption of the Smallholder Party, the theatrically rigged trials against opponents of the regime, and the fraudulent elections of August 1947. But he was not a Muscovite like Rákosi and the other top leaders in the Communist Party and may have been considered by them as a rival. In fact, he was much more popular among the Communist rank and file than Rákosi—a short, bald, fat "pocket Stalin."

By the end of July, Rákosi took yet another step to strengthen his position. This time the victim was Zoltán Tildy, the president of the Hungarian republic. A member of the Smallholder Party, Tildy stayed at his post while his party was disemboweled, its leaders arrested, and Ferenc Nagy, the prime minister, forced to stay out of the country and resign. Now Rákosi's murderous machine got hold of him, too.

Tildy's son-in-law, Victor Chornoky, was the Hungarian minister to Egypt. He allegedly maintained secret contact with Western powers and plotted to help his father-in-law escape to Austria. Chornoky was due to return to Budapest; he telephoned successively from Geneva, Paris, and Vienna but was able to speak only with his mother-in-law. Mrs. Tildy assured him over the telephone that it was safe for him to return. Of course, next to the telephone sat a security police agent forcing her to give that answer; President Tildy was already under house arrest. Thus, Victor Chornoky returned to Budapest, where he was promptly arrested, tried in secret, and hanged some time in August. Tildy's resignation was announced on July 30.

While these gangland-type events occurred, I was fully occupied with the talks with the Americans. But in August my private life underwent a momentous change. I accidentally met Rose on the street and, having become unimpeded and secure from the dangers of my Delilah, I was only too eager to renew our friendship and even more than that. I was overwhelmed to realize that despite my previous slights, she bore no grudge and was ready to reciprocate my interest. We henceforth met frequently.

There was only one other minor crisis in our relationship, when I was unable to keep an appointment with her—a dinner engagement at

Gundel's, the famous restaurant in Budapest. During the Labor Day weekend a number of officers of the United States Army in Germany, among them those who had previously handled the question of Hungarian displaced property, came for a three-day visit to Budapest. Dr. Sándor Hahn, our representative in West Germany, advised us to help the officers in every way possible. I was put in charge of Operation Hospitality, and the dinner we offered the Americans was on the same night as the one I had hoped to spend in the company of Rose. However, this cloud also passed, and I was able to restore my credibility with Rose by taking her on another night for a splendid dinner at Gundel's — one which she has remembered for a long time thereafter.

While I was awaiting confirmation of the agreement we reached with the American side — confirmation which was never forthcoming — it was announced in early September that MAORT, the American-owned Hungarian-American Oil Corporation, a subsidiary of Standard Oil of New Jersey, had been taken over by the government. Its American director, George Bannantine, was arrested, together with some Hungarian managers. The alleged reason for this step was that the company was sabotaging production. It should be remembered that MAORT's difficulties with the Hungarian authorities were among the problems we discussed and wished to eliminate as a result of the bilateral talks held from June to the beginning of August.

The takeover and arrest were a slap in the face of Washington, a little Pearl Harbor that could only have been performed with the consent or direction of Moscow. This was Rákosi's sly answer to the six-week attempt to settle differences with the Americans — talks to which he had given his consent.

Soon thereafter a presidential decree nationalized all industrial enterprises; only Soviet-owned corporations were exempt. The decree promised compensation to foreign owners. All the former enemy countries (except, of course, the Soviet Union) lodged protests against the discriminatory handling of their nationals; the peace treaty provided for most-favored-nation treatment of all these countries.

In October I was given the task of dealing with a rather sticky diplomatic question involving relations with Yugoslavia. In 1947 Hungary had concluded a wide-reaching trade agreement with Belgrade, which foresaw the delivery of huge quantities of Yugoslav timber in exchange for Hungarian electrical appliances and agricultural machinery. The agreement contained an arbitration clause: should any dispute as to the interpretation or application of the agreement arise, a three-member arbitral commission would adjudicate the issue.

After the expulsion of Yugoslavia from the Soviet bloc, Hungary stopped shipping goods to Yugoslavia. Belgrade retaliated by discontinuing the delivery of the timber so needed in Hungary for the construction industry. The balance sheet showed that at that moment Yugoslavia owed large amounts to Hungary. Budapest then invited Belgrade to resume the exchange of goods, but Yugoslavia demurred.

The Hungarian Communist leaders, never briefed properly by Moscow, were not quite clear whether the exclusion of Yugoslavia was to be a temporary measure or betokened a permanent state of hostility. On the other hand, Yugoslavia for many months did not openly condemn Moscow but only reacted against Hungary and behaved as if the friendship with Big Brother was to continue. Tito must have hoped that Stalin would reconsider his stand, but at the same time he was unwilling to make concessions on the really crucial issue: Soviet hegemony over Yugoslavia.

In this ambivalent situation the Hungarian Ministry of Commerce resolved to initiate the arbitration procedure foreseen in the agreement. I was named arbitrator on behalf of Hungary, and Belgrade was asked to name an arbitrator for Yugoslavia. By the end of October I was to travel to Belgrade and meet my Yugoslav counterpart. Together in accordance with the established procedure, we were to elect a third arbitrator, who would be chairman of the commission. It was suggested to me that I propose the Soviet ambassador in Belgrade to chair the commission; it was expected that this choice would be rejected by the Yugoslav member. The names of Czechoslovak and East German law professors who might be considered for the chairmanship were also put forward. But I was instructed not to commit the Hungarian side to any of these persons, at least not for the time being.

Rose was rather anxious about my trip to Yugoslavia. We were now meeting almost daily and, without openly discussing it, we considered ourselves to be engaged.

I went to Belgrade on October 24. The hotel—the only place where foreigners could live comfortably—was half empty. So were the shops, and people were walking about the streets in worn clothing. The effect of the Soviet boycott, which forced Yugoslavia to execute a volte-face in her political and economic orientation, was sorely felt. There was little food, all of poor quality, in the restaurants.

On October 25 I met the Yugoslav arbitrator, a certain Marković, an official of the Yugoslav Trade Ministry. He possessed no legal qualifications (he had used to be a shop clerk), but he had fought as a partisan against the Germans. Our meeting was reserved but friendly. I submitted to him the proposal to select the Soviet ambassador as chairman of our commission. He was slightly surprised and asked for time to consider the proposal. He promised to have his answer the following day. The next day, to my amazement, he told me that he agreed with my proposal. We then decided that the two governments should officially invite the ambassador to accept the assignment.

I informed the Hungarian Legation of our choice. It was not easy to enter the place; it existed in a state of siege, surrounded on all sides by policemen and probably a number of plainclothes agents. People in the legation told me that some pro-Soviet Communists might try to take refuge in the building; to prevent this, the Yugoslavs had placed a screen of policemen around the legation as well as around other pro-Soviet foreign missions.

I boarded the night train for Budapest, glad to leave the oppressive atmosphere of Belgrade. I was fast asleep in the berth of my sleeping compartment when I was awakened in the middle of the night as the train stopped at Subotica, the Yugoslav frontier station. A guard entered and took away my passport. From my window in the dim light of the station, I saw another passenger led away by guards amid loud protests and escorted to the station building. More than an hour later my passport was returned, and the train, with practically no passengers, moved on. Some twenty minutes later we stopped at the Hungarian border station. When the Hungarian police officer examined my passport (I carried a service passport), he said, "You are lucky. A member of the Hungarian Legation in Belgrade was removed from this train an hour ago in Subotica."

Back in Budapest, I went to my office in the morning and later reported to the Ministry of Commerce, where I told about the person being removed from the train. In the afternoon I was summoned to Lászlo Rajk, the minister of foreign affairs, to tell him personally about what had happened. Rajk, whom I saw then for the first and last time, was lanky, tall, and tight-lipped. He talked in rather a whispering voice. His comment on my story was short: the removal might have been retaliation against the arrest of a Yugoslav diplomat in Hungary who, he added in a monotonous voice that revealed no emotion, "did conspire." I vividly remembered this conversation when the following year Rajk was tried for, among other things, having conspired with Titoist Yugoslavia. He was sentenced to death and hanged.

The Soviet ambassador in Belgrade declined to serve as chairman of the arbitral commission, and that was the end of this attempt. When years later, after Khrushchev's apology to Tito and a reconciliation between Moscow and Belgrade, Hungary tried to mend fences with Tito, she had to pay compensation for the violation of the trade agreement before the exchange of goods was resumed.

THE OMINOUS JOURNEY

After the rupture with the Americans as a result of the arrest of George Bannantine and the seizure of MAORT, Nyárádi appeared to be in despair. He continually repeated to me that his usefulness to the regime was at an end. He was in constant fear that he would be dumped by the Communists, or even worse: "If they hanged Chornoky because he had Western contacts, what about me? I had contacts; they may as well hang me."

On November 3, 1948, a meeting of all the staff of the Ministry of Finance was suddenly convened. Nyárádi addressed the several hundred employees assembled and, after a few formal announcements, he unexpectedly began to discuss the conflict between the regime and the Hungarian Catholic church as personified by its primate, Jozsef Cardinal Mindszenty. The main thrust of his criticism was directed against the cardinal by reproaching him for wishing to encroach on affairs that rightly belong to the state. He quoted from the Bible: Render therefore to Caesar the things that are Caesar's, and to God the things that are God's.

The audience, mostly longtime civil servants, listened with perplexity, and afterwards I heard many adverse comments on Nyárádi's speech. I and a few others sensed that this harangue was a homage paid to the anticlerical and atheistic ideology of the Communists. I felt a sinister foreboding of what was to come next and what was to happen to Cardinal Mindszenty, who happened to be very popular not only among Catholics but also among the anti-Communist majority of the Hungarian people.

A day or so later Nyárádi called me into his office. He now seemed full of vigor—no longer despondent but still nervous. "I just saw Gerö," he told me (Gerö was deputy prime minister and second in the Communist hierarchy), "and he agreed with my plan to make a last-ditch attempt in favor of the restitution of displaced property. I laid out my plan: to go and see General Weems personally and to take Éva along because he likes her. I also want to return the visit of Monsieur Richard."

Gen. George Weems used to be the head of the American contingent to the Armistice Commission in Hungary and was now assigned to the American headquarters in Frankfurt. Éva was Nyárádi's wife now, but it was not she who had introduced Rose to me. Nyárádi had divorced his first wife in mid 1947 and had then married Éva de Roskoványi, who had been a secretary to the team dealing with displaced property. Richard was the French minister for restitution who had visited Budapest in early 1948.

Nyárádi continued. "You have to join me on this journey. It is very important that you come since you have been dealing with the Americans." Then he added, "But you must promise me to return. Otherwise, I would be endangered."

"Yes," I replied, "but you have to promise to do the same. Otherwise, I shall get into trouble."

"Of course," said Nyárádi. "I shall come back."

Preparations for the journey began; passports were issued, exit permits granted, and visas obtained. Nyárádi, as always, wanted to travel in style—in the ministerial Packard with a driver—and, besides his wife and myself, was accompanied by his personal secretary, Rezsö Csikszenty. It was understood that we would be back by early December, and Nyárádi made several appointments both official and private for that period.

I was not at all enthusiastic about leaving my mother and Rose for a period of several weeks. In those days many who left the country on official assignments never returned. Earlier, thousands had left Hungary illegally, which now had become practically impossible, the border having been completely sealed off with mines and barbed-wire fences. I promised my mother that I would return and told Rose the same when I last met her.

We left for Vienna on November 14. I went to the Nyárádi apartment to pick up Éva (Nyárádi was already on the road to make a speech in a border town and was to join us later). She appeared irresolute about taking their Scotch terrier. Pacing up and down the room, she finally decided to take the dog "because the servant would not take proper care of her." When I later remembered this scene, I realized that it was an act to allay any suspicion I might have had.

In Vienna our party was put up in the spacious Hungarian Legation. On the following day we were the guests of the Austrian minister of finance; then we departed in the early afternoon for Salzburg. It was still daylight when we reached the demarcation line—the border between the Soviet and American zones of occupation—along the river Enns. As we approached the line, Nyárádi became more and more restless. Suddenly he turned to me and said, "You step out and hand over our passports to the Soviet control officer."

When our car drove up to the Soviet booth, I jumped out and gave our passports to the stern-faced officer, who examined them carefully, peeped into the car, compared photographs, and eventually shouted, "Davai!" ("Let them go!").

The Packard slowly climbed the bridge over the Enns, and we soon saw the helmeted American military police waving to us to proceed. When we reached the middle of the bridge and started to descend, Nyárádi heaved a deep sigh.

On the road to Salzburg we stopped for a few minutes to stretch our legs and let the dog walk. Nyárádi led me aside. "You realize that the situation in Hungary is going from bad to worse. They will arrest Mindszenty. I saw this coming at the last cabinet meeting, so I am considering not returning."

I looked at him in astonishment. "Because of Mindszenty?"

"Yes, yes! But mainly because I do not feel safe. Look what they have done to Tildy's son-in-law."

"But we agreed, didn't we, that you and I would return?"

"Yes, yes! But I now see things differently. And it would be prudent for you, too, to give up the idea of returning."

I briefly explained that I must go back because of my mother and "other commitments." I also expressed a hope that he would reconsider his decision.

In Salzburg, where we spent the night, we met Dr. Sándor Hahn, the head of the Hungarian restitution team in Germany. He escorted us to Munich and then on to Baden-Baden, where we exchanged some words with the French occupation authorities. Except for Baden-Baden, which seemed untouched by the war, everything was still in ruins.

On November 19 we drove north on the autobahn to Frankfurt. Nyárádi continually insisted that his primary objective was to see General Weems. However, the general was absent from Frankfurt, and it was uncertain when he would return. In a gloomy frame of mind we continued the journey to Paris via Saarbrücken, Verdun, and Meaux. Csikszenty and the driver did not know why the rest of us were so morose and enveloped in our own thoughts.

In Paris, Nyárádi negotiated with some French officials concerning Hungarian property in France and French-occupied parts of Germany and Austria. On November 21 we had lunch with French minister Richard at his commodious apartment. In the evening Nyárádi came into my hotel room and again raised the question of returning to Hungary. He acted as though he was still hesitating over what to do, but I was convinced that he had already made up his mind. Our conversation remained inconclusive. Having gotten in touch with General Weems by telephone, Nyárádi wished to return with Éva to Frankfurt by train. The rest of our party was to drive to Geneva, where they would rejoin us.

Two days later we all met in Geneva. Nyárádi now appeared more cheerful and determined. I never asked him about his conversation with Weems; he must have talked of something other than Hungarian displaced property.

Dr. Hahn, who came with us to Geneva, was now informed of Nyárádi's plan to defect. Hahn himself had for some time been determined that he would not go back; he now sent word to his wife to join him as soon as possible.

Nyárádi, still acting as though he had not made up his mind, proposed going to Rome to call on the American ambassador, James Clement Dunn, whom he had met in Washington and who, Nyárádi hoped, could be helpful in resuming restitution. We moved on from Geneva to Milan where Nyárádi expected word from Rome.

The Hungarian consul general in Milan, Imre Gál, an old friend, came to my hotel. He confided to me that he had been called back to Budapest to report but that he had no intention of going. Rather, he was using every pretext to delay his departure and would eventually tender his resignation.

Nyárádi, embarrassed as he had been since our conversation on the road to Salzburg, sneaked into my hotel room. Now he began to speak of his future plans, evidently encouraged by his conversation with Weems. He intended to go to the United States, settle there, and eventually do some teaching at a university.

I was rather surprised because so far he had shown neither the inclination nor the aptitude to devote himself to an academic career. I did not ask him what he intended to teach, and though I knew there were great differences in quality among universities in America, I did not feel it my job to explain this to him. However, I warned him that he would not be acceptable to the Hungarian National Committee, which had been formed in New York under the leadership of former prime minister Ferenc Nagy. They would reproach him for having continued to serve as a cabinet minister after the coup that removed Nagy.

Nyárádi asked me to join him and his wife Éva in their room, where they again tried to persuade me to defect with them. "I shall share with you what I have," Nyárádi said. But I was so dispirited and disgusted that I did not even ask what he wanted to share with me.

I told the couple that if I failed to return, the security police would immediately evict my mother from the apartment I shared with her. She would lose all her cherished belongings and would not know where to go. In her state of health this could only mean a painful death. After all, I had promised her that I would return and I wanted to keep my promise. I was, of course, also thinking of Rose. She would not be able to follow me, and we would be separated for many years, if not forever. She would have to remain behind the Iron Curtain and would, no doubt, think me unworthy.

Éva then spoke. "Rákosi is a scoundrel. Don't put your faith in him." I almost burst out laughing. "I know very well that he is," I replied.

I explained to the Nyárádis that it was not in my interest to prolong my stay in Italy and that I wanted to return to Hungary posthaste. In fact, I wanted to be back when news of Nyárádi's defection reached Budapest. We consulted the railroad schedule and found that it was possible to reach Vienna quickly, but I would have to stay the night there for a connection to Budapest. So Nyárádi phoned his ministry to send a car to the Austrian border to pick me up.

I departed. Nyárádi gave me a letter to Gerö in which he explained why he wanted to go to Rome. Traveling overnight, I arrived the next afternoon in Vienna. There I rented a car, which took me to the Hungarian border, where the ministerial car was already waiting. At two o'clock in the morning on November 29 we reached Budapest. After a short sleep I went to the Ministry of Finance and reported to Undersecretary István Antos, who took me straight to Gerö. I handed him Nyárádi's letter.

Gerö exploded. "What on earth is he going to do in Rome? We don't care about the Americans or the displaced property." He turned to Antos. "Cable him to return *at once.*"

In the ministry I learned that during my absence the directors of the American-owned Standard Electric Company and of the Hungarian branch of International Telephone and Telegraph had been arrested, among them British and American citizens.

I saw Rose on the day of my arrival and shared with her my secret of Nyárádi's defection as well as the considerable discomfort I felt.

On December 4 Csikszenty and the chauffeur arrived with the Packard. They told me that they had left Rome after a one-day stay and had driven to Pavia with the Nyárádis. There Nyárádi entered the Certosa to pray at the tomb of Saint Anthony. When he emerged from the church, he told the dumbfounded secretary and the driver that they should return to Hungary and that he and his wife would stay behind. He gave them his letter of resignation. The two men drove back day and night and were exhausted and terrified when they arrived. Bearers of bad news faced danger in this part of the world.

The next day the defection was reported in the newspapers, which declared Nyárádi an enemy of the people and an agent of the Western powers. The Budapest grapevine spread the rumor (not without a certain schadenfreude) that the minister of finance had left with heaps of money under his arm.*

JEOPARDY AND MATRIMONY

The first blow in reaction to Nyárádi's defection came on December 8. Prime Minister Dinnyés, the Smallholder fellow traveler, was cashiered — even though he had been on bad terms with his finance minister — and replaced by an even more accommodating figure, István Dobi.

---

*Nicholas Nyárády made it to the United States, earned another law degree, wrote articles and a book, and became director of international studies at an American university. — ED.

A peasant known to be an alcoholic, Dobi was a mere puppet in Rákosi's hands.

During the next weeks the Ministry of Finance, thus far a stronghold of the Smallholder Party and of old-time civil servants, was flooded with new Communist appointees, most of them ignorant and unqualified clowns. The Communist István Antos continued to be in charge of the ministry.

In the section dealing with foreign financial questions the newcomer was a sinister personality: Endre Száberski, formerly a colonel in the security police. His outward appearance seemed to confirm the reputation that accompanied him: in a horror movie he could have played a sadistic torturer, and rumor had it that he was one. He had a crooked back and his features were distorted. There was an ominous, threatening look in his eyes. According to gossip, he was soon to become the head of the section.

My closest colleagues were rather happy to see me back and Undersecretary Vásárhelyi expressed the wish of many that I should continue, despite the change of minister, to handle the legal questions relating to war damages as well as to other foreign claims and obligations. However, contacts with foreign missions had become more difficult; instructions came that we could only make appointments with members of foreign missions through the Foreign Ministry and that an official of this ministry must be present at the talks. The same rule applied when a foreign diplomatic mission wished to contact somebody in the Ministry of Finance. But in practice almost all contacts, negotiations, and exchanges of notes between Hungary and Western powers seemed to have been discontinued.

On February 10, 1949, a short, youngish man dressed in a dark suit and flashing a sly grin came into my office. He wished to see me alone (generally my secretary remained in the office when I had visitors). He identified himself as Imre Molnár (surely a pseudonym), a lieutenant of the ill-famed State Security Section of the Ministry of the Interior—then known as the AVO. As if delivering a rehearsed speech, he quickly told me that his bureau knew all about me—about the felonies I had committed and my betrayals of state secrets. He recited such "affairs" as the Turkish affair, the Hardi affair, and the Nyárádi affair and referred to names I had never heard before. He then demanded that I make a frank admission in writing along with a formal promise to cooperate with him, as an officer of the security police. If I failed to do so, I would immediately be taken into custody and could end up on the gallows.

Mustering all the self-discipline I could, I replied that I knew nothing of these "affairs" and had committed no violations of the law. Then I stood up and invited him to accompany me to Deputy Minister Antos, before whom he could repeat his accusations as well as his offer to make me an informer, a job hardly compatible with the position of ministerial counselor.

Molnár immediately lost his arrogance and aggressive posture and instead tried to ingratiate himself, assuring me that everything would be alright if only I would cooperate. I told him to leave me alone and showed him the door; he left with threats on his lips. I must have been deathly pale when my secretary returned, because she asked me if I was feeling well.

My impression of this incident was that Molnár had been watching me for some time and that this move had been initiated by him – an act of derring-do to stampede me into confession and submission and thus assure my collaboration. On the other hand, he may have been authorized by his superiors to make this attempt.

I told only Rose of this experience; my mother would have been frightened to death. However, I was convinced that this was just the beginning of further intimidations and threats.

Eight days later, on February 18, it was announced in the papers that Ernö Gerö, the deputy prime minister, was going to take over the Ministry of Finance. When I arrived at my office the next day, two gorillas from the personnel department of the ministry came with a letter for which I had to sign a receipt. The letter informed me of my immediate dismissal from the ministry and ordered me to vacate my office without delay. Severance payment for six months was graciously offered. Two days later the dean of the Faculty of Law and Political Science at the University of Budapest asked me into his office and rather apologetically requested that I immediately discontinue my teaching because my position had been "abolished."

I felt down and out. A person who has lost his job without the hope of obtaining another of similar standing is bound to be hopelessly miserable. If this state is aggravated by the danger of being arrested by a Moloch who swallows up but never releases his victims, life becomes almost unbearable.

Still, life had to go on, and after a few days of sullen frustration I recovered my balance and even my innate optimism. In this evolution I was greatly helped by Rose. At first she was almost as despondent as I was, though she was trying not to show it. She instilled in me thoughts about a rosier future. After we had shared our anxieties, our togetherness helped us overcome our depression. We both held that we must somehow emerge first from the spiritual morass in which we found ourselves and only then fight our way out of the actual predicament.

I never formally asked for her hand. It simply became understood that we would marry. But now I began to be concerned about the possible consequences to Rose of such a union. "At present," I told her, "I am a suspect — a person haunted and one day possibly hunted by the AVO. You are not. If we get married, I could involve you. I could drag you with me to disaster."

But Rose insisted. "Never mind! If you go down, I don't want to stay out of it."

In those days one could never be sufficiently careful and I always found it useful to be more secretive than artlessly candid. I had not told my mother about Rose, though discrete as she was she must have guessed that something was going on. However, I believe she considered me an incorrigible bachelor and did not wish to interfere. In the past she had been approached frequently by her friends and well-meaning acquaintances with recommendations of a suitable match for me. I had invariably turned down such suggestions; I was even unwilling to enter into what I had considered to be a blind date. Then came Turkey and the years of suspense, uncertainty, and much work. Now my mother was highly surprised and extremely curious when I told her that I wanted to introduce a young lady to her.

Both Rose and my mother were terribly nervous at this first meeting. Rose had thought of her as an acquisitive mother who did not want her son to desert her. My mother, like all mothers, was uncertain whether this was the right girl for me. But they liked each other immediately. When Rose left, my mother said, "I never believed that you would marry a *beauty*." In her thoughts she must always have felt that I would marry a so-called intellectual (but otherwise plain) girl, if I married at all.

We were married on March 22 with only our witnesses and none of our relatives present. Then we spent three days at a resort in the Mátra Mountains just before the hotel was nationalized and reserved for Communist trade union members.

Rose and I had two principal concerns in mind. First, we wanted to explore every possibility for an escape to the West. Thus far I had considered it my duty to stay at my posts, both at the university and at the ministry, where I could at least in a modest way check the slide down into the Soviet maw. But now I had no hesitation—I was of no help to anyone; I had to think of myself first.

To enable us to escape abroad should there be an opportunity, we had to establish a household of our own, separate from that of my mother. This would prevent her being involved in our action and evicted, as she would have been had I stayed abroad with Nyárádi. After prolonged waiting and negotiations we exchanged our apartment for a smaller one and purchased another for my mother and her longtime housekeeper.

The second and no less urgent concern was to find a source of income. Rose, a graduate of the College of Arts and Crafts, where she had specialized in textiles, worked in her mother's dressmaking shop. They had recently undertaken a new venture: stuffed toy animals. Rose, with her natural artistic talent, designed ones far superior to those offered for sale in the state department stores. This enabled her, at least in a modest way, to provide for the maintenance of both of us.

For my part, I left no stone unturned to obtain a job, both to provide needed additional money for ourselves and also to help my mother, who lived on a totally insufficient pension that she had received since my father's death (he was a doctor) and that had been devaluated as had all retirement benefits of former employees. I had no chance to obtain a job suitable to my qualifications and ambitions. At the same time I felt that I was in constant danger of being arrested. My petition for readmission to the bar was turned down, though even membership in the bar did not guarantee a livelihood.

I tried many ways to find employment. I called on influential friends, such as Iván Boldizsár (now an undersecretary in the Foreign Ministry), István Gyöngyösy (who, however, was soon arrested), and also Robert Hardi. I remained in touch with some of my former colleagues in the Ministry of Finance, though many of them, including Rezsö Csikszenty and my own secretary, had been dismissed on the same day I was. Some of these friends appeared to be afraid when I approached them; others received me with friendly assurances but nothing more.

After a few months I was able to get a part-time appointment as legal adviser to the Hungarian branch office of IBM. This branch office was considered a commercial and not an industrial enterprise and, therefore, escaped nationalization. In addition, a few months later I obtained a receivership from the Tax Office to control a textile mill too small to be nationalized, where only the woman owner and one employee worked. The mill had been in arrears in paying its taxes and a receiver was needed to see that these debts were paid from current income.

At the university I was not the only person who had lost his job or had been prematurely retired. Professor Gajzágo was forced to retire before reaching the mandatory retirement age; he was left with a minute pension and was desperately seeking additional income. In comparison with him I should have felt fortunate: I was more than twenty years younger and was healthy, whereas his health was impaired. In 1951 he suffered a heart attack, and when I last saw him, he was still confined to his bed.

I had always regretted that I had not studied a Slavic language. Although Hungary was bordered on the north and the south by Slavic nations, I along with many of my contemporaries had preferred to learn Western European languages—German, French, English, and Italian. I could manage only a few words of Slovak as a result of my many travels in Czechoslovakia. Now it appeared that knowledge of the Russian language carried many advantages, as there were relatively few who had mastered that language.

I enrolled in the Russian course at the Gorki Institute, a new creation patronized by the Soviets. Rose felt uncomfortable when I practiced my Russian pronunciation aloud, pacing up and down the room; it reminded her of the Soviet soldiers after the capture of Budapest who roamed near her apartment house and of the many misdeeds these bullies had committed in those days. But although I condemned much of what Moscow stood for, I could never feel any animosity toward the Russian language or toward any language, for that matter.

After a year of study I was able to translate from Russian into Hungarian. Robert Hardi's wife, who worked for a publishing office, asked me to translate a Soviet book on criminology. This was a scholarly book and, since the topic was not alien to my qualifications as a lawyer, I found the work quite enjoyable. But it amazed me to learn that criminality, instead of decreasing (or disappearing, as was often alleged) in Soviet society, was, according to this scholarly publication, in many respects greater than during tsarist times.

In the summer of 1949 an official announcement told us that Lászlo Rajk, the minister of foreign affairs, had been arrested on charges of treason and conspiracy. At the same time, a number of high-ranking army officers had also been arrested as well as hundreds of Rajk's "accomplices," almost all of them members of the Communist Party. It appeared that Rajk's case— evidently an anti-Titoist display, because he was accused of having conspired with the Yugoslav leader—was being used as a pretext to eliminate a number of prominent Communists who were not Muscovites. These were persons who, like Rajk, worked during the Horthyist period in the Communist underground in Hungary or were connected during World War II with Western Communist parties. Some of those arrested had fought in the Spanish civil war.

The irony of the entire affair did not escape the eyes of observers. Rajk had masterminded the Communist Party's takeover after the initial setback in the elections of 1945; he directed the campaign against all those who were opposed or were considered dangerous to the Communist victory. He was the operator of the various show trials, the most conspicuous among them the trial of Cardinal Mindszenty, who was given a life sentence in 1949. Now Rajk had to face the same ordeal he had prepared for others. Evidently, he was tortured, drugged, and pressed into making confessions by the same methods he had used on the enemies of the regime. Rajk's sensational trial in September 1949 was broadcast over the radio. He admitted that he had been an informer for the Horthyist police, that he had been enlisted as a spy by the American and the French intelligence services, and that he tried with the help of Tito to overthrow the regime in Hungary and murder Rákosi. All the witnesses who confirmed the confession of the accused were held in custody by the security police, and none of them was released thereafter. I later met one or two of them in prison.

Despite some of the slips that occurred during this performance, it was so convincing that listeners to the trial must have felt there was some truth in what was said, even if they did not believe every word. However, the entire array of admissions and testimonies was, from beginning to end, lies and fabrications, as was fully revealed at the time of Rajk's posthumous rehabilitation in 1956.

The ultimate stage managers of this grizzly performance were the Russians. They had practice in these matters; Stalin's show trials in the 1930s provided the needed experience in the manipulation of human destinies. Rajk was duly sentenced to death, together with some of his "accomplices," and was hanged.

Among friends who belonged to the Communist Party and disappeared at the time of the Rajk affair were György Páloczi-Horváth, György Heltai, and István Gyöngyösy. It was only later that I heard of their ordeals and their condemnation to long prison terms. They had been accused — falsely, of course — of having been Western spies, Titoist agents, or conspirators to restore the capitalist regime with the help of the imperialists.

In the spring of 1950 came the turn of former Social Democrats. Hundreds of them — the leadership of this party, which was allowed to operate during the "fascist" Horthy regime — shared the fate of the Communists martyred by Rákosi. These Socialists, after the enforced merger of their party with that of the Communists, were still suspected and feared by Rákosi who, not unlike Stalin in the 1930s, wished to take revenge on his former rivals.

During the two and a half years that followed my dismissal from all my positions, life had become more and more difficult. The oppressive atmosphere of the totalitarian Stalinist rule that descended by then on every segment of the Hungarian population permeated all activities. It became dangerous to complain in a shop against bad service and in the streetcar against the incivilities of passengers or of the ticket collector. Anyone who could be suspected of belonging to the "bourgeois" class was exposed to rudeness or mockery by young thugs or ill-mannered hags — all ostentatiously displaying the Communist Party button.

In such a depressing atmosphere it was for us psychologically important, lest we lose our minds — to seek the company of those in whose presence we could express ourselves openly and without fear. We now saw more often than in the past the few friends we could trust.

I also felt a compulsion to have contact with those who were able to travel, to read Western newspapers, and thus to have a wider world outlook and more information about what was going on abroad. After waiting many months, I dared to approach some of my friends among the diplomatic corps in Budapest. I soon gave up seeing Latour, the French trade attaché, who acted overcautiously. All my American acquaintances had been expelled or had withdrawn from Budapest. But two members of the British Legation continued to show me friendship and understanding. Several times we were invited over by Henry Morris and Clive Eborall. Both Rose and I enjoyed the comfort, civilized environment, and entertaining conversation in their homes — a glimpse into the free world. All these contacts helped us to maintain our mental equilibrium and common sense. We knew that these meetings were risky but tried to take every precaution that they remain discreet.

During this time I did not sense that I was closely watched. Only later did I find out that my movements were being observed and registered. How many informers contributed information I shall never know. Only once did I become alarmed, when a telephone call came late at night and I heard Lia Gántay's voice. She said that she had found my name in the telephone directory and wanted to tell me that she was now happily remarried. I congratulated her, told her about my own marriage, and replaced the receiver with a rather shaky hand. But there was no consequence, and I believe the reason for the call was genuine. It was a relief, however, to have Rose standing next to me as I explained the conversation, for I must have been pale.

ARREST

In the spring of 1951 living conditions deteriorated even more. Not only had certain commodities become scarce or unobtainable but also production norms for industrial workers were raised to a level that turned them into robots — exploited and strictly disciplined human automatons. Dissatisfaction spread and, in the same degree, so did intimidation and terror.

The Western imperialists and their associates — the still unsubdued bourgeois elements in the country — were blamed for every evil. In order to counter proletarian discontent, those who were suspected of still possessing something were dispossessed and crushed. The government resorted to the large-scale expulsion to rural areas of "unreliable" elements.* From hour to hour families were forced to leave their apartments or houses and were transported to small villages in the eastern part of Hungary where they were confined to eke out some living by agricultural work, for which they had neither strength nor aptitude. Many of those sent into internal exile were elderly persons who died by the hundreds under these unsanitary and miserable conditions.

An aunt of mine, a widow in her seventies whose husband had died in 1925, was exiled. Her husband happened to have been the general

---

*The number deported is uncertain. A possible approximate figure is ten thousand. — ED.

manager of an important flour mill. She was already reduced to a meager living and already shared her apartment with a Communist family. Now she was taken into the Hungarian Siberia and forced to work in the potato fields until, one day, she collapsed.

The outbreak of the Korean War in June 1950 was looked upon with relief by many; at last the Cold War had turned into a shooting war and there might be a change for the better. The ominous news of the defeat of American forces and their withdrawal to the southern tip of Korea was received with despair. Reports of these defeats were given a prominent place in the Hungarian newspapers and on Hungarian radio. At one important intersection of Budapest the Ministry of Information placed a huge map of Korea, illuminated at night by electric candles, which showed the front line day by day as it advanced to the south. However, when General MacArthur's stratagem bisected the Korean Peninsula and drove the Communists north, the large map was immediately dismantled and all news from Korea was suppressed.

Warfare in Korea was another reason for increased internal terror. The AVO, which had separated from the Ministry of the Interior and become the State Security Authority (AVH), continued to arrest people, knocking at their door during the night or early morning and taking them away. We constantly heard the names of acquaintances and friends who thus disappeared, never to be heard of again. But one experiences the greatest shock when lightning strikes in one's own neighborhood, as when the wife of János N., a close friend of ours, came to us with the tragic news that her husband had been taken away the night before. This happened at the end of July 1951, a time when Rose and I were constantly concerned that my mother or Rose's parents would be exiled. We were less concerned for ourselves; perhaps exile was better than arrest. At least we could remain together in that case. But János N.'s arrest impressed us as particularly baleful.

János N. was legal adviser to the archbishop of Kalocsa, Jozsef Grösz, who had been arrested in May and given a life sentence by late June. Half a year before, as I remembered then, János N. had handed me two precious sixteenth-century ecclesiastical books and had asked me to have them taken by one of my diplomatic friends to Vienna. Diocesan libraries were frequently ransacked by the security police in those days, and many valuable old books were destroyed. These two volumes, my friend insisted, should not fall into the hands of these iconoclasts. I did as I was asked; I would have considered myself a despicable person had I turned down such a request.

Now it came to my mind that poor János N. was being threatened, pressured, and even tortured to force him to admit all his misdeeds and to disclose the names of his "contacts," that is, his accomplices. He was somewhat bohemian, an amusing but capricious fellow, likable but with many weaknesses. He was hardly a person who could resist such pressures; he would surely tell everything — even more than everything. Soon my name would come up in the course of his interrogation. Since I was already on the list of suspects, they would not hesitate to arrest me — perhaps that night or even earlier.

Peeping out from our window on the fifth floor, we saw a man standing across the street opposite the entrance. A few hours later the man was still standing there. Time and again we saw him casting glances toward our windows. There was no doubt we were being watched, and watched rather conspicuously. It meant that the AVH was no longer anxious to conceal their surveillance; it meant that they wanted to make sure that I should not escape. For an arrest the signature of Péter Gábor, the head of the AVH, was required; it might take many hours, perhaps even days, before this bureaucratic formality was accomplished.

Different people react differently to such a challenge. Many just sit in despair and wait until the waves close over their heads. My reaction was not to submit without attempting to escape. At the same time, I did not want to overreact. Perhaps all this was a false alarm, and no arrest would follow. It was the beginning of July, the time when most people who could afford it left for vacation. Why should we not go into hiding under the pretext of going for vacation and wait to see what would happen? We could still pretend to have gone on vacation should our concern prove unfounded. What was important was to escape without raising suspicion. The person who had to be informed of our departure was the house commissar. Every apartment house had a commissar who, of course, was a person of confidence — not to the tenants but to the party and the authorities. He was a professional informer. We knew that he was reporting on us, so we tried to be on good terms with him and his wife. Since I held no fixed employment, I could leave whenever I wanted.

The house commissar, Comrade Lajos Gondos, lived on the ground floor near the entrance. He was an elementary-school director and a devoted party member. He arranged two weekly sessions of the tenants, at which excerpts from the Communist press were read and questions relating to politics and the house were discussed. Not many attended and generally no one talked except for Comrade Gondos and his wife.

Once we witnessed an extremely comic scene at one of these sessions. In the middle of an article read to us by Comrade Gondos, his wife arrived, unusually late, disheveled, and weeping. She admitted that she had lost her Party card. Her husband rose in a fit of rage. "So you lost your card? Then you lost everything! Didn't Comrade Rákosi say that the Party card is our most cherished possession?" The meeting soon came to an end, and we never knew how this question was eventually resolved between the couple and between them and the Party.

I went down to the apartment of the commissar and told his wife that we were going on vacation to Lake Balaton. I asked her to check on our door while we were away. In the meantime Rose had packed a few essentials in a suitcase. The man on the street — or was it a different man now? — was still gazing toward our window. Quickly, before the commissar could say anything to anyone, we slipped out through the back door, having made certain that no one was watching us from the empty lot behind the house.

Fast walking enabled us to reach the main boulevard and to get on a streetcar. On the Buda side of the Saint Margaret Bridge we changed to a local train, which took us to Szentendre, a small town some twenty miles from Budapest on the banks of the Danube. Here Rose's parents had a tiny summer cottage. We knew where the key was hidden and were able to enter. We spent the night mostly deliberating on what to do next. We were certain that we had not been followed.

The question was how to find out whether the AVH wished to arrest me, and in that case — in any case — how to manage, despite the almost insurmountable risks, to escape to the West. For all this we needed a place in Budapest with a telephone where it would be possible to arrange appointments or make other contacts. But we were unwilling to risk staying with either my aged mother or Rose's parents.

Next morning I walked to a public telephone booth and called István and Éva D., two very close friends, who shared our desire to leave the country. It was Sunday, and they immediately came out to meet us in Szentendre, where we discussed the situation. They offered their small apartment as a hiding place for us. At first we refused, because we did not wish to endanger them, but eventually, since we had no other choice, we accepted their generous offer.

For the next four weeks we lived in their apartment, remaining silent while they were out working. Rose occasionally left the apartment furtively—so as to escape the attention of the janitor—to do some grocery shopping. But after the first ten days we decided to take certain inevitable risks. I knew that the husband of the woman who owned the weaving mill where I acted as a receiver had taken some preliminary steps to prepare their escape to Austria. So I left the apartment and went to see Paul H.

Paul H., a stocky and pouchy former businessman, was unemployed. He had spent half a year in jail in the city of Szeged for alleged violations of trade regulations. He confided to me that he was in touch with the captain of a steamer that plied the Danube between Budapest and Vienna; it was a cargo vessel and had no regular schedule. Sometimes the steamer went down the river to Belgrade, but it invariably stopped in Budapest to load goods for Vienna. At present—so Paul said—the steamer was in Belgrade and might be in Budapest on any of the next few days, but it would stop only for a few hours and quick action was necessary to reach it. Paul appeared convinced that the captain would take us on board—for money—and would hide us there. Paul also wanted to leave with us. He did not mention his wife; my impression was that he wanted to leave her behind.

With considerable reluctance I gave Paul the telephone number of the apartment where we were hiding. I had to trust him; there was no alternative. I also told him that two of our friends would probably come along with us, and he had no objection. There would be plenty of hiding places on the boat.

Soon it was already the month of August. We anxiously waited for Paul's telephone call. After a few days I contacted him again, only to be told that the ship had already passed Budapest for Vienna but would be back within another week to pick up cargo in Budapest before returning to Vienna. He also said that the captain was willing to take all of us.

This news came to us on a Saturday. On Sunday, we decided to take an excursion to a beach on the Danube north of the city so as to give István and Éva a chance for some privacy.

It was August 5, 1951, a beautiful, sunny day. We sneaked out of the apartment and the house and took the streetcar some blocks away.

The car was crowded; we were standing on one of the platforms. It occurred to me that a young girl was looking at me and made a movement as if she recognized me, but immediately she became indifferent and left the car at one of the next stops. We reached our destination—the ruins of the ancient Roman city of Aquincum. We walked about half a mile to the beach called, most appropriately, the Roman Shore.

After a pleasant swim, we sunbathed and then went again into the water. It must have been well after noontime when we sat down to eat our lunch, which we had brought with us from the apartment. At that moment three young men in dark suits came toward us and crouched down so as not to arouse the attention of other bathers next to us.

"Identify yourself," said one of the men to me. I realized that all was lost. Still, I refused to give up.

"Please, you have to identify yourself first."

The man showed me a card that revealed him to be an agent of the AVH. Then I showed him my identification card and he nodded approvingly.

"We have to take you to our office. We have a few questions to ask you."

"All right, but please show me a warrant or other paper that shows I am wanted for questioning."

"It is Sunday, and we had no opportunity to get these papers. But you have to come with us; otherwise, we shall have to use force, and you will pay heavily for having resisted us."

We dressed and followed the three men to a car with a driver that was parked at the edge of the beach. The girl who had been on the streetcar stood there triumphantly.

I kissed Rose and was shoved into the car. Two of the men who arrested me sat down, one on either side of me. One man and the girl stayed behind with Rose. I looked back at her as the car turned and drove away. I felt that I would never see her again.

Váli participates in the survey for the International Boy Scout Jamboree, Godollo, Hungary, 1930.

Váli receives the Ph.D. at the University of London, 1932.

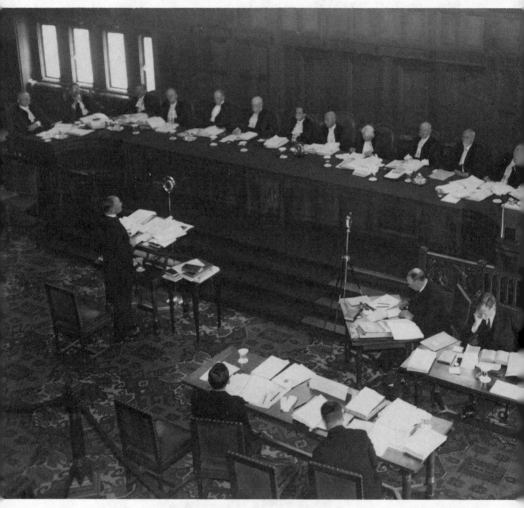

The International Court of Justice, The Hague, 1937. Váli sits on the right at the table in the foreground. The American judge, former Secretary of State Frank Kellogg, is the sixth judge from the left.

The professional staff of the Harvard Center for International Affairs, 1959–60. Váli stands in the fourth row, far right. Below Váli is Zbigniew K. Brzeziński. Henry A. Kissinger stands in the first row, second from right. Robert Bowie stands to the right of Kissinger.

Váli receives an honorary doctorate at Wayne State University, June 18, 1962. Robert Bowie stands to Váli's right.

Rose and Ferenc Váli, early 1960s.

Váli in his office at the University of Massachusetts.

III

Political Prisoner

For it is better to suffer for doing good, if that should be God's will, than for doing evil.

1 Peter 3:17

INTERROGATIONS: THE INITIAL PHASE

I sat in the police car between the two security police agents. We reached Budapest, and when the car failed to turn left toward the Saint Margaret Bridge, I became certain that we were heading toward the notorious prison and chief investigative section of the AVH, the State Security Authority, on the Fö-utca.

I probably made some nervous move because one of the agents took a small pistol out of his pocket.

"Do you know what this is?"

"I know."

"These pistols are manufactured in Czechoslovakia and are very good. So beware."

The heavy iron gate opened for the car and closed behind us when we rolled into the courtyard. The tone of the agents suddenly changed.

"Get out, you swine! And turn to the wall! Put your hands back!"

Soon I was shoved into a kind of reception office, where the plain-clothes agents handed me over to uniformed AVH guards. Again shouting — "Turn to the wall!" — and my forehead was pushed against the plaster.

After a while I was ordered to turn around, empty my pockets, and undress. Then I was given back my clothes (I was wearing shorts when I was picked up on the beach), but my belt and shoelaces had been removed. I had to sign an inventory form, where my money, wedding ring, and wristwatch were listed. Then I was moved to an elevator amidst curses and threats. There were several floors, I observed, and we stopped on the third level. I was made to hurry along a gallery. Safety nets had been stretched between the galleries on each floor. Heavy carpeting muffled our footsteps, and there was deadly silence as if the whole building was empty. The heavy metal door of a cell was opened and I was unceremoniously jostled into it.

When the door slammed behind me with a resounding bang that broke the prevailing silence, I was able to recover my breath and look around. It was a small cell with two wooden benches and a toilet bowl without a seat; a bare light bulb hanging down from the ceiling burned day and night. A small window high up was covered with an opaque glass and allowed only dim light to enter.

I sat down on the bench wondering what would happen next. I was not terrified but felt a mixture of curiosity and disquiet. I had become a denizen of that netherworld from where nobody emerged. But I felt anxiety for what might happen to Rose.

Later in the afternoon some food was pushed in through a little door; it was tasty but scanty. I ate it to the last crumb, resolved to keep my strength. I also discovered that there was a judas hole in the door through which I could be observed without my noticing it. The heavy carpet on the corridor dampened the sound of the jailers' boots.

In the evening the door was opened and a guard entered and grabbed me: "Put your hands behind your back and move!" While we walked, he cursed me, using obscene and blasphemous language. I wondered why all these curses were alike. Evidently, the guards — peasant boys from the country — were trained to swear in a uniform pattern; they were to be accustomed to such profanities, the use of which might strengthen their atheistic feelings and their loyalty to Marxism-Leninism.

I was led — pushed, rather — along the corridors into another wing of the building. Some parts of this edifice were familiar to me; it used to be the District Court of Buda, and in my days as a practicing lawyer I had attended hearings here. But now the entire complex had been taken over by the AVH.

We entered an office where a small morose man in civilian dress sat behind a desk. The guard withdrew. There was a chair in front of the desk, and the man gave me a sign to sit down. For at least ten minutes he looked at me and I looked back. Finally, he broke the silence:

"Why are you here, Váli?" he asked.

"Because I was arrested."

"Why were you arrested?"

"I don't know. You should know why."

"So you don't know? Well, just think about it and get out of here!"

The guard took me away while the man at the desk cursed me.

At about 9:00 P.M. a jailer entered my cell and brought me a blanket. He told me that I could lie down but in a manner that my face and both my hands should be visible.

I then lay down and hoped that they would let me rest until morning. But soon I was awakened and, with the usual brutishness, taken down to the same interrogator.

"Why did you leave your apartment?" was his first question.

"You know that many people are deported these days. You can prevent this happening or delay it, at least, if the deportation order cannot be served. So we preferred to stay elsewhere, as many people are doing these days."

But the officer was not at all satisfied with this explanation.

"What was the *real* reason for going into hiding?"

When I refused to give any other explanation, my interrogator banged the desk and shouted:

"If you refuse to answer my question and confess, I shall have your wife arrested. We know everything about you and have been waiting to arrest you for a long time!"

"You see, I had a good reason to go into hiding."

"Look here, Váli, don't be so smart. Don't you dare to *provoke* the State Security Authority!"

This expression, that I should not provoke the AVH, I had to hear oftentimes thereafter. It was said in Hungarian, but it was a translation from the Russian.

Our "dialogue" lasted for many hours. I was made to stand at attention and not move. A few times the officer withdrew from the room, but I was left with a guard. It must have been well after midnight when once more he came back, telling me that they knew about my activities in the

Grösz affair. But that was nothing—there were much more serious matters for which I had to account. Finally, he sent me back to my cell, where I had only a few hours to sleep.

At about 5:00 A.M. (so I guessed) the deadly silence was broken by the thundering noise of the opening of doors. A guard was at my door shouting: "Stand at attention. Any complaints?" Before I could answer, the door was slammed shut.

Slowly I became conscious of the significance of the various noises. A clatter of the little doors signified that breakfast was being served. A canister of ersatz coffee and a piece of bread were just about thrown into the cell.

During the following days I was almost permanently interrogated from the morning hours until late at night. I was made to sit on a chair in the middle of a large office, where men in civilian clothes or in uniform joined my interrogating officer and asked various questions—questions swiftly following each other, like artillery salvos. Some of the persons only came in and stared at me as if I were some sort of rare animal.

The questions embraced all kinds of subjects—my education, my prewar activities, my foreign travels, my stay in Turkey during the war years, my work for the government, and my association with IBM.

Many of these visitors looked brutal and ferocious; others looked intelligent, spruce, and trim. Some of these persons approached me menacingly and uttered threats; others made flattering remarks and expressed satisfaction that such a "famous spy" had at last been captured. Their questions also varied: some were cleverly put; others were stupid and made little sense. I realized that this activity around me served a double purpose: to make it possible for AVH agents to recognize and identify me, and to weaken my will to resist.

The principal threat so far used against me concerned my wife and my aged mother. They would be arrested unless I admitted everything, I was told. Supposedly, our friends had already been arrested and had made a "full confession." What this confession was about I was not told.

On the fourth day I was brought before a new interrogator. He was in the uniform of a chief lieutenant and announced that he had been assigned to be my "rapporteur," or special interrogator. Neither he nor any other interrogator ever revealed their names. The AVH personnel, not unlike conspirators in a plot, preferred to remain anonymous. This anonymity was intended to forestall subsequent possible recriminations or accusations—so I presumed.

My new official interrogator, a dark-haired, swarthy man in his late twenties or early thirties, started with a lecture:

"Váli, you are here to admit everything. Otherwise, you will be *punished*. I also will see to it that your wife is arrested, and she will also be punished."

While he administered this sinister admonition to me, a guard walked in and whispered in his ear (but so that I could overhear it), "The major wants to see this man."

The major, a stout man trying to be affable, offered a complete contrast to the preceding ominous discourse when he gave what sounded like friendly advice:

"Look here, whatever is said of us, no force will be used against you. After all, you did not commit any grave offense; otherwise, you would have been arrested long ago. You will have to serve a sentence of a few years, that is all. Then you will be released and can start a new life. You will not be too old to have a sex life. We are, however, aware that you have given some information to foreign diplomats. So the best thing would be for you to make a frank confession in writing, and we shall make it possible for you to do so."

The chief lieutenant was also present, and he then took me back to his office. With this intermezzo, his line of attack was lost, and he continued in a less menacing tone. Nevertheless, he insisted that my wife would be arrested if I refused to talk.

I was then taken to a "writing room"—a room with a bed and a straw mattress on it. There also were a table, a chair, and a typewriter in the room.

My instructions were to write down my entire life story, with emphasis, of course, on the misdeeds I had committed against the people's democracy in Hungary along with the names of all my accomplices.

I wrote down all I could think of about my life. I tried to point out that I had contact with foreign diplomats because of my official position and my knowledge of foreign languages. I mentioned a few names of the people I had met. After having typed a dozen or so pages, I knocked at the door and gave them to the guard. He soon returned and handed back the paper: "You should write down everything again. But this time it should be three times longer than what you wrote before."*

As the night advanced, I typed in greater detail all that I had done previously, adding a few more events and names. This time the guard returned with permission for me to lie down. After the hard wooden bunk, it appeared a great luxury to rest on a mattress. I fell asleep at once but was soon awakened by the screams of a woman in the neighboring room and the shouting and swearing of a guard. The woman, in a shrill, hysteric voice, pleaded to be released and, for this purpose, asked to see an officer. The shouting match continued:

"Shut up, you whore! Be quiet!"

"The whore is your mother, who shit you into this world!"

Soon the guard must have realized that he could not rival the language of his interlocutor and went to call an officer. An officer came, and after renewed exchanges of curses and obscenities, the woman was taken away from the room and I had a short time to sleep.

Next morning the chief lieutenant received me with an ominous look:

"You have confessed nothing. But you will, eventually. I have some practice in this sort of thing. Here, in the chair you are sitting in, I faced an even more determined and reluctant prisoner. He was Archbishop Grösz. He started like you but eventually admitted everything."

At that moment it dawned on me that I had read the name of my chief interrogator before. In late June three AVH officers were named in the papers who had been decorated because of outstanding work in the unmasking of Archbishop Grösz's "conspiracy." There was one chief lieutenant among the three, and his name was Gábor Ginály. The archbishop had been arrested in May and sentenced in late June.

An imprisoned person, isolated from the outside world, may develop faculties that were weak while he was at liberty. He may develop more acute hearing, the ability to recollect events and names otherwise forgotten, and a new sense of reasoning and association of events. He can observe, concentrate, and ratiocinate better and faster than before his detention. With such improved faculties I was able, despite the secretiveness of the AVH, to discover the names of many of my interrogators and jailers.

Gábor Ginály (over the telephone he occasionally spelled out his

---

*On this Soviet method of interrogation see F. Beck (pseud.) and W. Godin (pseud.), *Russian Purge and the Extraction of Confession,* trans. Eric Mosbacher and David Porter (New York: Viking, 1951).—ED.

first name, thus confirming my recollection) proceeded to let me know that the close connection I had maintained with the British diplomats Morris and Eborall was well known to the Security Authority. He added:

"We are certain that you are an agent of British intelligence and also of the American Secret Service. You also worked for the French and for the Turks as well as for the Vatican."

All this appeared so preposterous to me that I almost burst into laughter, which prompted this remark:

"So you are laughing! You will stop laughing soon."

My interrogator then asked me to name all the foreigners with whom I had any contacts in the past.

"This would be a rather difficult and long-drawn-out endeavor," I warned him.

For hours he wrote out the names I listed, having great difficulty with spelling. Most of the persons I mentioned I had not seen or heard of for twenty years or so. Ginály after a while realized that this was an unproductive approach.

"Only mention to me those persons whom you have seen in the past three or four years."

My impression of this exercise was that the omniscient State Security Authority really did not know what to do with me or on what accusations to concentrate.

The next morning Ginály began drafting a long protocol on my mission to Turkey between 1943 and 1946. I described to him what was generally known of the Hungarian effort to conclude a separate armistice with the Allies.

"I want you to tell me," he insisted, "what was planned in Turkey against the interests of the Soviet Union and the working class. You and your associates' endeavors were directed toward preventing the Soviet Union from liberating Hungary. Isn't this the truth?"

"I deny this," I answered, "but, even if this were true, would you please tell me what crime that would be under Hungarian law?"

"You damn lawyer! We are not interested in your law. In any case, it was a crime against the people!" he shouted.

After a long discussion he succeeded in writing down a text describing my stay and activity in Turkey, which I signed since there was nothing incriminating in it.

But the following day Ginály sprang another surprise on me:

"We are in possession of written proof that you have betrayed state secrets to the Americans and the British. More specifically, you told these secrets to Edward Mag, on the American side, and to Clive Eborall, on the British. You also caused damage to Hungary amounting to three or four million forint by an act of sabotage."

"All this is absurd. I should like to see this written proof," I answered.

Ginály then read out to me two statements written on sheets of paper. In the first it was stated that the person who had made this deposition had firsthand knowledge of the matter in question. I had admitted to him that I had given a list of American and British assets in Hungary to the previously mentioned foreign representatives. I had also given away to them the Hungarian "legal arguments" concerning wartime damages suffered by American and British owners, arguments that Hungary wanted to use against claims of restitution by these foreign citizens or corporations.

I guessed that Jozsef Száberszky, the AVH colonel who had joined the Ministry of Finance, masterminded these accusations. But the wording of this text made it immediately clear to me that the author of this statement was Pál Makay, a colleague of mine in the Ministry of Finance, a frail and sickly person who was dismissed from the ministry at the same time as I was. I had heard that in 1949 he had mysteriously disappeared for a few days. Like a shot, it came to my mind that when I had met him more than a year ago on the street, he, with a furtive look on his face, quickly stepped aside so as to avoid speaking to me.

"I know exactly," I burst out, full of indignation, "who has made these false statements. It was Pál Makay."

The interrogator appeared perplexed. He had been so careless that he had previously read the date of this deposition: November 27, 1949. I continued:

"If you believed these statements to be true, why did you not arrest me at once instead of waiting for one and a half years?"

After having composed himself, Ginály gave a stereotyped answer: "We wanted to wait until you had committed some further misdeeds before arresting you."

As to the accusation itself, I responded, "I never held in my hand a list of American and British properties in Hungary, and I doubt that such a list existed at all. Of course, Washington and London have their lists but not we — and certainly not I. As to the 'legal arguments' concerning war damages, these arguments were submitted first to the French in Paris in 1948 by Undersecretary István Vásárhelyi, and I was not even present. In any case, it was my duty to explain these arguments to the American and British representatives in order to defend the material interests of Hungary. And how did I do damage to the Hungarian treasury in the amount of three or four million?"

The chief lieutenant got up from his seat and, raising his finger at me, exclaimed as though he were accusing me of a most abominable crime:

"It is stated here" — and he pointed to the other written statement — "that you used certain words and omitted others in a letter you drafted for Finance Minister Nyárádi and addressed to Selden Chapin, the American envoy in Budapest."

"What were these words, if I may ask?"

"I cannot tell you now, but we shall find out."

"Yes. I drafted such letters, which the minister signed. But it is absolutely nonsensical to state or believe that by adding or omitting a word or two (which I cannot remember and you are unable to quote) one could cause any material damage. I drafted such letters to persuade the Americans to resume the return of displaced Hungarian property. You think that the words I allegedly omitted would have changed the American decision to stop the return of these articles? The whole thing is a sheer fabrication similar to the one you mentioned before. Poor Makay must have been hard pressed to invent such stupidities. He probably invented them because he was certain that no person even distantly familiar with these matters would believe them."

But Ginály furiously and menacingly insisted that I had committed grievous misdeeds and done damage to Hungarian interests. It was quite futile arguing with a person who had been instructed to raise these accusations and who had not the slightest familiarity with the questions involved.

During the days and nights to follow I was constantly pressured to admit that I had been enlisted as an American or British spy. The questions generally were put in this manner: "When and where were you recruited as a spy? When and where were you sworn in as a professional informer?"

While I was being squeezed under a constant barrage of questions on that one subject, Ginály was occasionally reinforced by the presence

of an AVH captain to whom I first gave the name Wild Boar, because he
was stocky and unshaven with a red face; later on I found out that his
real name was Béla Bátor.

I was urged, under repeated threats, to reveal whether I was enlisted
as a spy while working in the Boy Scout movement or during my university studies in London or during my stay in Turkey. Denying all these
charges only led to new threats. At the end of one of these sessions
Ginály declared, "Due to your uncooperative attitude and stubborn de-
nials, we have been forced to arrest your wife."

When I told him that I could not believe that they would arrest an
innocent person, he had his retort ready:

"Here is the inventory of your wife's belongings that we confiscated
from her when she was taken into custody."

He held before my eyes a sheet of paper with the inventory but
covered the date with his hand. However, a day later when he again
waved the inventory and let it slip to his desk, I was able to recognize the
date: August 7, 1951. This was ten days before the inventory was shown
to me. So for ten days I was threatened with the arrest of Rose when she
was already imprisoned. While terribly upset by this news, I was somewhat relieved to know that even my "confession" would not have prevented her arrest. But all this once more confirmed my conviction that
not one word from these AVH people was to be trusted.

INTERROGATIONS: THE ROUGH PHASE

Ever since my imprisonment began, I was determined not to lose
track of time. In this I was helped by the fact that interrogations were
generally not held on Sunday, and on this day supper was served much
earlier. Thus, I knew exactly that it was August 19 when I received a
cellmate.

This was most unusual, I thought. Although I never practiced
criminal law, I had studied the law of criminal procedure, from which I
learned that a suspect in custody was to be isolated during his interrogation by the police until he was surrendered into the custody of the public
prosecutor. But it was also provided that this period of complete isolation was not to last longer than forty-eight hours, a period that could be
extended with the permission of the public prosecutor by another
twenty-four hours. The AVH was evidently above the law, and no such

restrictions applied to its prisoners. However, the assumption that a suspect could obtain advice and encouragement from another prisoner during the time of his preliminary interrogations also applied here. Thus, from the very moment of his arrival I suspected the newcomer of being an informer or stool pigeon. That he was pushed into my cell under obscene curses by the guards did not allay my suspicions.

The newcomer introduced himself as Jozsef Bányay. Before his arrest, he told me, he was a staff captain in the Hungarian army. He was about thirty years of age, well educated, and intelligent. But he had an unhealthy look and had difficulty in climbing stairs (when once a week we were taken together for a shower); nonetheless, he smoked cigarettes incessantly until his stock was exhausted and then was extremely unhappy. Every second day he was taken out for interrogation — or so he pretended — and returned with several packs of cigarettes.

Bányay without much reluctance narrated his life story. He had participated in battles against the Russians in Hungary and had surrendered to the Russians a few weeks before the end of hostilities. He then was recruited into the new Hungarian army but was eventually arrested, though he told me he had not yet been sentenced. Later, in the convict prison, I heard from other prisoners that by the time he came to my cell, he had already been given a life sentence and was being used by the AVH as a stool pigeon.

Nevertheless, at first I found his company entertaining and even useful. I never let him know about my suspicions. He denied that he had been a member of the Communist Party, an assertion I disbelieved; after 1948, no officer — let alone a staff officer — could have avoided becoming a Party member.

A few days after Bányay's arrival I was taken for interrogation, no longer to Ginály but to Béla Bátor, the Wild Boar. He talked to me in an ominous voice.

"It's time that you stop playing around with us. We tolerated it, hoping that you would come to your senses. But you have to realize that I am not a person who would just use empty threats."

There was a ten-minute silence while he looked at some papers. Then he whispered in an icy tone, "Who were your contacts?"

"I had no contacts."

"Who were your contacts?"

"I had no contacts."

"Who were your contacts?"

"I had no contacts. I have friends and acquaintances."

"Who were your contacts?"

"If you mean spy contacts, I had none."

Then he began asking me names of contacts. I repeated that I had no contacts but that I was ready, as before, to list friends and acquaintances.

When Wild Boar saw that he could not frighten me into admitting my "contacts," he asked for names of "connections." I told him I was ready to mention connections with the understanding that these were not spy connections.

"Tell me about the spy reports you made to Morris and Eborall," he inquired.

"I have given no reports to either of them, let alone spy reports."

"Didn't you talk politics with them?"

"We talked politics, but I did not give them any information. I knew nothing that they did not already know."

"Didn't you talk about people being arrested? About the Rajk affair, for instance?"

"We may have talked about the Rajk affair. Everybody talked about it at that time."

"You were in contact with Philip Clock of the American Legation, were you not?"

"Yes, I had official contact with him. It was my duty to have such contact."

"Didn't you know that Clock was the security officer of the legation?"

"I didn't know that. But even if I had known it, I never discussed security questions with him—only official business on behalf of our authorities."

"And what about the secret reports of Sándorfi to his company in New York?"

It was at this moment that I realized that Gyula Sándorfi, the director of IBM in Hungary, also had been arrested and that an investigation was in progress against IBM.

"I have known of no secret reports. I may have seen one or two letters dealing with legal questions. That's all."

Captain Bátor then worked himself up into a rage. He shouted that he would give me one night to reconsider my attitude. Otherwise, I would see that he meant business.

Back in my cell, I told Bányay about my interrogation. He strongly advised me to admit everything.

"But there is nothing to admit."

"Then invent something; otherwise, they will run over you until you have come up with something. Later you can always withdraw everything."

I felt certain that he would repeat our conversation to his interrogator, who may have been identical with mine. I thus thought it useful to share my problem with him, though I was by no means willing to follow his advice.

When I was brought down the following morning to Wild Boar and he found that I had nothing to add to what I had already said, he burst into vehement shouting and swearing. He wrote some instructions to the guard and sent me back to my cell at once. In the evening, shortly after I lay down on my bunk, I was ordered by the guard to get up and stand through the entire night. A special jailer stood outside and watched me through the peephole. During the day I was also watched, for when sitting on my bunk I would dose off or fall asleep, the guard would immediately kick the door and order me to stand.

For a week I was prevented from sleeping or resting properly. This was an uncomfortable time for my cellmate also, but I felt no sympathy for him.

Exhausted and suffering from a sharp headache, I was led down to Captain Bátor, who hissed at me, "Now you can appreciate the consequences of your recalcitrant behavior. You know now what you can expect if you don't confess. Even much worse things may happen to you."

I expected that he would then force me to admit something in return for permission to sleep. But that did not happen. Instead, I was taken back to my cell and allowed to sleep during the following nights. For about two weeks I was left to rot in my cell, as the interrogators called it when a prisoner was spared days of interrogation.

During that period I had ample time to converse with Bányay. In discussing my case he again urged me to admit everything because the AVH would sooner or later discover everything. One should even admit what was not true if the interrogator insisted, because they had the means to force anybody to confess whatever was required irrespective of its veracity. He referred to his own case, in which finally he had had to admit that he knew of a general's conspiracy of which he had no knowledge whatsoever. Now he was treated better and received cigarettes.

Bányay was taken out for "interrogation" several times during these two weeks. He was rather vague about his encounters with his interrogator. But one day he returned and announced that his interrogator had shown him some English and American newspapers from which he learned that the American forces had been completely ousted from Korea, the Turkish expeditionary force had surrendered, and the Chinese Communists had captured Taiwan.

At the time of my arrest in early August 1951 the front in Korea had stabilized more or less along the thirty-eighth parallel, and I had no reason to believe that Bányay's story had any foundation whatsoever. The news concerning the surrender of the Turkish corps was also intended to discourage me and to weaken my will to resist.

It was the middle of September when I was again taken to be interrogated, this time before a new person—a young sublieutenant. I only discovered his first name—Lászlo—but soon I began in my mind to call him Missing Link, after the hypothetical creature connecting the ape and man. His intelligence was on that level. He acted strictly under the supervision of a superior officer; he had some typewritten questions hidden in the drawer of his desk. Whenever he asked a new question, he pulled his drawer out a little bit and peered onto the paper. He was probably selected to be my interrogator because he would blindly do the rough work expected from him. Sometimes he displayed an unexpected friendliness; otherwise, he was brutal and possessed animal-like ferocity.

But when Missing Link was not peeping for questions into his drawer, he occasionally became quite loquacious. While being rather secretive in a clumsy way he still revealed to me some details of how I had been watched ever since my return from Turkey. These checks on my movements were intermittent, taken up again and again after intervals of one or two months. I must have been followed on the street and in public transportation. There was a spy in the Ministry of Finance and another in the IBM office reporting on me and others. Information was collected from, among others, Dezsö Ujváry, the former Hungarian consul general in Istanbul, as well as from prisoners like Páloczi-Horváth and György Heltai.

Missing Link asked me questions during the following weeks about my numerous friends and acquaintances. The first questions invariably were: When and where did you first meet this person? Who introduced this person to you? Of course, the assumption, although not spelled out, was always that meeting new persons or making new friends was a conspiratorial action for the purpose of gathering state secrets or recruiting new informers.

I tried to remember all names but naturally some slipped my memory. One morning Missing Link jumped at me:

"You failed to mention Ferenc Kalmár. Surely he must have been one of your accomplices?"

Feri Kalmár was an employee of the Ministry of Finance in the Bureau of Currencies and Foreign Exchanges. He was an old friend and occasionally came to visit me in my office.

"Why was it when Kalmár came to you and when you two were sitting in your office, you always stopped talking when somebody entered?"

In a flash I remembered that a typist in the office adjoining mine frequently entered or passed through, especially when Kalmár was with me.

"Oh! Was it Juci Varga who reported this?"

Missing Link looked embarrassed. "It doesn't matter who reported it. Why did you stop talking?"

"I'll tell you. Because Ferenc Kalmár was telling me salacious jokes, and he naturally stopped when a girl entered."

There was nothing that Missing Link could say. I thought he would be interested in some of these jokes, but he did not ask. I was hardly in the mood to recall any.

In this manner the long array of my friends and acquaintances, Hungarian and foreign, was passed in review. In an often silly manner the questions were drawn up so as to force me to admit directly or indirectly that some espionage was being carried out. For instance, the question was put to me whether I went to the Soviet embassy in Ankara to spy. Since I did not deny having been to this embassy, I could not answer the question with a simple yes or no.

My ingenious interrogator wrote out protocol after protocol, typing very slowly, like a child, and considering often for minutes how to write one or two words. He insisted that I sign all this nonsense, often in bad orthography, which he had laboriously put together. Most of it I refused to sign. He retaliated by all kinds of rough treatment. He observed that I was sensitive to loud noises, so he would come up to me and shout into my ear or would stand behind me and suddenly hit my head. Sometimes he made me stand and kicked me from behind. He actually invited me to hit him back; but I restrained myself, knowing that this would only be an excuse for beating me even more savagely.

But there were evenings when, to my great satisfaction, Missing Link exclaimed in half despair: "Again you have admitted nothing today! Again we cannot arrest anybody because of your refusal to talk!"

This creature tried out some other tricks on me. With great gusto he ate pears and peaches before my eyes (it was the autumn fruit season), hinting that I would get one if I confessed. In a similarly childish fashion he laid a number of cigarettes out on his desk one morning and invited me to take one and light it. Throughout this and other series of interrogations the officers refused to believe that I was a nonsmoker and that cigarettes meant nothing to me. Some prisoners could be induced into admissions by cigarettes, but others gave up smoking completely so as not to be vulnerable to such rewards.

One day Missing Link exploded:

"You are a spy. You are a traitor to the fatherland."

He repeated this charge several times. I looked at him, dressed up in his Russian-type uniform with the sprawling golden epaulettes on his shoulders, a parody of a Soviet KGB officer, and asked myself, "Who is the traitor among us?" But I withheld any comment for it only would have boomeranged on me.

"We also know," the sublieutenant continued, "that you had a cover name as a spy."

I just smiled.

"Do you know what this cover name was? It was Well. That's what your superiors called you."

Perplexed when I burst out laughing, he still continued, "Do you know how we found this out? Here is the text of a conversation you had with one of your bosses."

He put a piece of paper before me, and I read these English words in Hungarian spelling: "Well, we are glad to have you here. Well, let's have a drink. Well, let's go over to the other room now."

Evidently some chambermaid or butler overheard my conversation with one of my American or English friends. Despite my miserable condition, I couldn't help laughing and laughing again.

"Do you know what 'well' means in English?" He wanted to know, but I told him to ask somebody else who knew English and then raise the matter again.

By the end of October, Missing Link's operation had probably been found unsatisfactory, because a new interrogator came to his assistance. He was a tall, black-haired, muscular, youngish man with brutal features. In contrast to the sublieutenant, he was astute and tried to pose as a well-educated person. He liked to discuss some scholarly point (he displayed his superficial knowledge of practically everything), but he more often was churlish and ferocious. He wore civilian dress, and my impression was that he really worked in the investigative side of the AVH and was called to interrogate only when special brutality was to be employed. I suffered more from his brutishness than from that of any other interrogator. I considered him the meanest person I had ever met. I was never able to catch his name, but it gave me some satisfaction when I came to regard him as a kind of lycanthrope, a werewolf, whose task was to torment humanity.

The first morning when I was taken before Werewolf, he wished to impress and frighten me, both with his brutishness and with his erudition.

"It is a pity," he began, "that you were not beaten half dead when they brought you in. That would have saved us much time."

He discussed my education and previous career, dropping a remark or two to show that intellectually he was on the same level as I. Then he said, "You realize by now that there is no way to escape from this prison." I could only agree with him. "Further, you must also realize that we can do with you whatever we like. We can kill you and nobody will ask questions."

"If that is so," I replied, "why do you bother to press people to confess?"

"Aha!" he exclaimed. "It is not you who is of any importance. We want to find out who the enemies of the people are who are still at liberty. If you help us in this work, you might save your skin. You may even relieve your bad conscience, and if you really cooperate with us, you could leave the prison with your head raised."

The interrogation proper began with another review of my mission to Turkey. Werewolf wanted me to admit that, after the separate armistice with the Allies proved to be a failure and the Germans occupied Hungary, I must have joined the American or British intelligence service and worked against the Soviet Union. Eventually I was sent back to Hungary to carry out this work there.

"This is only logical, you must admit."

"There are different kinds of logic," I answered.

"Who said that? Was it Kant?"

I couldn't help smiling. "Logic is a tool for correct thinking. Some use the tool correctly; others do not."

He reacted violently by pushing me to the wall and hitting me in the face with his fist. He then drafted a paper in which I was to admit that I joined the Western intelligence agencies in Turkey. I refused to sign.

"Look here, we can force you to sign. One method will be to throw you into the cellar, which is damp and full of rats and insects. You will not die there immediately, but after several weeks you will develop arthritis or rheumatism, which will stay with you for the rest of your life. Another method will be to hand you over to the Russians."

He was taken aback when I retorted, "I will be glad if I am handed to the Russians. From what I have heard, the treatment in the Lubyanka or Butyrskaya prisons is incomparably better than what I experience here."

He dismissed me, but the next day he took up my stay in Turkey again: "You were sent by the Americans to spy on the Soviet Embassy in Ankara."

I guessed that there was in this building or in the AVH Headquarters on the west side of the Danube a Soviet liaison officer who might have been interested in such questions. But I refused to sign a paper admitting anything to this effect. He then threw himself on me with a truncheon he displayed on his desk. He beat me on the head and the kidneys until I fell to the floor. I must have fainted because a guard poured water over my face.

After this prolonged ordeal I invented some Turkish and Russian names of nonexistent persons who had given me information in the Soviet Embassy in Ankara.

Early in November the duress practiced on me reached the upper limit. For two weeks continuously—this time even on Sundays—I was prevented from sleeping. In the nighttime Missing Link interrogated me until dawn (he, I am sure, slept during the day), and during the day Werewolf belabored me. Very seldom was I allowed even to sit down, generally only when I quickly ate one or two meals a day. There were also days when I was punished and not given anything to eat. Most of the time I had to stand at attention before my interrogators. My legs were swollen, and I collapsed several times. Soon I became almost insensitive to beatings. Seeing my condition, Werewolf assured me, "You will be interrogated even if we have to bring you in on a stretcher. After you confess, you will see a doctor. We have excellent ones."

During these weeks of torment the guards who accompanied me to and from the interrogation were equally brutal. It was like running the gauntlet through those empty corridors (red lights signaled that a prisoner was being transported so that two prisoners should never meet), being pushed and squeezed by the jailers who yelled and cursed all the time. They kicked me when I was not fast enough and spat at my face when I lost my breath.

In addition to these physical pains I was also subjected to mental cruelty. Missing Link told me, "You speak about your wife. I must warn you that she has been unfaithful to you. She hates you, detests you. She only married you because of your position and not because she loved you."

I, of course, knew that all this was untrue and a cliché (I already had lost my position when we were married), but since I felt wretchedly alone and abandoned, it hurt.

Werewolf assured me that I would be lucky if they would simply hang me; this was a rather unpainful death. But I could expect no such quick demise; it would be a slow, extremely painful death for me.

But these predictions left me almost unmoved. I genuinely wished that everything would be over. I was not thinking of suicide, which was in any case impossible, but I was longing to be dead. I must have answered incoherently and signed everything placed before me. Now I was ready to admit anything but was anxious not to involve anybody else. Only occasionally did I revolt against some preposterous accusation. I had hallucinations during my nightly interrogations and spoke of all sorts of things that came into my mind. Werewolf predicted, "In another week you will go mad, and that is what you deserve!"

INTERROGATIONS: THE SOFT PHASE

On the evening of November 26 when again I was led to Missing Link, he unexpectedly invited me to sit down.

He was preparing a little speech and was looking down into his drawer to find the words. The essence of what he said was, "I have ceased to be your interrogator." Whereupon I couldn't help exclaiming, "Thank God!"

He took no notice of my reaction but added a sort of farewell admonition, searching for expressions in his drawer.

During the next six months while I still enjoyed the hospitality of the AVH, I never saw him again, nor did I see Werewolf. The latter failed to say good-bye to me, a failure I did not regret.

I was taken back to my cell without the accustomed savageness and was allowed to sleep. But for many hours, despite my exhaustion, I could not find sleep.

On the next day another surprise: a set of my clothes was brought to my cell (they must have been picked up at our apartment) and given me to wear. Up to that time I was still wearing the shorts and the shirt in which I was arrested on the Danube beach. The air had become quite chilly, and my clothes were most welcome.

In the afternoon of that day I was called and guided by a guard to the interrogation section and into a large room where, amidst a staff of officers, sat a man in civilian dress. Subsequently, I was able to find out his name— Tamás Gerö, then a major in the AVH. He had a reddish face and red hair, and looked to me like a fox. He had an ingratiating, soft voice.

"How are you, Váli?"

"For a moment I did not reply; I was still under the impact of weeks without sleep. Then I answered, "Tired and sleepy. They did not let me sleep for two weeks."

The major smiled. "Please do not exaggerate. This has happened to many—inside and outside this prison."

"As far as I can see," I said slowly and reluctantly, "it was duress."

"I see you are a lawyer. Well, legally we are entitled to interrogate people at night. And, as you must know, sleeping in the daytime is forbidden under the prison regulations."

I just looked disdainfully at this schoolish example of sophistry.

"But let us speak of something else," the major continued. "You have given us a mass of untrue statements." And he pointed to a bundle of papers on his desk, the product of my interrogations over the past weeks.

"All this is due to the constraints to which I was subjected." He did not interrupt me, so I continued. "These papers do not represent what I have said. And I was forced to sign what the interrogators wrote down."

"You are again exaggerating. How did they force you?" the major retorted with a benevolent smile.

"Threats to arrest my wife, to submit her to duress, to send me to the cellar, by beating me and not letting me sleep."

"Well, well, I do not see any sign of beating when I look at you. But you can go to our doctor if you have such complaints. It is impractical now to speak of what has happened. This chief lieutenant"—and he pointed his hand toward a short, stocky officer with a broad, yellowish face—"will be your interrogator and with him you will go through all your statements. I hope he will find you cooperative."

When asked whether I had any further questions, I asked for the release of my wife. The major replied, "We still have business with her. But you may as well know that she will be transferred to another prison more suitable for women. And it will depend on your future attitude whether she will be released."

When back in my cell I considered the meaning of this conversation. I was convinced that all the sweetness and friendliness was just a facade to counteract the psychological effects of my previous treatment. My opinion of the State Security Authority did not change; it was quite evident to me that I was in the clutches and at the mercy of a criminal association, the security arm of the regime. I had no doubts that before a Nuremberg-type tribunal this organization would have been condemned as a criminal conspiracy against mankind, just as the Gestapo was in its time.

During the next five weeks I was interrogated almost daily by the chief lieutenant (his name was Szabo). My cellmate Bányay was suddenly removed. In a way, I was sorry for his departure, because he was an entertaining companion. While his being an informer made me uncomfortable, I was convinced that, in fact, he had not hurt me; apparently, he had invented nothing nor had he lied to the AVH, as he could easily have done and caused me much harm.

Shortly after Bányay's disappearance I overheard a heated dialogue between two guards just outside my cell. Something must have excited them greatly, otherwise, they would have avoided talking so loudly. They were complaining to each other about a rumor, which they said was widespread, that soon the regime in Hungary would be swept away.

"What does this man want? He wants us to return to our villages and work on the farm in poverty? How does this man dare to interfere in our business?"

This man, as it became clear, was nobody else but Winston Churchill, who had evidently returned to be prime minister of Great Britain again. So outstanding was his nimbus, even in this part of the world, that the Hungarian public, infused by wishful thinking and catching at any straw, believed that this change of government in Great Britain could save them from their predicament.

With my new interrogator I went through all the previous protocols, most of which I refused to recognize as valid and truthful. Szabo, who had common sense but little education (though he had an overdose of Communist indoctrination), himself recognized many of these statements as pure fantasy or nonsense. He said to me, "We knew that you were not an enlisted spy. Páloczi-Horváth told us so."

All that remained as "incriminating" material were talks I had had with Morris and Eborall concerning the Rajk affair. These were no secrets; everybody in Budapest knew that the witnesses in this "trial" had been arrested and sentenced later. I tried to explain to Szabo that what is common knowledge cannot be a secret.

"But you have spoken of these matters before foreigners. It will be for the court to decide whether these are secrets or not."

"You have no other evidence of these conversations than my own statements. Without corroborating evidence this is insufficient for an accusation or conviction."

But Szabo was no lawyer and, even if he had understood these distinctions, he had to act as he did. Nor did he understand that I had the right, under Hungarian law and the laws of civilized nations, to remain silent. The burden of proof rested with the prosecution.

"That may have been the case in bourgeois Hungary and with common criminals. But a Communist society has the right to defend itself against its enemies and, in this case, *you* have to prove your innocence."

"How can one prove something negative? Especially without counsel, incommunicado as I am in this prison?"

"You are a suspect. That is the view of the AVH. And that is what matters."

There was no question any more of the nonsense of having caused three to four million forint damage. The alleged betrayal of "legal arguments" was also quietly dropped. But by the end of December the IBM matter came up again. I continued to deny having known anything about the "narrative reports" of Gyula Sándorfi, but I could not deny having talked politics with him.

Just before Christmas Szabo declared, "In this prison, unlike in

Horthyist Hungary, the prisoners have the right to petition. Do you want double rations or, as an alternative, warm underclothes?"

I answered, "The right to ask for something is not a right. Only what *must* be given to the prisoner if he asks for it is a right. In vain have I asked to see a lawyer or to exchange letters with my wife. Whatever is said about Horthyist Hungary, prisoners, even the few political ones who existed, had the right to ask for a lawyer and for visits from relatives. You may ask any of your older Party members whether what I have told you is correct."

I opted for warm underclothes because temperatures in the cell were pretty low and heating was insufficient. I received the underclothes, but after a while when I asked for replacements, I received none. So I decided to stick to those I had, even when by the end of the cold weather they became yellow and disgusting. But the important thing was to keep healthy, even under these difficult circumstances.

I also asked Szabo whether I could not have a cellmate. For a few days a naive young worker of the Csepel Icarus bus factory shared my cell. He was no informer. In protest against the Party secretary he and some of his friends had staged a slowdown. They were promptly taken into custody. Upon returning from one of his interrogations, he complained that he was subjected to threats in order that he betray his "accomplices." He had not.

Through the views of this young workman I obtained a glimpse of the thinking of the real proletariat, the element that was supposed to practice the dictatorship in Hungary and other Soviet-dominated countries. My cellmate had only contempt for the Party of which he was a member. His father, now retired, had been a conductor on the local electric railroad that operated between Budapest and Csepel. He had once asked his father, "Which regime would you prefer—the royal government under Francis Joseph, the Horthy era, or the present Communist regime?" His father replied, "The time of Francis Joseph." But I told myself that this had been the time of his youth and, therefore, he may have been prejudiced.

After a few days the young man failed to return from an interrogation. For the remaining five months of my stay in the Fö-utca prison I had no other cellmate. This short companionship was just an injection to keep me sane, as conceived by the AVH psychologists.

Christmas 1951 was beyond doubt the saddest holiday season I ever experienced. I felt forsaken, lonely, and wretched. My only solace was in my thoughts—my hope in Providence and my conviction that I had been martyred for a good cause.

Early in January I was brought before a pleasant-looking young officer by the name of Ferenc Toldi-Kiss. He raised only irrelevant questions. Evidently he was given the task of speaking to me so that I should not "rot" any longer in my cell. He then asked me to tell him something about international law. So I "lectured" for several afternoons; some other interrogators joined to listen in. They probably had nothing to do; the inflated personnel of the AVH at that moment was lacking victims. But I was convinced that sooner or later they would discover new cases of espionage or conspiracy.

For another five weeks I was left undisturbed in my cell. In vain did I ask for a book from the guards; they just laughed and cursed.

On February 12, 1952, I was brought before another interrogator, whose name, however, I was unable to discover. I learned only that his home was in Pesterzsébet, a suburb of Budapest. A lieutenant, he was quite intelligent and better educated than any of my previous questioners. But he appeared highly ambitious and probably ruthless in serving his superiors. In his preliminary warnings he, like the other interrogators, uttered threats.

I responded, "You are again trying to force me to sign untrue statements. A major whom I saw some months ago reproached me for having done so, and you must know that all the absurdities I admitted had to be reviewed and eliminated."

He then somewhat changed his tone and used subtleties and persuasion. His main concern was the alleged unlawful activity in the Budapest IBM bureau. I soon sensed that Sándorfi was being questioned simultaneously, and the AVH was attempting to use his testimony against me and vice versa. The intensity of this investigation made me believe for some time that the regime was preparing a rigged show trial against IBM, a cause célèbre similar to those undertaken in previous years against the Hungarian-American Oil Company and against the directors of the American-owned Standard Electric Company and International Telephone and Telegraph. I further felt that since my arrest the AVH had been hesitating between two courses: whether to explode my case into a big espionage affair—a pretext for the expulsion of American and British diplomats—or to focus on so-called abuses of IBM. Eventually both alternatives were abandoned.

A copy of the Hungarian state budget bill for the year 1949 was found when the offices of IBM were searched by the security police. This was a copy that had been distributed among members of the National Assembly and representatives of the press. Actually, it was the last Hungarian budget that was fully published before the complete Communist takeover. Its figures appeared in the daily press. Sándorfi must have told his interrogators that he received this copy from me. This was true, and I had no hesitation in admitting it. It was not a confidential or secret document and, therefore, it was not unlawful to give it away. Sándorfi may have quoted some of the budget figures in the economic reports he sent to New York. Now the AVH jumped at this act as espionage.

The security police had taken the trouble to have many of the English-language texts found in the IBM office translated into Hungarian. This had been a Sisyphean task, and nothing interesting for the AVH could have possibly come out of it. Nevertheless, I was endlessly questioned on these letters, accounts, and papers, of which I knew nothing and could be of no use. But all this senseless examination lasted until the middle of March. Then I was again left to rot in my cell for another seven weeks.

I had become a kind of household fixture in the Fö-utca prison. Most of the guards had been assigned to this place after my imprisonment. Some of them inquired how long I had been there. When they heard that I had been an inmate of this interrogation prison for eight months, they shook their heads. Once or twice an officer of the guards came and asked me the same question.

Occasionally now I was allowed to leave my cell and clean the corridor, which, for lack of regular exercise, was the only way to get into fresher air. I asked to be taken to a doctor and he examined me superficially. He also inquired how long I had spent in the prison. He showed some amazement but did not prescribe anything. From the way he looked at me, I guessed that I must have appeared run down and unhealthy.

It was the second half of April when I was taken once more before the lieutenant of Pesterzsébet.

"I have been assigned to draw up the final protocol in your case. This alone will be forwarded to the state attorney."

He began to write out this masterpiece. I told him that if the words *espionage* or *spy* were mentioned, I would not sign it. He avoided these expressions but included bits of conversations I was supposed to have had with Morris and Eborall. These included statements that Rajk was arrested a few days before his arrest was made public; that the witnesses of his trial were all prisoners; and that Endre Sik, head of the Political Section in the Ministry of Foreign Affairs, had previously been a professor of anthropology at the Leningrad State University.

These phenomenal pieces of confidential information were collected from the revised edition of my admissions. They were there because no sane person outside the prostituted environment of Stalinism would have thought to construe them as secrets not to be told to foreign citizens. The budget bill was also mentioned in this draft.

I refused to sign. After hours of useless persuasion I was led to a major (whose name I was unable to discover), who must have been in charge of this operation. He asked me the reason for my refusal to sign.

"As this final protocol is phrased," I replied, "it conveys the impression that the facts listed therein constituted criminal acts. Whereas it must be clear to anybody that these were pieces of an innocent conversation involving no state secrets. Besides, I cannot now recall with certainty that such statements really were made. I have mentioned them only as examples of talks that could have taken place. I know you will tell me that the court will decide this question. But I was frequently told by your interrogators that the courts will do what you, the State Security Authority, will tell them to do."

The major was a quiet, slim, small, matter-of-fact type. "Look here. Of course, you may refuse to sign, but in that case we shall send all your confessions to the state attorney and the court. If so, you will be hanged, because there is so much incriminating material in these protocols of yours." And he raised a big bundle of papers lying on his desk. "Of course, you will say that you have made these confessions under duress, but nobody will believe you. On the other hand, if you sign this final protocol, which includes only bagatelles, you may get only a slight conviction, a sentence of a few years. You will be able to recover your liberty before you are too old; you may still be able to use your tool when you are out. Another alternative for us, if you insist on not signing, is to keep you here. We can do that indefinitely, even until you die. Nobody can question us."

I asked the major about Rose.

"Your wife was transferred to Marko Prison many months ago. She has not been sentenced yet. Whether she will or not depends on your behavior now and during your trial. If you sign this protocol, you will be allowed to write her a letter and I shall see to it that you receive an answer."

Because I still appeared undecided, the major continued. "As to your reasoning concerning the information you have conveyed to foreigners, I must tell you that our definition of a state secret is broader than it was before. Practically, the disclosure to a foreigner of any fact, politically or militarily relevant, whether generally known or not, is punishable. This is the Soviet practice, and they know why they have adopted it; our practice is now to conform to theirs. But you may feel free to use any legal argument—I repeat, legal argument—before the court. We only insist—and you should well remember—that you should not alter or revoke your admission of the facts mentioned in the final protocol. If you should do that, the worst might happen to you and your wife."

I asked for one day to consider whether to sign or not. The major consented.

In my cell I had to make a decision that was not easy. By now I had spent nearly ten months in this AVH prison, sleeping throughout on a wooden bunk in a position so that my face and hands were visible to the guards, with the light bulb shining day and night. I lived without exercise and without fresh air or sunshine, in a cell with only a small, frosted glass window. Although I did not believe in any of the promises of the major, there was a possibility that Rose would suffer less if I agreed to sign and cooperate. I decided to sign.

In the major's office I wrote the letter to Rose:

"I was allowed to write you this simple letter to tell you that I am in good health and that all is well with me. I was promised that you will be permitted to reply. I want to know how you are. I love you very much."

This was all I was permitted to write.

One week later a well-meaning guard whispered that I would be transferred to some other place on the following day. He may have thought that I would be released.

On May 17 I was taken to the receiving office and my belongings were given back to me. I was then blindfolded and urged not to utter one sound. Thus, I was guided (I assumed) into a prison van. Another prisoner was seated next to me. I heard his heavy breathing.

The van rolled into the street, turned twice left and then to the right. From the noise of the road, I could sense that we were crossing the Saint

Margaret Bridge into the Pest section of the city. Then another turn to the right, and in a few minutes the van stopped. We were ordered to step down and the blindfold was removed. I then saw that my fellow passenger was Gyula Sándorfi.

It was Marko Prison, the court prison, to which we had been transported. Again, a body search followed—the surrender of the scant contents of my pockets. Then I was taken up the stairs and shoved into a cell that was teeming with humanity—perhaps fifteen younger and older males sitting on straw mattresses. A white-haired, dignified-looking man stepped forward. He gave his name and added, "I am in charge here. Welcome to our midst."

THE TRIAL

The cell I entered was more than twice as large as the one I had occupied in the AVH prison. There were only two cots, one on either side, but a number of mattresses were heaped on them and a few were lying in a semicircle on the floor. The atmosphere in this cell, despite its crowded conditions, was more relaxed than the sordid, silent, and threatening atmosphere that pervaded the prison from which I had just come. The guards here were not AVH men but were ordinary prison jailers.

The white-haired man who had welcomed me so cordially introduced the others. They were all politicals—at least, they were treated as though they were. Not all of them had spent time in the Fö-utca. As I could make out, the majority of these prisoners were accused of such crimes as attempting to cross the border illegally or having sabotaged or otherwise infringed on work discipline. But a few of them were branded spies, conspirators, or wreckers.

I talked with them about my experiences, and they told me about theirs. Some of them had already been there for several months, but most of the men for only a few weeks. There was a fast turnover: some were being taken out for trial, others had already been sentenced and would soon be taken away to their respective convict prisons. Only a few expected to be sentenced to long terms of imprisonment, and one or two might face a death sentence.

Soon the midday meal was handed in. It was abundant compared with what was provided in the AVH prison, but its quality was of a lower grade.

In the afternoon, the cell leader arranged a general conversation. I was invited to talk on international politics, but from lack of information on developments during the past year I could hardly be expected to provide useful material. However, the discussion soon turned to topics of history, and in this field I could contribute something of general interest.

In the evening the mattresses were removed from the cots and laid on the floor. The cell leader and the senior inmate — not according to age but according to the date he arrived in the cell — were entitled to lie on the cots. This seniority system was generally applied; I, as the latest arrival, was assigned the least advantageous site — the one near the toilet.

When the signal for night recess was heard, the light was extinguished from outside the cell, and for the first time in nearly ten months I was able to relax in the dark.

Just after daybreak the mattresses were stacked up on the cots, and breakfast — ersatz coffee and a piece of bread — was handed in. Soon the door of the cell was opened and the guards shouted, "Out for exercise!" But when I tried to follow the others, the guard stopped me, saying "Only after you have seen the state attorney!"

My cellmates had warned me that the newly arrived would be "examined" by the prison doctor. Unless one could demonstrate some physical evidence of having been beaten, one should deny that one had suffered any mistreatment. Otherwise, the AVH would violently retaliate against the complainant. I was also told that the doctor was a fervent Communist.

Later in the morning a guard opened the door, shouted my name, and made me step outside. Before the doors of neighboring cells other prisoners were standing. The doctor, an elderly man, slowly approached along the corridor, addressing each of the prisoners. When he came to me, he gave me a cursory look and asked, "Did they hurt you?" When I silently shook my head, he moved on. The medical examination was over.

In the afternoon I was suddenly called to step out with all my belongings. I had no belongings. I was led to the guards' room where, to my surprise, Chief Lieutenant Szabo was waiting. He handed me a paper.

"This is from your wife, in answer to your letter."

With great excitement I read:

"I am so happy to hear from you and to know that you are well. I too am well. Let us hope that we shall soon be together again living in contentment and happiness as before. Whatever should happen in the meantime, this hope should keep us alive. I love you very much and I am proud of you."

"Where is she?" I asked.

"She is here, and as she wrote, she is well. Now I have something else for you. I shall take you out from your crowded cell and place you in a better environment."

I was taken up to the third floor. Szabo discreetly disappeared and an AVH guard, together with a prison guard, showed me to the new cell. It was smaller and had only one bed. The second guard seemed to look at me with great interest. When the AVH man left, he told me in a whisper, "You may relax here, lie down whenever you like. Knock at the door whenever I am in service and I shall do everything possible to help you. If you want more food, just ask me. You have been given library privileges."

"So, can I have a book?"

"Yes, I'll bring you the list of books we have in the prison and you may choose one or more. You will get those that are available."

After the crowded cell I felt quite lonely, but I was happy to be able to lie down on a regular bed.

As I slowly discovered, the third floor in Marko Prison was reserved for special prisoners of the AVH. Regular prison guards were supervised here by an AVH man on duty. I assumed that Rose was also on this floor.

The obliging, polite guard brought me a catalogue of books on the following day. "Look through this and make your choice."

The list contained much Communist literature but also a number of works of fiction by Hungarian authors as well as translations of foreign authors. Most of the foreign books were Russian; whoever had screened this library after the Communist takeover evidently had not dared eliminate books of tsarist Russian origin. As far as I was concerned, this would be an excellent opportunity once more to get thoroughly acquainted with Marxist-Leninist political writings so that I would be fully able to discuss questions with promoters of such ideology. During the coming month, which I spent in this prison, I was able to peruse all the works of Marx, Engels, Lenin, and other similar authors. I was famished for books, having been so long deprived of them. The books I was seeking were always available; nobody else in the prison wanted to read them.

On my birthday, May 25, the lenient guard entered my cell and somewhat reluctantly addressed me. "I really don't know whether I should do this, but I have to tell you that your wife is on this floor and sends you her congratulations on the occasion of your birthday. She also sent you this." And he gave me a plate on which there was some gooseberry jam and a spoon. "She has tasted this jam with this spoon."

I was moved and thanked him. Now he trusted me. My wife, in her prison memoirs, has given him the nickname Cricket, and I shall also call him by that name.* It gave me some peace of mind to know that he was taking care of Rose as well as of me.

One day in early June I was roused and told to step out of my cell. An evil-looking guard—short, bony, and with piercing black eyes—stood at the end of the corridor.

"Stick out your arms!" he ordered, and he put handcuffs on my wrists in a manner that hurt me. "Come along." He grabbed my arm and pulled and pushed me as the AVH guards had done during my weeks of rough treatment in the Fö-utca prison.

The guard who was so brusque with me conspicuously wore a Party emblem. He must have been some important person in a local Party cell, perhaps the Party secretary, because he was obsequiously greeted by guards and some civilians on the way through corridors and staircases to the other section of the building. The section of the Marko complex where the courts and the state attorney's office were located was familiar to me. Not only criminal but also civil tribunals operated here; I had represented clients in these halls during my days as an attorney. We were heading toward the office of the state attorney.

The repulsive guard entered the office with me after he had removed my manacles. At a desk sat a man, one of the state attorneys, whom I remembered slightly. He had been my contemporary in law school, not a brilliant student. He must have known who I was, but he acted as if he did not recognize me. He did not invite me to sit down but asked bluntly, "What is your name? When and where were you born?"

I then remembered his name, which was László Egri. He was a rather stout, small person with an apoplectic, red face that made him

---

*Rose Váli, *Black Nightshade: The Hungarian Prison Memoirs of Rose Váli,* narrated in English by Theresa de Kerpely (New York: Morrow, 1965). —ED.

look angry. Or did he have some personal grievance against me? I did not know.

"You are now placed in preliminary detention, pending trial."

"Preliminary detention? I was arrested ten months ago. What was that?" I asked, just to embarrass him.

"That's different. You were in the custody of the State Security Authority."

Then he must have realized that I could not have been ignorant of these legal distinctions and looked into a paper that lay on his desk.

"I shall now read your indictment."

And he read the text so fast that it was hardly understandable.

"Now, sign it!" he ordered curtly. Sensing my reluctance, he continued, "But if you don't sign it, it will make no difference."

"I would like to read it. Couldn't you give me a copy?"

"No. But you can make written observations, should you want to."

"To write observations I would need a copy or at least to read the indictment once more slowly."

"I'll not. You should have listened with greater attention. But you will have a counsel to defend you."

"When can I speak to my counsel?"

"He will come to see you. Just wait your turn."

Now the gorilla-like jailer intervened. "Enough of all this talk. Your hands!" He handcuffed me again in such a way that I thought my circulation would stop. He hurried me back to the cell and relieved me of the oppressive manacles as he half shoved me through the door.

I asked the AVH guard for paper and pen. Then I drafted my observations, once again pointing out that the acts listed in the indictment did not constitute a crime because the information I was supposed to have conveyed was generally well known or did not hurt state interests. But I now doubted that these observations would be read at all by the state attorney or the members of the court.

Three more weeks passed. I was avidly reading the books that Cricket was diligently bringing me. Despite having seen the state attorney, I was still prevented from exercising. I had hoped that I could possibly see Rose during a walk in the courtyard.

In the middle of June a sleek, quiet AVH officer visited my cell. He let me know that my trial would be forthcoming within a week or so. He wished to warn me against retracting my admissions. He would be present at the trial. In return, I asked him about my counsel for defense;

he also promised that this mysterious person would see me before the trial.

More than a week passed. On June 25 Cricket came to tell me that I was to be tried on the following day. The next morning I was shaved and given a necktie to wear and a brush to clean my clothes. But no defense counsel showed up. This time a more considerate guard came for me, handcuffed me, and led me to the other section of the building. As I walked erect and proud through the corridors filled with people, I looked right and left to see whether I recognized anyone. People looked at me with regret in their eyes.

In the vestibule of the courtroom Sándorfi was sitting on a bench, also handcuffed. I had hoped that possibly Rose would be one of my codefendants, but in vain. Nor did I see any witnesses; there were none.

A case was being tried in the courtroom and a strident voice, presumably that of the presiding judge, was often heard. We sat silently at opposite ends of the vestibule. The guards did not talk.

After about a half hour the door opened and two young prisoners in rags stepped out, accompanied by two guards. Then Sándorfi and I were taken into the huge, empty hall of justice. Our handcuffs were removed, and we were told to sit down on the bench of the accused facing the high table of the court. The guards sat between Sándorfi and me.

On both sides of the platform of the court were longish tables. On the right from us sat a balding, middle-aged man reading papers. I asked my guard whether this was the attorney for the defense.

"I don't know," he answered.

"Please ask him or I will ask him, because I want to talk to him."

"You are not allowed to talk to anybody."

A door opened and the members of the People's Court entered. I recognized the presiding judge. He was Vilmos Olti, who had presided over many prominent political trials — rigged trials — in the past, such as the infamous Rajk trial and Cardinal Mindszenty's trial. Before and during World War II Olti had been a clerk in the Ministry of Commerce. He became compromised because of his collaboration with the Nazis and then allowed himself to be blackmailed by the Communists. Under their auspices he obtained a lawyer's diploma and was made a judge. It was known that he was a tool of the security police and, therefore, was assigned to pass the arbitrary and often murderous sentences demanded from him by the AVH.

Olti took his seat in the center of the high platform. Two pairs of persons—the people's assessors—clad in black suits and wearing the party emblem, took their seats on either side of the presiding judge. Together with the members of the court László Egri, the state attorney and public prosecutor, had also entered and took his seat at the table left of where we sat. I glanced behind my back and saw only an AVH officer in the empty hall.

Judge Olti looked around and at the accused. In a sonorous voice he declared the session opened. He stated that the public prosecutor and the attorney for the defense (whose name was Bolgár) were present. Then he proceeded to request the personal data of the accused. I asked whether I could talk with the defense attorney, but Olti retorted that he would allow no interruptions. He read the indictments, which were affirmed by the public prosecutor. Then came the examination of each of the accused.

"By having revealed such important secrets," Olti addressed me, "you have unmasked yourself as a counterrevolutionary!"

None of these "secrets" was explained, and I was supposed not to disclose what they were. So I just answered, "These were not secrets, because everybody in Budapest knew about them."

"You were not to speak of these things before foreigners, let alone foreign diplomats. You, as an international lawyer, should have known that if the embassies wanted to obtain information they could have acted through official channels."

"One does not ask for something which is on everybody's lips. Besides, as an international lawyer I know that every foreign embassy is gathering information, in a lawful or unlawful manner. But to converse on such matters as are here in question is lawful. Every Hungarian mission abroad tries to obtain information, and so does the Soviet mission."

"Don't you dare to speak about our Soviet allies, who saved us from such reactionary fascists as you."

Sándorfi's examination proceeded in a tone similar to mine. After less than ten minutes Olti addressed the public prosecutor: "Your motion, please."

Egri got to his feet. "Now he is going to have his revenge," I said to myself. I was at the top of the class in law school, and he must have been envious of me.

"Honorable Comrade Chairman! Honorable People's Court! It must be clear to all of us that this man Váli is a class enemy. He is well educated and very dangerous. He has committed grievous crimes by revealing state secrets to the enemy. He has done so out of hatred against the people's power. There can be no doubt that he perpetrated high treason through espionage. Such miserable guttersnipes have no place in our people's democracy. I ask for the most severe penalty."

Similarly, the public prosecutor accused Sándorfi of having committed treason and in his case also asked for the harshest penalty. Olti then asked if I had anything to say.

"I only repeat that the statements in question are not secrets under any standard of law. They have harmed the interests neither of the state nor of anybody else. No definition of state secret can ever apply to them. To declare such utterances as punishable would mean that you are forbidden even to speak to foreigners. No such prohibition exists. I was no longer in government service when these talks occurred. I have not infringed any law. I ask for an acquittal."

After Sándorfi had expressed himself in a similar vein, the presiding judge turned to the counsel for the defense, who up to now had not said one word. Bolgár stood up and with some embarrassment (he must have known me, too) submitted his statement:

"There may be some substance in what the accused have said in their defense. Please take this into consideration. As to the accused Váli, he may be a learned man, but his education in Marxism-Leninism is that of a ten-year-old child. This should also be considered as an alleviating circumstance. In any case, I ask for a merciful judgment."

The People's Court then withdrew. But Egri and Bolgár looked away from us and read papers. After less than five minutes the members of the court reappeared. The people's assessors, dummies in the entire procedure, appeared to be more animated. One of them even gave me an encouraging look. I tried to interpret it. Did it mean no death sentence?

"In the name of the Hungarian people," Olti declaimed, "both accused have been found guilty as charged. Ferenc Váli is sentenced for high treason to fifteen years imprisonment, Gyula Sándorfi on the same account to imprisonment for life. They are deprived of their citizens' rights for the term of their conviction. All their properties are confiscated. Do the accused wish to appeal?"

"I do," I said.

"I do," said Sándorfi.

Bolgár rose: "On behalf of the defendants I also appeal."

Manacled, the guard led me back to the cell, where Cricket was waiting. "What happened?" he asked. "They gave me a fifteen-year sentence." "So much? I was not expecting it." "Please don't tell this to my wife, or at least put it to her mildly."

On July 2, a hot and sultry day, Sándorfi and I were transported in a Black Maria. We had not been blindfolded, but from the inside of the van one could only guess the direction the car was heading. It was out of the city, and I soon calculated from the distance we covered that we were nearing the suburb Köbánya where the Central Prison, Gyüjtöfogház, was located.

The van stopped; it must have been at the gate. Then it proceeded and finally came to a halt at a smaller building, not the main prison edifice (which I once visited as a law student). I was taken into a well-aired cell with an open window and freshly whitewashed walls. A straw mattress lay on a cot.

The commander of this prison building, a short, wiry lieutenant of the guards (his name, as I later learned, was Mihalicska), gave me a warning: "Here you have to follow the instructions and rules blindly. Otherwise you will fare badly. When somebody opens the door, you stand at attention, tell your name, but speak only when asked. The chief warden of the prison is likely to visit you sooner or later."

In the evening I listened to some disturbing noises: voices that became louder and louder. I heard shouts of terror, threatening yells, as if people were being beaten by frantic assailants and were crying out in pain. Then silence followed. After half an hour I heard the drumming sounds of the iron doors being opened and slammed shut and, intermittently, sounds of despair and fear.

Suddenly the door of my cell flew open and Mihalicska appeared grinning in the door while other guards stood behind him. I sprang up and began to report, but before I could finish, the lieutenant slapped my face. I stumbled toward the bed.

"Why don't you report, you scoundrel, you miserable villain!"

I straightened up and stood silently; the guards outside were laughing. "He is taking it out on him," one said.

Mihalicska calmed himself. "What is your name?"

I told him my name and added, "You know, I was just brought in here a few hours ago, and I don't know why you hit me."

"You will know soon enough," the lieutenant shouted, and he turned his back on me. The door slammed shut.

During the night, I heard agonizing cries, sounds of groaning and anguish and pain as if people were being tortured. I had come to a death prison.

THE DEATH PRISON

The building where I spent my first night and where I began to serve my sentence of fifteen years was known as the Little Prison. It was used for many purposes, including as a reception house for newly arrived prisoners and as a prison for those to be isolated for disciplinary punishments. Newcomers generally spent two to three weeks here before being transferred to the large building where most of the inmates were housed. As I understood some two years later, my stay in the Little Prison was cut short by the events of my first night. There had been an alleged escape attempt, which was the excuse for the indiscriminate beating and chaining of prisoners. Many of them were to undergo disciplinary punishments, and for this reason isolation cells were needed.

So it happened that around eleven on the following morning the door of my cell opened wide and a group of officers and guards stood there, headed by a small, bald, ugly man in a colonel's uniform. He was István Lehota, the much-feared and ill-famed chief warden of the Central Prison and a former ironworker from the town of Diosgyör. Next to him stood Mihalicska, the lieutenant who had struck me the night before.

I reported as was required, and Lehota looked at me with his bloodshot grey eyes. He exchanged a few words with members of his entourage (I only overheard "This one, too") and the door was closed.

An hour later I was escorted to the main building: a three-winged and three-storied edifice, a so-called star prison, because the three large wings extended from a central point wherefrom all the corridors and cell doors were visible.

I was handed over to the commander of section B, Sergeant Pintér, a well-built and rather stout man who smiled and roared alternately. I was assigned cell 208 on the second floor. Soon I was given prison clothes and boots; my civilian garments were taken away.

For five more months I lived the life of a convict in solitary confinement. The monotony of existence was only broken three times a day when meals were pushed in through the slot. This was not done here by guards but by orderlies, privileged prisoners who during the daytime moved around the corridors completing certain duties. I only left my cell once a week at night when I was taken alone and hurriedly to the bath-house adjacent to the prison building.

The orderlies mostly were condemned Hungarian war criminals or Hungarian Nazis. Previously they had been Horthyist gendarmes, offi-cers, detectives, or policemen. They tried to please the guards and espe-cially section commander Pintér. This man was a sadist and had the power to mete out disciplinary punishments. Apart from the unofficial beatings, the usual punishment was to put the prisoner into "short iron," a corporal punishment that had been in use in the old Austro-Hungarian army but was applied only to young persons and not longer than for two hours. A physician had to be present during the punishment. But in this death prison even sixty-year-old prisoners were put to this torture for as long as five to six hours.

To be short ironed means that your right and left ankle are chained to your right wrist. The iron chains are shortened while the guards push your back so as to fold you up. An iron bar prevents you from lifting your knees. Your whole body becomes numb and you experience extreme pain. Many victims faint after screaming in vain and sobbing in agony. Older people never completely recover from this ordeal. On my first night I heard the moaning of prisoners being short-ironed, and during the next year I would have to listen to such expressions of pain several times each week.

I tried to behave according to the rules, even if the rules were un-written and arbitrarily interpreted by my jailers. I did this not out of conviction or fear, but I hated any contact with the often brutish guards and their subservient, ill-willed orderlies. Fortunately, they were not sup-posed to talk to us unless there was a request or an instruction.

After a week of complete isolation a guard opened the little door and handed in a piece of soap and a brush. I soaped my face. Then the door was opened, and under the supervision of a guard, a prisoner with a razor shaved my face without uttering one sound, as if he were a deaf-mute slave in the harem of the sultan. Then he quietly disappeared.

Once a week the chief orderly of the section handed me a bucket of water and a brush to scour the wooden floor. There was generally little concern for cleanliness, but the floor was different: it had to be white.

This requirement was to serve Sergeant Pintér as an excuse to teach me a lesson. Whether I deserved it or not made no difference. I had to be taught that lesson.

For several weeks I failed to obtain that bucket of water to clean the floor despite asking for it from the orderlies. Then one day Pintér entered the cell, looked around, and uttered something about it being "as dirty as a pigsty." Next morning I was taken downstairs, and with a cruel grin Pintér announced that I would be punished by spending twenty-four hours in the dark cell. At that moment I felt quite fortunate to have escaped the short iron.

The dark cell was so completely deprived of light that one's eye could not get accustomed to it in any degree. I only had my sense of touch to substitute for my sense of sight, like a blind person. I could touch the contours of the walls and find a mattress of straw where I could rest. The door was only opened for a brief time to allow me to eat a meal. Especially at the beginning of this dark-hole existence I had to fight hard to overcome the inevitable claustrophobia. After twenty-four hours I was returned to my cell and given a bucket of water to scour the floor.

Almost once every week reveille was delayed for about an hour. When I asked the reason for this, one orderly whispered, "Hanging." All these executions were carried out in an oppressive silence. Later I was told by prisoners who were able to catch a glimpse of the proceedings that the person to be hanged had a gas mask over his head while his hands were manacled. Earlier, courageous victims (such as Victor Chornoky, the son-in-law of President Zoltán Tildy), while being taken out for executions and before the hangman's noose was tightened around their neck, shouted insults on the regime and its leaders. The executions took place in the courtyard of the Central Prison and the shouts could be heard by other prisoners. Such protests were now prevented by a gas mask. I sadly recalled the savage humor of Voltaire, who wrote that "nothing is more annoying than to be obscurely hanged."

This technique, introduced by the Stalinist rulers of Hungary, made me reflect on previous Hungarian regimes and the public executions practiced during the first Communist rule in Hungary in 1919. As a boy of fourteen I witnessed such an execution in mid June 1919. It was held on the square in front of the parliament building in Budapest after the "counterrevolution" by the cadets of the Ludovika Military Academy had failed. This event had stuck deep into my memory.

A cordon of Red Guards held back the crowd. A man was led to the stairs of the building; he was made to kneel down and was blindfolded. He shouted words that, however, were not understandable from a distance. Some ten soldiers lined up before him. At that moment the curses of the condemned man became more audible. A salvo from the execution squad silenced him, and he tumbled down the stairs. Years later whenever I passed that spot, I could still detect the marks of the bullets on the side of the steps.

This scene called back to my memory other events of that ominous year. My high school of the Piarist religious order was subjected to special measures by the regime. Our teachers were constantly threatened by a commissar with a distorted, scar-ridden face. Rumor had it that he had suffered a head wound in the war and was mentally unbalanced. Teaching had to continue (one of our history teachers even had to teach Marxism), but the commissar supervised the performance. He walked along the corridors in boots and a Russian-style uniform; around his hip was fastened a belt with a holster in which his pistol was quite visible.

I recalled the time he entered our classroom while the teacher was explaining some algebraic formula and writing it on the blackboard. The commissar listened, and after a while he interrupted the teacher: "How can you add a and b to become c? That makes no sense." The class, already sophisticated in algebra, burst into laughter.

"Stop laughing, you bastards!" the commissar shouted, and he pulled out his gun, directing it alternately at the class or at the frightened teacher of mathematics. My schoolmates and I ducked under the benches, but the poor teacher stood trembling in the far corner of the classroom. Then the commissar replaced his pistol and left the classroom.

This and other incidents left vivid memories in my mind. In 1919 most people were convinced that the Communist regime would not last, and that time they were right. The Béla Kun regime collapsed as suddenly as it was created. Soon Rumanian army columns marched into Budapest. Some persons were ready to greet the Rumanians as liberators, but this sentiment quickly changed. Everybody began to feel the humiliation caused by the presence of a despised foreign army. Although the Rumanians did not enter private houses and apartments, they looted public buildings and factories.

Then rumors circulated about the approaching White Army (to distinguish it from the Red Army of Béla Kun), led by Admiral Horthy, as well as rumors about atrocities committed against Jews and persons suspected of being Communists. But we were all looking forward to the end of Rumanian occupation.

At last, on a humid November day, our class was led out with other schoolchildren into the streets when Horthy and his army entered the city. I stood in line with my schoolmates when the admiral, riding his legendary white horse, passed by. Jokes about "the admiral on horseback" were rampant ever since.

During the following twenty-four years of Horthy's regency I stood close to him only once. This happened in 1926 at the Hungarian National Boy Scout Jamboree, held on the shore of the Danube north of Budapest. The regent had come to visit the camp. Besides a few thousand Hungarian scouts, several groups of foreign Boy Scouts also attended the rally. Horthy walked among the foreign contingents, and I, a liaison to these foreign guests, followed him and his entourage closely. Whatever objections may have been raised against the regent, he showed himself to be an accomplished linguist. He addressed the Austrian Scouts in a genuine Viennese accent, and he talked with the French and the British in their native tongues. He spoke Italian with the Italian Catholic Boy Scouts (Mussolini had not yet dissolved the movement at that time) and exchanged some words in Croatian with the few Yugoslavs.

I must admit I was terribly impressed by this performance and vowed to myself to become a person of many languages. The Latin adage *quod linguas calles, tot homines vales* (the more languages you know, the stronger you are) was brought home to me. Horthy's multilingual prowess stemmed from his past life and experiences. He had joined the Austro-Hungarian navy as a young man, a navy whose official language was German but whose sailors were mostly Dalmatians who spoke Italian or Croatian. Horthy for a number of years was the naval aide-decamp of Emperor-King Francis Joseph, and in the court of Vienna he had an opportunity to practice French and English. In his professional capacity as a naval officer he visited the then mecca of naval skills, the British naval installations. By the end of the world war he had risen to become the last commander of the Austro-Hungarian navy. When listening to him, I was even able to discern a slight accent in his Magyar speech, his mother tongue, no doubt due to his long absence from his native soil.

From Horthy I came to meditate on the long reign of Francis Joseph. He ruled from 1848 and was first considered, after the defeat of the Hungarian War for Freedom of 1848–49, to be the oppressor of the Hungarian nation. The so-called Compromise of 1867 restored Hungary's statehood and established the dual monarchy, in which Francis Joseph ruled as both emperor of Austria and king of Hungary.

I only once saw Francis Joseph. It was in 1913, when I was eight years old. But I still remembered that one afternoon I left our apartment and was walking on the nearby street when I observed an unusual number of policemen scattered along the pavement. Soon a lonely carriage driven by two horses approached and passed. A hussar in his flamboyant uniform sat next to the coachman. Two officers, the older one in a general's uniform, sat in the open coach. Pedestrians on both sides of the street lifted their hats, and the old man in the general's uniform raised his hand toward right and left in a military salute. Only when the carriage was gone did I realize that this was our king, the eighty-three-year-old ruler, witness and partner to nearly a century of European history.

I was rudely aroused from my historical daydreaming by a kick on the door. A jailer was peeping through the slot: "Stand up and walk if you cannot sit without falling asleep!"

I did not find solitary confinement as unbearable as could have been, say, being locked in an overcrowded cell with uncongenial cellmates. I was living in the past most of the time, except when taken back to the unpleasant reality of the present. I remembered many events of my previous adult life, often in the greatest detail, as well as long-forgotten particulars of previous studies. I wandered back into the pages of history. One day it was the Ancient Orient, next day the Greek and Roman worlds, another day the Middle Ages or the Modern Age that I went back to in my thoughts. I traveled over the world map in my reveries and thus visited many countries where I had been or where I would like to go. I remembered my own past travels, people I had met, scenes I had witnessed. In my thoughts I followed my past career, my love life, and my romance with Rose. I started to speak to myself in the different languages I knew, recalled quotations in foreign tongues, and practiced words and expressions. Once I must have been reciting numerals in Turkish when the little door opened and a relatively well-meaning jailer asked, "What are you saying to yourself?" "I am counting in Turkish." "You must be crazy," he replied and slammed the door.

During my solitary confinement three more indiscriminate beatings of prisoners took place. Fortunately, convicts in solitary were spared this ordeal. But it was quite a trial to listen to the cries of the innocent victims. I began to doubt, despite my innate optimism, whether one could survive for a number of years—let alone fifteen—such a life, surrounded by scenes of horror, without exercise or human contact. As I subsequently learned, several of the inmates either were beaten to death or succumbed later to such beatings. Others were incapacitated physically or mentally for the rest of their lives.

In early November I was led down to the guards' office on the ground floor, uncertain as always what would happen to me. The section commander in charge (Pintér was absent) held a paper in his hand.

"The Supreme Court has rejected your appeal of your sentence." As I stood impassively, he continued: "Have you any comments to make?"

"Yes. According to the law of criminal procedure, I should have been informed of the hearing and, if I so requested, summoned to be present."

The sergeant looked at me in surprise; for a moment he hesitated whether to yell at me or to say something without making a fool of himself.

"So, you are a lawyer? Do you wish to write this down?"

"Thank you," I said. "It will not help me."

"Then get back to your cell, you scoundrel!"

Strangely, this announcement of the finality of my judgment did not depress me or drive me into despair. Perhaps I never expected my appeal to succeed. But I had to realize now more than before that I might have to spend the next fourteen years in jail, unless I died before then or unless "something happens." I remained determined not to abandon hope.

Soon my solitary confinement came to an end. At the end of November, after I noticed Pintér peeping several times into my cell, the door was opened and a tall, terrifyingly thin man entered. Because of his emaciated, pale, and haggard look, his age was undiscernible.

With an awkward smile he mumbled something by way of introducing himself. Finally, I made out that his first name was László, or Laci. His last name was Aradi, but he said that the prison authorities insisted on using his original family name, which was Szüts.

Laci remained throughout a somewhat mysterious individual, and his narrative about himself was not devoid of contradictions. At first he had difficulties in articulating and speaking. He excused himself for this deficiency by telling me that he had been in solitary for many years. He had spent more than a year in the Lubyanka Prison in Moscow.

His story was confused and complicated. He explained that he was a Catholic priest trained in Rome. He had been kidnapped by the Russians in the Soviet sector of Vienna. After endless interrogations in Moscow the Russians did not know what to do with him (he was supposed to have conspired against them), so they dispatched him to his native country. Here he was given an eight-year sentence; the exact grounds for his condemnation were never made clear to him.

As he gradually regained the ability to speak that he had lost during the long years of solitary confinement, Laci proved to be an entertaining companion. He had interesting stories to tell, some of them fantastic, beginning with his childhood and later training and education. The many inconsistencies in his narrative I never attempted to solve.

In early December I was taken to the Little Prison to be once more interrogated. But this time the subject of the questioning was neither me nor any other person, but some bizarre conspiracy. The AVH interrogator inquired whether I knew the inside of some public buildings in London. He expressed special interest in the British prime minister's office and in the premises of the BBC. I had some difficulty in persuading him that despite my prolonged stays in London, my inside acquaintance with public buildings was restricted to university buildings, museums, and the law courts.

After putting my negative answer to paper, the AVH officer asked: "Do you know of persons who are in our custody and should know the interior of such buildings?"

"I don't know all the people who are in your custody. The only prisoner I knew who would possibly be able to provide such information would be Páloczi-Horváth." The officer waved with his hand in a sign that he had already been questioned on this topic.

When back in my cell, I was left guessing for what purpose the Hungarian security police wished to be acquainted with the interior set-up of such buildings. I was never able to find out.

Before Christmas another prisoner was put in our cell. He was György K. (we called him Gyuri), a forestry student who had been sentenced because of alleged participation in a conspiratorial group. On his wrists and ankles marks of the short iron were clearly visible. He was fairly young and full of energy and could endure the monotony and isolation of prison life less well than either Laci or myself.

There was no change in the routine of life during the first half of 1953. However, we noticed that beginning in March a new wave of even more violent terror had descended on us. The brutal behavior of guards became more intensified, the incidence of prisoners placed in short iron became more frequent, raids into cells occurred more often and were carried out in a brutish fashion, accompanied by wild threats and beatings. For several weeks we were not taken out for our usual Sunday showers.

Our cell was not spared any of these brutalities. Once, several guards led by an officer entered and searched everything, turning over our mattresses and trampling on our towels. Another time, members of such a raiding squad, while we were standing at attention, hit us with their fists and pushed our faces against the wall.

One had the impression that the regime wished to forestall a revolt in the prison or that some major conspiracy among the inmates had been discovered. Guards looked sullen and apprehensive, the orderlies were in constant fear and behaved viciously and maliciously.

By the end of June it appeared that the storm was over. From one day to the next there appeared a change in the air. Guards began smiling; they talked to us, even making jokes. One guard asked me, "What did you do outside?" "I taught in the university." "You must have been a bad teacher."

In the first days of July the explanation came to us.

AFTER STALIN'S DEATH

It was a warm July Sunday when in the morning (not at nighttime, as before) we were called out to be led to the bathhouse. We were not taken in an isolated group but in a long line with inmates of neighboring cells. Walking the two hundred yards to the bathhouse allowed me to enjoy a short spell of sunshine, which I had missed for two years.

In a group of twenty to thirty prisoners we stood under the shower. The usual shouting — "Hurry up! You have only two minutes!" — was not heard. Looking around we discovered that there was no guard present, not even in the forepart of the shower room. Like in a beehive, whispered exchanges of names, greetings, and information passed between the members of the group. We were jumping from under one faucet to the next to speak with as many persons as possible. The palaver continued while we were drying ourselves and only ended when a guard appeared to take the group back into the cells. Our faces were shining; each of us had picked up some important news.

Three months after the fact, we only learned now of the death of Stalin. This news item was passed on by a prisoner who had been arrested after March 5, the day the sadistic tyrant died. But Laci picked up some news that concerned us more closely. One fellow prisoner told him that Rákosi had been replaced as prime minister by Imre Nagy, who was considered to have more liberal leanings. However, Rákosi remained the leader of the Party. This prisoner had been able to overhear a speech by the new prime minister, broadcast in the guards' room, in which he promised to have the sentences of political prisoners reviewed.

On the following morning a call reverberated in the large hall of section B:

"Prepare for exercise!"

Exercise? An exciting new experience in our prison life. But this novelty reminded me that prison regulations had always made mandatory a daily exercise period of one hour, which could only be barred to prisoners under disciplinary punishment and only for one week. Perhaps now some other provisions of the prison rules, such as those regarding visits by relatives, food packages, and correspondence would also be observed.

All the cells of section B were opened and the prisoners streamed down to the ground floor. In lines of four we were led out into the courtyard, where officers and guards, headed by a new chief warden, witnessed the event.

It was a scene not to be forgotten—a replica of the scene in Beethoven's opera *Fidelio* where tormented prisoners emerge from their dungeon. Like living corpses, emaciated, pale, often sickly persons of all ages lined up. Some could hardly walk and had to be assisted by their cellmates. It was as if Hungarian history had been revived by the resurrection of once well-known political figures from their graves. Gen. Béla Magasházy, the aide-de-camp and chief adviser of Regent Horthy, was there; so were István Tasnády-Nagy, speaker of the parliament under Horthy, and Prince Paul Esterházy, the wealthiest landowner of the country. Members of the Catholic clergy, the entire leadership of the former Social Democratic Party, and prominent victims of various show trials were there. Among the accused of the so-called Ministry of Agriculture trial I recognized the principal defendant, Béla Perneczky. Many others I could not immediately identify; they had changed because of age, sufferings, and sickness.

Now the days were spent more cheerfully. One could always look forward to the exercise. Of course, you were not supposed to speak during the walk around the courtyard, but it was possible to exchange a few words with a friend or acquaintance when distant from the guard on duty.

I also was now able to get fully acquainted with the layout of the prison buildings. In the star prison the B and C wings were reserved for political prisoners, either in solitary confinement or crowded together in threes or fours (the cells were originally intended for two people). Wing A was occupied by politicals working in the button factory of the prison. There was also a hospital building—the little house where I spent my first night in the Central Prison—and a mysterious smaller building, facetiously referred to by the prisoners as the Little Hotel, which was also known as the House of the Engineers. There were some smaller buildings as well, such as the kitchen and the bathhouse.

In September I was suddenly transferred from section B to section A. Life in this working section of the prison immediately appeared to be more relaxed. My cell was shown to me not by a guard but by the chief orderly of the wing, Ferenc Palotás, a former sergeant of the gendarmerie. I do not know whether he had participated in any of the excesses, particularly against Jews, of which the gendarmerie had been accused; but he immediately took a fancy to me. He asked me a straightforward question: "Do you want to work?" I had heard so much of the high working norms in the button factory and the skills required there that I gave him a straightforward answer: "Not if I can avoid it." "All right, then I shall assign you to be my daytime assistant when most of the inmates are out at work."

For the next four months I lived a relatively pleasant prison life. I was allowed to walk around the corridors and up and down the stairs of the wing and to talk to fellow prisoners at leisure. Even after the working group returned to their cells, I could visit them. I became known as a storyteller, somebody who could teach them languages and talk to them about history and international politics.

Palotás had access to Hungarian newspapers. I was thus able to read all the news the Hungarian press reported. I now knew that General Eisenhower had been elected president of the United States earlier that year. This event, like the previous return of Churchill, had raised hopes for an early deliverance both for us in prison and for the country as a whole. Characteristically, however, the more sophisticated but still not fully informed segment of the prison inmates placed their hopes on the rearmament of West Germany, which shows that historical memory counted for much in that part of the world.

But what remained completely inexplicable to all of us was the slowness in the implementation of reforms promised by Imre Nagy in regard to political prisoners. For a time it was believed that he would be more influential than the arch-criminal Rákosi, the prime Hungarian pupil of Stalin. Nothing seemed to move toward a release of the political prisoners or, at least, a review of their sentences. The Central Prison and other political prisons remained a hodgepodge of all kinds of "criminals": war criminals, enemies of the Communist regime (the so-called counterrevolutionaries), former capitalists, western "spies," Social Democrats, and, last but not least, Communists (alleged Trotskyists, dissidents, traitors to the Party, and so on). This seeming incomparability of all types of political convicts strongly reminded me of the prison scene in Dumas's *Count of Monte Cristo,* where the main hero was imprisoned because he allegedly conspired in favor of Napoleon, whereas his fellow prisoner, the Abbé Faria, was imprisoned because he allegedly conspired *against* Napoleon.

During these months in section A I was twice interrogated. These interrogations demonstrated, on the one hand, the cooperation between the security organs of the satellite countries and, on the other hand, the continued activity of the AVH against members of the Communist Party itself.

In September 1953 my former interrogator, the lieutenant from Pesterzsébet, came to question me about a man named Ferdinand Stossel, a Rumanian citizen from Transylvania whom I first met in Istanbul in 1943 or 1944. He had been a sportswriter, but during the war he worked in Turkey for the British. By the end of 1945, when the Germans were no longer in Rumania, he returned to his homeland. In 1947 I accidentally met him in Budapest when he accompanied a Rumanian football team to Hungary. Later I was told that he had joined the Communist Party, where his former British connections were known. I could tell the AVH officer nothing more. I was wondering how Stossel's name came to be associated with me. Perhaps I had mentioned his name during the earlier ordeal of my interrogations.

In November 1953 I was interrogated about Robert Hardi, who from 1945 to 1948 was one of the architects of foreign trade in the Ministry of Commerce. Later he became manager of the State Chemical Export Corporation. The interrogating officer wanted to know whether I knew about his contacts with foreign citizens, especially members of the consular or diplomatic corps. I felt amused to notice how the AVH was trying to dig up compromising evidence at all costs against such an influential Party member. My answer to the question was that I knew nothing of such connections. Finally, the AVH officer came out with a direct challenge: "Do you know of Hardi's contacts with Mr. Chambers, the British commercial attaché in Budapest, during the early war years?" I knew nothing of this either.

A step toward "normalization" of the prisoners' status occurred in November 1953. Postcards were distributed by the jailers, and the prisoners were invited to write to their nearest relatives for the first time in nearly two and a half years for me and in many more years for some others. We were warned, however, to write only about our sentence and that we were well, nothing else.

I was somewhat in a quandary to whom to write. I hoped that Rose was free, but at the same time I was convinced that she was not. In any case, I did not know her address. I did not dare to write to my mother. Finally, I decided to write to Rose but to the address of her parents.

Weeks later, at the end of that month, I received a reply written by my father-in-law. He informed me that Rose had been sentenced to a four-year term and that she was in a work prison in Kalocsa, in southern Hungary, but that otherwise she was well. He also wrote, in as tactful words as possible, that my mother had died in the month of June, just five months before.

As happy as I was to learn that Rose was well, I was struck dumb by the news of my mother's death. Nothing could afflict me more—more than my own predicament—than the thought that my mother had died without knowing whether I, her only son, was alive or not. At that moment I could have forgiven all the cruelties and misdeeds committed against me except the one by which a criminal regime had caused a mother to die in ignorance of what had happened to her only child. The memory of this villainy has haunted me ever since.

In early December we were allowed to send postcards to relatives inviting them to visit us on certain scheduled Sundays. This was intended to be another long overdue measure to normalize or legalize the status of political prisoners. In January I was visited by my mother-in-law. I was terribly happy to hear from her that she personally had brought my postcard to Rose when she saw her in prison in Kalocsa. But there was little else she was able to communicate to me; a rail reaching to the ceiling divided the visitor from the prisoner during such interviews, and next to each of the prisoners stood a guard listening in on the conversation. Both prisoners and visitors were enjoined to discuss strictly personal matters only.

In January 1954 section A received a new inmate, who by his own request was permitted to remain secluded in his cell. His real name escapes me, but he was known to other prisoners as Captain Thomson. He used to be an AVH informer, whose particular skill was to pose as an American army captain in mufti in order to smuggle people out of the country. He had his "office hours" in a coffeehouse in Budapest, and gullible persons came to seek his advice and help. He reported their names to the AVH and they were forthwith apprehended. However, Captain Thomson became alarmed, and he himself tried unsuccessfully to escape over the border. He was given a stiff sentence. Many of his victims now shared the prison with him, and he was rightly fearful for his safety.

I talked to him once or twice in my capacity as an assistant to the chief orderly of the section. He appeared to me a very simple but crooked man who did not know one word of English. It is amazing how such a dullard could have misled so many people. Later, after I was transferred away from section A, I heard that Captain Thomson had been tossed down a staircase by unknown assailants. He died in the hospital from head injuries.

In January my days in the button factory section were already numbered. In February I again found myself in section B, where I shared the cell with three prisoners, two of them Social Democrats and the third a victim of the Agriculture Ministry trial. Like life in general, prison life has its ups and downs, only both the ups and the downs are more unpleasant there.

At the time of my return to the more isolated section B, the Foreign Ministers' Conference in Berlin had just ended. It was the first of such conferences after Stalin's death, and on its agenda there was a vague item on East-West conflicts. Through the obscure channels by which prisoners gathered information about events outside the prison walls — short remarks or innuendos by visiting relatives, utterances by jailers — but mostly through the wishful thinking of the prison constituency, an idea developed that the question of Hungary and particularly that of the Hungarian political prisoners had been discussed at this conference. In my previous assignment in section A I was able to read details of this conference and especially its absolutely negative final protocol.

However, I drew upon myself the wrath and indignation of my fellow prisoners when I steadfastly denied that this conference had anything to do with Hungary and, furthermore, that it ended in a complete fiasco. I could not reveal the source of my information (I did not want to harm Palotás); nobody believed me that nothing was to be expected from this ministerial gathering. During a walk Béla Perniczky insisted that although the participants to the conference had gone home, they soon reassembled and ratified important decisions that must be of a nature to affect Hungary. This was a wholly unsubstantiated pipe dream, one of the many that spread among political prisoners. Thereafter I felt reluctant to discuss international politics, not wishing to demolish their castles in the air—the hope for a sudden liberation both of Hungary from Soviet domination and of themselves from imprisonment.

My cellmates and I were not in a work section of the prison. Nevertheless, we were occasionally called upon to perform certain chores, such as carrying mattresses or beds from one place to the other or shoveling coal, all this within the walls that surrounded the prison complex. These were welcome events, opportunities to move around in the fresh air and see something of the world outside the cell. On any of these occasions my colleagues and I cast nostalgic eyes on the enigmatic Little Hotel, which had windows without bars and where privileged prisoners lived an intellectual and comfortable life. I had no inkling that because of certain circumstances I would soon enter the gates of this prisoners' Eldorado.

THE TRANSLATION BUREAU

In July 1954 it became known that Communist Party members (actually, former Party members, because they were deprived of membership when sentenced) were to be picked up and taken away from the prison. It was assumed that they would soon be released. I was glad to hear this welcome news; I had met István Gyöngyösy in section A and knew that he was one of those who had left the Central Prison.

On August 4, almost exactly three years after my arrest, the section commander called me to come down with all my belongings (now I owned a handkerchief and some foodstuffs that arrived in one of those packages we received every three months). A guard escorted me across the courtyard to the Little Hotel. It was a T-shaped building with two floors. Indeed, inside it looked like a modest hotel. I reported to the commander of the building, who happened to be Lieutenant Mihalicska, my old acquaintance from the Little Prison. He acted as if he did not recognize me (he may not have) and passed me on to another old acquaintance from the outside world, namely Zoltán Horváth, the former foreign policy expert of the Social Democratic Party whom I visited shortly after my return from Turkey.

I learned that next to the engineers and another group, the artists, there was a translation bureau in the Little Hotel. This entire setup was the Hungarian version of the Soviet *sharashka,* a special scientific and technical institute staffed with prisoners and run by the state security police.

Zoltán Horváth was the prisoner head of the translation bureau. He gave me a friendly but rather businesslike welcome. I was given a room (not a cell, because it had ordinary windows and an ordinary door that could be opened also from the inside) with a bed, a table, and a typewriter on the table.

Horváth explained to me that the Communist members of the bureau were recently transferred elsewhere and there was a need for their replacement. He mentioned Páloczi-Horváth and György Heltai among those who had thus left. According to him, Páloczi-Horváth had tried to have me brought to the bureau several times, but the earlier policy was that only former Party members could be employed here.

The remaining translators were, without exception, former Social Democrats (and former Communists, since the Social Democratic Party was merged with the Communist Party in 1948). I soon met the other members of the group, among them Imre Vajda, formerly undersecretary in the Ministry of Commerce, Pál Ignotus, a noted writer, and Sándor Szalai, a sociologist.

I was immediately given texts to translate from English, French, German, and Italian into Hungarian. Zoltan Horváth was an exacting taskmaster; his goal was to provide fast results. He defended his attitude by referring to the need to please our "customers." The books and articles we had to translate were given us by the AVH or the Ministry of the

Interior. Many of these texts were political and anti-Communist by nature. We were considered safe to handle these "inflammable" texts because we could not communicate with the outside world. But each of us was delighted to translate such books and articles, and we rendered into Hungarian with gusto passages attacking Communist regimes and their leaders. Sometimes Russian texts had to be translated; the AVH was also interested in what was written in the Great Socialist Fatherland.

A few weeks after my transfer to the Little Hotel, Horváth came to see me with a short Rumanian book. It was a first-aid manual. "This was given to me today and should be translated without delay. I think the Ministry of the Interior wants to publish the Hungarian version of this book. We have nobody among us who knows Rumanian. But you know Latin, French and Italian, and have traveled in Rumania. You must do the job; we cannot refuse to do it."

"Well," I said, "I speak no Rumanian. But if you let me have a Rumanian grammar and a dictionary, I shall perhaps be able to translate this book." Fortunately, we had a short Rumanian grammar in our library, and the engineers had a Rumanian dictionary. I set myself to work. The technical expressions were easily managed, but for some passages of the text I had to rely on my imagination and on my own command of first aid, acquired in my Boy Scout days. The translation was ready within the required time, and I subsequently heard that it had been published by the ministry. I only hope that any error I may have made in the translation did not cause physical harm to those who used that manual.

Movement within the building was entirely free during the daytime. It was thus easy to make contacts with the engineers, by far the largest contingent, as well as with the artists, a smaller group. During our exercise in the courtyard one could join any of the other inmates and even talk to them. In our case, the guard simply ignored the prohibition against speaking since we could speak with each other in the building. I particularly recall the conversations I had with Simon Papp, a world-famous geologist and oil expert who had been convicted in the Hungarian-American Oil Corporation trial on charges of having sabotaged the production of oil. In fact, Papp had warned that excessive production eventually would reduce oil outflow. After he received a life sentence from Judge Olti, his prediction proved correct. Then Rákosi turned to him for advice on how to remedy the situation. Papp pointed out that he would have to visit the oil wells to do this. Since this was tantamount to setting him free and therefore clearly impossible, he was unable to provide any advice.

Among the artists I became well acquainted with were two painters, Sándor Bodo and Tibor Dánielfy. Bodo was serving a life sentence because when designing the bond certificate for one issue of the Peace Loan,* he added in small print: "Nobody should expect that this loan will ever be paid back."

Dánielfy had been an art student and had belonged to a group of highly gifted students who met to discuss the achievements of contemporary artists and to visit art exhibits. The wife of Communist Party leader Mátyás Rákosi was interested in art and sometimes participated in the meetings of this group. But this fact did not help them: they were arrested and sentenced on charges of conspiracy. Madame Rákosi could not or did not want to intervene in their favor.

In September I experienced a joyful reunion. I was informed by postcard that Rose had been freed on parole and that she would seek permission for a special visit. This special visit took place on a Sunday when no other visitors were present.

I dressed up and shaved as best as I could for this occasion. One of our guards in the Little Hotel accompanied me to the hall where such visits took place. In the corridor I saw my wife approaching. Although "kissing visits" were forbidden, I ran to her and held her in my arms. The guard, who knew that this was a first visit and that Rose had been in prison, tactfully looked the other way.

Rose looked fine, better than I expected after her prison term of three and a half years. However, I was frightened to hear from her that soon she would have to undergo a thyroidectomy, an operation required as a result of the enlargement of her thyroid during her incarceration. She told me that the services of the best specialist in this field had been retained. "I shall try to see you again as soon as I recover. Perhaps I shall obtain another special permit for a visit or just wait until the regular visit is allowed. When my operation is over I shall undertake everything to set you free."

A few weeks later Rose wrote that the delicate surgery had been successful. Fortunately, she has never experienced any further traces of this erratic ailment.

---

*One of various semicompulsory government bond issues. —ED.

Also in September I was interrogated once more, this time again about Páloczi-Horváth. I guessed that a revision of his sentence was under way. This interrogation was not antagonistic toward the subject of the inquiry; on the contrary, it was leaning toward the exoneration of the accused. The principal question put to me was whether I knew of the reason for Páloczi-Horváth's return to Hungary in 1947. Was he sent there by the British? I told the interrogator that I had no direct information on the circumstances of his return. What I knew about it I heard from Páloczi-Horváth himself.

Finally, the AVH officer asked me, "In your *opinion* was he sent to Hungary by British intelligence?" I replied, "I do not believe that he was sent. He came on his own initiative and without any assignment from anybody." Strangely, this "opinion" of mine was taken on record.

That same month a new member was added to the translation bureau. I failed to recognize him before he muttered his name. He was a schoolmate, some years below my class, and I had not seen him for many years.

Iván Meznerics was a lawyer employed by the Hungarian National Bank. Once, on an official mission to London, he met his former boss, Lipot Baranyai, a past president of the bank, who lived in London. Meznerics, upon his return to Hungary, was arrested and forced to admit that he betrayed secrets to his former chief. He had nothing to admit and eventually, in agreement with his AVH interrogator, invented some secret which he was supposed to have revealed. He was given a lenient sentence of only ten years.

Meznerics began serving his time in the prison at Vác, another place for political prisoners. He had been transferred to the Central Prison and assigned to the translation bureau. By some administrative error, however, he was delivered to the nearby Mental Observation Institute for Criminals. He almost lost his sanity while he vainly pleaded to speak with a doctor or the director; he was just put off with promises. Somehow the error eventually was discovered, and he was brought to our place. It took him several days before he could recover from this frightful experience.

Soon I was to realize a speedy prison career: I became the head of the translators. In the first days of November 1954 the Social Democrats, among them Horváth, Vajda, Ignotus, and Szalai, were transported away. The assumption was that they would be released soon. Upon the recommendation of Horváth the colonel in charge of translations appointed me to head the reduced staff of the bureau. In anticipation of what was coming, some new members had been previously added from among the ranks of the prisoners in the principal building. I was trying to have Sándorfi transferred but succeeded in this only much later.

To head the translators' group was not an entirely welcome job. It assured the possibility of greater freedom of movement and of acquiring useful information. But discussing the work with the colonel (who was in charge of the economic affairs of the prison) and with a subintelligent person like Mihalicska, the commander of the Little Hotel, was not a pleasant task.

As long as the translation bureau was located in the same building as the engineers, that is, in the Little Hotel, the operation was relatively smooth. However, this favorable situation was not to last very long. From early 1955 our guards circulated rumors that the translators and the artists would be transferred from the Little Hotel to the main prison block. I tried to enlist the support of the head of the engineers for the maintenance of the status quo but found none. On the contrary, it appeared that while our numbers were decreasing, the engineers were expanding and needed space. They were found so useful (and inexpensive) that various state agencies flooded them with projects, for which they were drawing up plans.

In March we had to move to section B of the principal prison building together with our tables, typewriters, and books. A row of adjacent cells was assigned to us; it included a guards' room, which I shared with Iván Meznerics.

To operate in an ordinary prison where other politicals were housed created many inconveniences. We had to remain in contact with each other to share dictionaries and exchange views; therefore, our cell doors had to remain open, at least during the daytime. To explain this to the prison guards, who were changed often, was a task strewn with difficulties. They did not care whether we performed our work. To complain to the section commander or the colonel was a double-edged endeavor that called for diplomacy, persuasion, and insistence on my part. It was also clear that some of the dull-witted jailers regarded us as pampered and pretentious intellectuals and handled us accordingly.

After April 1955 a hardening of the treatment of prisoners was noticeable. A number of ill-willed guards had returned, and though they were careful not to relapse into the excesses they committed prior to Stalin's death, their presence itself served as a warning that "socialist legality" was a passing phenomenon. The reason for this recrudescence was not unknown. In April, Imre Nagy had been removed from the prime ministership, which meant that again Rákosi was the sole master. New conspiracies were "discovered," among them one named after the former detective inspector Jozsef Fiala. Cells were crowded with the members of this plot, and the ringleaders were hanged.

At the same time there were some hopeful changes. The head of the AVH and some high-ranking security police officers had been arrested. The news reached even me that Jozsef Száberszky, who must have had a hand in the accusations brought against me, had committed suicide to forestall arrest. While in the bathtub, he opened his arteries and bled to death.

But there was no movement, no sign in regard to the release of political prisoners. Although the former Communist Party members had been released back in September (and many of them readmitted to the Party), the rehabilitation of political prisoners otherwise had come to a standstill. In the spring of 1955 the Social Democrats, after having undergone innumerable interrogations in the Fö-utca, were returned to the Central Prison. Horváth and Szalai, upon their request, rejoined the translation bureau and were placed in adjoining cells.

I personally did not lose hope; I felt certain that I would not have to serve out my fifteen-year sentence. Still, this delay appeared inexplicable and a waste of time. Every three months I felt the approach of Rose's scheduled visit as an incomparable stimulant. Fortunately, she never did try to mislead me with false expectations. She handled the situation realistically, in a matter-of-fact manner, by providing me with a well-balanced appraisal of developments. She was living at her mother's apartment (my father-in-law had died in early 1954) and worked with her on a stuffed toy animals business that proved to be remunerative.

Later in the spring of 1955 there was another development. Cricket, the loyal and helpful guard of the Marko Prison, was assigned to the Central Prison and by good luck to section B. My wife, after her release, had not forgotten him and his good deeds and had contacted him to thank him for all he had done for her. Now Cricket became an indispensable link of communication between Rose and myself. It was also gratifying to her to know that at least on certain days and at certain hours a guardian angel in a jailer's uniform was able to look after me.

Cricket occasionally brought me some fresh fruit and, what was most important, clippings from newspapers on international and domestic developments, which Rose sent to me. He concealed these clippings under his tunic, and when he opened my cell in the morning, he slipped the clippings to me. I quickly read them in the corner of the room, where I could not be seen through the judas hole, and then disposed of them in the toilet. For this operation to remain safe it was indispensable that my cellmate should be absolutely reliable. When Meznerics chose to share his cell with a friend of his, another newly enlisted translator, I was at last able to recruit Sándorfi as a translator, and henceforth he shared the guards' room with me.

In July, at the time of the Geneva summit conference,* a wave of completely unwarranted and unrealistic expectations swept the prison. It was widely held that the question of Hungary and of her political prisoners would also be discussed.

A visit with Rose was scheduled for July 24, the day following the end of this meeting. She was able to whisper to me that there was nothing in the final protocol, published in that morning's newspapers, that could in any way affect Hungary or the political prisoners. Characteristic of the prevailing naive optimism was the fact that most of my fellow prisoners who also had visits on that day came back carrying unfounded reports of an impending change.

The events that followed the summit conference were no less discouraging. The much-heralded release of Cardinal Mindszenty to help Hungary get admitted to the United Nations was only a sham release. He simply was transferred from prison to a house in the country, where he remained under house arrest. As to the admission of Hungary to the world organization, I found it rather depressing and it strengthened my skepticism about an overly idealistic approach to international politics. Few of my fellow prisoners knew as I did that the Charter of the United Nations included several provisions concerning human rights and fundamental freedoms, which the member states promised to respect. The Soviet Union was a founding member of the United Nations, and nothing could be done about its disregard for these principles enshrined in the charter. But the admission of a country such as Hungary, which had crudely and overtly violated these provisions and continued to violate them, appeared to be highly hypocritical and a slap in the face of

---

*The 1955 Geneva summit was a meeting of the leaders of the United States, Great Britain, France, and the Soviet Union, which failed to achieve any of the ideas proposed there—e.g., Eisenhower's open-skies plan—but which may have relaxed the Cold War somewhat.—ED.

decency. Of course, I understood the unfortunate realities of international politics, the necessity of reaching compromises. Still, in my own position and as an international lawyer, this slight of international commitments was painfully felt.

The only encouraging event, as far as I was concerned, following the otherwise ludicrous Spirit of Geneva was the release of Archbishop Grösz and some of his codefendants from prison.

Another wave of uncalled-for optimism inundated the prison when the news was heard that the Russians were to pull out of Austria. Since nothing had been announced in regard to Soviet forces in Hungary, I cherished no hopes that this pullout would be followed by a similar move in our own country.

But there were some other interesting developments in the Central Prison. A large contingent of prisoners of war, mostly officers and kidnapped civilians released from Russia, arrived in the prison. Shortly thereafter they were subjected to criminal trials before special sessions of the People's Court held within prison walls. Those poor devils! After having survived the Russian prison camps, instead of being released immediately, they were to serve sentences of short duration for acts they had never committed. All this was done — probably after some Soviet model — to prevent them from conveying their close impressions of life in Soviet camps and to help them to forget their sufferings in the land of our great ally.

A similar interpretation was given by many of us to the procrastination practiced in the case of our liberation: we should be given time to forget the brutalities committed against us during interrogations and our treatment in prison before the death of Stalin. Some of us noticed that "the food is improving," and this phrase became synonymous with the idea that release was just around the corner.

Following the pilgrimage by Khrushchev to Tito in May 1955 and the apologies he expressed to the Yugoslav leader, the Hungarian regime was also eager to normalize its relations with Yugoslavia. There were numerous Yugoslav prisoners held by the Hungarians: officials, refugees, kidnap victims, and members of the Yugoslav minorities. Rákosi, in a way typical of his attitude toward political prisoners in general, was dragging his feet in regard to the release of these Yugoslavs.

In December 1955 the Yugoslav inmates in the Central Prison and in section C, after having been transferred from one prison to the other, staged a kind of revolt. They were taken out together for exercise; as a closely knit unit, they must have agreed to stage a demonstration to draw attention to themselves. They suddenly began to destroy the contents of their cells, to smash furniture and windows, and to tear apart the mattresses. There was an uproar that was heard throughout the prison. The guards rushed along the corridors, officers and representatives from AVH headquarters came to parley with them. Because of the awe the AVH men felt for Tito (who had been placated only with difficulty by Khrushchev), no harsh methods could be used against the Yugoslav prisoners. Now immediate release was promised; within a week they left the prison, evidently to be allowed to return to Yugoslavia.

In November 1955 I was once again questioned, this time about László Veress. The main point raised was whether I could tell the AVH officer with whom Veress (now in London) was corresponding in Hungary. I laughed in the interrogator's face: "I have been in prison for over four years. How should I know about such things?" The officer disappeared without drawing up a protocol.

Khrushchev's secret speech of February 24–25, 1956, in which the Soviet leader described Stalin's evil deeds, reached our prison by some obscure channels a few weeks later. Of course, the original version did not come to our ears, but rather an exaggerated and overcolored account of the meaning of the speech. I remember that it was Zoltán Horváth who first mentioned it to me. The Social Democrats at that time possessed good sources of information—perhaps the prison guards, themselves former Socialists. Having heard so many hyperbolic stories in prison, I first doubted the veracity of this news. However, it was soon evident that the Twentieth Party Congress of the Soviet Union had set into motion an avalanche that was impossible to stop.

At the end of April I saw a long line of Social Democrats forming up on the ground floor of section B, and the orderlies reported that they would be set free within a day or so. Since I had read in one of the clippings I received that Khrushchev was visiting England, I could easily imagine (this was subsequently confirmed) that the British Socialist ministers had intervened in favor of the Socialist prisoners within the Soviet sphere of domination.

In the following weeks I read with interest and surprise of the debates in the Petöfi circle, a club of intellectuals, where all aspects of the regime underwent serious and sharp criticism. To read Hungarian newspapers in June 1956 was exhilarating: they began to acquire the marked quality of a free press, at least in their denunciation of domestic abuses. My own and my fellow prisoners' presence in jail appeared to be more and more an anachronism, a bureaucratic tardiness that would have to be corrected in due time.

What must have been inevitable after the condemnation of Stalinism at the Twentieth Party Congress was the ouster of the Hungarian Stalin, Rákosi. This finishing stroke to the era of terror was delivered at the end of July, and the news spread like wildfire in the corridors of the prison. Everybody expected a quick denouement of their individual tragedies of unjust imprisonment. However, the denouement was slow and painful.

The relaxation and gradual loosening of Party discipline was felt throughout the prison. The jailers, even the most infamous among them, approached us timidly and often apologetically. The worst among them were the most courteous; the hunters had become the hunted. We occasionally reminded our cruel erstwhile tormentors of some atrocities they had committed. Now their usual comment was, "I did not see it! I was not there at the time! I protested in vain!" And when they were told, "I saw you there; you did this or that," they shrugged their shoulders and replied, "I was ordered to do that. I could not prevent it!"

The slackening of prison discipline meant that we, the translators and the artists, could freely visit each other in our cells. I spent much of my time in the company of my particular artist friends, Sándor Bodo and Tibor Dánielfy. The latter expected to be released soon, because he heard that some of the codefendants in his case already were free. Indeed, in August Tibor was set free; he visited Rose and gave her all the details she wished to know about my life and doings.

Because I was still considered a good source for the discussion of foreign politics, Bodo conceived a brilliant idea that would permit me to spend my evenings in the company of the artists. He told the colonel in charge of translators and artists that he wished to practice portrait painting, hinting slightly that one day he might paint him, too. Thus, he obtained permission for me to sit in his cell so he could practice on me. During the month of August and the beginning of September Bodo painted me several times until he was satisfied with the result.*

Other prisoners also profited from the relaxed situation. Béla Király, the general who had been sentenced to death and for over a year

---

*This portrait is reproduced on the jacket of Váli's *Rift and Revolt in Hungary* (1967). The original hangs in the Váli Room in Thompson Hall at the University of Massachusetts at Amherst. —ED.

expected to be hanged until he received information that his sentence had been commuted to life imprisonment, visited me in my cell in order to use the typewriter. He was also eager to learn English, and we were able to provide him with reading materials in that language.

In the late summer of 1956 political prisoners of all kinds were being sporadically and erratically released. Now former members of the Smallholder Party received pardons or suspensions of their prison terms. One day in September I was happy to inform Meznerics that he could pack up his belongings because he too was to be set free. Some days later Béla Király was released.

In early October another outstanding event occurred, which was given wide publicity in our prison. This was the reburial of Lászlo Rajk and his associates, who had been executed in 1950. All had been rehabilitated earlier, but the burial, a demonstration against the injustices and crimes of the Stalin-Rákosi regime, was a call for revenge against those who had been responsible for these and similar misdeeds. The crimes that had been committed were thus openly admitted, but the criminals—practically the entire Party leadership—tried to avoid punishment. And it appeared (at least to those of us still in prison) most anomalous that after the recognition of such abuses the release of all political prisoners was still delayed.

On Sunday, October 7, Rose came to visit me. At that time it was possible to speak freely about everything during such interviews; the guards failed to interfere. Rose told me, "In the last weeks I saw the supreme state attorney and several leaders in the Ministry of Justice. I have handed them petitions for your release. I was encouraged by some, but there were also those who were reluctant to support your case. However, there is yet another development that may be far more important. Two directors of IBM from New York recently have been negotiating with representatives of the Hungarian government, which wishes to rent or purchase one of the up-to-date computers required for the national census to be held next year. Don't ask me how I know it, but I heard reliably that these directors have raised the question of IBM employees imprisoned in 1951, and you, as their former legal adviser, have also been mentioned. I was given to understand that the deal to be concluded, or already concluded, contains a hidden clause that will secure your release."

Upon my return to the cell, I told Sándorfi the good news, which I was certain would affect him as well as myself. But I tried to dampen my expectations; there had been so many frustrations in the past that I preferred to await developments in equanimity rather than excitement.

The next week passed without anything happening. Thursday, October 18, also passed uneventfully, and by four in the afternoon I was ready to wind up my work for that day, when a guard came rushing to the door:

"Váli! Bring your belongings! Hurry! If you are quick, you can be processed right away and released at once. Hurry!"

IV

Release, Revolution, Escape

All that is necessary for the triumph of evil is that good men do nothing.

Edmund Burke

RELEASE

I quickly said good-bye to Sándorfi and the other translators and packed up my belongings in a bundle. They now included several books, a sweater, and a few pieces of underwear.

When I told two orderlies, "Good-bye, I am going to be released!" they thought I was joking. Nobody was released so late in the day. But when I got to the section commander, he announced, "We just received instructions to release you at once; if you hurry, you can still make it. The cashiers close at five."

I was taken to the cell on the ground floor for prisoners about to be released. A guard brought me a sack with my civilian clothes. They were moth-eaten and in rags. He seemed most eager to secure my early release. "I have to get you some new clothes. I will tell the colonel."

The clothes arrived quickly. They were ill-fitting, but I took them. I changed in a hurry, rushed to the cashier's office, and asked for my valuables; I remembered having given up my watch, my wedding ring, and a wallet with some money.

"I am sorry, there is nothing in your box. You know, some years ago these boxes were ransacked."

"You thought I would never get out alive, didn't you?"

The clerk smiled in embarrassment. "I was not here at that time. I know nothing." But he did pay me my translators' wages, though he forgot to deduct the cost for my "maintenance." I signed a receipt.

The section commander then took me to the Warden's office, where an officer gave me my release paper. I read it carefully: "Ferenc Váli, sentenced on June 26, 1952, to fifteen years imprisonment for high treason. His sentence is hereby suspended for the period of six months. He is to be released at once." The paper was signed by the deputy attorney general; the signature was unreadable. The officer shook my hand, and so did the section commander.

I crossed the courtyard and reached the outer gate. The gatekeeper, a sergeant and one of the brutes of the Stalinist era, checked my release paper. "Behold! Fifteen years and already out!"

"Some who had life sentences were released before me, were they not? Of course, those who were hanged or died could not be released."

The sergeant did not answer. He opened the narrow door next to the big gate and let me out.

I walked slowly toward the streetcar stop I saw in the distance. About halfway there I was overtaken by the obliging jailor who had brought me the clothes. "I just phoned your wife to let her know." He hurried back to the prison entrance. I did not know that this man was also in contact with Rose. Now I wished that Cricket could have been there, but he was not on duty that day.

I waited, somewhat uneasy at being alone with nobody watching me. Soon the streetcar arrived and I stepped aboard. It was almost empty, and I sat down in a corner. The conductor stood before me.

"I want a transfer ticket," I said, remembering that I would have to change cars. He handed me the ticket.

"How much is the ticket *now?*" I asked. The conductor looked at me and my ill-fitting clothes with understanding. "Seventy-five fillér," he answered. I gave him the money.

"How long have you been inside?"

"Five years and three months."

The conductor whistled: "Quite a long time. Political, of course?"

At the subsequent stops the car gradually filled up. Passengers watched me and the bundle on my lap but said nothing.

The streetcar reached its terminus at the National Theater. I stepped out. It was seven in the evening and already dark. Crowds of people rushing home from work surrounded me in the glare of the streetlights. I felt dizzy, as if a million well-dressed persons, among them beautiful women, were around me. "Agoraphobia," I told myself. But I felt unable to cross the busy boulevard. A taxi stood at the corner and I got in it.

"Where to?" the driver asked.

It took me a few seconds to remember. "Number seven, Váci-utca."

In about ten minutes we arrived at the large apartment house in the very center of the city. The driver got out and opened the door for me. I gave him a good tip and he thanked me profusely. "At your service, sir."

Before entering the arched doorway, I looked at the nearby shopwindow where the stuffed toy animals, the products of my wife and of my mother-in-law, were on display. Then, slowly, I entered the gate and climbed up to the second floor. At the door of the apartment, I don't know why, I hesitated before ringing the bell.

Seconds after the bell sounded, the door opened, and my mother-in-law stared at me. She stretched out her arms to greet me and shouted: "It's true! Rose, it's true!" Rose came running and crying. "It's true, it's true!"

After embracing me, she explained, "Last week I had a phone call from the guard that you had been released. We prepared a dinner for you. But you did not come. This time, I did not believe him when he called. But Mother went out to buy you some good food."

She kept repeating, "How good it is that you are here. How good it is. Thank God, you are here. Are you healthy? You are, aren't you?"

"I am all right. But you look pale. Are you overworked?"

"No, no, it is just all this waiting and waiting. And now the excitement. I'll have to tell you everything. So many people were asking about you. Especially those who refused to see me when I was released. Now they are phoning or coming here almost every day."

She mentioned a few names, among them Iván Boldizsár.

"Of course, your fellow prisoners who were released in the last two months are also coming. Your former cellmate Laci, and also Tibor Dánielfy, and others. István and Éva D. have also been released. You will meet all of them, sooner or later."

"Have you tried to see Gajzágo?"

"Yes, but unfortunately he is no longer alive. He died in 1953; heart failure, I believe. I only spoke with his sister. I was very sorry to observe how they lived; he must have died in abject poverty."

It was a shock to learn that such a scholar, a luminary of international law for whom I had the greatest respect and affection, had passed away in such isolation from the Western world to which he always considered he belonged.

The dinner was excellent. I was given a little wine, but not too much, as Rose said, "You must take time to get accustomed to free life." But I already felt accustomed.

The apartment was now much smaller than when I last saw it. The authorities had requisitioned two rooms. My mother-in-law, who ran her shop in the apartment, managed to separate her part from the rest of the apartment by making it into a self-contained unit. Rose showed me our room, a small but comfortable chamber behind the kitchen. It used to be the maid's room.

We retired early. Rose said, "Our doctor advised me to spare you in the beginning, that you may not be ready yet."

But I was ready. So we disregarded the doctor's advice.

OUTBREAK

My first errand on Friday, October 19, was to the local police station to obtain my identification card. Without such a card in a Communist country you are a nonentity and liable to arrest. One has to carry this card at all times.

At the police station a female clerk, a Party emblem on her bosom, questioned me. "Did you just arrive from abroad?"

"No, from prison." I showed her my release paper.

"Now don't tell me you were innocent," she remarked in an arrogant tone.

"You evidently don't believe that people had been innocently imprisoned? What about Rajk? He was a Party leader and he was innocently hanged. Or you think he was guilty?"

The woman said nothing; there was nothing to be said. After she wrote down my personal data, she told me, "Bring your photograph next week and you will get your card."

My next destination was to see S. M. P., a lawyer friend who had advised Rose and drafted the petitions for my release. S. M. P. had been a legal adviser to prominent people in pre-1945 Hungary—landowners, aristocrats, and high officials. Almost miraculously he escaped deportation and continued to counsel many persons of importance. Previously, he had run a large office with many lawyers and a sizable clerical staff; now he was reduced to operating in a small apartment with no employees. He devoted much of his time to advising victims of the regime, and he was well informed in political and financial matters.

I wished to thank him for the assistance he had given to Rose and at the same time to discuss with him the prospects for a revision of my sentence. How was I to use the six months while my sentence was suspended?

S. M. P. gave me the following political survey: "The leadership of the Communist Party is divided. Gerö, the first secretary, is just as hated by the anti-Stalinist wing as was his predecessor, Rákosi. These anti-Stalinists want Imre Nagy to become their leader. He has now been readmitted into the Party, but his return to power is opposed by Gerö and his group. These Stalinists have one desire: to save their skins. Therefore, they fear Nagy. And there is a third group around János Kádár, who is considered an anti-Stalinist because he has been imprisoned. But Kádár also is afraid of Nagy and of the right-wingers in the Party. Nobody knows whom Moscow will ultimately support, and that is what really matters."

About my own personal problem he said, "If Imre Nagy is returned to power, there will be no difficulty in having your sentence quashed. And if the situation thus improves, you as a non-Party person may even have a chance to obtain a decent position. You could work as a practicing lawyer again, perhaps for an import-export trade corporation; they need people with your international background and knowledge of languages. As for a university job, this is less likely. But who knows?"

We also discussed events outside Hungary. S. M. P. offered this comment: "The Soviet-bloc country that is in even more turmoil than Hungary is Poland. The Poznan uprising in June has not been forgotten. We can expect interesting developments to occur in Warsaw."

I left S. M. P. with the impression that my future, as had been in the past, was closely dependent on political events and all that I could contribute was to make the best use of whatever opportunities might offer themselves.

When I returned to our apartment, I found it crowded with friends, acquaintances, and well-wishers. I could not guess how the news of my release reached all these people.

On the following day, Saturday, Rose took me to a number of shops to purchase clothes and underwear. She absolutely refused to see me in the outfit I brought home from the prison. In my new sartorial garb I visited several people: an aunt, Laci, Tibor, and others. Rose's birthday on October 25 was approaching, and I invited Tibor for dinner on that day.

On Sunday we again had many visitors, and we were also invited for dinner. The dramatic developments in Poland were now central to all conversations. On October 19 the Polish Central Committee elected Władysław Gomułka as leader of the Party and it did so without the approval and probably against the objections of Moscow. Gomułka, a victim of Stalinism who had been in prison for many years, had the reputation of being a liberal in the Communist context. In Hungary, it was obvious that he could be compared with Imre Nagy, although the parallel was in many respects inaccurate.

On the night of Gomułka's election a group of top Soviet leaders descended on Warsaw to enter into discussions with the Poles. Simultaneously, Soviet troops moved toward the Polish capital and Polish units prepared to defend the city. But by Sunday, October 20, an agreement was reached; Gomułka was accepted by the Soviet leaders, and the Soviet forces were withdrawn.

In Hungary, as elsewhere in the world, the outcome of this crisis was interpreted as a Polish victory. At that point nobody knew what Gomułka had discussed with the Soviet leaders and how he would behave in the future. But the refusal by Poland to submit to Soviet threats and the eventual acquiescence of Moscow created an atmosphere of satisfaction and a euphoria that electrified large segments of the Hungarian population.

A mutual revolutionary contagion has long affected Hungarian and Polish history. Every Hungarian and every Pole is aware of the traditional friendship between their two nations. They were neighboring countries for a thousand years but never waged war against one another. Hungarian kings had been Polish rulers, and vice versa. They had fought common enemies: Turks, Germans, and Russians. During the Hungarian War of Liberation in 1848–49 Polish officers, among them the celebrated General Bem, fought on the Hungarian side. After the Polish uprising of 1863 many Hungarian families had a Pole, that is, a refugee houseguest. When Germany and Russia invaded Poland in 1939, two hundred thousand Poles escaped to Hungary, where they enjoyed warm hospitality. After such historic precedents it was only natural that in Hungary the

"Polish October" gave rise to exhilaration and that the alleged victory of the Poles over the Russians received an unrealistic and exaggerated emphasis.

On Monday, October 22, meetings were held in celebration of the events in Warsaw in many Hungarian universities and professional associations, such as the Writers' Association. Resolutions were adopted and disseminated through handbills. Some were even published in the daily press. The best known were the "sixteen points" of the students and workers of the Technological University for Building Industries. These resolutions included demands for the withdrawal of Soviet troops from Hungary, the appointment of Imre Nagy to the premiership, the prosecution of Stalinist criminals, the release of political prisoners, economic reforms, and greater freedom of the press.

To commemorate the Polish events, a mass demonstration was to be held on Tuesday, October 23, before the statue of General Bem in Budapest. On that morning I went to pick up my identification card at the police station; this card thus bore the memorable date of October 23, 1956.

Soon after twelve noon the radio announced that the Minister of the Interior had forbidden the demonstration. But to my surprise, at about two-thirty the prohibition was withdrawn. At the same time it was announced that First Secretary Gerö, who had just returned from Yugoslavia, was to make a speech over the radio at eight in the evening.

In the afternoon I witnessed groups of students marching to the statue of the revolutionary poet Petöfi on the Pest side of the Danube, which was close to where we lived. Then these groups crossed over one of the bridges to the Buda side, where the statue of General Bem was located. These were enthusiastic, unarmed, mostly young men and women. There was nothing to indicate that this was to be anything different from other well-attended peaceful meetings that had occurred in recent months.

Rose and I listened over the radio to some of the speeches made in front of the Bem statue. The speakers reiterated the demands already expressed in the various points. Subsequently, the radio reported that there was a large crowd before the Parliament building waiting to hear an address by Imre Nagy. I did not hear Nagy's address, but later an eyewitness told me that he behaved in an awkward manner, as if he had spoken against his free will.

We did listen with great interest to the speech Gerö delivered at eight o'clock. At that time several hundred thousand people were in the streets—not to fight, but to celebrate. Under the circumstances Gerö's speech was provocative and stupid. Instead of appeasing the crowd and saying something sympathetic about Poland, he spoke of the achievements of the people's democracy, which was threatened by enemies of the working class. He mentioned hostile endeavors aimed at "loosening the relations that link the Hungarian Party to the glorious Communist Party of the Soviet Union." At a moment when almost all Hungarians derived pleasure from the defeat Moscow had suffered in Warsaw (or was supposed to have suffered), he incited the crowd by his reckless words. Gerö called the students "impudent propagandists" because they felt that Hungary's relations with the Soviet Union were not based on equality. He rejected the allegation that Hungary's independence should be defended against Moscow. His outworn expressions and Stalinist slogans exasperated the crowd. He shouted that his listeners clearly had to choose now between a socialist democracy or a bourgeois democracy. At that moment the term *socialist democracy* was considered synonymous with nothing else but Stalinist dictatorship.

Our windows looked down on the Váci-utca, the fashionable street running north-south. Around nine o'clock we saw many thousands of persons—not only students but people of all ages and callings—singing, shouting, and marching south in spontaneous but still disciplined order. Many carried the national flag, but these flags now looked different: they had cut out the Communist hammer and sickle from the center of the flag. An empty hole showed where this ideological emblem had once been.

It was a mild evening, and all the windows were open. From these windows the residents admired the crowd, joining in their singing and shouts, waving the national flag with the gaping hole. This flag with the hole in its center had suddenly become the symbol of the movement.

So far no violent attack against the Soviets had occurred in the speeches and in the press, only restrained demands for equality and the withdrawal of their troops. Now, probably in the aftermath of Gerö's provocative speech, a new rhythmic cry was intermittently heard: "Ruszkik ki!" ("Russians out!"). Soon the street reverberated with this cry: the crowd now had become overtly anti-Soviet.

Since we did not anticipate that this demonstration would result in anything violent or momentous, we quietly went to bed when the street became empty.

It was a surprise the following morning when no newspapers arrived and the radio announced, "Hooligans and reactionaries are attempting an armed revolt. The Hungarian government has asked the Soviet forces stationed in the country to help it in suppressing this revolt. Hungarian and Soviet forces are on the way to restoring order and peace in Budapest." There was a further announcement: "Imre Nagy has been appointed chairman of the Council of Ministers. The government has declared martial law."

Soon the telephone rang. It was Tibor Dánielfy. "I am sorry," he said. "Because of the situation in the streets, I shall not be able to come to the dinner party tomorrow."

I answered, "Oh, I am sure you will be able to come. Everything will be over by tomorrow. You know, of course, that the Soviets have intervened."

Tibor, who lived in the Eighth District of Budapest, replied cautiously, "It does not appear to me that everything will be over by tomorrow. I don't want to go into detail, but from what I can observe here, things will not come to an end soon."

As I soon found out, the Eighth District was the area where most of the fighting had taken place the previous night. It also was the area where the radio station was located. But our part of the city was quiet. From Tibor's words I gleaned — after the words used in France in 1789 — that this was not a revolt: it was a revolution.

REVOLUTION MILITANT

Thereafter we sat and listened to the radio almost the entire day. There were quite a few days in my life when waiting for news absorbed my undivided attention: when Hitler invaded Poland, when the Battle of Britain was being fought in the air, I sat at the radio in my Budapest apartment; when the landing at Normandy occurred, I crouched by this news-disseminating device almost day and night in my Istanbul room. Once again one's existence had become dependent on events that were to be reported across the airwaves.

Hungarian news broadcasts became sporadic; in between there was music. But I was able to catch the BBC reports from London and the Hungarian-language broadcasts by Radio Free Europe, for jamming of them had miraculously stopped.

The official Hungarian announcements were blatantly contradictory: first they claimed that the government forces had restored order; next they announced that the fighting continued. In an address purported to have been that of Prime Minister Nagy but read by somebody else, the rebels were invited to surrender before a certain hour, otherwise martial law would be applied against them. These deadlines, however, were constantly being moved forward both on that day and on the following day. Finally, no deadline was announced, only that the fighting still continued. Silence surrounded the operations of the Soviet forces.

Later that day telephone calls from various parts of the city confirmed that the reports of government troops fighting the insurgents were completely untrue. Only Russians, moving with their armored troop carriers and tank columns from place to place, engaged in combat. Russians fought Hungarian guerrilla groups, who soon were called freedom fighters.

The story of how the fighting started and how the insurgents were able to obtain arms gradually came to light. Security police troops guarding the radio station prevented the broadcast of the "sixteen points" demanded by the demonstrators. These security policemen started shooting at the unarmed demonstrators, who, however, quickly obtained arms from nearby police stations, the regular police siding with the demonstrators. As the night advanced, workers at arms factories brought out light arms by the truckload and distributed these weapons among the crowd. And when Hungarian infantry was brought to the scene, they refused to fight the students and workers and handed their rifles over to them. It must have been this hopeless situation that induced the Party leadership to appeal for help to the Soviets.

To any eyewitness of these and the preceding events it must have been obvious that the uprising was spontaneous; it was neither premeditated nor planned by anybody. Had there been any conspiratorial planning to organize such a revolt, it would—in view of the widespread informer system—have come to the attention of the security police. As it happened, the events tumbled down on everybody—the Hungarian government, the Hungarian public, and the world at large—as a complete surprise.

Furthermore, it should be recalled that Hungarians have never excelled in conspiratorial endeavors. I cannot remember any Hungarian conspiracy that was not prematurely disclosed or betrayed. None of them has ever been successful, whether because it is against the national character to conspire in secret or because of the talkativeness of individual Hungarians.

It is absolutely certain there was no preconceived plan for this uprising. Nobody could seriously point to any person or group of persons who could have been the organizers of a coup. The Communist propaganda, which declared that Horthyist officers, aristocrats, and big landowners masterminded the revolt, is a cock-and-bull story without any foundation. The accusation that inflammatory broadcasts by Radio Free Europe or the Voice of America fomented the revolt is equally incorrect. The demonstrators in front of the Bem statue, in front of Parliament, and in front of the radio station were not and could not have been influenced by such broadcasts. These demonstrators and the subsequent freedom fighters were acting instinctively, led by their hatred of the regime and its representatives. Finally, when Soviet forces intervened, this fact aroused nationalist passions even among those who up to that point had remained unmoved by events.

The events came so unexpectedly that our household, like other Budapest households, was unprepared for them. We lacked basic food items. In Hungary, as in other parts of continental Europe and even more so in Communist countries, grocery shopping is a daily activity, partly for lack of refrigeration, partly for monetary reasons. There was always the possibility that one who bought surplus supplies would be accused of hoarding.

Since intermittent shooting could be heard, one was reluctant to leave the safety of one's lodgings. Still, I saw passersby in the street, sometimes running for safety to the entrances of houses or to the few shops that were open. Several times I ventured out myself to purchase such items as bread, milk, and vegetables. I had to walk several blocks, but I took cover or quickly returned because of shooting. Once I saw Soviet armored cars followed by tanks. Soldiers discharged their handguns, perhaps in the air or at distant targets. There was no response.

In the evening a somewhat clearer picture evolved of what was really happening. I exchanged phone calls with friends in several parts of the city who themselves had been in touch with others. It was remarkable that in spite of everything, the telephone continued to function unhindered. Also, some foreign broadcasts in various foreign languages confirmed the reports that came to me through telephone conversations.

The brunt of the fighting took place in the Seventh and Eighth

Districts on the Pest side and around the Széna-tér, a large square on the Buda side where roads and streetcar lines from many directions meet. A number of freedom fighter groups had organized themselves and established headquarters in some public buildings in these parts of Budapest. From there they defended certain strongholds against Soviet attacks and made attacking sorties themselves.

A more positive description of the fighting reached me from Tibor and Laci and some other inhabitants of affected areas. Evidently, when the Soviet forces ventured into the streets of the city, they had no preset ideas nor any inkling of whom they were called upon to fight and how to conduct the fighting. I assume they were instructed to spare the lives of civilians and avoid unnecessary damage to houses. They had no infantry, except those in armored cars, and no supporting artillery. When a Soviet tank column entered an often narrow street, young Hungarian fighters managed to throw a Molotov cocktail onto the leading vehicle and also one onto the last. Thus prevented from moving in any direction, the terrified crews left their tanks and ran for safety while being shot at from the houses.

Practically all young Hungarians — both students and workers — had to undergo some military or paramilitary training under the Communist regime. They were taught how to use rifles and many of them were specifically instructed how to fight "imperialists" in the streets. They were shown how to handle a Molotov cocktail. Now these young men and women practiced their knowledge against those who had instructed them.

October 25 was Rose's birthday. To substitute for flowers or other gifts I told her that her birthday present was the Revolution. "I couldn't expect anything better," she responded.

Despite the promises of the Hungarian radio broadcasts that order and peace would soon be reestablished, other sources confirmed that the fighting was spreading into many other sections of Budapest, into its suburbs, and into many provincial towns. Fighting, of course, meant shooting at the Russians. However, at certain isolated spots shooting erupted between freedom fighters and members of the security police. In the town of Magyaróvár, near the Austrian border, security police shot at unarmed demonstrators, killing many. The retaliation was terrible: the local AVH headquarters was besieged, and its occupants were wiped out.

The first reports about the events in Magyaróvár came over the BBC and Radio Free Europe. Reporters were now able to cross the unguarded frontier in both directions and to send their news reports from Vienna.

When I wanted to witness some fighting with my own eyes, Rose prevented it. "You have just come out of prison, you are not young enough and have never handled guns. Let the fighting be done by others!" But in the early afternoon we decided that the coast was clear, and we both left the apartment and quickly walked toward Saint Stephen's Cathedral, stopping and listening on the way for more shooting. There were only a few pedestrians in the street. In accordance with the fraternal spirit that prevailed throughout the revolutionary period we exchanged words with those we met. "No danger in that direction. No Russians, no fighting there."

We reached the house where our friend S. M. P. lived. He was expecting us and offered us coffee and sweets; since it was Rose's birthday, he persuaded us to accept. "The Party is unable to decide what to do," he informed us. "The Russians are losing face. Imre Nagy is not a free agent; he is held by Gerö at Party headquarters, where the latter is still in control. Of course, only at headquarters, because it appears that the Party is about to disintegrate. In many provincial towns local Party offices have been taken over by revolutionary committees. The Party secretaries are in hiding. In Csepel [a major industrial suburb of Budapest] workers have ostentatiously torn up their Party cards, and the streets are full of these shreds."

We listened to some noise in the street and saw persons running in great excitement from the direction of Parliament. One shouted up to us in the window, "The security police opened fire from the roof of the Agriculture Ministry on demonstrators who wished to see Imre Nagy. There are many dead. We are calling for freedom fighters to do away with them."

Our host turned on the radio. There was no report on the bloodbath in front of Parliament, but soon there was another announcement: "The Political Bureau of the Party has relieved Erno Gerö as first secretary and appointed János Kádár in his place." Then Kádár spoke: "Antidemocratic and counterrevolutionary elements have caused peaceful demonstrations to degenerate into armed attack. When peace is restored, we shall conduct talks with the Soviet government for a just settlement of all questions pending between our two Socialist countries." As soon as Kádár was off the air, Imre Nagy's voice was heard: "We shall proceed with all-embracing reforms. We shall open discussions with the Soviet Union concerning the withdrawal of Soviet forces stationed in Hungary."

When walking in the streets, one witnessed curious and contradictory scenes. On a square not far from our apartment I saw a column of Soviet tanks in a stationary position. The crew sat outside doing nothing. But the group was surrounded by heavily armed sentries. When you approached any of them, they would shout: "Stoi!" ("Stop!") and would reach for their weapons. Evidently, they were apprehensive for their own safety.

Half a mile away, on the Rákoczy-ut, one of the main thoroughfares, I saw two Soviet tanks slowly moving as if in a procession. On top of the tanks sat members of the Soviet crew and Hungarian fighters, boys and girls holding each other, singing and chanting. I could only infer from this scene that the morale of the Soviet forces must have been pretty low. They had probably been stationed in Hungary for some time and now enjoyed the opportunity to fraternize. Before their arrival in Budapest they had been told that they were being sent to fight fascists and counterrevolutionaries; instead they met students and workers as their adversaries—not aristocrats and not Western imperialists.

Simultaneously with these incidents, some two miles away heavy fighting was in progress around the Kilián barracks where two days earlier Colonel Maléter with five tanks under his command went over to the freedom fighters. He and his soldiers and the insurgents now held these buildings against the onslaught of the Russians.

Grocery shopping had become easier. Although many shops were still closed and others lacked supplies, the farmers from the countryside came to the rescue of the townspeople. We saw pedestrians walking in the street with vegetables, fruits, and loaves of bread wrapped in newspaper. They told us that on certain squares peasants were selling or distributing food from their horse-driven carts.

Rose and I walked down to one of these squares. Indeed, there were the carts and smiling farmers handing down vegetables—mostly potatoes—and some fruit and bread as well. They accepted money, but if a person had none, they willingly gave the articles away without it.

The peasantry had no opportunity to participate in the fighting. There was hardly anybody in the countryside for them to fight—no Russians, hardly any security police (if so they would have fled, especially after the Magyarovár incident), and what Communist Party members there were offered little or no resistance. It was in this way, by generously providing food, that farmers expressed their gratitude to the inhabitants of Budapest for having saved them, or so they hoped, from the pressures of collectivization and for having possibly enabled them to keep their formerly collectivized land.

On Friday, October 26, fighting continued in many sections of the city, but the Soviet forces in other sections refrained from aggressive actions and only responded to defend themselves. It was now much safer to move in the streets. Signs of shooting could be observed everywhere. Broken windows in the principal thoroughfares were evidence of past fighting. What was perhaps most remarkable was that despite the open shopwindows, there was no sign of looting. The contents of these windows, including those of jewelers, were intact, and nobody thought of touching or taking anything. This contrasted sharply with behavior in other great cities of the world where such situations were considered an invitation to loot and pilfer.

One day Rose and I stopped in front of the British Legation in the Harmincad-utca, where a crowd had gathered. They were waiting to be admitted in order to make inquiries or to press requests for assistance, but they were only admitted one by one. A Hungarian police officer appeared in the entrance. He still wore the official hammer-and-sickle emblem on his cap. The crowd shouted, "Away with that horrible badge!" The officer smiled. He took a rosette in the national colors out of his pocket and replaced the Communist badge with it. The crowd cheered.

Then another man, evidently a driver, joined the group. "I just met a colleague of mine who came from the Austrian border," he told us. "The United Nations forces have just crossed the frontier." The people shouted enthusiastically and embraced each other. Poor naive souls, I told myself. Not one word of this was true; people deceived each other through wishful thinking. That morning I had learned from the BBC that at long last the Hungarian issue, upon request by the United States, Great Britain, and France, had been placed on the agenda of the next Security Council meeting, which was to be held on October 28, that is, in two days. I wanted to say something to the crowd, but Rose prevented it. "Don't say a word! They will lynch you. They will think that you are a Communist," she whispered.

It was on the following day, October 27, that all the political prisoners in the Central Prison were freed. As I was told by former fellow prisoners, after the outbreak of the Revolution a commission arrived in the prison to arrange for the release of political prisoners. The commission worked slowly, interrogating inmates alphabetically and then ordering their release. By October 27 the commission had only reached the letter *F* when a group of freedom fighters broke into the prison. The guards opened all the cells; those of bad conscience, including the gatekeeper, fled. Cricket was cheered by the prisoners, who now simply walked out. Had my sentence not been suspended on October 18, I would also have been freed nine days later. But I had the advantage of a release paper and an identification card, which were most helpful during later developments.

For the new leadership under Imre Nagy and János Kádár the principal task was to end the fighting and to reestablish governmental control. But this was only possible if the demands of the people were met — demands expressed by workers' councils, various national councils, and the freedom fighters. These demands included the withdrawal of Soviet forces, equality in the relationship with the Soviet Union, the dissolution of the security police, free elections, freedom of the press, freedom of speech, freedom of assembly, and freedom of worship.

Under these irresistible pressures, and perhaps following his own inclinations, the prime minister gave in: on October 28 the radio announced a unilateral cease-fire and ordered Hungarian units to stop fighting the freedom fighters. This was only a symbolic gesture, because no such fighting took place. But at the same time it was reported that the Hungarian government had come to an agreement with the Soviet command, according to which Soviet forces would be withdrawn from Budapest.

We all felt that a new era had begun. The monopolistic rule of the Communist Party had come to an end. The press was free (even the Communist daily *Szabad Nép* now openly attacked Moscow), and the director of the Hungarian radio apologized on the air for having disseminated so much "untruth." Members of the various freedom fighter groups now openly appeared with their weapons. Soon they would be united and legitimized as the Hungarian National Guard. The political parties that had been suppressed seven or eight years ago began reorganizing themselves. The government had to yield; the Revolution was won.

But in viewing these developments, I constantly asked myself, What is Moscow doing? Can the Soviet leadership be expected to acquiesce in the secession of one of its satellites? The declaration of the Soviet government of October 30 was widely publicized in the Hungarian radio and press. This declaration admitted "violations and errors that demeaned the principle of equality among Socialist states" and promised to review the economic and military ties binding these countries together. But it also emphasized that Soviet units were stationed in Hungary in accord with the Warsaw Pact and therefore the stationing of troops on the territory of another member state had been done by agreement among all the members of this treaty organization. On the other hand, the declaration expressed regrets over the bloodshed in Budapest and announced that instructions had been issued for the withdrawal of Soviet military units from the city.[1]

The pullout of Soviet forces from Budapest created an atmosphere of euphoria, particularly among the freedom fighters themselves, a euphoria which I could hardly share when I realistically considered power relations and the wording of the Soviet declaration. The Soviets certainly had lost a battle in Budapest but not yet the war. Nonetheless, it was pleasing to hear the freedom fighters half-jokingly boast, "There are three superpowers: the United States, the Soviet Union, and the Eighth Budapest District." At the same time it appeared illusory to believe that Moscow would be ready to relinquish Hungary from its sphere of influence without an agreement between the world powers.

The Hungarian foreign service remained infiltrated by pro-Soviet agents. This was demonstrated in the meeting of the United Nations Security Council on October 28 when the Hungarian representative, Peter Kos (alias Leo Konduktorov, the oil expert who came to assist me in my 1948 negotiations in Switzerland), submitted that the Hungarian government had requested the intervention by Soviet forces and, therefore, the council had no right to discuss the matter. Whereupon the council meeting was adjourned *sine die,* that is, without any resolution whatsoever.

Another ominous development occurred on that day to distract completely the world's attention from the Hungarian question. Israeli forces invaded the Sinai desert, and on October 30 Great Britain and France presented an ultimatum to Egypt demanding the evacuation of the Suez Canal area. On the following day British and French military action began.

I listened, horrified, to the news relating to the Suez crisis as announced by the BBC. A new world confrontation was in the offing in which Hungary would play a secondary role. But in the streets of Budapest people were frolicking, enjoying their hard-won freedom.

---

1. *Pravda,* Oct. 31, 1956. See also Ferenc Váli, *Rift and Revolt in Hungary* (Cambridge: Harvard University Press, 1961), pp. 345–347.

REVOLUTION TRIUMPHANT

On October 30 Prime Minister Nagy announced the abolition of the one-party system and the formation of a multiparty coalition government. This meant a return to the pre-1948 system, which was a coalition of four political parties—the Communists, the Social Democrats, the Smallholders, and the National Peasant Party. But in 1947–48 the Communist Party was a powerful, aggressive, and expanding organization, whereas now it was a compromised, decomposed, disheartened, and moribund body.

However, there was an attempt, perhaps by Imre Nagy or by the remnants of the Stalinists in the Communist Party, to prevent the reemergence of a genuine coalition based on the equality of all the participating parties. Thus, when the first coalition government was announced, the majority of the ministers were still Communists, and among the representatives of other parties figured many compromised persons who had collaborated earlier with the Rákosi regime. It was only on November 3 that a coalition government was formed that had only non-Stalinists among the Communists, and persons untainted by collaboration from the other three parties. Pál Maléter was promoted to general and became the nonparty minister of defense. János Kádár was one of the Communist ministers, but as we shall see, he soon disappeared from the scene for a while.

My former fellow prisoner Béla Király was not only given back his military rank of general but was appointed commander of the National Guard, a body organized from the members of the freedom fighters, and also made military commander of Budapest.

Cardinal Mindszenty was also freed and arrived in Budapest to be extolled and cheered by an enthusiastic crowd.

One of the first acts of the coalition government was the recall of Peter Kos as Hungarian representative to the United Nations and the appointment of another person to that post.

After having removed their destroyed tanks, the Soviet forces evacuated Budapest on October 31. I watched near one of the Danube bridges as tank column after tank column moved across the river, evidently to regain their previous headquarters near Lake Balaton. The tanks moved slowly, and members of the Hungarian National Guard walked along with them to protect them from possible attacks by the crowd, which observed these movements in disdainful silence.

I received a phone call inviting me to visit the Faculty of Law and Political Science of the University of Budapest. There I found that all the professors of the faculty had failed to show up during the last days, and the administration had been taken over by a revolutionary committee, headed by a lecturer, Dr. László Révész. He assured me that my formal reinstatement would take place within a few days as soon as the reorganization of the university had been completed.

I also received a call from the Ministry of Finance, from which I had been dismissed in February 1949, just about the time I was banned from my university post. Undersecretary István Vásárhelyi inquired whether I would be willing to return and take up my former job. I withheld a final reply because of other possible commitments that now appeared in the offing.

The Ministry of Foreign Affairs, heavily staffed as it was with former security police officers, Muscovite Communists, and disguised Soviet citizens, proved a special headache for the Imre Nagy coalition government. On November 1 the prime minister himself assumed the post of minister of foreign affairs and appointed György Heltai, a former prisoner and member of the translation bureau, as his deputy.

It was feared that the unreliable elements and Soviet agents in the ministry might destroy important documents and remove foreign exchange that was kept there. A careful plan was developed, therefore, for the sudden takeover of the building and reinstatement of dismissed employees. Imre Nagy was privy to this scheme, which was to be implemented in the early morning hours of November 5. A detachment of the National Guard was to assist in the operation. I was also asked to participate.

In the meantime, my mother-in-law's small apartment was transformed into a busy office or conference hall where visitors on official, semiofficial, or private errands spent many hours. When I was absent, Rose entertained them or simply asked them to wait. These callers were real friends or former friends who wished to renew contact. Some came apologizing, others asked for my help or simply wished to make an appearance lest I forget them. Iván Boldizsár was one of the most insistent callers. Our small back room was used for confidential parleys with friends or visitors.

It was amusing and exhilarating to walk in the streets during these few days of national enjoyment. Reconstruction had begun and shopkeepers were preparing to expand their businesses, just as in the good old days. The nightmare of Soviet Communist oppression seemed to be over. Few realized how chimeric this new status happened to be.

But this was not a time of happiness for all. Many Communist Party members who had built careers upon their membership in the ruling body were afraid of losing their jobs or suffering degradations. Among intellectuals there were different types. Some openly admitted that they had joined the Party for reasons of opportunism. These individuals often hoped that such sincerity would bring them rewards or, at least, would prevent major disadvantages. Others professed that they had been misled to believe in a future ideal Communist regime. They were now utterly ashamed and wished to make amends for their mistakes.

I vividly remember accidentally meeting Robert Hardi in the street. He walked stealthily, his head hanging down, and with an uncertain gait. When our eyes met he stared at me as if I were a ghost. I could not help telling him, "Do you know that this wonderful Party of yours, which you served with such devotion, was at the same time trying to find an opportunity to arrest you, perhaps to hang you? Do you know that I was subjected to the ordeals of interrogation because of you?" He turned on his heels and ran away as if I had threatened to shoot him.

I had never changed my basic political philosophy; I opposed any totalitarian regime, any authoritarianism, and considered genuine democracy as generally the best form of government. I was, therefore, always opposed to Nazism and Fascism, but equally to any Soviet Communist dictatorship. I spent my prison years in the conviction that I had been martyrized by a cruel, inhuman, and unjust system. Five years in jail were far too long and wasteful for my life. But otherwise I felt enriched by my prison experience. I had learned about people and acquired new capabilities, and it did not prove harmful to my health. Erich Honecker, the East German Communist leader, who spent ten years in jail under the Nazis, is reported to have said, "Prison is good for your health — if it doesn't kill you."

But the Communists and Communist collaborators who had been arrested and tormented and who spent years in jail experienced a double frustration: they had been innocently imprisoned, and by the very system they were eager to serve. I almost felt sorry for them. They had helped a vicious system and its wicked leaders to accomplish villainous objectives. They now saw themselves as fools, and some hated themselves. Many promised that after their release from prison they would never again serve this system. Some kept this promise, others did not. Many of the younger Communists, erstwhile devotees of the system and subsequently its fanatical enemies, joined the freedom fighters and revenged themselves upon those who had misled and seduced them to participate in misdeeds.

One did not ask during the revolutionary period whether a person had or had not been a Party member. The question was always: did he do something that was criminal or harmful to others?

But these considerations and others were iffy. Everything depended on the great question that Napoleon's sober-thinking mother had so concisely expressed concerning the viability of her son's political system: "pourvu que ça dure!" ("provided that it last!"). In my mind this question overshadowed all the cheerfulness that I otherwise felt about the unexpectedly happy turn of events.

I had no doubt that everything depended on the attitude of Moscow. It had been announced that two emissaries of the Soviet Presidium, Mikoyan and Suslov, had arrived in Budapest on October 30. They must have been able to assess the situation here much better than during their earlier visit a week before. At that time everything was in flux, and they might have hoped that a Gomułka-like solution could be reached with Imre Nagy and the Hungarian Communist Party. But now they faced an entirely new situation. The Party had collapsed and lost its hold over the country and the armed forces; a coalition government had been formed and free elections were to be held. They could have had no illusions of what the results of such free elections would be, namely, the elimination of the Communist Party as a factor in the political life of Hungary.

Among the demands urged on the government was withdrawal from the Warsaw Pact. A concurrent popular demand was for the immediate withdrawal of Soviet units not only from Budapest but from all of Hungary. All this would have serious consequences for Moscow: first, a loss of real estate where it could exercise control; second, a strategic setback in the balance of power in Central Europe; third, an invitation for other satellite countries to follow the example of Hungary. Could the Soviet leadership be expected to acquiesce in such a diminution of status unless forced to do so by overwhelming odds?

We could only guess that neither Mikoyan nor Suslov had given any promises to the Hungarian Communist leaders who had asked for help. Shortly after the departure of the two Soviet emissaries Kádár announced the reorganization of the "rejuvenated" Communist Party, one that now was resigned to collaborating in a multiparty system and doing away with past crimes and errors. On the same day Kádár also voted for Hungary's withdrawal from the Warsaw Pact and in favor of neutral status.

Everything appeared to be at its best on November 1. Imre Nagy proposed negotiations for the pullout of Soviet troops, a proposal that had been accepted. But later that day there appeared some foreboding signs: Soviet troop movements along the northeastern borders of Hungary and a gradual penetration of Soviet units into Hungarian territory were reported.

Hungarian radio now informed the public of these developments on an hourly basis. Upon the protest of Imre Nagy, Soviet ambassador Andropov* gave reassuring answers: the troop movements were aimed only at relieving other Soviet troops stationed in Hungary; the takeover of Hungarian airports by Soviet forces was to protect the evacuation of Soviet civilians from Hungary.

At 4 P.M. the Hungarian cabinet met. News of further entry by Soviet tank forces into Hungary had reached Budapest. In view of the Soviet violation of the treaty and upon the recommendation of Imre Nagy the cabinet unanimously approved the withdrawal of Hungary from the Warsaw Pact. Hungary declared itself to be a neutral country, invoking the example of Austria.

Notes were immediately sent to the great powers informing them of this decision. The prime minister also informed the secretary-general of the United Nations about the events and asked that "the question of Hungary's neutrality and the defense of this neutrality by the four Great Powers" be placed on the agenda of the General Assembly.[2]

The news of these decisions became known that evening and the following morning and was received with general rejoicing and satisfaction. It was as if the country had been relieved of a nightmare. The painful shackles of the hated Warsaw Pact had been thrown off, and Hungary had undertaken a historic step toward genuine international independence. In such an atmosphere of exhilaration few took notice of the imminent and menacing Soviet military buildup.

Yet the military movements, unmistakably directed against Buda-

---

*Yuri Andropov, later head of the Soviet KGB and general secretary of the Soviet Communist Party from November 1982 until his death in February 1984.—ED.

2. United Nations, *Report of the Special Committee on the Problem of Hungary* (New York, 1957), p. 58.

pest, could hardly be misunderstood. I believe that the instructions the Soviet General Staff sent to its forces stationed in the southwest corner of the Soviet Union and in Rumania preceded by some hours the final decision by the Soviet political leadership to intervene for the second time in Hungary and to restore a dependable Communist regime in that country. Simultaneously, they must have decided to use all possible tricks in order to deceive Hungarian and world leaders of their real intentions.

In view of this state of affairs the renunciation of the Warsaw Pact was not the motivation for the Soviet decision. This decision had been taken earlier. But the motivation for the Hungarian withdrawal from the Warsaw Pact was the Soviet menace, which threatened to suppress the Revolution.* For Imre Nagy this was an act of despair, the last straw of hope. He and his advisers might have thought that a neutral Hungary had a better chance to obtain assistance from the West and from the United Nations in particular.

While these dark clouds gathered on the Hungarian horizon, I watched developments in the West with desperation. Listening to the BBC broadcasts, I was able to learn and analyze the impact of these happenings on the fate of Hungary.

Unlike many other (even well-informed) intellectuals in Budapest, I considered it neither possible nor even wise for the Western powers, the United States in particular, to risk starting a third world war on Hungary's behalf. That was unrealistic to expect. But it was not unreasonable to believe that these powers would undertake everything short of war to preserve and strengthen the achievements of the Revolution, namely, a genuinely democratic and independent Hungary. The question was only superficially one of Hungary; it was more profoundly a question of Soviet control over what had become known as Eastern Europe. It was a question of Soviet imperialism and even of Communist expansion.

I remember discussing all this with some close friends in the seclusion of our back room. In view of the Cold War the East-West cleavage in the world should have demanded the closest attention of the leaders of the Western World. But these same leaders were now at loggerheads over the issue of Suez, an issue, whatever its outcome might have been, that

---

*Here Váli is arguing against the often-stated view that the USSR might not have intervened in Hungary if its leaders had not withdrawn from the Warsaw Pact. —ED.

was secondary in comparison with the global confrontation of our times.

It was quite evident from the handling of the Hungarian issue in the West that it occupied only subordinate attention there compared to Suez. Whereas the United Nations Security Council, and subsequently an emergency session of the General Assembly, promptly handled the Israeli and Anglo-French attacks on Egypt, for more than three days nothing was done concerning the Hungarian complaint to the United Nations. Prime Minister Imre Nagy dispatched not one but many such notes asking for speedy action. None of these were acted upon promptly, and the credentials of the new Hungarian representative were left unnoticed for many days on Secretary-General Hammarskjöld's desk, an oversight that later caused irreparable and unnecessary delays.

It was exasperating to realize that in this death-agony of a nation nothing was done. And when something was eventually done, it was too little and too late. There was a government in Hungary that would have readily cooperated with any action the United Nations might have taken. The secretary-general, a team of international observers, or a United Nations peacekeeping force would have been welcomed with open arms on Hungarian soil. Such actions would not have been inconsistent with international law, but there was no move in any such direction.

It was clear that the United States would have been less able to reach out militarily toward Hungary, as it was able to do two years later in Lebanon. However, there were other options: a military demonstration, a diplomatic initiative for an international meeting on this issue, or some collaboration with Yugoslavia,[3] a country anxiously watching these developments along its northern borders. Any such actions might have helped, though none were even attempted.

It is, of course, far from certain that any action might have prevented the Soviet onslaught. But it was known at that time, and confirmed later, that the Soviet Presidium had passed its ominous resolution only after considerable hesitation and that some members objected to it because it would have placed Russia in a bad light before the world and before the international workers' movement. Should the Soviet Union have been put in a more unpredictable situation before proceeding with renewed military aggression against Hungary, who knows, perhaps there

---

3. This was doubtful. Tito had personally endorsed the Soviet military intervention. See Nikita Khrushchev, *Khrushchev Remembers,* trans. and ed. Strobe Talbott (Boston: Little, Brown, 1970), p. 421. —ED.

would not have been a majority for the decision to eliminate the Imre Nagy government.

At any rate, as we saw it then, there was no reason, no excuse, for inaction. Moscow was allowed to play its cat-and-mouse game with Hungary by agreeing to negotiations for the withdrawal of Soviet forces at a time when the noose around Budapest was tightening hour by hour.

To delude the Hungarian leaders, on November 3 Soviet representatives began official talks with Prime Minister Nagy on the subject of Soviet military withdrawals. It was even decided that a political and a military committee should further discuss the details. A meeting of the military committee was set to take place on the same day at 10 P.M. at Tököl, the Soviet military headquarters south of Budapest.

On Saturday, November 3, the United Nations Security Council was scheduled to meet at 3 P.M. New York time (9 P.M. in Budapest) to consider the appeal of the Hungarian prime minister, between breaks in the Suez discussions. Upon the renewed assurances of the Soviet representative that negotiations were being held between Hungarian and Soviet delegations concerning the pullout of Soviet forces from Hungary, the discussion was again adjourned. A few hours later the Soviet attack began.

On that Saturday evening I sat together with a few friends in our apartment. We all concluded that the situation appeared dark. Still, some of us thought it was not hopeless. One of my friends said, "Even if the Russians should move to attack Budapest, they would meet resistance just as before. And even if they succeed in taking the city, what can they achieve? The country is now governed by workers' councils and national councils. The Communist Party is in shambles. The security police has been wiped out. If all Hungarians refuse to cooperate with the Russians, if Moscow is unable to find responsible persons to form a government (it will not dare to experiment with Stalinists), then what can it do? It will have to deal with Imre Nagy and the leaders of other parties. And eventually the Russians will have to pull out again."

I could not agree with such undue optimism. I responded, "Unfortunately, the Soviets will be able to find people who will be ready to cooperate with them and accept their conditions. What about Kádár, for instance? He participated in the cabinet meeting of November 1, that is, last Thursday. Then he disappeared. I was told that his whereabouts are unknown. And as to the people generally, they can be moved to cooperate by sheer force or by the necessity to survive. And some leaders will emerge to pull the Communist Party together once again. I am sorry to admit, if there is no help forthcoming now, there will be much less chance of it after the country is subdued. As a student of international affairs, I am too conscious of the tendencies to accept a fait accompli. Unpleasant accomplished facts in which the international community has eventually acquiesced are to be noticed in every corner of the globe."

While waiting for the news from the BBC, we thus discussed the events in a somber mood. When later, past midnight, it was announced that the Security Council had again adjourned without passing a resolution on Hungary (it was about to take up the Suez issue once again), we ended our discussion as well.

Rose and I went to bed. We were, however, awakened at four o'clock in the morning by cannon fire.

REVOLUTION SUPPRESSED

The cannonade became more and more intense. The telephone began ringing. Friends from various parts of the city reported their experiences. It was evident that the Soviets had attacked from all directions, but the thrust of the attack was on the Pest side. Now they came with infantry and heavy artillery. The BBC had earlier reported that ten new divisions with three thousand tanks had crossed the Hungarian border during the past few days.

This time the Soviet fighting behavior was ruthless. Upon meeting resistance, they would destroy the house from which shots were fired. They cared even less for civilians. The National Guard erected barricades with cobblestones and sandbags across the main thoroughfares, but it was easy for the heavy Soviet tanks to smash through these obstacles. They bypassed, however, certain centers of resistance and aimed for Parliament and to secure the Danube bridges.

At half past five Budapest radio, which up to that time had been silent, announced that the prime minister was to speak. "This is Imre Nagy speaking, the chairman of the Council of Ministers of the Hungarian People's Republic. Today at daybreak Soviet troops attacked our capital with the obvious intention of overthrowing the legal Hungarian democratic government. Our troops are in combat. The government is at its post. I notify the people of our country and the entire world of this fact."

This announcement was followed by the Hungarian national anthem. Then silence set in.

Rose and I now listened to the broadcast by the BBC from London. The United Nations Security Council was called into session at 3 A.M. New York time (it was 9 A.M. in Budapest). United States ambassador Henry Cabot Lodge informed the council that Budapest was under Soviet attack. He submitted a resolution that called on the Soviet Union to stop all forms of intervention in Hungary. It was vetoed by the Soviet representative. Then the Security Council decided by a vote of 10–1 to refer the question to the General Assembly.

Later in the morning we heard a radio message from an unknown station that shed light on the events to come. It was announced that a "revolutionary worker-peasant government" had been formed (it was not said where) under the chairmanship of János Kádár. The speaker also disclosed that Kádár and his friends were prompted to establish this new government because Imre Nagy had become a tool of the reactionaries.

An hour later I was listening to the Kádár government's program. It had some good words for the Revolution, which was directed "against the grave mistakes of Rákosi and Gerö." But soon, the broadcast continued, the well-meaning patriots were misled by reactionaries, and thus the movement ended by becoming a counterrevolution. The new regime promised to defend national independence, the democratic and socialist system, and the management of factories by the workers themselves. It even vowed that after the restoration of order it would start negotiations for the withdrawal of Soviet forces from Hungary. But there was no word of a multiparty system or about free elections.

In the afternoon I learned from telephone calls that Prime Minister Nagy and his close collaborators had sought refuge in the Yugoslav Embassy. The BBC announced that Cardinal Mindszenty had fled to the United States Legation. We also learned of the fate of General Maléter. He and the members of a military delegation had gone to the Soviet military headquarters at Tököl to discuss the promised withdrawal of Russian forces when they were duplicitously arrested at midnight. Thus, at the moment of the Soviet onslaught Hungary was deprived of most of her reliable military leaders. To lure opponents to one's camp and then arrest them was not a new feature in Hungary's history: this had happened several times earlier and was especially practiced by the Ottoman

Turks in the sixteen and seventeenth centuries. There is a Hungarian saying, "soon will come the black soup," which means that something ominous is going to happen. The black soup was the coffee usually served at the end of a meal when the unsuspecting guest was taken prisoner or even killed. Now, many centuries later, the Russians had resorted to the same trick.

There was, of course, no chance of venturing out into the streets. Fighting continued throughout the day in many parts of the city. We heard that the bulk of the National Guard, led by General Király, had taken up positions in the Buda Hills. There was also considerable combat in some provincial towns, but the situation appeared to be hopeless.[4]

Still, some of my friends placed their hopes in the United Nations, or expected Western powers (especially the United States) to react against this overt aggression. It would have required lengthy explanations to disabuse these credulous persons of their erroneous ideas. There were in my mind several questions about both the determination and even the capability of these putative saviors of our country. Moreover, my friends would hardly appreciate the fact that this was the end of the presidential campaign in America and that in two days, on Tuesday next, the presidential election would take place. It would have been mental cruelty to disclose to my friends that whether Eisenhower or Stevenson would be elected president weighed more strongly on the minds of most Americans than the tragic fate of Hungary.

Late that night while listening to the BBC, we heard that the emergency session of the United Nations General Assembly had approved a resolution by a vote of 53 in favor, 8 opposed, and 7 abstentions, which invited the Soviet Union "to desist forthwith from all armed attack on the people of Hungary . . . and to withdraw all its forces without delay from Hungarian territory."[5] I remembered that a similar invitation addressed to Great Britain and France to withdraw from the Suez Canal area was promptly complied with by these two states. But I felt certain that it would fall on deaf ears as far as Moscow was concerned.

Also irrelevant now was the request made by the General Assembly and addressed to the governments of Hungary and the Soviet Union to permit observers designated by the secretary-general to enter the terri-

---

4. Khrushchev writes that "our troops found themselves faced with well-organized defenses" (Khrushchev, *Khrushchev Remembers,* p. 422).

5. Resolution 1004 (ES-II). See U.N. General Assemby. Official Records. Second Emergency Special Session. Supplement no. 1 (A/3355), p. 2.

tory of Hungary. Had such a resolution been proposed and accepted two or three days earlier, the government of Imre Nagy would only have been most eager to receive such observers as well as the secretary-general himself, who attempted in vain to go to Hungary a week or so later. I do not think now, and did not think then, that the presence of observers would have prevented Moscow from using aggression. But who knows? Nevertheless, the uncertainty of success is no excuse for inactivity. As it happened, this and subsequent resolutions of the United Nations to assist Hungary proved to be whistles in the wind.

On the following day, Monday, November 5, we were forced to step out into the streets to try to purchase some food. Armed struggle still continued in some parts, but the center of the city was peaceful with the peace of a graveyard. There were hardly any people outside; traces of past fighting were to be seen everywhere. The only vehicles that moved were Soviet military automobiles or troop carriers. But on these vehicles one could discern some Hungarians — security police officers, who now joined the Soviet forces of occupation and provided them with advice and acted as interpreters.

In fact, Budapest and much of the country had become an administrative void; the prerevolutionary personnel had not yet returned, and the revolutionary institutions — national councils and new organs — had ceased to function, except for the workers' councils in the major factories. For the time being, the entire city and much of the country had come under the military administration of the armed forces of the Soviet Union.

The puppet government of Kádár entered Budapest only on November 7. It set up headquarters in the Parliament building, but it took several weeks and even months before it was able to exercise a modicum of authority over the country. The daily press, still somewhat free in its reporting, described the struggle Kádár had to wage in order to defeat the power of the workers' councils. On November 14 these even organized themselves into the Greater Budapest Workers' Council, which was able to declare strikes in protest against the regime and the army of occupation. But with the help of the Soviet army and the newly reorganized security police, the new regime gradually managed to extend its control. The instrument used for the intimidation and elimination of all elements of resistance was the old one; arrests were made by the Soviet security forces, and most of those arrested ended up somewhere in the Soviet Union or were never heard of again.

Members of the National Guard and the freedom fighters were the prime targets of persecution, but other participants in the revolutionary movements were also picked up and either deported to Soviet territory or, pending their condemnation, imprisoned in Hungary. Oddly enough, as we learned, Iván Boldizsár was apprehended by members of the Soviet intelligence services. However, after three days he was released, and his critics ironically hinted that he had "come to a new agreement" with them.

The danger of being arrested was brought home to me on November 9 when the house where we lived was surrounded by Soviet troop carriers and Soviet soldiers took up positions in the entrance and staircase of the building. Thereupon uniformed Hungarian security police agents invaded the apartments in search of freedom fighters and counterrevolutionaries. Two such uniformed agents with submachine guns on their shoulders entered our apartment. They were muscular, silent characters with deadpan expressions, possibly the result of their being forced into hiding during the successful days of the Revolution. "Is there anybody present in the apartment who does not live here?" they asked first. They perfunctorily searched all the rooms and then turned to Rose, my mother-in-law, and myself. They were mainly interested in me.

"Show us your identification card."

I gave them my card, which they examined very carefully. Then one asked: "Why were you registered on October 23? Have you been abroad?"

"No," I replied, "I happened to be in prison. Here is my release paper."

They read the paper with great attention and seemed hesitant. Finally, they returned the card and the paper, and without another word they left the apartment. It was a relief. Had they decided to take me and hand me over to the Russians, as frequently happened in those days, who knows where I would have ended up?

In every person's life there are problems that are mulled over in one's inner self, sometimes subconsciously, without admitting it openly even to oneself. Then comes a moment when, as if lit up by a flashbulb, the unconscious emerges, and one realizes what one wants or does not want.

That night when Rose and I retired, we said almost simultaneously to one another, "We must get away from here." There was no hesitation; we were determined. The only question to be resolved over the next few days or weeks was how and when to realize this objective. Although many people were leaving and escaping to the West in those days, it was still imperative to keep the plan secret. But in order to implement it, we had to seek advice and assistance.

We discussed it with our old reliable friend, S. M. P. "There is no future here for me, while there is plenty of danger," I told him. "If by staying here I could be of some help to our country, I would not think of leaving. But I don't think I could do anything useful. Ten years ago I returned from Turkey, though I could have gone to one of the Western countries. But it made sense at that time to come back. I felt it to be my duty. But now I have to think of Rose and myself. Even if I manage after six months to have my sentence invalidated, in this Hungary of Kádár I would still be a tainted person. I feel I have a calling to write, to publish, and to teach. Here all this is precluded to me. I would remain a frustrated person who had missed his purpose in life."

S. M. P. fully agreed with me. "You have to think of yourselves first, and I strongly advise you to leave as soon as possible."

"Wouldn't you like to join us?" Rose asked.

"No, I am sorry I cannot. I am too old to begin a new life abroad. Besides, I am much less vulnerable than you two are. And I can still perform useful services to my friends and others who might be in trouble. I am determined to stay."

When we left, we promised to see him once more before our final departure. In the meantime we had to work out our plan as best and as quickly as possible.

The so-called technical obstacles along the Hungarian-Austrian border—the barbed-wire fences and minefields—had been dismantled during the summer, so this risk factor could be ignored. From reports I was able to gather that the Hungarian border guard was still disorganized, operating only sporadically and unreliably; therefore, they would not interfere with persons wishing to leave the country illegally. The only danger along the border was presented by the Soviet forces, which now had deployed along that stretch of territory and had received orders to capture would-be escapees. But I was also assured that these Soviet units and individual soldiers were highly unfit for that task; they did not know the terrain, operated in large units, were not in touch with the local population, and were frightened by the possibility that groups of freedom fighters would fight their way through to Austria.

The main problem appeared to be how to reach the border area.

Railroad trains had ceased to run since the Russian invasion, at least not on a regular schedule. To rent a car or truck and proceed by road would be extremely risky. The Russians had set up roadblocks at various points to check passengers, and now they were assisted by the Hungarian security police in many provincial towns. To walk, of course, would be the safest way but would take a very long time, and Rose and I could not undertake such a strenuous endeavor. So we had to wait until the railroad trains started to run again.

News from Radio Free Europe and the BBC announced almost daily how many Hungarians had reached Austria. The number was impressive. In the second week of November it was already near fifty thousand. We were naturally impatient to leave, but we had to wait until a propitious time.

Upon meeting with friends in those days, the inevitable topic of conversation was, "Are you leaving for abroad or not?" We decided to keep our decision to ourselves and remained noncommittal. This was necessary because some of our friends and acquaintances approached us with the proposal, "Would you join us?" or "Could we join you?" We wanted to choose our own partners and not burden ourselves with persons who, in our opinion, were unfit to stand the test.

But we had friends who were determined, whatever might happen, to stay. Some had serious, others only flimsy reasons. Some had what was known as the piano or furniture complex; they were sorry to leave behind a piano or their furniture. Others had a good job they did not wish to give up for the hazards of a new existence abroad. We did not persuade anybody either to leave or to stay. But we were sorry to see some tragic situations. For instance, there was a friend of mine who had been an officer in the Horthy army and spent many years in Russian captivity. He had no job, but his wife had one, which she refused to abandon; so they stayed behind.

But there were also people who were optimistic about the political future. An old friend, who had been a Social Democrat all his adult life and for this reason had been imprisoned by the Communists, insisted that the present situation was only transitory and that the bad Stalinist times were over once and for all. I had a long discussion with him; he guessed that we were planning to get out of the country, and he tried to persuade me to stay. "Kádár," he explained, "is now in a vise between the Soviet army and the Hungarian people. He has spent years in prison and therefore is aware that totalitarian government is wrong. If you read his pronouncements, you can see that his efforts are directed toward establishing a socialist but not a dictatorial regime. The Russians are urging him to resort to terroristic measures in order to restore order and Communist Party rule. But he prefers to use persuasion. He will ultimately be successful in convincing Moscow that the Soviet system will not work in Hungary. The Soviet leaders have already learned by experience that Stalinism may be a danger to themselves. In Hungary you will see the ideas of Imre Nagy triumphing, that is, the emergence of a democratic socialism. Stalinism is a unique phenomenon, never to return."

I asked him a straightforward question: "Do you intend to work for this government? Haven't you said earlier, 'Never again'?"

He seemed somewhat perplexed, but eventually he replied. "Yes, I am ready to accept any public position. Actually, one has already been offered to me. It is a university post, not a political one. I want to cooperate to build *real* socialism in this country, and we shall be able to do so as soon as the Soviets cease interfering in our internal affairs. And they will eventually cease, as they already have in Poland."

"But how is it that you changed your mind?"

"I'll tell you. The Revolution was a wonderful thing. But in retrospect, it was senseless. We have to consider our geography. We live in close proximity to the Soviet Union and many thousands of miles from America. In foreign policy and in questions of defense we have to cooperate with Moscow. I am an admirer of Imre Nagy, but it was tragic that he was unable to understand this, or rather, that he allowed himself to be persuaded to abandon this principle."

"Don't you think that he only accepted what the Hungarian people wanted him to do? Don't you think that he wished to follow the desire of the people to achieve genuine independence?"

"There are times in politics when you should not follow the will of the people, especially if this will is based on emotion or the people's ignorance of the facts of the international situation."

"What you say involves two points: first, that you should oppose the people when you think you are right and they are not; second, that Imre Nagy should have conspired with Moscow in order to defeat the most important goals of the Revolution. He is evidently a person of integrity who was not prepared to do either, not the first nor the second."

"But a national leader also must have other qualities beyond integrity and character. He must have flexibility and astuteness, and foresight."

"What you are saying is really that Imre Nagy was wrong because he was unsuccessful. This is an argument I do not find convincing. It is a fallacy to believe that only a successful leader is right, and an unsuccessful one is wrong. These are different categories. And often he who appears to have been unsuccessful and, therefore, wrong may eventually, in history, prove that his ideas were correct and, therefore, that he was right from the beginning to the end."

My friend continued. "In my view, and this is really why I changed my mind, the Marxist-Leninist idea of unity in leadership and the social objectives can only be achieved by force. The outcome of the Revolution has proven this to me. But I do not subscribe to anything that sounds like Stalinism, which has nothing to do with either Marx or Lenin. The Stalinist excesses will not be repeated either in the Soviet Union or in Hungary or anywhere else in the world."

Now I realized where in fact our ways of thinking parted. I responded, "It is wrong to try to dissociate Lenin and Stalin, or Marx and Stalin for that matter. It was Lenin who created that system, a system partly based on Marxism, which Stalin used for his purposes. Without such a system, without such a mechanism, Stalin would not have been able to establish his brutal regime. After all, you know and I know that our imprisonment was made possible because, under the Leninist system, law and independent courts were abolished. This gives license to any future leader or leadership to imprison thousands, execute many, and terrorize an entire people. I do not deny that authoritarian and totalitarian governments are possible elsewhere. I only am convinced that the Leninist Soviet system provides the mechanism for leadership abuses, and it does so constitutionally and organically. I don't want to live in a country where the person in supreme power may at any time, that is to say, by the nature of the system, play with the lives and fate of his subordinates. And since the highest-level decisions are not really taken in Hungary but in Moscow, I even more strongly refuse to live in an environment where anything may—not necessarily will, but may—be determined by some oriental despot. In other words, the likelihood that excesses will be committed are infinitesimally greater under the Leninist Soviet system than under any other governmental system I know of. And it is this likelihood that I want to avoid after having once burned my fingers."

We parted as good friends, and I wished him luck. I do not know whether he has since changed his mind. I have not changed mine.

ESCAPE

Rose and I chose to escape with István and Éva D., and also with Laci, who would bring along his cousin. They had relatives in Western Hungary, not far from the border, and that might be important when we reached the frontier area. For this reason we also decided to travel first to the border town of Szombathely and not to a point near the direct Budapest-Vienna railroad line. I had a friend in the administration of the Hungarian state railroads. He promised to let me know as soon as scheduled trains started running again in the desired direction. On November 19, he informed me that the first regular train for Szombathely was leaving the Budapest-South station at 8 A.M. on Wednesday, November 21. We were eager to board that train.

The Danube bridges were still guarded by Soviet soldiers. We were uncertain whether they would let us pass in the early morning hours. On Tuesday afternoon all six of us crossed the Elizabeth Bridge (as we were used to calling it although a new name was given to it by the Communist regime) and entered the apartment of friends on the Buda side. The couple received us with sincere hospitality; they had given shelter to many refugees in the past weeks. The wife was ready to join us, but her husband, who had a steady job, opposed the move.

The apartment was not far from the Budapest-South station. At the crack of dawn we quietly left our friends' apartment and walked to the station. Many hundreds of people were already there. When the train pulled up it was stormed by this crowd; we had to fight our way into one of the passenger cars. The travelers were packed like sardines into the compartments and corridors. The six of us pressed ourselves into the toilet, where two could sit while the others stood. There was no use of the toilet for us or for anybody else in the car. It was impossible to move in the corridors.

The scene evoked a memory of my early youth. In the summer of 1914 my parents and I were vacationing in north Germany on the island of Rügen in the Baltic Sea. When the news of the Austro-Hungarian ultimatum reached my father, he immediately returned to Budapest. On July 31 my mother received a cable from my father enjoining us to return to Hungary at once. A general mobilization had been declared in Germany, and the outbreak of World War I was imminent. With my mother I entered a railroad station, where an immense crowd stormed the incoming train headed for Berlin. Robust German men with their wives and children fought to get into the cars. Many had been called to the colors, while some were going to replace others in their jobs. My mother was unable to climb up the steps amidst this mad scramble. She stood crying before the doorstep until a Hungarian lady friend pulled both of us up to the door and inside the car. The five-hour journey was most unpleasant; the toilets could not be used because they were crowded with passengers, as was happening on our present journey to western Hungary.

The journey to Szombathely lasted eight hours and was not without excitement. We carried knapsacks, as if we were on a walking tour, and if we had been questioned, our answers would have been that we were traveling to purchase food to take to Budapest. Still, at every stop (and these were often long stops) we feared a search by Russians or by the Hungarian security police.

At one of these prolonged stops I overheard two young men talking to each other in the corridor. "Do you have your gun ready?" asked one; and the other said, "Sure I have." These evidently were freedom fighters, prepared to shoot if necessary. I realized that a large military or police unit would be required to surround the train and to overcome its passengers since so many of them were armed. At the Sárvár station, about one hour before our destination of Szombathely, the freedom fighters left the train, evidently to move on foot and cross the border during the night.

So far no attempt had been made by railroad personnel to examine tickets; up to then a conductor would not have been able to walk the corridor. Now, the conductor appeared and almost jokingly asked, "Who has tickets?" We knew that the railroaders sided with the refugees.

It was almost dark when our train rolled into the station at Szombathely. In the station hall we noticed travelers being stopped and questioned by armed men at the exit. While we stood there not knowing what to do, a railroader approached us.

"The AVH is questioning passengers. I'll show you out through the back door."

We quickly walked away from the station to a house where István and Éva's relatives lived. It was a three-storied apartment house. Our hosts were surprised to see us. They were a frightened couple; the man was afraid of losing his job. They constantly warned us, "Softly, please, softly. One of our neighbors is a Communist Party member. They

shouldn't see you." The couple offered us hospitality for the night but no
further help. "Szombathely is surrounded by Soviet troops," they said.
"It would be very hazardous to try to cross the border from here." We
decided instead to move north, where many villages lie along the frontier.

The next morning we walked back to the station and boarded a local
train. We looked like a rather disheartened group, and Laci continually
repeated, "I don't know what to do, I don't know what to do."

It was a very slow train, but by early afternoon it reached the station of Csepreg, where we stepped out and hurried along the road that
led to the village. We were told where Laci's relatives lived, and we soon
found the spacious house in the middle of a large courtyard with stables,
horses, and poultry.

In contrast to our friends in Szombathely, we were met here with the
unperturbed calm of steadfast farmers. The head of the household was a
matriarch, a dignified woman in her sixties who must have been a beauty
in her younger days. When we told her the purpose of our visit, she
quickly issued the required instructions. "You will stay here tonight and
have a good rest. Tomorrow morning"—she addressed herself now to
one of the men—"you, Peter, will take them, with the necessary precau-
tions, to Alsovis, to a cousin who will guide them over the border."

We were given a hearty meal, and our beds were assigned us. The
next morning, November 23, we were invited to an opulent breakfast. At
the table Peter spoke. "Last night I listened to Vienna radio. Do you
know that Imre Nagy and his associates left the Yugoslav Embassy yesterday and were kidnapped by the Russians, who took them to some
unknown place? The radio also said that Kádár has promised Nagy that
he will be allowed to return to his home. At least, this is what I heard,
and whether all this is true, I don't know."

Despite the innate skepticism of Hungarian farmers, I was convinced that the news was true. Evidently, the Yugoslavs wished to get rid
of Imre Nagy and his entourage, and Kádár's promise gave them an
excuse to rid themselves of a cumbersome guest. There was no news of
Cardinal Mindszenty, who was a guest at the United States Legation.

We gave our thanks and said good-bye to the matriarch. Peter
waited at the door with a long, open cart driven by two hefty horses. All
six of us laid down on the floor of the cart. We were then covered with
cornstalks up to the level of the railings on both sides. It felt stuffy down

there, and at first I had some difficulty breathing on account of my recurrent claustrophobia. But soon I became accustomed to the position and was able to get fresh air through a hole.

Peter told us not to move and not to utter a sound, especially when the cart stopped. Russians, he said, often patrolled the road.

I had carried with me an old, detailed Austro-Hungarian military map of the region, on which I had checked the distance we had to cover and direction we had to proceed. The distance was no longer than eight miles, so I expected we should be there in two hours.

The horses trotted or walked. We stopped a few times. Once I over-heard a conversation. It was in Hungarian; but, of course, Russians used Hungarian interpreters. Then the cart was moving again, and eventually it turned left and then right, and stopped. I heard friendly voices and then laughter. The cornstalks were removed by quick hands, and we saw that we were in the courtyard of another, smaller house. It must have been in the village of Alsovis.

A middle-aged man and a woman greeted us cordially. We said good-bye to Peter, who returned with the cart to Csepreg. When we entered the house, we found about twenty persons, all refugees, waiting to be taken across the border. Our host was most reassuring. "I'll manage them all. Just wait your turn. First come, first served."

In the early afternoon our host selected seven or eight persons. A few of them were to carry hoes and rakes, as if they were going out to work in the fields. "These stupid Russians," our host remarked, "they don't know that there is no agricultural work done this time of the year."

After about an hour the man returned. "They are now over the border and safe," he announced.

Some time later he collected another group of five or six. They left, but after less than half an hour all returned. "The Russians have just arrested two people out in the fields. It's too risky to go out again."

During the day our hostess was cooking all the time. We were of-fered first potatoes paprika and later in the day potatoes in tomato sauce. Our host frequently conferred with neighbors, who evidently had similar problems at hand. Young boys were coming and going with re-ports of where the Russians were.

Around eight in the evening our farmer returned from the village street. "I will take all of you now. The Russians have withdrawn into larger units; they are afraid in the dark. But they may be on one of the hills. You will have to follow me one by one, and if I throw myself to the

ground, you do the same. You may have to run, so leave behind everything that may hinder you in running. And do not utter a sound."

The group of about twelve people assembled in a barn. It was pitch-
dark there. We left our knapsacks behind, keeping only a toothbrush.

Then our leader led us out of the barn and into an open field. There
was dim moonlight. At places the ground was covered with light snow
and was uneven, a fact that impeded rapid movement. Rose had a cold
and had difficulty going fast. I held her arm. Then our guide threw
himself to the ground, and we all followed his example. In the distance I
saw some shadows moving silently. It must have been another group of
refugees.

Soon we moved again. Rose said, "We must be in Austria now. It
seems that we have been running for two hours." "No, no," I said, "less
than twenty minutes, I think. The border is about a mile and a half from
where we started."

The dangerous hill loomed on our right, but we passed under it
without anything happening. Then we reached a narrow, uncultivated
stretch. "This must have been where the minefield was placed," I told
myself. Then we entered a vineyard that our host had mentioned as
being on the Austrian side of the border. At an open space our guide
suddenly halted.

"You are now on Austrian territory. Do you see dim lights in the
distance, on the right and on the left? Those are Hungarian villages.
Don't stray away in those directions. Go straight forward, then you will
reach the first Austrian town."

The man never asked for a penny. Now we gave him most of the
Hungarian money we had on us and thanked him.

One of our fellow refugees carried a bundle over his shoulder. He
now opened it, and out tumbled a puli, a small Hungarian sheepdog.
The dog ran around happily and sniffed our feet. The man should have
been reprimanded, at least, but we were all so happy that nobody said a
word.

We marched forward, now at a slower gait. I remembered that my
map had shown that an Austrian town by the name of Lutzmannsburg
was at the bottom of a steep declivity. We soon reached the edge of a
cliff; below us the lights of the town were clearly visible. We descended a
steep incline and entered a street. We met a passerby, and I asked him,
"Is this Lutzmannsburg?"

The man answered, "Yes, it is. And if you are Hungarian refugees, go to the school building. There you will get a hot meal." He even showed us the way.

There were more than a hundred refugees in the school. We got our meal. Then I inquired of a person in charge about our further prospects. He said, "If you have no possibility of going elsewhere, a bus will pick you up in a day or two and take you to a camp. There you will be processed further."

Éva's father was in Vienna, and she was desperate to get in touch with him. I went with her to the nearby gendarmerie station and spoke to the sergeant in command. "We would like to place a call to Vienna. But we have nothing except some Hungarian money, which is worth little here."

The sergeant smiled. "I also speak Hungarian. But your German is perfect. We will make it an official call."

It was 11 P.M., but there was no answer at the number. Despondent, we returned to the school. Half an hour later the sergeant appeared. "I called the number again, and there was an answer. They are coming by car to pick you up. So you all are to come to the station, where they will look for you." We moved to the gendarmerie station and tried to get some sleep in the empty jail, but we were so excited that this was hardly possible.

At four o'clock in the morning the car arrived. We were soon on the road to Vienna. It was about eight and dawning when our car entered the former imperial city. About eight years had passed since I had been there last as an official member of a Hungarian ministerial delegation. Now I entered as a destitute refugee. A full circle, indeed.

V

The Career of a Political Refugee

And thou shalt prove how salt to taste is e'er
Another's bread, and how the path is hard
Which goeth down and up another's stair.

Dante, Paradiso, XVII.58–60

FREE, DESTITUTE, AND STATELESS

I told Rose that as soon as we crossed the Iron Curtain, everything would be all right. I did not deceive her. "Everything" is relative; and with this relativity in mind, everything was all right, though not at once. There were many obstacles to overcome, many crucial decisions to make, many mistakes to avoid before everything turned out for the better. But despite being destitute and practically stateless individuals in Austria, we already felt incomparably better than we had in Hungary.

Vienna, we realized, was for us the gateway to another world. After ten years behind the Iron Curtain (including five of them behind prison bars) Vienna represented more than a recovery from a fatal illness for Rose and myself. It was like a reincarnation from a lower life form into human existence.

Looking back to those few weeks in Vienna, I can only think with gratitude of all those who generously helped us. The people of Vienna showed us so many instances of kindness that it would be difficult to remember all of them. There was the hairstylist who refused money from Rose, and there were the streetcar conductors, whose union voted not to require tickets from Hungarian refugees. Vienna's Soviet sector and lower Austria had been relieved of the incubus of Soviet occupation only a year before, so their people felt a special sympathy for those who had managed to extricate themselves from the constraints of foreign oppression.

We felt very much at home in this city and liked the happy-go-lucky temper of its inhabitants. In my boyhood (it was Austria-Hungary until my thirteenth year) I had spent much time in Austria, and Rose had spent a year in school in Vienna.

We encountered many expressions of individual goodwill and generosity. I called on friends from my time in Turkey: Prof. Clemens Holzmeister and his gracious wife, Gunda, who had both experienced the anguish of exile. Professor Holzmeister, a famous architect, had planned the new Parliament building in Ankara and happened to be in Turkey when Hitler invaded Austria. A leading figure in the Christian Socialist Party, he refrained from returning to Austria and instead accepted a teaching post at the Technical University of Istanbul. At the end of the war he returned to Vienna and to the chair of architecture at the University of Vienna.

The Holzmeisters arranged a party in our honor and invited a number of prominent people who were also ready to help us. After the dinner the professor took me aside: "Please, no undue modesty. You need money." And he almost forced on me a handsome amount in Austrian schillings.

Another friend was Alfred Verdross, an internationally known professor of international law. In 1947 Verdross, with a group of jurists, visited Budapest. Vienna was still starving, but I was able to offer him hospitality and good food, which was abundant in Hungary in those days. Professor Verdross introduced me to the rector of the University of Vienna, who told me, "A representative of the American Rockefeller Foundation came to see me yesterday. He is here to look for Hungarian refugee scholars who may need some help. I will talk to him about you and suggest you go and visit him in his hotel."

The very next day I called on Dr. John Maier, who after a brief introductory talk asked me point-blank, "Do you want to submit a study project? If it is approved in New York, you may obtain a fellowship for one year."

I immediately began preparing a project. It had to be a somewhat tentative one. I planned to follow up the study that originally had been my dissertation topic for the doctorate I obtained from the University of London and that subsequently was published in England. That had been some twenty-three years ago, and I wished to examine pertinent developments that had taken place since then in the world. I took the project to Dr. Maier, who promised to forward it to New York. Since we soon were to leave Vienna for London, he gave me the address of the Rockefeller Foundation's London office, where I could inquire after arriving there.

Professor Holzmeister had a further surprise for us. "You are exhausted, you need a rest. I have a chalet in the Tyrol, on the Hahnenkamm above the town of Kitzbühel. Take two of your friends and go there for a week or so. I have already informed the housekeeper of your arrival."

With Éva and István D. we took the train to Kitzbühel, a famous ski resort, ascended by cable car to the Hahnenkamm, and found the Holzmeister chalet with ease. Snow and sunshine were abundant and the high mountain air filled our lungs.

Later, back in Vienna, I made arrangements for our trip to London. It was in England, where I had been a student, that I had friends and acquaintances who could help me to embark on a new academic career. At the British Embassy in Vienna I met an old acquaintance by the name of Leslie Szilagyi. He was the scion of a Hungarian family and had settled in England many decades before. Leslie had joined the British diplomatic service, but he retained his name, rather cumbersome for the English to pronounce. He spoke fluent Hungarian and was therefore assigned to Vienna to assist Hungarian refugees, whose numbers by now had swollen to one hundred fifty thousand.

Leslie placed us on his list; we would be taken to England with the next transport. After a few days we were instructed to board a bus at noon on December 17. This was one of the buses that brought gift packages to Hungarian refugees in Austria and returned to England with refugees on board. Our particular bus had come from the city of Bristol. Three buses with a complement of two hundred fifty refugees left Vienna on the road across the continent to a channel port.

We traveled leisurely for five days until we reached London. After our Hungarian quarantine and prison isolation it was a most exhilarating journey. Our travel companions were mostly young men and women who had never left Hungary. Many of them had never eaten an orange or a banana, spoke only Hungarian, and had received a Communist education.

An English doctor accompanied our transport. He was in constant search of a patient, but, to his disappointment, everybody was healthy. At long last, after a few days, one young worker complained of having some stomach disorder. He hoped, as he admitted to us, that the doctor would prescribe the traditional Hungarian remedy for such an ailment, namely, a glass of brandy or a similar hard drink. To his consternation, the doctor ordered him to drink milk several times a day.

We reached the English Channel at the French port of Boulogne. Our doctor hoped, I believe, to provide medication to those who became seasick during the usually rough voyage. Another disappointment! The sea happened to be as calm as milk. I have never experienced such a smooth Channel crossing.

We spent one night in a London hostel but, to my sorrow, had to go on to Bristol the following day. It was just before Christmas. In the Bristol hostel men and women slept in separate dormitories. It was a very cold winter for England, and heating was minimal. The first morning Rose, who had never been in England before, told me, "The matron in my part of the building gave me a hot water bottle. She advised me that I should purchase such a bottle with the first money I earn, for it is the most important utensil in England."

I was deeply touched by the people of Bristol—laymen and clergymen, men and women—who came to entertain us on Christmas Day. There was the language barrier for practically everybody—I had to translate, assisted by a Hungarian lady who had married a local businessman. Still, our visitors tried their best to organize games and provide amusements in the English Christmas tradition for these refugees, who were so forlorn in this unaccustomed environment.

On December 27, following the English Boxing Day, Rose and I went to the nearby police station, where we were given our identification cards and were permitted to leave for London. Friends of ours had made reservations for us in the Basil Street Hotel until we could find an apartment.

I hurried to call Miss H. B. Lynn, the secretary of the Rockefeller Foundation. My name was familiar to her, and she exclaimed, "I have a check for you!"

"What about my application for a fellowship?" I asked.

"I don't know about that. The papers have probably been sent to Vienna. But come and collect your check."

The "papers" also arrived later, and I was informed that a fellowship had been awarded to me. Few people who have not experienced the same predicament would realize how miraculous it was for a destitute refugee to obtain a comfortable allowance for a full year. We certainly considered ourselves fortunate.

We rented a small furnished flat and I endeavored to reestablish ties interrupted by the war years and by my incarceration. In my old school, the London School of Economics and Political Science, I was given the status of a visiting scholar. I was thus able to use the library and to eat with the faculty in the refectory. Among my former teachers only Charles Manning was still active there. Professor and Mrs. Manning proved to be extremely helpful. Prof. L. C. B. (Jim) Gower and his wife Peggy befriended us and gave me useful advice. They introduced us to Ed Jaegerman, an American visiting scholar who worked for the Securities and Exchange Commission. Both Rose and I were happily impressed when they invited us to stay at their home, should we come to Washington, D.C.

Dr. Lauterpacht, my principal instructor in the London School of Economics during the years 1929–32, had risen to become professor of international law at Cambridge University. More recently he had been elected the British judge at the International Court of Justice at The Hague, and he had been knighted. I wrote to Sir Hersch (as he now was called) and received an immediate reply. On January 31, 1957, I met him in the London Athenaeum Club. I explained my situation, and he gave me excellent advice: "You should prepare a revised and extended edition of your book, *Servitudes of International Law.* This book is sold out, and you were correct in proposing to the Rockefeller Foundation that you work along this line. Many new developments have taken place since the book was published in 1933, and they deserve analysis and inclusion in the new edition. We have here in England the International Law Fund, which could support the publication of your manuscript."

I told Sir Hersch that we wished eventually to go to the United States. "I can only agree with your plan," he said. "We are too congested on this small island. It would be very difficult to get a decent university appointment in Britain. In the United States there are some two thousand institutions of higher education. I shall recommend you to some of my friends in that country, and I have no doubt that you will be successful in getting an appropriate job."

I had started to revise my earlier book upon our arrival in London. But now, with the encouragement of Sir Hersch, I was eager to complete it as soon as possible. However, I was slowed down in this endeavor because I was often called upon to speak on the events in Hungary. Malcolm Muggeridge, the well-known writer and television commentator, interviewed me. I gave talks to several groups of students, British and foreign. Professor Manning was instrumental in arranging a public lecture for me at the London School of Economics. Its title was "The Hungarian Revolution and International Law," and it was held on April 30. I had a large audience and entertained many questions.

In my application to the Rockefeller Foundation I foresaw the possibility of travel to France, Switzerland, and the Netherlands for the purposes of my research. I wished to complete my manuscript at The Hague, where the Peace Palace Library offered a unique collection of international treaties and related material. But travel was not a simple matter for refugees. Technically we were not stateless, because we had not lost our Hungarian citizenship. But we had no travel papers, and it would have been inconceivable for us to ask for Hungarian documents. Hence de facto, we were stateless.

Fortunately, in the 1950s the West European states had entered into an agreement to provide travel documents to stateless persons, most of them refugees from behind the Iron Curtain. We applied for and received British "certificates of identity, in lieu of passports," as they were officially named. They somewhat resembled British passports, but we required visas for entering any country. The French issued visas for several entries without much ado, but I had difficulties with the Swiss and the Dutch. We obtained our visa for Switzerland only in Paris, when I named as my reference the undersecretary in the Swiss Trade Department with whom I negotiated the oil deal in 1948. We were still waiting for the Dutch visas to arrive. I then wrote a letter to Ambassador Van Kleffens, who was accredited to NATO as the Dutch representative and whom I had met many times while in Holland. The result was quite explosive: the Dutch Embassy phoned three times urging us to come and get the entry permits. I felt sorry for other refugees, poor devils, who had no such high-level contacts.

We spent more than a month in Paris, enjoying the amenities and splendor of this city of lights. We met Tibor Dánielfy and many other friends, among them Paul de Auer, the former Hungarian ambassador to France. I called on the Rockefeller Foundation's office and again saw Dr. Maier. As a former legal advisor to IBM Budapest, I also had the chance to meet Arthur K. Watson, president of the IBM World Trade

Corporation and later American ambassador to France.

We left at the end of June for Geneva, where we again met Professor Verdross, who was the Austrian member of the United Nations International Law Commission, which was in session there. I had several interviews with United Nations officials that I needed for my research. Then we proceeded to The Hague. My old school, the Academy of International Law, gave me the address of a pension, where we settled comfortably and inexpensively.

My main occupation at The Hague was to do research in the library of the Peace Palace. But I also attended lectures at the Academy and listened to cases tried before the International Court of Justice. The court being in session, Sir Hersch Lauterpacht was in residence. He lavishly entertained us in his home, and we also enjoyed the hospitality of some Dutch friends. To my deep regret I learned that my closest Dutch friend, L. H. J. J. Mazel, had been executed by the Germans at the end of the war. He was one of the hostages killed in retaliation for the deaths of German soldiers.

We returned to London on August 9. Jim Gower soon sent word that he wanted to introduce me to his friend, Gray Thoron, dean of Cornell Law School. The meeting took place, and the dean encouraged me to contact him when I got to the United States.

During the following weeks I completed my manuscript. I applied for a grant-in-aid from the International Law Fund, as Sir Hersch had suggested, to subsidize its publication. The subsidy was approved promptly and the printing of the book, by Stevens & Son, was assured.

Since our return to London I had been busy with securing our admission into the United States. We would have been taken to America from Vienna without many formalities, but from a "secondary country of immigration," such as Great Britain, the bureaucratic formalities were more lengthy. We became frequent visitors to the U.S. Consulate General to fill out various application forms. In one of these we were expected to declare under oath that we had never before been sentenced for a crime.

"I can't possibly sign this," I told the vice-consul, "you know I spent five years in jail."

The official was somewhat puzzled, but then told us, "Add to your declaration, 'Except that I was sentenced to fifteen years imprisonment for high treason and conspiracy.' That will do." With this proviso I signed, and so did Rose.

This took place at the end of August, and for nearly two months there was no response. I corresponded with several friends in the United States, who gave us advice on what to do or attempted to intervene to hasten matters. I even retained a lawyer in Washington to expedite the decision.

One of my American friends was of long standing. I had met Francis Birch in 1926 at the University of Dijon in France. In the following years, while he was still in Europe on a scholarship, I had traveled with him in Germany, and a few years later he visited me in Budapest. But by the late 1930s, because of the various crises, the war, and my postwar difficulties, we had lost touch. I knew that Francis was a geophysicist and a graduate of Harvard University. At random I wrote to him at Harvard and received a quick reply. He had become a professor of geology and had participated in the Los Alamos experiments with the atomic bomb. In fact, he was quite a famous man in his field. He was able to provide me with useful information.

At the end of October, Hungarians in Great Britain, joined by many groups in that country, commemorated the anniversary of the Hungarian Revolution. The developments that had taken place since Rose and I left Hungary were most depressing. A wave of violent repression had begun against participants in the revolt as well as against all those who displayed attitudes considered inimical to the regime. Many thousands had been arrested, hundreds sentenced to death and executed; the Writers' Association had been dissolved, and the workers' councils silenced. My mother-in-law wrote us in veiled language that detectives had questioned her about my whereabouts. The secretary-general of the United Nations attempted in vain to go to Hungary; he should have gone earlier, during and not after the collapse of the revolt. Resolutions by the United Nations General Assembly remained whistles in the wind. A special committee set up to prepare a report on the events was also refused admission to Hungary. Its report, which was made public in June 1957, was an impressive but academic condemnation of the Soviet intervention and of the Kádár regime imposed on the people of Hungary.

Although the permit for our admission to the United States came by mid-November, we still had to undergo another screening. We were summoned to the American Embassy, together with other Hungarians, to be interviewed by an official specially experienced in dealing with these refugees. He certainly was familiar with their circumstances. When I was admitted to his office, he asked for my military booklet, which every

Hungarian male was expected to carry. Mine had miraculously survived my prison term, and I gave it to him. He immediately turned to question 10 on page 3 of the booklet, dealing with party affiliation. When he read "nonparty," he nodded approvingly and only asked some general questions of us.

But not all the Hungarians who were there passed the scrutiny with flying colors. In the case of one young man, the answer to question 10 was smeared and unreadable. Evidently, he was a Communist Party member and was trying to conceal his affiliation. He was told to leave. Under the McCarran Act, Communists needed a State Department waiver to be admitted.

The Rockefeller Foundation was prepared to pay our fare to the United States. We hoped to cross the Atlantic on the French liner *France*. But the American Consulate General informed us that we had to take transportation arranged by the Immigration and Naturalization Service.

After a waiting period of several weeks word was sent to us that the plane that would take us to New York was leaving on December 16. The flight originated in Frankfurt; it carried some eighty Hungarian refugees, and half a dozen more were added in London. For good measure, before leaving Frankfurt, some twenty German orphans were placed in the laps of the travelers, children sent for adoption to the United States. The plane was a rather outmoded DC-4.

After our departure from Heathrow Airport we landed in Shannon, Ireland, to refuel before crossing the Atlantic. At around 6 P.M. we left Shannon and were two hours out over the sea when the plane suddenly lost altitude. Being the only passengers who spoke English, we asked the stewardesses what was going on. "We have lost one engine and are returning to Shannon. But don't tell the others; we don't want a panic on board."

Later the captain emerged from the cockpit and loosened the cords of the rubber boat, while Rose and I sat in silent dread. When lights appeared on the ground, the lights of Ireland, our Hungarian fellow passengers exclaimed, "America, we are over America!" There was considerable disappointment when we landed at the same place from where we started four hours earlier.

Our party spent the next four nights in Shannon. Once we took off again but immediately returned to the airfield. Finally, spare parts arrived from London, and we restarted our voyage across the ocean.

This time the plane made it. After a record flight of fourteen hours we landed in Gander, Newfoundland. It was midnight; we had to wait there several hours, because New York would not receive the plane before 6 A.M. During the last leg of our journey we encountered a violent thunderstorm over the Boston area that buffeted the craft as lightning struck on both sides. The passengers screamed, and the German children wept. In contrast, we flew over Manhattan in clear, dark weather and admired the skyline of the city and the lights of the skyscrapers. It had been a record slow flight, but we had at last come to the New World.

From Idlewild (as Kennedy Airport was then called) we were taken to the Saint George Hotel in Brooklyn for final processing. Our friends in England had warned us that New York was much colder in winter than London, so we were wearing heavy winter coats and sweaters. As it happened, that December 21 was unseasonably warm, and the hotel was overheated. While moving from one room to the other in our heavy clothing and with our luggage (we now had acquired certain "belongings"), we felt unbearably hot. We were all lined up once more in the hotel hall to be interviewed by the U.S. Immigration and Naturalization Service when Rose fainted. We gained at least one advantage from this unpleasant episode: we were quickly interviewed.

The other Hungarian refugees who had individual sponsors, relatives, or friends were immediately dispatched to them, even if it meant traveling by train to California. Our sponsor, through the good offices of the Rockefeller Foundation, was the National Science Foundation. Therefore, we were given a room at the St. George Hotel at Uncle Sam's expense until we could find a place to live. Exhausted, we went to bed but were frequently awakened by friends in New York who phoned to ask whether we had arrived. Well, we had.

IN THE NEW WORLD

Many years after our arrival in the United States I was asked by a friend, "What was the most striking single characteristic that, in your view, distinguishes this country from those you have known in Europe?" I answered, "Egalitarianism." Indeed, there is far less submissiveness, if any, in the contact between Americans of all strata than one can experience in Europe and most other parts of the world as well. It is not without cause that Teddy Roosevelt declared that the first requisite of a

good citizen be that "he should be able and willing to pull his weight."
Well, he does and she does.

I have found this emphatic egalitarianism to be most refreshing and
seldom disturbing. Prof. Philip C. Jessup, then on the faculty of Columbia University, had served the Truman Administration as ambassador-at-
large, and also as the United States permanent representative to the
United Nations. When I first visited this globally respected scholar of
international law at his Columbia office, I was struck that his secretary
addressed him as *Mister* Jessup. I recalled that in Communist Hungary,
whereas Party members were "comrades," non-Party persons were nobo-
dies; a minister expected to be called Comrade Minister, a professor
Comrade Professor, and the wife of a minister did not refuse to be
addressed as Your Excellency.

This egalitarianism was particularly noticeable in New York, where,
from the newspaper boy to the taxicab driver, from the coffeeshop at-
tendant to the cleaning woman, all displayed a cheerful and free direct-
ness.

Another important impression I gained was the friendly attitude
toward immigrants, especially recent immigrants. This attitude may not
be found throughout the United States at present, but it certainly prevailed in New York then. In the subway we read a poster: "Immigrants
welcome, it is you who made America great." Of course, we also realized
that New York was, so to speak, saturated with relatively recent immigrants, more so than any other city in America. As a janitor jokingly
remarked to me, "You don't have to go to Europe; Europe is coming
here."

If it had been only Europe, it would have been a simple experience.
But I found New York to be the crucible of the entire world, of all the
five continents. If one were to undertake anthropological or ethnic stud-
ies, one could do it in New York alone. The abounding humanity of New
York is overpowering. I had to remind myself that the population of
Greater New York equaled that of a country—of Hungary, for example.

At the time when we came to the United States, everybody still
remembered the Hungarian Revolution. If other immigrants were
welcome, Hungarian refugees were more welcome. I wondered whether
there was a kind of collective guilt complex for not having helped
Hungary, or was it rather admiration for a heroic revolt? Or was it both?
Whatever the cause, there was a spontaneous willingness everywhere to
help the Hungarian refugees, both by individuals and by public bodies.

The days when immigrants from that part of the world were derisively called "hunkies" were evidently gone.

It appeared to us that there were many more Americans of Hungarian descent than were listed by statistics. Those who had only one Hungarian ancestor (for instance, one Hungarian grandparent) often proudly proclaimed themselves to be Hungarian. In Columbus, Ohio, a university faculty member proudly confided to me that his wife was the descendant of a Hungarian-Transylvanian prince. In Brooklyn a shop assistant mentioned that she too was Hungarian. When addressed in this language, she ruefully admitted not being able to utter even one Hungarian word; a grandparent on her mother's side had come from Hungary.

My Rockefeller Fellowship was extended for another year, so that I would have time to look for a job at leisure. My contacts in Great Britain now became useful in the New World. As he promised, Sir Hersch Lauterpacht had written to Philip C. Jessup, and on January 17 the latter invited me to lunch at the Columbia University Faculty Club. Jessup was accompanied by a colleague, Oliver J. Lissitzyn, who also taught international law. At the table there was no end of questions about my antecedents, prison experiences, and future plans. Thereafter, Philip Jessup, a charitable and charming man of the world, became the mainstay of my future employment and career in the New World.

At Columbia University I also met old Hungarian friends: Tibor Halasi-Kun, professor of Turkish studies (whom I had met during my stay in Turkey), and Charles Szladits, adjunct professor of comparative law, whose father had been one of my law teachers in Budapest.

Dean Thoron of the Cornell University Law School invited me to give a lecture. He was amazed when I arrived by train. He said I had been the first visitor in his experience who had traveled to Ithaca by this conveyance. For me, the natural thing was to travel by train and not by bus or plane.

On February 22 I went to Columbus, Ohio, to participate in a panel discussion, called a "town meeting," on Eastern Europe. One of the panelists was none other than Walter Birge, the wartime American vice-consul in Istanbul, who had exchanged his State Department post for one in industry.

We left a hospitable and impressive New York on April 18 for Washington. Ed Jaegerman and his wife meant it when they invited us back in London to stay at their house in Bethesda, Maryland. There we became acquainted with the intricacies of an American household. They had five children, and in the daytime, while both father and mother were out to work, a nanny watched over the smaller children. Ed was in government service, and Midder was a high school teacher. Rose was terribly touched when she was told, "Whenever you want something, just open the refrigerator and help yourself." Later we realized that this was what the children did when they wanted something to eat.

One day Rose was alone in the house, and a black car, seemingly huge enough to be a limousine, pulled up the driveway. Out stepped an elegantly dressed middle-aged man, who rang the bell. Rose believed that he must be an important visitor, perhaps a colleague of Ed's, and she prepared herself to act as the substitute hostess. She asked the man to sit down and offered him coffee or tea. But the visitor, smiling, declined: "I am the exterminator. I came to look around the house to see if there is anything to be done." Fortunately, Rose was already acquainted with the profession of an "exterminator"; otherwise she might have had a fit.

In Washington I visited several people to whom I had introductions, among them Colonel Townsend, an undersecretary in the Department of Justice. He had been instrumental in issuing the permit for our entry into the United States. I also saw officials in the Department of State, those at the Hungarian desk and those dealing with United Nations affairs (where the Hungarian question was still pending). We also did some sightseeing and were impressed by the layout of Washington (resembling Paris) and its public buildings.

By May 9, however, we were back in New York, but only for a few days. I had invitations to go to Yale and Harvard universities. At Yale our host was Eugene V. Rostow, then dean of the law school and later an undersecretary in the Department of State. He gave Rose and me a dinner party; he even delivered a welcoming address in which—most flatteringly—he recalled that Erasmus, the Dutch philosopher, had been a political refugee in England and taught at one of the Oxford colleges, where an inscription commemorates the event. Rostow also recalled that in almost every epoch scholars had been forced to leave their native land because of intolerance and persecution.

In Cambridge, Massachusetts, we met Francis Birch and his wife Barbara. But one of the main purposes of my visit to Harvard was to call on Professor Robert R. Bowie. I came to see him upon the recommendation of Philip Jessup, who hinted that Bowie might have an opening for me. Formerly a professor in the Harvard Law School, Bowie had joined the State Department and in the years 1955–57 had been assistant secretary of state for policy planning. He then returned to Harvard, where he joined the Department of Government.

After a preliminary conversation Bowie, in a refreshingly business-like manner, raised the question that was all important for me. "We are setting up a new research center here, named the Center for International Affairs, where the research staff — research associates, assistants, and fellows — are to work on individual assignments or collective group assignments with the purpose of eventually writing book-length studies. Among others, we are planning to have a European program where both West and East European topics will be handled. I have already approached a young assistant professor, Zbigniew Brzezinski, to do research on the relations of the Soviet Union with the East European countries. Should we choose to have somebody to do research on the recent revolutionary events in Hungary, would you be willing to accept such an assignment?"

Although at that moment I was still thinking of international law as my main focus of interest, I said, "Yes, I possibly could undertake such research."

Bowie continued. "I see from your curriculum that your original area of specialization is in international law. I myself, before I worked in the State Department, had been teaching law. But I assure you my transition from law to politics was not difficult."

"Tomorrow," I told him, "I have an appointment to see Dean Griswold to discuss with him the possibility of securing a job in a law school to teach international law. But I would like to ask you to keep open for me the assignment you have just mentioned."

Bowie smiled. "Go and see him, by all means. In any case keep me informed of your whereabouts so that I can reach you, should we decide to have something done on Hungary."

Jim Gower had written from London to Erwin Nathaniel Griswold, dean of the Harvard Law School (he later served as solicitor general). Griswold, an outspoken and stern personality, listened to me carefully when I appeared before him on the following day.

"We have no opening here for somebody in the field of international law," he explained. "And it will not be easy for you to obtain an appointment in this field anywhere in this country. Only a few law schools, only the bigger and better ones, have international law positions. Generally, if international law is taught at all, it is done on a part-time basis by a person who teaches other branches of law. But leave your curriculum vitae here, and I shall think of you and let you know what could be done in your case."

When we returned to New York I received a four-page letter from Dean Griswold. I was impressed that he had taken the trouble to write me at such length, although the contents of his letter were less encouraging.

Griswold set out in detail why it was mandatory that a faculty member of an American law school possess an American law degree. Most probably he would have to teach, aside from international law, an American legal subject. He stated that an American law school is a professional school, that is, one which trains its students to practice law. He suggested that I enroll in a school of law, obtain a degree, and then I could hope to get a teaching job in law. As an alternative, he suggested that I secure a position at a liberal arts college, where international law is part of the curriculum in international relations. He listed the names of several prominent international law teachers who taught in such colleges and who did not hold a law degree.

By the time I received Griswold's letter, I already realized that as a topic of instruction international law was handled differently in America from the way in which it was handled in other countries. I believe that the reasons for this different approach ultimately were twofold. First, the geographical and longtime political isolation of the United States from Europe diminished the relative value of international law. It was not a bread-and-butter subject; only a tiny elite of lawyers needed such an education. Secondly, because legal education in this country follows college, unlike in England and the Continent (where the study of law begins after secondary school), the majority of American law schools are legal trade schools rather than professional schools; that is, they dispense with providing a philosophical or theoretical background for their students. At the same time, however, America has given the world many prominent international legal scholars.

The singular way in which international law is generally taught in this country may also have contributed to its sidetracking. The case method, the method practiced in England and in the United States to teach common law (which in its essence is a judge-made case law), was extended to provide instruction in international law. However, since judicial procedures are extremely scarce in the international context, the overwhelming body of principles and rules of this branch of law is not based upon judicial precedents. Rather, international law emanates from the practice of states and from international treaties. I think the case method is deficient and inadequate for the purpose of teaching international law.

All this differed from what I experienced in Europe. In England you could choose international legal studies as a kind of major without neglecting other fields of law. But in the United States a person may be admitted to the bar and even become a judge without ever having taken an international law course.

It is true, as Griswold pointed out in his letter, that international law is being taught in liberal arts colleges. But it is somewhat anomalous to teach students this branch of law when they have not been exposed to other legal studies. Nor am I convinced that, as a rule, the teaching of international law by nonlawyers is a happy solution.

Nevertheless, as the American system was explained to me, I felt sufficiently flexible to conform to it. I did not try, as did some other European exiles, to "fight city hall." Since back in Hungary, and in my teaching and writing both there and in Turkey, I had always included international politics, I was easily prepared to abandon the idea of teaching in a school of law. Henceforth I directed my main attention to questions of international relations.

I wrote to Dean Griswold and thanked him for his advice and comments. I told him that at my age (I had turned 53 in 1958) and after my past career I would feel rather odd enrolling in a school of law. I reminded him that I was the author of the standard book on a question of international law, the second edition of which was about to be published. On the other hand, I welcomed his suggestion to seek a position in a liberal arts college or a university where I could teach international relations and also international law. Some years later I heard from Griswold again; he expressed satisfaction that I did not follow his first but only his second suggestion. I am certainly grateful to him for having devoted time to consider the problem of my career.

In fact, the revised and extended edition of *Servitudes of International Law: A Study of Rights in Foreign Territory* came out some time later. I was eager to and did present a copy to Dean Rusk, the president of the Rockefeller Foundation, under whose auspices I prepared this volume. At that moment I could not have predicted that Dean Rusk would soon become secretary of state in the Kennedy and Johnson administrations.

We spent the summer of 1958 at Cornell University, where I was engaged in research on various subjects. I was still in search of a job; the Rockefeller fellowship was to expire at the end of that year. Gray Thoron, the dean, offered me a one-year appointment. I was to participate in a research project funded by the Ford Foundation, and in the spring semester I would substitute for Prof. Michael Cardozo, who taught international law and was to go on sabbatical leave. This, in my eyes, was a makeshift solution, but I had nothing better at hand.

However, in early August I received a telegram from Robert Bowie offering me the position of research associate in the newly established Center for International Affairs at Harvard University. He invited me to come to Cambridge to discuss this assignment once more. On my way there I stopped in New York and sought advice from Philip Jessup. He told me, "I strongly recommend that you accept Bowie's offer. You could still teach at Cornell in the spring semester if Thoron and Bowie agree to this. It will be strenuous to commute between Cambridge and Ithaca, but it is important that you establish your reputation as a teacher in this country. Only a teaching position will provide you tenure. Without tenure, you will continue to hang in the air." I was becoming aware of the number one of academic desiderata: a teaching job *with tenure,* a still distant objective.

Bob Bowie (I learned how easy it was in this country to switch to first names, even with your future boss) showed great understanding and approved of my commuting to Cornell during the spring semester of 1959. In Ithaca, Gray Thoron shared Jessup's opinion as to the advantage of a Harvard appointment. He suggested a Monday schedule for teaching in Cornell, which would allow me to fly to Ithaca on Sunday and return to Cambridge by Monday night.

On September 26, 1958, we moved to Cambridge, and for three weeks, until we were able to obtain an apartment, we stayed as houseguests with Barbara and Francis Birch. While we searched for an apartment, I took up my position and Rose acquainted herself with the new environment. She also tried to be helpful in the Birch household. Once she offered to prepare a Hungarian dinner, chicken paprika. Unfortunately, in the supermarket, instead of sweet paprika, she purchased cayenne pepper by mistake. The dish was served; it was extremely spicy and hot. At first, out of politeness, nobody said a word. Finally, the Birches' adolescent daughter burst out, "Is this a joke?" But the chicken was still eaten, with plenty of iced water, of course.

On October 22 we moved into our rented apartment on Ware Street. It was small, and we had no furniture at first but slept on blankets on the floor. Slowly we acquired pieces of furniture. One day Gray Thoron, on a visit to Boston, telephoned that he had some kitchenware, inherited from an aunt, which he would like to give to us. Should we have no use for it, he would give it to the Salvation Army. Soon the entire Thoron family, parents and children, entered our apartment in a procession carrying tableware, trays, plates, glasses, knives, forks, and spoons. Suddenly, wonderfully, we became amply supplied with all these useful utensils, which enabled Rose to invite people for dinner.

My appointment to the Harvard Center for International Affairs proved to be an intellectual bonanza, a springboard for my future career, and gave me an opportunity to write another book. The Center was created for the primary purpose of throwing light on and analyzing world affairs. It was also to become an intellectual meeting place where scholars and senior officials from many parts of the world could mingle.

Besides Robert Bowie, who was the director of the center, other Harvard faculty members participated in its proceedings. Henry Kissinger was the associate director, and soon I met Prof. Edward S. Mason and Prof. Thomas C. Schelling. During my three years at the Center twenty to twenty-two research associates and assistants were employed there and worked on diverse research projects. These included Zbigniew Brzezinski (with whom I shared an office for one year); Max Weston Thornburg, an internationally known oil expert; Raymond Vernon, a professor of international trade and later director of the Center; and Lincoln Gordon, a professor of Economics and later ambassador to Brazil and president of Johns Hopkins University.

Another group at the Center comprised the fellows, experienced officials from the United States and fourteen other countries. Each year we had six Americans, three military and three civilian, among the latter one or two on leave from the State Department; other fellows came from various countries. Some have since become prominent persons: Capt. Arnold F. Schade rose to become vice admiral; Walter J. Stoessel, ambassador to Moscow; Il Kwon Chung, prime minister of South Korea; and A. Duncan Wilson, British ambassador to Moscow.

My own primary task at the Center was to prepare a study on the developments in Hungary that led to the Revolution in 1956 and those of the aftermath of the revolt. To analyze the internal rift in the Communist Party of Hungary, the popular opposition against a regime protected and dominated by the Soviet Union, provided a challenging topic. But the Hungarian events could not be separated, in my view, from some developments that took place outside Hungary. The changes in the leadership in Moscow following the death of Stalin, the events leading to the secession of Yugoslavia from the Soviet camp, and the convulsions in neighboring East European countries could not be ignored. Nor was it possible to bypass other foreign factors—Titoism, the attitudes of the West, and the Suez conflict, in particular.

In addition to this work, I also participated in other activities at the Center, including seminars and the research of my colleagues. I myself conducted seminars on topics related to my study. Later I also led seminars at Eliot House on questions of international politics.

Besides the scholarly cooperation and exchange of ideas that prevailed at the Center, it also gave us an opportunity for social contact with members of the Harvard faculty and the faculties of neighboring teaching institutions, such as Boston University, the Fletcher School of Law and Diplomacy, and the Massachusetts Institute of Technology.

We felt particularly gratified when Bob and Teddy Bowie invited us to spend our first Christmas Day in their house. Before that, we experienced our first Thanksgiving dinner as guests of Capt. Brown Taylor, a fellow of the Center, and his wife Myra.

Henry Kissinger, the associate director of the Center in 1958–59, was already a famous author. His book, *Nuclear Weapons and Foreign Policy,* published in 1957, was a pioneer study in this field and was a selection of the Book-of-the-Month Club. He was already a consultant for various federal agencies before he became the national security adviser to President Nixon in 1969 and subsequently secretary of state.

When I first visited Kissinger in his office, he showed great interest in my narrative of the Hungarian events and evinced no little familiarity with this subject. He told me we must have lunch together. We never did, but I frequently met him in the Center's cafeteria. Rose and I met his first wife, Ann, and visited them in their house in Belmont. After I left the Center in 1961 and moved to Amherst, I continued seeing him. Once he came to Amherst to lecture at the University of Massachusetts, my new place of employment. Even much later, when he was secretary of state, he continued to have an interest in my work. It was probably because of his recommendation that I obtained a grant from the Department of the Navy in 1974, which enabled me to do research on the countries of the Indian Ocean region.

Zbig Brzezinski and his wife Mushka also helped us to overcome our newcomers' difficulties. They often invited us to their home and brought us together with Harvard faculty members and their wives. Soon Rose developed a circle of friends, which enabled her to become completely acclimatized to an American and academic environment.

Zbig, an assistant professor of government at that time, invited me to address his East European government class. He certainly showed much sympathy with the ordeal of the Hungarian people, which was not dissimilar from that which Poland had to endure. He was fortunate that his father, a Polish diplomat, chose to be appointed consul general to Montreal (instead of to become consul general in Kiev) in 1938. Thus, Zbig attended McGill University and subsequently gained his Ph.D. at Harvard. In a way, I shared his trauma when he was forced to leave Harvard in 1960.

Harvard University has a peculiar system for faculty promotion and tenure. Assistant professors are appointed for five years and, unless promoted to associate professor and given tenure, have to go elsewhere. Because tenured positions are limited, only a fraction of assistant professors manage to gain permanent faculty status. In the case of Brzezinski, he failed by one vote to get his promotion. He was immediately offered positions at the University of California at Berkeley and by Columbia University. I wholeheartedly supported his decision to go to New York, which suited his vibrant and dynamic personality.

He soon had the pleasure of getting his satisfaction from Harvard. Two years later that university offered him a full professorship if he would return. But Zbig turned down the offer, something that probably had never before happened to Harvard. Instead, he was promoted to full professor by Columbia University and became the director of the Research Institute on Communist Affairs (later the Research Institute on International Change). That was only the beginning of his meteoric career, which (at the time of this writing) culminated in his appointment as national security adviser to President Jimmy Carter.

As agreed between Bowie and Thoron, in the spring 1959 semester I commuted from Cambridge to Ithaca to teach a seminar on international law at Cornell. It was a physically demanding but intellectually rewarding effort. I taught American law students, that is, students on a graduate level, and it was an interesting and educational experience for me. Thereafter I could refer to the fact that I had teaching experience not only in Hungary but also in the United States. Dean Thoron praised my accomplishment and quoted one of my students, who had said, "He is a terrific teacher."

By the end of my second academic year at the Center in the spring of 1960 I had completed a rough draft of my book on Hungary. I received valuable assistance from a colleague at the Center, George A. Kelly, who was willing to read and edit my original manuscript. I submitted my draft to Bowie and he circulated it among a few experts: Prof. Merle Fainsod, an eminent scholar of Soviet affairs, John C. Campbell of the Council on Foreign Relations in New York, and Prof. Andrew Gyorgy of Boston University. I showed it, in turn, to Zbig Brzezinski and to William E. Griffith of MIT. They gave me helpful and critical suggestions. Fainsod, Campbell, and Gyorgy all expressed enthusiasm for the study.

With Max Hall, the Center's editor of publications, I went through the manuscript once more. His stylistic improvements were most valuable. I chose for my book the title *Rift and Revolt in Hungary: Nationalism versus Communism,* which expressed the fundamental issues and the ideological theme of the work. It was accepted for publication by Harvard University Press in early 1961.

As a happy coincidence, my portrait, painted in prison by Sándor Bodo, had just arrived. When released from prison during the Revolution, the artist took my portrait with him and, before his escape to Austria, deposited it with my mother-in-law (Rose and I were already gone). She managed to mail the picture to America. Harvard printed it on the flap of the book jacket.

While I worked on my book at Harvard, the news from Hungary was far from encouraging. Most conspicuous in the prevailing terror was the judicial murder of former prime minister Imre Nagy. On June 16, 1958, it was announced in Budapest that Nagy, Gen. Pál Maléter, and two of Nagy's advisers had been sentenced to death and that the sentences had already been carried out. It was a secret "trial," if a trial it was (not even the names of the judges were made public), and a secret hanging. The last act of this period of terror was the forcible collectivization of agriculture, which was "successfully completed" in 1961.

Both Rose and I were eager to get acquainted, as best as we could, with our newly adopted country. In the spring of 1959 we purchased our first car and became "motorized," another feature of American life. That summer we decided to drive across the continent to the West Coast. Well-meaning people warned us, "It is a distance of three to four thousand miles, and you have to cross high mountains and deserts, with which you are unfamiliar." But nothing could deter us.

In late June we took off for California. It was a memorable experience to reach the great Mississippi, to cross the green cornfields of Iowa, to climb gradually to the uplands of Nebraska and Colorado. We met Hungarian friends in Denver, then crossed the continental divide high up in the Rocky Mountains, entered the highlands of Nevada, and drove down into the steaming-hot plain of California. A cool breeze signaled the approach to San Francisco and the Pacific.

In Muir Woods we met the Thornburgs; then we moved south and stayed a few days on the beach at Santa Barbara. In Los Angeles we were the guests of Prof. Andreas Tietze and his Turkish wife. Andreas is an Austrian, a great Turkish scholar whom I met in Istanbul. Now he taught at the University of California at Los Angeles.

We turned back east and crossed the Mojave Desert; we marveled at the Grand Canyon and the Painted Desert. We recrossed the Mississippi at Memphis. At Nashville we visited Sándor Bodo and his family; he was well on his way to becoming a famous painter. Finally, we passed along the Blue Ridge Parkway and through Shenandoah National Park. I think this was the best way to realize the magnitude, extent, variety, and richness of this country.

In the summer of 1960 we made another journey, this time to Canada. We were not American citizens yet and had no passports, but we could travel to Canada with certificates of permanent residence, which we possessed.

I was to complete my assignment, the writing and publishing of a book on the Hungarian issue, by the end of the academic year 1960–61, and I was expected to leave the Center for International Affairs at that time. But I still had no new job, no "teaching position." It was essential to find a permanent post. I was therefore reluctant to accept any new temporary appointment that was offered to me, such as substituting for a teacher on sabbatical leave, without prospects for a permanent appointment or tenure.

CITIZEN AND TENURED

In the years 1960 and 1961 the economy of the United States suffered from a slight recession. The academic world reacted, as always, and the expansion of teaching institutions generally came to a standstill. It was not easy to get a position, especially in my specialty.

On the other hand, I soon came to realize that I complied fully with the three criteria that were generally required for an academic appointment: a Ph.D., teaching experience, and publications. My Hungarian legal degree alone would have been found insufficient; it was of little value in this country. But my doctor of philosophy degree from the University of London was considered not only adequate but by some people even superior to the average American doctoral diploma.

I also could rely on my teaching experience in Hungary, Turkey, and, last but not least, in the United States at Cornell. In addition, I had published, and even in English. My new book, *Rift and Revolt in Hungary,* would help counter possible objections in a political science department that I was "only" an international lawyer.

The people who undertook to help me find a position were aware that I had a strong case. The Center for International Affairs considered it its duty to set into motion a campaign to secure a teaching position for me. I cannot thank enough all those who wrote letters of recommendation for me. Bowie, Kissinger, and Benjamin Brown, the executive secretary of the Center, divided among themselves the chore of letter writing to prospective employers.* I saw the copies of some, but not all, of these letters. What I found remarkable was that in these letters not only had my qualifications been emphasized but also my wife Rose had been favorably mentioned. Thus, Bowie wrote of her that "she is most attractive and will be an asset to her husband wherever he might settle." For some time thereafter I referred to Rose as "my asset."

In my European experience wives were not taken into consideration when academic appointments were determined. But it would have been a wise precaution; wives influence the performance, or the quality of performance, of their husbands. A wife who is inadequate to the position her husband is holding may be a calamity, especially in a small community.

Despite the many laudatory letters of recommendation written in

---

*A letter addressed on October 21, 1960, by Kissinger to John S. Harris, Department of Government, University of Massachusetts, Amherst, reads in part: "[Vali] is a very broad-gauged man whose fields of scholarly interest and proficiency include Political Science and Eastern European History. . . . He is qualified for appointment at professorial level. . . . He is a first-class scholar who communicates with ease and is, I am sure, a very fine teacher. He retains astonishing balance and objectivity after his trying experience in Hungary." Reprinted with the permission of Henry A. Kissinger. —ED.

my favor, despite the excellent references, which included those of Philip Jessup and Gray Thoron, the replies were appreciative but rather negative because of the economic uncertainties. No concrete offer came. There was mention of an opening at the University of Massachusetts at Amherst in the correspondence Henry Kissinger maintained with that institution. But in January 1961 Prof. John Harris, the head of the Department of Government, wrote that the vacancy had been filled.

At the beginning of the spring, with the help of Bob Bowie and Andrew Gyorgy of Boston University, I had already made a tentative arrangement for the next academic year. It was to be two part-time appointments, one at Harvard and the other at Boston University, strictly limited to one year. I declined an offer by Swarthmore College to fill in for one year for a professor on sabbatical leave. I did not wish to move away from the Cambridge-Boston area and then start job hunting again from an unfamiliar environment. Bob Bowie thought that I was foolish to refuse such an offer, but I stuck to my point.

However, on April 5 the telephone rang in my office. John Harris of the University of Massachusetts was on the other end of the line. "We would like you to come to Amherst for an interview next week," he said.

"But you wrote in January that the position had been filled."

"Yes, yes. But this is another position. We would very much like if you could come so that we can discuss the matter."

I agreed, and on April 12 I drove to Amherst. Several department members interviewed me. I ate lunch with the members of the executive committee, which, in addition to John Harris, consisted of Prof. Loren P. Beth and Prof. John H. Fenton. I was quizzed on my views about international politics and on my previous teaching. I had the impression that one faculty member had had a bad experience with a Hungarian or other East European refugee politician, who obtained an academic appointment and then behaved like a prima donna.

Evidently, all those who interviewed me had become convinced that I had the intention and capability to become a responsible member of the department. It was suggested that I teach international relations, international law, and Soviet government.

John Harris explained to me that while the University had at present only eight thousand students, the Massachusetts state government was determined to expand both its faculty and student body. Private colleges and universities were no longer willing or able to expand to enroll the growing number of applicants. Like California, Massachusetts wished to build up its institutions of higher learning. It was their intention to improve the quality of the faculty, and they determined to hire only the best-qualified scholars. Soon the university would be granted fiscal autonomy so that salaries could be raised to compete with the offers made by the best universities and colleges in the country.

I saw plenty of evidence of the coming expansion. Many classroom and office buildings as well as student dormitories were being constructed. I was favorably impressed and hoped that this time I would not fail to obtain an appointment.

A few weeks later John Harris telephoned again and informed me that my appointment had been approved by the dean and the provost, so that I could consider it final. At last I had a "teaching position" with the prospect of gaining tenure.

On May 20 Rose and I drove to Amherst to find an apartment or house to rent. When our car moved down from Pelham Hill and Rose saw the pretty houses on our right and on our left, the green meadows and blooming flowers, she immediately fell in love with Amherst. She had been afraid, as she admitted to me, that she would find it a desolate place in the backwoods.

We were shown around by Frank Beturney, a real estate agent, but the houses for rent and the few apartments available were unsuitable. These were old, neglected cottages or dreary, dirty dwellings that students rented. The pretty houses were not for rent. The big building boom in Amherst was yet to come. After some wandering, Beturney asked, "Why don't you want to buy a house? Here everybody owns one."

"Buy a house? Right now? We shall perhaps buy a house in a year or so, after we have lived here and become acquainted with the neighborhood and had an opportunity to look around," replied Rose.

"I have for sale something very suitable for you—a three-bedroom house. One bedroom may be used as a study. There is a small cottage on the same lot, which is rented. The rent would pay the mortgage on both houses." Frank took us straight to the property for sale. It was a handsome prefabricated house, just off campus. And there was the tiny cottage behind the house.

We could afford a down payment. I made a quick calculation; indeed, the rent would cover more than the mortgage payments. The deal appeared to be advantageous. It was Saturday afternoon, and we had to return to Cambridge on Sunday night. We promised Beturney an answer by the next morning. We discussed the question with John Harris and his wife Lois, for we were staying in their house for the night. John was doubtful, but Lois persuaded us to buy.

To the European mentality the purchase of real estate was an issue that required major consideration. We only realized later that Americans bought and sold their houses as they did their automobiles. Still, we had to come to a decision at once. Rose considered the purchase a gamble, but she also realized that we must have a decent place to live when we moved to Amherst.

On Sunday (you could do such things in a small place) Beturney took us to the home of the vice president of the Amherst Savings Bank, and we filled out an application for a mortgage loan. We deposited the down payment with the owner of the house and were ready to sign the contract. The purchase proved to be a bargain, especially when real estate prices soon began skyrocketing in Amherst.

In early June I took Rose to Amherst (I still was attached to the Center), and she painted the empty house; at night she slept on a mattress. By the end of July we moved into our house with the few pieces of furniture we had. When we moved there in 1961, Amherst was an even smaller college town than it is now.

The fast-expanding university (it reached a student population of twenty-three thousand in 1975) somewhat overshadowed Amherst College (with fifteen hundred students) in the eyes of some college faculty who looked upon the university as an upstart. Still, Amherst College remained the prestigious East Coast college, but the number and variety of its course offerings could hardly compete with those of the university.

I became the eleventh member of the Department of Government (the name of which was later changed to the Department of Political Science because some of us experienced disadvantages in foreign research as professors of "government"). By the early 1970s the departmental faculty rose to thirty-eight. We could therefore offer a great variety of courses, often taught by professors with differing approaches: political theory, public law, federal, state, and municipal administration and politics, and international studies. In area studies we covered many individual countries and all the major regions of the world: Western Europe, Eastern Europe with the Soviet Union, the Middle East, South and East Asia, Latin America, and the British Commonwealth. The university included a graduate school with many of its students specializing in political science.

Amherst College was more selective in its admissions policy and could give closer individual care to its students. The admissions policy of a state university was bound to be less selective (even so, three out of five applicants were refused admission) and tuition here was incomparably lower. But the low-quality students were gradually weeded out; the juniors and seniors I taught were mostly dedicated and capable students. Whereas undergraduates were mainly Massachusetts residents, the graduate students came from all parts of the country and from overseas. During my years of teaching, the quality of graduate students continually improved.

The intellectual ambience of the town of Amherst was further enhanced by the neighboring teaching institutions — Smith College in Northampton and Mount Holyoke College in South Hadley. In addition to the university and Amherst College, another college was established in Amherst in the late 1960s by the name of Hampshire College. These five institutions cooperate and exchange students and faculty members.

The large number of teachers and their spouses, together with the administrative staffs and persons attracted by the intellectual and other amenities of the place, created the background for all kinds of social and artistic activities. I found that Amherst combined the advantages of rural living with those of urban culture.

I started my teaching career at the University of Massachusetts under auspicious circumstances. A few weeks after the opening of the fall 1961 semester my book, *Rift and Revolt in Hungary,* was published. It was the first fully documented and detailed analysis of the events in Hungary. The book was forthwith reviewed on November 22, 1961, in the *New York Times Book Review* by Henry L. Roberts of Columbia University, who called it "an admirable study" and in conclusion wrote that "we are very fortunate in having, so soon after the event, such a solid, mature — and readable — history of this tragic drama." And the *Times* of London, in a review published on January 18, 1962, characterized my book as "contemporary history at its best."

It was mainly due to this publication that one year later, on June 21, 1962, Wayne State University conferred on me the honorary degree of doctor of laws. William R. Keast, president of the university, hosted a dinner for the persons on whom honorary degrees were to be conferred. Each of them was invited to say a few words. When my turn came, I was overcome by a dramatic coincidence as I spoke:

"This is a memorable day for me. But, by some strange coincidence, it is as well a memorable anniversary. Exactly ten years ago, on June 21,

1952, I stood before an entirely different audience. It was the so-called People's Court in Hungary, one of those Stalinist kangaroo courts, meeting in secret session. It consisted of a professional chairman (he was a former Nazi, who two years before had sentenced Cardinal Mindszenty); there were four people's assessors, sinister-looking silent characters, faithful Party members. There was a public prosecutor, and my defense counsel, with whom, however, I was not allowed to exchange one word either before, during, or after my trial. There were no witnesses, in fact, no evidence except my 'confessions,' statements wrung from me during the ten months of interrogation in the dungeons of the security police.

"The trial—tragic travesty of a trial, indeed—lasted ten minutes, and I was sentenced to fifteen years for treason and conspiracy. The words pronounced by the defense attorney differed little from those of the public prosecutor, except that the former asked the court to take into consideration, as an alleviating circumstance, my lack of ideological knowledge, which, he said, was equal to that of a ten-year-old child. I must have improved since.

"This lurid scene is still in my memory. I derived much value from it: the significance in a man's life of the benefits of the rule of law—public trial by jury, independence of the judiciary, presumption of innocence, equality of accuser and defendant, the benefit of doubt, due process, and others. Those who always have lived under the regime of these time-honored principles hardly ever realize what a blessing it is to be governed by the rule of law. You often only realize what you have when you come to lose it.

"I spent 'only' five years in prison (I still owe them ten). You will appreciate my feelings when I consider myself extremely fortunate, and that I am grateful to Providence when comparing my situation as it was ten years ago with the privilege I am enjoying to be here tonight."

It was also fortunate that my performance at the University of Massachusetts was recognized as more than satisfactory. Within the minimum time, after three years of service, I was given tenure in 1964.

Our citizenship status was resolved within the shortest required time, as well. This was basically due to an act of Congress of July 25, 1958, which conferred retroactively the right of permanent residence on Hungarian refugees who entered the United States following the Revolution of 1956. Under this provision we were entitled to request citizenship five years after the day of our entry into the country.

On February 14, 1963, we were invited to appear with two witnesses at the Immigration and Naturalization Service office in Boston. Our witnesses were Francis and Barbara Birch. Francis had known me since 1926, and both had met us soon after our arrival to the United States; we could not have produced better witnesses. Rose and I and the two witnesses were separately interviewed. An elementary knowledge of the Constitution was expected of us. I was asked whether I could list three of the original thirteen states; I listed all thirteen. Rose also passed with flying colors.

On February 25, before the U.S. District Court in Boston, we took the oath of allegiance. Soon thereafter we were able to apply for American passports. As soon as the spring semester was over we set out on a three-month journey to Europe. Rose wanted to meet her mother, who had been given permission to leave Hungary for three weeks, and I was deeply involved in a research project on the German reunification problem.

In the spring 1964 semester I took a leave of absence to work on my book concerning Germany. In that year Rose became involved in a book of her own.

Soon after we settled down in Amherst, we became acquainted with Theresa de Kerpely. She was born and educated in England, and with her husband, who was in the British foreign service, she had lived in several European countries as well as in South America. After her first husband's death she married a celebrated Hungarian cellist, and they lived in Hungary until after World War II, when the couple emigrated to the United States. Following her Hungarian husband's untimely death Theresa embarked on a career of her own. She wrote novels and was writer-in-residence at the University of Massachusetts. She remained interested in Hungary and, therefore, in our past experiences in that country.

Rose told Theresa about her prison ordeal and in long conversations revealed to her detail after detail. Theresa, as she admitted, identified with Rose's traumatic experience, much in the way a novelist identifies with the protagonist of her novel. The result of this cooperation was *Black Nightshade,* published in 1965 by Morrow in New York. The title is symbolic. It refers to a weed with attractive white flowers and edible berries but poisonous leaves; it represents the apparent attractiveness of the Communist system and its vicious essence, the victim of which was the heroine of this autobiography.

STUDENT UNREST

The peaceful and constructive educational activity of the University of Massachusetts, as of many other universities, was rudely interrupted in the late 1960s by the Vietnam War. The pernicious impact of this event culminated in 1970, began to ebb in 1971, and gradually disappeared in the subsequent years. The riots and irrational convulsion were less violent and disruptive here than on some other campuses. Still, remembering these events, I cannot help feeling shame and frustration, not for my own actions or inactions, but for what some students and some members of the faculty indulged in doing.

It is not the correctness, rightfulness, or alleged immorality of the Vietnam War that should be weighed here. Opinions on these questions differed at that time, but by now the overwhelming view was that involvement in this war and its escalation were tragic mistakes. To engage in a major land war in Southeast Asia, with no direct American vital interest at stake, was wrong. The belief that the North Vietnamese were just a cat's-paw of the Chinese was erroneous. Presidents Kennedy and Johnson and their advisers should have been aware of this state of affairs. Even the domino theory, if valid in that region, should not have justified the engagement of half a million soldiers — fifty thousand killed — and the waste of billions of dollars.

But by 1969 the new administration in Washington, under Nixon and Kissinger, had already given up the intention of fighting this war "for victory." It was fought in order to achieve the most favorable, least damaging denouement, a disengagement from a messy predicament. Every sensible person should have understood this. A world power such as the United States could not just pull out from Vietnam, leaving bag and baggage behind, without losing face, that is, the prestige it requires in its worldwide involvements. An American president could not just beg the North Vietnamese "on his knees" (as suggested by a presidential candidate in 1972) to release the American prisoners of war. Great Britain could not have been expected to relinquish the rebelling thirteen colonies without a reasonable treaty arrangement; Khrushchev was not to be cornered into a humiliating capitulation during the Cuban missile crisis. Similarly, the United States could not accept the opprobrium of running away from its commitments in that part of the world.

The violent demonstrations, irrational outbursts, and unreasoned criticisms were counterproductive; they did not shorten — on the contrary, they prolonged the war by at least two years. Neither the administration nor the Congress were sufficiently impressed by these commotions to alter their attitudes, which favored a contractual, and not a unilateral, ending of hostilities. Not so the North Vietnamese; they took these outbursts as the sign of an impending change of regime in Washington that would render *their* complete victory possible. Self-appointed representatives of the antiwar movement thronged to Hanoi, which action gave encouragement to the Communist government to hold out against pressures. If it had been a declared war, these persons could have been indicted for treason. Under such circumstances the peace negotiations were bound to be extremely difficult, cumbersome, and prolonged.

Had all the American people, especially large segments of the intellectual and college community, shown greater discipline, self-restraint, and rational thinking, the hostilities could have come to a close by 1970 and not 1973. That inexperienced students, who hated the draft and who, among others, carried the brunt of the war, were unable to understand why and how the United States government could not, from one day to the next, extricate itself from this tragic situation is regrettable but understandable. But that their elders, some of them faculty members and self-styled experts on international politics, showed no understanding is less excusable.

Though one had to feel utter compassion for those young men who suffered, died, or were mutilated in the jungles of Indochina, one had to be moved to dismay and disgust when envisaging this delirium of hatred, misconception, and ignorance that swept the academic world in those years. Scientists and scholars of humanistic studies discovered an aptitude to pronounce incontrovertible judgments on complicated questions of international politics, opinions that were widely quoted and relied on by their constituents on the campuses. Nobel Prize winners in science could readily answer the question of how to get out of Vietnam: "By ship," they replied with simplistic ease. The war was proclaimed by them to have been illegal under international law, unethical or immoral, as if such characterizations could be made in a peremptory manner. Inanities were widely quoted, such as the words of one war veteran before a congressional committee: "How can one expect anybody to be the last soldier killed in this war?" As if in every war there did not have to be somebody who was killed last.

The most furious reaction against the war erupted at the time of the American incursion (incursion it was, because it lasted only six weeks) into Cambodia in May 1970. The North Vietnamese had invaded the area of Cambodia adjacent to the Vietnamese border many years earlier. From the battlefield point of view it was a rational decision to try to dislodge them from this sanctuary. It was not, as was alleged, a violation of Cambodian neutrality; the enemy had used this area as a staging ground for its military deployments, and, if anybody, it was the North Vietnamese who had violated Cambodian neutrality. In any case it was not an escalation in intensity, nor an extension into thus far unaffected areas of the war; the response to it was, therefore, both irrational and out of proportion.

On the Amherst campus the news of Cambodia and of the Kent State University tragedy prompted a strike, a shutdown of classwork, dictated by the usually dominating tiny minority of students. This strike was backed up by some members of the faculty and handled most tolerantly by the university administration. This abstention by many from classes happened in the last three weeks of the academic year; it was welcomed by those students who wished to avoid final exams. The complacent administration ordered that the students be given final grades without final exams; we, the faculty, were instructed to assign them grades according to their academic standing when the strike began, that is, with incomplete study material and with incomplete knowledge of their erudition.

I ignored the strike and continued my classes with student attendance reduced by 60 to 70 percent. My undergraduate international law course depended heavily on the final exam for the evaluation of students. I held the exam; but because students were to be given semester grades even if they did not come to take the exam, only about half of the class "volunteered" for this purpose. Therefore, I distinguished between the grades *I* gave to the students and those I *had* to give them as instructed by the administration. Later I was unwilling to give recommendations to those who had not attended the final exam.

The student strike appeared to me most anomalous and unreasonable. In industry, workers strike against their employers for higher wages. A strike by students against the university is really one against themselves. Neither the university nor the commonwealth of Massachusetts could be held responsible for the Vietnam events. The federal government, which conducted the war in Indochina, remained unaffected by this strike; President Nixon completely ignored the student excesses.

Unfortunately, however, the North Vietnamese watched them carefully and gained encouragement from them.

The Vietnam imbroglio poisoned the otherwise delectable and gratifying intellectual atmosphere of our campus and relations with some of the faculty members in the neighboring colleges. The arrogance of ignorance displayed not only by some students but also by many faculty members turned social encounters into emotional bickerings. My field being international politics, it was painful to be exposed to apodictic pronouncements and opinions by ignoramuses who now posed as experts on international relations and international law.

Graduation ceremonies had become occasions for propagandistic political outbursts. At the 1970 commencement exercises of our university the speaker of the graduating class shouted that he and his peers "wanted freedom" and "an end of the American police state"; he was applauded by thousands of other students. How ridiculous this was to somebody like me who had come from behind the Iron Curtain! Where was the lack of freedom or the police state, when this speaker was permitted to use such language without risking anything?

But intellectually it was even more painful when the commencement speaker, the recipient of an honorary doctorate, Kingman Brewster, the president of Yale University, condemned the Saigon government for "rejecting both democracy and peace." Well, it must have been known to the illustrious speaker (later the American ambassador to London) that there has never been a democratic government in Vietnam since the dawn of history, and least of all in Hanoi.

In 1971 the commencement speaker at Amherst College, the poet Robert Bly, referred to United States foreign policy as "shadow murdering on an international scale"; he urged the graduating students not to join corporations, which he described as "earth murderers" and whose executives were "telling lies for money."

It had become a widespread obsession by some students to hold that the United States was one of the most reactionary, most oppressive countries of the world. Many expressed the desire to emigrate to places where "there is freedom." When I asked one of these deficient students, "Where would you like to settle down?" the reply, after some hesitation, was, "Well, just let me think!" Poor ignorant souls, they did not know what was going on in most parts of the world!

One gifted but radicalized student joined the Peace Corps. From countries in Africa he wrote me long letters in which he described his experiences, the oppression and misery that he observed with his own eyes; there he suddenly discovered his respect and admiration for his country of birth. This reminded me of John Berryman's dictum: "A man could live his whole life in America and never be scared." And he will never find out whether he is a coward or not.

In my experience naturalized immigrants were often the "best" Americans. Native citizens frequently failed to appreciate the advantage of having been born in this country. People valued more highly what they had to struggle for than what was given them.

I considered it extremely ill-conceived when faculty bodies or the university passed resolutions on the Vietnam War or on any international political issue. Although individual faculty members should be free to express political opinions, it is inappropriate for teaching bodies or institutions to indulge in expressing political opinions. I have never wavered in maintaining that the major if not exclusive task of a university and its faculty is to teach, to spread knowledge, without committing themselves to partisan issues. Furthermore, it should be illicit and contrary to the professional duties of a teacher to incite students to commit violent actions or even to strike against the university.

I found it odd, to say the least, that no disciplinary actions were instituted against faculty members who had committed such, in my eyes, grave acts of misconduct. Even to join a strike I consider a neglect of an instructor's duty. In 1970 former presidential candidate Hubert Humphrey was to address our students. He was prevented from speaking by organized shouting, invectives, and obscenities hurled at him by a minority of the audience, who were trained in this endeavor by an assistant professor. No disciplinary action followed that disgusting event.

Most regrettably, the entire mentality of many educators and administrators had been put to the test by these student disorders, and they generally failed in maintaining their dedication to the ideals of education. Students had come to be regarded not as disciples but as consumers, who should rather be satisfied according to their predilections than taught or educated as deemed useful and appropriate by their teachers. Students, and not the faculty, should decide what is to be taught; students should be amused, entertained, rather than confronted with serious studies. Students should decide what is relevant and what is not. Time-honored intellectual standards should be abandoned in favor of exciting innovations just to please the consumers.

Such tendencies coincided with the demand to "democratize" the university. Of course, nobody could or should deny that the university is *for* the students, but that does not mean that the university should be ruled by them. It must be spelled out clearly that the university, like other institutions of learning, cannot be democratic institutions if they are to be educating institutions. Democracy has its limits and limitations. It is therefore ludicrous to juxtapose or equate a faculty senate or an administration with a student government. Autonomy of the student body must be restricted to matters of welfare and leisure but cannot extend to decision making on questions of curriculum and faculty appointments or promotions. At the same time, students should be consulted on all these issues.

In the mid 1970s it appeared that many of the aberrations caused by the Vietnam War would be abandoned and the universities would return to what I consider normal. The university should be restored to what has so wonderfully been expressed by John Masefield, the English poet laureate: "There are few earthly things more beautiful than a University. . . . It is a place where those who hate ignorance may strive to know, where those who perceive truth may strive to make others see; where seekers and learners alike, banded together in the search for knowledge, will honor thought in all its finer ways, will welcome thinkers in distress or in exile."

TEACHER, RESEARCHER, WRITER

The teaching staff of quality institutions of higher learning is generally evaluated according to three criteria: teaching, research and publications, and service to the college or university community. The last measure is considered supplementary to the first two. Thus, the qualification of a college or university professor hinges essentially on the quality of his teaching and the value of his or her research and publications. Hence the threatening slogan "publish or perish," which, like a sword of Damocles, hangs over the head of instructors, especially those who hope for promotion, salary increase, or tenure.

While it can be maintained, in the abstract, that an excellent teacher does not necessarily have to publish in order to be recognized as such, this is an unlikely occurrence. The question is further complicated by the quantity and quality of publications required. An article in a professional journal may be more valuable, more original and educational, than a book-length volume. Furthermore, it could be possible that somebody would be able to produce a good manuscript but be unable to find a publisher. Such a calamity may be (but is not always) a reflection on the quality of the manuscript.

It should, therefore, be rather hazardous to pronounce any definitive judgment on the justification of the publish-or-perish issue because of the variables of the individual cases. Still, I venture to hold the view that the quality of teaching largely depends on the well-organized and systematic presentation of the teacher, on his or her analytical skill and factual knowledge. A teacher having such competency must feel an urge to communicate his or her talent not only to the class but to a much larger circle, to become available even years later. As expressed in the Latin saying *verba volant, scripta manent* (words fly away, what is written lasts), a good teacher should be a publishing scholar. Furthermore, a printed text is generally more precise and better structured than an oral allocution.

To evaluate a teacher on the basis of his or her classroom performance alone is almost impossible. One has to rely on "witnesses," his or her students, who are generally biased or less than competent arbiters. A written or printed text, a book or an able article, reveals incontrovertibly the talent of its author. On the other hand, a lack of publications is mostly due to a deficiency in organizing, assembling, and articulating one's ideas.

I do not deny the importance of the manner in which teaching is performed. It is highly important. Confused peroration, mumbling, disorganized and unsystematic presentations are deplorable. It happens sometimes that scholars write good books but are poor lecturers. Still, they are better teachers than those who are articulate performers without a command of the substance of their discipline.

I, for one, always felt the need not only to express myself orally but to prepare texts and publish. For me the slogan "publish or perish" meant "publish or suffocate." I would have felt extremely unhappy and frustrated had I been prevented from publishing, as I no doubt would have been had we stayed in Hungary.

After having completed my study on Hungary, I immediately immersed myself in a research project on the question of Germany's division. Having visited Germany so many times and in various periods of its turbulent recent history, I was driven by an almost spontaneous urge to examine its major post–World War II problem and to write on it.

As I mentioned earlier in this book, the first time I was in that country was as a young boy of nine in the summer of 1914, at the time of the outbreak of World War I. At the Anhalter station my mother and I camped for three days, waiting for a train to Vienna. Before our eyes an unforgettable event unfolded—the mammoth clockwork-like German general mobilization. Train after train was moved into the gigantic glass-roofed station; unit after unit of the German Imperial Army boarded the cars—soldiers with their spiked helmets covered with cloth, carrying their knapsacks on their back and their rifles in their hands. One train rolled out to give way to the next, all in almost complete silence, as if directed by remote control. It was this general mobilization that so much impressed the young Adolf Hitler, who as an Austrian then enlisted in the German army.

I must admit, it impressed me too. It was a herculean preventive action (which ultimately failed) to forestall the dreaded two-front war. This was the implementation of the Schlieffen Plan to marshal practically all the German forces for a lightning attack across Belgium and to destroy France before Russia could assemble its sluggish millions for action against Germany's eastern flank.

The scene remains indelible in my mind, and I have never ceased to meditate upon its implications. The necessity, legality, or morality of carrying out what has come to be known in the nuclear context as a "first strike," that is, to prevent, forestall, or preempt the impending attack of an enemy, has ever since occupied my mind. Much later I foresaw it happening in 1967 when Israel considered herself cornered. I am haunted by the thought that such a preemptive first strike might one day descend on the world with our nuclear "balance of terror."

It was nine years later that I next visited Germany, this time in the company of a few schoolmates after we had graduated from high school. In 1923 the ill-famed German inflation peaked. In early July, when we came to Germany, one dollar was worth eight hundred thousand German marks; three weeks later it was worth six million marks. All monetary and other values confusedly tumbled, fortunes disappeared, and lives became destabilized; the misery and humiliation we encountered was unbelievable. The individual and collective suffering these people endured boded ill for the future.

In the next years, until the outbreak of World War II, I traveled to or across Germany at least once a year. Whenever I passed through that country on my way to London or Paris or The Hague, I tried to spend at least a few days there. I visited it shortly after the Nazi takeover, after the annexation of Austria, and between the Munich Conference and the invasion of Czechoslovakia in 1939. Then again I saw Germany, both East and West, in 1948, the giant prostrate and his former capital, Berlin, divided.

One year before obtaining American citizenship and being able to travel, I had already devoted myself to the study of the German question. I became aroused by Germany's national predicament and postwar division. Historically, German political unity was a fairly recent development, but German ethnic, linguistic, and cultural unity was of long standing. I was fascinated by the question of whether the present division of the German ethnic body will, in the long run, defy the forces for unity.

Under a grant from the Rockefeller Foundation I spent the summer of 1963 with Rose in Germany. I worked in the library of the Federal Parliament in Bonn, interviewed members of the German Foreign Office and the Federal Parliament, scholars, publicists, and members of foreign embassies. I visited Munich, West Berlin, Stuttgart, Frankfurt, and Hamburg and met with experts on the topic of my research. In 1965 I returned to Germany once more. I completed the final text of my manuscript in that year. The result was a book entitled *The Quest for a United Germany,* published by Johns Hopkins University Press in 1967.

Before my book on the German question had come out, I had already embarked on yet another research topic, this time about Turkey. This jumping from Hungary to Germany, from Germany to Turkey, was no madness; there was a method in it. I had spent the years from 1943 to 1946 in Turkey, a rather critical time, when Ankara was faced with the dilemma of joining the war against Germany (its leaders had foreseen by 1943 that Hitler would lose) or of remaining nonbelligerent. I had come to know and understand the motives, the goals, and the difficulties of Turkey's leadership. Ever since those years I have felt compelled to express my interpretations of Turkey's puzzling international situation and problems. And like Hungary, or even more so Germany, Turkey also stood at the divide of the East-West cleavage, looking with one eye to the Soviet colossus north of its borders and with the other to the industrial West, to which it wished to belong.

Although Great Britain, the United States, and the Soviet Union pressured Turkey in 1944 to participate in the war against the Nazis, Turkey's leaders declined. They were convinced that Germany even then remained strong enough to strike back at Turkey. The Russians would then move in to "rescue" the Turks, and at the end of the war they would be reluctant to withdraw.

But there also was internal pressure. The Turks, prompted by their historic tradition, are bellicose, and since 1922, for over twenty years, they had lived in peace — an unusual occurrence. Their officers were eager to win laurels on the battlefield.

I have always believed that moderation, restraint, and coolness of mind are the most valuable qualities statesmen can possess. Turkey's wartime president, Ismet Inönü, was a famous general. Against the counsel of some of his ministers he refused to yield to temptation or pressures and enter the war. He was known as a stubborn, heavy-handed leader, who ruled a one-party state in an autocratic way. But Inönü proved to be much more flexible, much more up-to-date than was then believed. He realized that Turkey, if it wished to gain the sympathy of the West, had to move toward democracy. Wasn't it Atatürk, the founder of modern Turkey, who wanted his country to become a European nation and state? So after the war Ismet Inönü agreed to hold popular elections and hand over the government to the elected democratic opposition.

Turkey's aim had been not only to adopt Western technology (as had Japan) but also to become modernized according to the European model without, however, abandoning its ethnic culture and the Islamic faith. Turkey has so far been the only Islamic nation to set before itself such a far-reaching goal and advance at least halfway toward it. It therefore has become — in my eyes — a kind of human laboratory, a political and social experiment station.

This challenge offered me a very special topic of research. But it was also Turkey's geopolitical location between Europe and Asia, between the Russian giant and the Middle East, the Black Sea and the Mediterranean, that turned the country into one of far greater significance than might have warranted by her military, economic, and demographic weight.

In 1965 I traveled to Istanbul with Rose. For me it was a sentimental journey, a return after nearly twenty years to the place where I had spent three eventful years of my life. For Rose it was new, unexplored territory, but she was only too eager to be exposed to this experience.

I had been so enthusiastic about my new project that I could hardly wait to start with the research in depth. In the fall 1967 semester I lectured in Freiburg, Germany, but I also visited London, Paris, Bonn, and Brussels (where I interviewed NATO and European Common Market officials) to collect information and material on Turkey. In February 1968 we proceeded to Turkey. I held fellowships both from the American Research Institute in Turkey and from NATO. In Istanbul we stayed in the mansion on the shore of the Sea of Marmara that belonged to the Köprülü family (which had given two grand viziers to the Ottoman Empire in the seventeenth and eighteenth centuries) and was rented by the institute. A month later we moved to Ankara, where the most important of my interviews were to be conducted. I became a frequent visitor to the Ministry of Foreign Affairs and to the Parliament building, where I met those officials who managed Turkey's foreign policy and the parliamentary leaders who had experience in the international field, including Sen. Niham Erim, chairman of the Foreign Relations Committee who subsequently became prime minister. I also talked to party leaders, to scholars, and to journalists. Such firsthand enlightenment on the motives, strategies, and aims of Turkey's foreign policy proved to be extremely valuable when I drafted the text of my book.

The most exciting experience was one I gained from my visit to the island of Cyprus. In Nicosia I saw Glafkos Clerides, Speaker of the House of Representatives, and Rauf Denktaş, leader of the Turkish community. These two were conducting negotiations for the settlement of the ethnic problems between the Greek and Turkish populations of Cyprus, a settlement that was thwarted by the shortsighted intransigence of President Makarios. During the previous years a considerable portion of the Cypriot Turks had been compelled to flee from their ancient living places; they were refugees on their own island, living in crowded slums and defended not so much by the United Nations Peacekeeping Forces as by their own fighters. The most important of these Turkish enclaves was located in the northern section of Nicosia and along the Kyrenia highway.

With my American passport I was able to cross the "green line," the demarcation line of the Turkish enclave, and travel along the Kyrenia highway. On one of the picturesque mountaintops, at Saint Hilarion Castle overlooking the harbor of Kyrenia, I visited one of the many defense outposts and talked to the Cypriot Turkish fighters. A sergeant introduced me to the commandant, who, he warned me, did not speak

English; Cypriots generally all spoke some English. The conversation with the commandant (the sergeant translated, although I was able to follow what was said in Turkish) revealed to me that he was a regular Turkish officer who, evidently, had been seconded to the Cypriot Turkish fighters. This incident, if nothing else, gave me a foreboding of what would inevitably happen if the plight of the Turkish refugees was not remedied.

The Turks twice previously had been prevented by Washington from coming to the assistance of their suffering co-nationals. However, in 1974, six years after my visit, having waited for such an opportunity, they invaded the island and occupied the northern third of it. Now the sufferings, on an even larger scale, of the Greek population commenced. Some two hundred thousand Greeks fled from the north or were evicted by the Turkish invaders. Such a tragedy could have been forestalled and prevented had the United States and Great Britain, with or without the United Nations, intervened to end the predicament of the Turkish Cypriots and forced Makarios to accept an equitable settlement that would have safeguarded the status and human rights of these sufferers.

The Cyprus problem has festered since 1974, and at the time of this writing no prospects of its solution are in sight. An arms embargo voted by Congress against Turkey has only resulted in the closure of American bases in that country and a further alienation of the proud Turks from the United States and NATO. However, this action has not improved the relations of the United States with Greece.

For a solution I take the heretical view that Cyprus be divided between Greece and Turkey in a measure more approximate to the numerical proportions of the two ethnic groups. Thereby the desire of Greeks—islanders and mainlanders—could at least partly be satisfied, and Turkey's strategic requirements could also be met. Cyprus would not, in that case, be the first island divided between two states. The Soviet Union and the Cypriot Communists would oppose such a deal but could not prevent it if the Western powers, Greece, and Turkey agreed. Moreover, the world would be relieved of an incubus that threatens the peace in the eastern Mediterranean and weakens the southeastern flank of NATO.

After Cyprus we spent some more months in Turkey and returned to the United States only in July. For another year I worked on my manuscript, and I had it ready by late 1969. I gave a symbolic title to the book: *Bridge Across the Bosporus,* referring to the Turkish endeavor to interlink with Europe. The book was published in early 1971, again by Johns Hopkins University Press.

The follow-up to this book on Turkey was another volume, which dealt with the Turkish Straits—the Bosporus and the Dardanelles—their legal and political status, and the role these strategic straits play in the defense plans of NATO. The Hoover Institution on War, Revolution and Peace, in California, invited me to carry out this project. I accepted the assignment with genuine interest; it was a task both relating to the international regime of the Turkish Straits, that is, international law, and to the variables of politics affected by this legal regime, which at the same time impinge on the efficacy and interpretation of that regime.

The role of international law in the shaping of international politics always captivated me. I perceived that some international lawyers exaggerated this role, while some political scientists, politicians, and the man in the street belittled its importance. The examination of the regime of the Turkish Straits, as laid down in the Montreux Convention of 1936, offered an almost unique opportunity to analyze the impact of these treaty provisions on the policy of interested governments, including the Soviet Union, and how maritime users of these waterways exerted influence over the application of that convention in conformity with their actual interests. I felt particularly suited to conduct such an inquiry.

In the summer of 1970 Rose and I drove for the second time to the West Coast, this time not omitting a visit to the wondrous Yellowstone National Park and charming Lake Tahoe. We spent two months at Stanford University. I worked in the Hoover Tower, where I found a useful library for my research. The end result of this effort, a book entitled *The Turkish Straits and NATO,* was published by the Hoover Institution Press in 1972.

It was this work which led me to my next topic of research. My examination of the political and strategic status of the eastern Mediterranean guided me, so to speak, through the Suez Canal (even if it was closed after the 1967 war) into the Red Sea and then on to the vastness of the Indian Ocean.

The withdrawal of the British from their last strongholds in the Indian Ocean, which prior to 1947 was well-nigh a British lake, and the simultaneous emergence of a Soviet naval presence in these waters heralded a significant shift in the balance of power in that part of the world.

In my teaching I conceived the balance of power as the major regulating and stabilizing mechanism on the international scene. It may not always operate in a satisfactory manner; still, it is the concept that is responsible for the relative order and stability we have. I was aware that some scholars and idealistically oriented persons deprecated balance of power and wished to replace it by a world order policy. However, I asked myself how a world order could be secured if not by the instrumentality of balancing power.

Attempts to set up a working collective security system by the League of Nations and, more recently, by the United Nations—a world order guaranteed and supported by these world organizations—have proved to be wanting. Although the United Nations remains a most valuable, almost indispensable "marketplace of the world" and occasionally contributes to the maintenance or restoration of peace and order, ultimately the relative order we have rests on a cluster of regional or local power balances and, when the general equilibrium of great powers or superpowers is at stake, on the global balance of power, which is also expressed as the nuclear balance of terror.

To reject or ignore the significance of this elusive but still operative regulating force of the balance of power is replete with dangers, and favors aggressors. The British and the French learned this lesson when in the post–World War I euphoria of hoped-for disarmament—the illusory "peace in our times"—they neglected their own security, while Hitler rearmed Germany. Fortunately, the post–World War II leadership in the West was reluctant to rely for its security on the United Nations, whose Security Council had become paralyzed because of the use of the veto.

The shift in the balance of power in the Indian Ocean, caused by the vacuum created by the British pullout, has not as yet proved so portentous as to create a complete imbalance in the global equilibrium of forces. Still, it was important enough to draw the attention of political leaders, the press, and the world of scholars to the new situation. Since 1971 several scholarly institutions have arranged conferences—in Washington, Southampton (England), New Delhi, and Tehran—to discuss the problems of the Indian Ocean region. Many of the contributions to the published proceedings of these conferences were highly valuable, but others were one-sided, biased, or insignificant. As is generally the case, articles in such collections are *disjecta membra*—"disjointed limbs," essays without a central theme, dealing with disparate matters and uncoordinated with one another.

My ambition was to write a book on the Indian Ocean region by examining it from a synoptic view, investigating its geopolitical and geostrategic unity and the alleged vacuum created by the British departure. A single conspectus would be able to concentrate on both the conflicts between the littoral powers of the region and the rivalries of the nonregional maritime powers, as well as on the interrelations of both these potential or actual confrontations.

For my research I was able to enlist support from the Naval War College in Newport, Rhode Island, and from the Earhart Foundation. In 1973 I visited Western capitals – London, Paris, Bonn and Lisbon – and collected much valuable information. In the first half of 1974 I traveled with Rose around the periphery of the Indian Ocean, from Australia to South Africa. All along this itinerary the American, British, and West German embassies provided advice and assistance.

I had interviews in Canberra, in Singapore, and in Kuala Lumpur. I was in Colombo for ten days and then had many interviews in New Delhi. Then we proceeded to Pakistan and later to Tehran.

From Iran, after a short stay in Egypt, we moved on to Ethiopia, where Emperor Haile Selassie was to be removed a few months later. In Addis Ababa I met the deputy secretary-general of the Organization of African Unity, who very openly revealed to me the organization's master plan: the step-by-step elimination of white domination, first in Portuguese Angola and Mozambique, then in Rhodesia, in Namibia (South-West Africa), and lastly in the hardest nut of all, the Republic of South Africa. Our next stop was the hospitable and enchanting island of Mauritius followed by Antananarivo, on the island of Madagascar, where I first encountered some difficulties in my interviews; but with the help of the American Embassy these were soon overcome.

The last leg of our odyssey was South Africa. I had meetings with faculty members of two universities in Johannesburg and commuted to Pretoria to interview Foreign Ministry officials and members of the American and German embassies. When I thought I had completed my interviews, I received a call from Dr. E. M. Rhoodie, state secretary for information. "Would you like to come and stay a few days in Pretoria?" he asked. "I could arrange some more important meetings for you, and your wife could do some sightseeing here."

I accepted, and we moved to Pretoria. I was taken to meet some interesting people: Major General Jan Robbertze, deputy chief of the South African defense forces, Professor J. H. Moolman of the Africa

Institute, and others who gave me the Afrikaner side of the story. On the second day my guide told me, "Now you are going to see General Hendrik van der Bergh."

"Who is he?" I inquired.

"He is the head of the BOSS, the Bureau of State Security."

This was quite unexpected. So I was to see the second most powerful man in the country (after the prime minister), whom few have met. He was the person in charge of internal security affairs, and his security police handled the delicate, difficult, and cruel business of watching over millions of discontented nonwhites in South Africa. He received his instructions from and reported directly to the prime minister.

In a rather inconspicuous house I was led to an elevator and on the third floor was ushered into a comfortably furnished room, which, however, had no windows. While waiting, remembering my interrogations by the Hungarian security police, I developed a mild claustrophobic anxiety.

The general, a tall, lank Boer with whitish hair, entered and talked to me in a paternal, soft voice. Coffee was served, and my claustrophobia receded.

"I am glad to have an opportunity to talk to you," he began, "because I saw your curriculum vitae and noticed that you had been a prisoner of the Communists. So you will appreciate what I have to say." When applying for a South African visa to carry out research, I had given the consulate a copy of my curriculum vitae. It had reached the hands of General van der Bergh.

The security police chief gave me a short résumé of South African history, in fact, the history of the Boers. Then he continued: "The greatest danger for today's South Africa is not the African states. Our defense forces are vastly superior to theirs. The real danger stems from the hostility of the West, which unwittingly promotes Communist influence. The South African Communist Party was founded in 1918. It first wished to enlist the support of the Afrikaners, whom it considered oppressed by the English. That didn't work. Then Communists decided to infiltrate the black masses. An ideal Leninist situation, indeed: an oppressed proletariat hating their white capitalist oppressors! During World War II they at first agitated against the war effort; after the German attack on the Soviet Union they supported the war but, at the same time, attempted to subvert the masses."

He stopped for a moment and took a sip from his coffee. I was taking notes, but he did not object. He went on: "My security police staff consists of dedicated, competent persons. We were able to eradicate the Communist leadership. I myself arrested the leader, a certain Bram Fischer, who, I must shamefully admit, was a Boer. I discovered the Communist blueprint for the subversion of our country."

"The new Portuguese government wants to give independence to Angola and Mozambique," I interrupted. "Wouldn't this greatly affect your strategic status?" In April 1974, just before we came to South Africa, the Portuguese autocratic regime was overthrown in Lisbon, and the future of Mozambique had become a major problem, widely discussed in Pretoria and Johannesburg.

"We are watching developments," the general said. "Last week I met with General Gomez in Beira. He told me that free elections are planned for Mozambique. Nonsense! In any case, it would be uncomfortable to have a hostile government in Mozambique, but it would not basically change the strategic picture." The general straightened himself up in his seat. "You must realize that Afrikaners will not look back over their shoulders. Unlike the French in Algeria or the Portuguese in Mozambique, we have nowhere to go. Afrikaners will stay and fight. They would rather die. In South Africa 'one man–one vote' is impossible. Black rule would ruin the country and destroy the whites. This is what Moscow and Peking want. But the Western Christian world should not be trapped into this conspiracy. South Africa should be given time to implement a workable program."

I asked him about Rhodesia. "Charity begins at home," he declared. "No military assistance to Rhodesia. In 1927 Rhodesia was offered provincial status in the Union of South Africa. Prime Minister General Smuts proposed it. But the Rhodesians refused; they said they would be unwilling to serve under 'Boer bosses.' Nor shall we interfere in Mozambique. Our principle is, Do to others what others do to you."

The audience had come to an end. I considered it most valuable. It provided a direct and succinct insight into the thinking of the South African leaders and also into the insoluble aspect of the South African problem, where two ideologies—the claim to human rights and equality and the religious missionary belief of being a chosen people in a promised land—clashed head on. I was suddenly reminded of something that Henry Kissinger had written in one of his books: "No power will submit to a settlement, however well balanced and however 'secure,' which seems totally to deny its vision of itself."

This was my last interview during our long aerial circumnavigation of the Indian Ocean. I felt immensely enriched by all the impressions I had gained, by the acquaintances I had made. Although I had little time outside my interviews, I managed to join Rose in some sightseeing as well. We had visited Bali, a gem of an island with a specific artistic culture; we went to Agra in India and admired the Taj Mahal; we marveled at the Great Sphinx and the pyramids of Gizeh in Egypt; nor shall we forget the beaches and the lush flora of Mauritius.

When I completed my manuscript, I soon found a publisher, this time not a university press but a commercial firm. The Free Press in New York published my book, *Politics of the Indian Ocean Region: The Balances of Power,* in late 1976. This was the sixth book I had published since we had arrived in the United States. I certainly had acquired some experience in the arduous business of having one's manuscript published.

PUBLISHING

When writing about publishing, I am not complaining. I am one of those fortunate scholars whose manuscripts without exception have reached the public and have not encountered major difficulties. Still, in my publishing career I have met certain stumbling blocks and have been exposed to some irritating experiences, which seem worth recording.

To have one's manuscript published, one first has to run the gauntlet of finding a publisher who is willing to read it. That is perhaps the greatest difficulty in this steeplechase because your manuscript may be turned down without being read, even if by all standards it is an excellent one.

University presses offer easier access for scholarly studies because they are supposed to appraise the product not on the basis of its salability but on the basis of its intrinsic scholarly merit. In practice, however, the criterion of salability, even if not admitted, is never ignored by the editors of university presses. They, like their commercial confreres, are longing to obtain manuscripts on "hot topics," or those written by well-known authors or scholars. The search for a publisher who will accept a book on a less exciting topic and by an unknown author, however good the product may be, is often almost hopeless. In the recession period of the mid 1970s university presses were compelled to live with reduced subsidies from their parent universities, who themselves often were in financial trouble. Consequently, university presses were forced to become more selective and to reduce the number of their less remunerative or unremunerative publications. Several of the university presses I approached for the publication of my Indian Ocean manuscript were ready to consider it, but only after a waiting period of a year or so, because they were "overcommitted in international political topics."

The second hurdle on the arduous path of publication is met after the manuscript has been accepted *for consideration*. This means that the editor will read it and then pass it on to one or two readers, alleged experts in the field. The publication of the book will then largely depend on the findings of these readers.

With the readers two kinds of difficulties might be encountered: first, they often move with glacial speed, that is, they sit on the manuscript for several months, even half a year; second, they may be biased or have certain hobbyhorses of their own. For instance, if one of them happens to be a historian who has to evaluate a book on some contemporary political problem, he may insist that the historical introductory chapter is deficient and does not include a discussion at length of some historical precedent he considers indispensable. An extension of the historical chapter could upset the balance of the entire book. If the reader has written something on the same topic (a most likely contingency), he may condemn as incorrect any deviation from the point of view he has taken. But it also happens that the reader may be a superficial or enervated person, or even an incompetent who himself has never published a book-length volume and, therefore, does not know how to write a book. All this depends on the choice of the editor, who sometimes may find it impossible to enlist a competent and conscientious reader. The author is therefore at the mercy of a judge whose name will never be revealed to him (a modern version of the *Vehmgericht**). Of course, it may also happen that the manuscript is really no good.

When I submitted my manuscript on the German question to a university press, the first reader must have suffered under more than one of these debilities. He must have been a historian because he objected that I had failed to record in full detail the story of the unification of

---

*Fehmic court: a medieval court in Westphalia and other German states noted for its secrecy and brutality. It was revived during the Weimar period by rightists and used against their opponents. —ED.

Germany under Bismarck. His other remarks showed that he probably published only on some narrow and limited subject, because he seemed to have no idea of how to write about a broader issue. Finally, as a historian he criticized the lack of documentary evidence of my theses. When writing on a contemporary subject, you generally have no official or archival records to rely on. I quickly gave up and found another university press, which promptly published the book.

My manuscript on the Indian Ocean was submitted to a reader who procrastinated for over three months with the manuscript (he was supposed to return it within three weeks) and eventually wrote a short report, which was partly critical, partly commendatory. I was grateful to him for the latter but amused by the former. He must have made no notes because he forgot what he had read in the beginning of the manuscript. This was clear because he reproached me for having omitted matters I had included. He questioned why I had discussed Australia's attitude and not also that of New Zealand. Had he looked at a map, he would have seen that New Zealand is in the Pacific and has no Indian Ocean shore. However, in fine, he still recommended the book for publication, and The Free Press ignored the ineptitudes of his report.

The last obstruction in the process of publication is the disregard for the time element. The period between the availability of a copyedited manuscript and the emergence of the final product — the book — is excessively long, sometimes ten months or even one year. It may be that in countries other than the United States this process is even longer, but it seems to be unwarrantable that in so highly industrialized a country as the United States this typographical operation should be slow. From the final approval of a manuscript until the end of the publication process sometimes one and a half or even two years may pass. For a book on some contemporary political question such tardiness may have a disastrous result; the book may become outdated, and at least parts of it may suffer from obsolescence. Editors remind the author that texts should be drafted in such a manner that their contents should not easily become "perishable." To follow this advice one would be compelled to make the text less precise, more ambivalent, and less up-to-date. This does not help the book become successful. For disciplines other than international politics these delays may be less harmful, but they still constitute a disadvantage. When facing this problem, I often wished I were a writer on archaeology or ancient history, where the time element would be less important.

When your book is finally published, the worst is over. But sensitive authors may still be nervous and await the reviews of their books with trembling. Here my advice would be to ignore all reviews except those written by competent and fair-minded reviewers. In periodicals whose review sections are well managed, such as the *American Political Science Review* or the *American Journal of International Law,* the reviews are generally reliable and well balanced; but the majority of book reviews in periodicals and daily newspapers are often unreliable.

Reviewers are frequently inclined to disclose their own views on the topic of the book and to add only a few sentences describing and evaluating it. Or they grab one relatively unimportant section or aspect (perhaps even one paragraph) of the book and subject it to a devastating criticism while leaving the other ninety-five percent of the volume unmentioned. It even occurs that the reviewer has failed to read the book in its entirety; there are scandalous instances when the reviewer has evidently read only the introduction and the final chapter. One rather candid reviewer of one of my books complained that he had to read "the entire book" to understand what message the work was meant to convey.

I really have little cause to complain; fortunately, all my books have been generally well received. But I should mention a few specimens of frivolous or prejudiced reviewing in my experience.

My book on the Hungarian Revolution was the first detailed and comprehensive work on this topic. A few of my émigré countrymen felt slighted or felt some jealousy because they believed I stole from them an opportunity to which they felt entitled. None of them has subsequently written anything of consequence on this subject.

One of my Hungarian American critics accused me in a review of having "falsified history" by not having listed the full membership of the executive committee of a political party that reconstituted itself during the Revolution. Another such critic blamed me for not having mentioned a "resistance movement" of which, evidently, he had been the chief protagonist. I failed to mention it because such a movement never existed.

My book on Turkey's foreign policy was sharply criticized by a reviewer because I had not "used" an article, published in an American periodical, that according to this reviewer was the most pertinent source on Turkish attitudes toward the United States. I did "use" a different article on the same topic by the same author, which was published in a Turkish periodical, and in my view it was less than authoritative.

My book on the Turkish Straits was written, as I mentioned earlier, under an assignment from the Hoover Institution. I had been invited to write a "policy-oriented" publication. Therefore, I included a last chapter, entitled "Issues and Options," in which I suggested a certain strategy and possible legal solutions in the event that the Montreux Convention might be revised. A reviewer in the *Middle East Journal,* who evidently had received no legal education, objected that I was suggesting decisions "from a lofty tower," that I was speaking in "imperatives," and that my suggestions could not be taken seriously. This reviewer may be disappointed to learn that the book generally received high praise from competent quarters and that the State Department Subcommittee on Straits, which prepared American positions for the Third Conference on the Law of the Sea, took my suggestions very seriously.

Before my book on the Indian Ocean was published, I had reached, in May 1975, the then mandatory age for retirement. Friends had warned me of the frustrating and traumatic effects of this ominous occurrence. For one moment even Rose pondered how to find something for me to do. I myself saw no problem. Nothing essentially was to change except that I should cease to do regular full-time teaching. Thereupon my good wife called me a "work addict." She may have been right.

EMERITUS

Farewell cocktail parties are generally offered to retiring professors. I declined. It would have been absurd to submit to a valediction when I knew that we were not leaving Amherst and that I would continue, if not my teaching, then my research and literary activity. But I agreed to be honored at the annual potluck dinner of the department.

The event was observed in the way I hoped it would be. Glen Gordon, the chairman of the department, addressed Rose and me in a few cheerful words and added a well-wishing sentence, which he read out from a piece of paper in quaint Hungarian. I responded in the same humorous vein, which was perhaps unexpected. People are accustomed to a melodramatic allocution from a retiree. I said the following:

"I feel very lucky to have been a member of this department, where everybody is my friend. It is an excellent department. A story from behind the Iron Curtain does not apply here. There, a Party functionary came to inspect a factory. At the entrance he asked the receptionist: 'How many people work here?' 'Only half of them,' was the answer. Well, in this department everybody is working.

"I have spent fourteen years at this university. That has been my longest continued activity at one place since I reached adulthood. Neither as a practicing lawyer, nor as a teacher at the Budapest University, nor as a political prisoner, did I serve for such a long time. I have thus become attuned to a philosophy of impermanency. Nothing in this world is constant but inconstancy.

"Thus inured to change, I feel no difficulty in retiring de jure, though de facto I shall not. Age is relative, and I am a believer in relativity. It is incorrect to assume that all fools are old fools. There are many young fools too, only nature has a way of taking better care of old fools.

"Nothing proves the relativity of age better than this experience. I remember an eighty-year-old gentleman eying a luscious Lolita type and exclaiming, 'I wish I could be seventy years old once again!'

"Or take the case of Franco. When he was eighty, he refused to accept as a gift a pet turtle (known for longevity) with the response, 'I cannot suffer seeing a pet die.'

"I recall the story about Adenauer, who was arrested in 1944 by the Gestapo when he was nearly seventy years old. A jailor checked on him in his cell several times during the night. The next morning Adenauer asked him, 'Did you think I would commit suicide?' 'Yes,' replied the jailor. 'After all, you are an old man, you are a prisoner, and you have nothing more to expect from life.' Well, five years later Adenauer was elected chancellor of the Federal Republic of Germany and stayed in that post for fourteen more years."

There was friendly laughter in my audience. The university had just received a new chancellor, and a vice-chancellor was present. I quickly added, "Don't misunderstand me! I have no ambition to be a chancellor or even a vice-chancellor!" And I ended, paraphrasing Churchill, "For me this is not the beginning of the end, nor the end of a beginning. It is the beginning of a new beginning!"

Shortly thereafter I was given the title of professor emeritus. I continued to occupy my office, and I was treated as a de facto member of the department. I taught in the fall semesters.

I spent the spring 1977 semester as a visiting fellow at the Australian National University in Canberra. Rose accompanied me on the journey.

We left Amherst in early January, visited Tahiti and New Zealand, and arrived in Canberra at the end of that month, the height of the Australian summer. We were comfortably accommodated at the University House. I joined the Strategic and Defense Studies Center, headed by Dr. Robert J. O'Neill, and I participated in its proceedings and collaborated with its competent research staff. My work was a follow-up of my study on the Indian Ocean; the assignment included writing a paper on the conflicts and arms races between littoral states of this ocean and conducting seminars on the same topic.

The four months I spent in Canberra gave me a welcome opportunity to look closely into Australia's foreign policy and defense problems. Australia is a young country, but its independent foreign policy, differentiated from the British, is even younger. Only when the protective shield of the British navy was withdrawn and serious doubts as to the efficacy of the American safeguard mounted did Australia genuinely embark on a course of its own.

Ensconced behind the Pacific and Indian oceans, with a small population (then only fourteen million) but with an expanse of territory as large as the United States (without Alaska), Australia seemed to suffer from a phobia of insecurity. This insecurity developed in the aftermath of the traumatic Japanese advance during World War II (now Japan is a close friend), and it is supported by the emptiness of its land, which may invite aggression. But as far as I could see, there was no aggressor in sight. Still, the attempts and probes of this young nation to find and secure its place in the world shed light on many problems of the contemporary international system. Watching the ferment in the orientation of Australian foreign relations was like looking through a test tube into the intricacies and pitfalls of present-day world politics. It also proved fascinating to observe the flow of international events from this distant corner of the globe, from a Western democracy washed ashore on the antipodes; for much appeared either clearer or dimmer depending on the sometimes unique Australian interpretation provided in this remote and exotic environment.

My stay in Australia coincided with the transfer of administration from President Ford to President Carter and also with the fledgling beginnings of the new administration. In such a period the vagaries of American foreign policy—as seen from this corner of the world—increased in bewildering motion. The quadrennial temptation to be different, to do better, and to create something conceptually novel was hardly resisted by the new administration. Since in foreign policy, as in other endeavors, it is not easy to distinguish between style and substance, the American campaign rhetoric and an apparent lack of continuity created uneasiness among the members of the Australian foreign policy establishment.

A retired Australian diplomat, trained in the best British traditions, told me, "Prior to World War I the foreign policies of the principal great powers could be characterized as follows: France sets a foreign policy goal and marches straight toward that goal; the British also have a goal, but they approach it cautiously, often in a roundabout manner; the Russians have no definite goal, they just move ahead whenever and wherever they can. Nobody at that time tried to describe succinctly the foreign policy of the German kaiser because it lacked rationality. But if I would try to describe in a similar vein United States foreign policy, I would say that Washington takes three steps in one direction, retraces its steps, takes three steps in another direction, then turns back again and repeats the same motions."

I asked him how this description was to fit the new Carter administration's foreign policy.

"I believe that if Carter embarks on new ventures in the foreign field he will be mostly unsuccessful," he replied. "Eventually he will be forced to return to continuity. Until he realizes that, he will place many foreign countries in jeopardy, and a number of mistakes will be committed, some of them irreparable. Consistency and continuity are the most important concomitants of a successful foreign policy. Unlike domestic policy, foreign policy depends on relations with other countries, on many variables that even the most powerful state is unable to control. Therefore, only a long-term foreign policy, one that is adjusted to the policies of other major powers, can guarantee success. No one state can disregard the traditional and generally practiced methods and usages of other nations. Commitments to do away with secrecy, to replace balance of power politics, to stop arms sales, to befriend other countries according to the degree they respect human rights (however laudable such an endeavor might be), and at the same time to promise not to meddle in the affairs of other nations are unrealistic, often contradictory goals and are certainly counterproductive."

I shared these anxieties. But having come to settle in the United States at a mature age and being already familiar with the intricacies of international politics, I felt better able to discern the positive and negative aspects of American foreign policy practices and activities.

The United States, since its inception as an independent state, has historically vacillated between an extremely idealistic and an extremely pragmatic or realistic foreign policy. This oscillation has often generated waves of bewilderment or discontent in other nations — those which, on the one hand, relied on unfulfilled idealistic commitments, or those which, on the other hand, were hurt by acts or pronouncements that revealed a disregard for the interests of friends and allies. Even the Monroe Doctrine was alternately given an idealistic and realistic interpretation: in principle, to protect the independence of Latin American countries; in practice, to secure United States predominance in the Western Hemisphere. It was its favorable geostrategic location and simple good fortune that amidst these meanderings saved America from major disasters. As Bismarck remarked in the 1880s, "God Almighty protects children, drunkards, and the United States of America."

In 1917 Woodrow Wilson entered the war against Germany, avowedly "to make the world safe for democracy" but in fact to prevent Germany from tilting the balance of power in Europe in her favor. But after the war Congress and the new administration dropped the new stance and returned to a selfish isolation, letting democracy and the League of Nations fend for themselves.

Before and even after the outbreak of World War II Congress dillydallied with neutrality acts. Eventually the United States had to be bombed into the war at Pearl Harbor and thus catapulted into becoming a world power. At the Yalta Conference, Stalin pricked up his ears when Roosevelt spilled the beans that the Senate would not consent to the stationing of American troops in Europe for longer than two years after the end of hostilities. The Russians were counting on such a withdrawal. I believe that even after the experience of World War II the United States would have pulled out from Europe and reverted to its accustomed stance of neutralistic indifference had the Soviet leader's greediness and aggressiveness not forced Washington to leave its forces in Europe and remain a vigorous actor on the world scene.

As long as the United States remained an isolated power enjoying its detached and distant situation, it could afford to set special standards in its foreign relations, with little harm to itself. It could act as an outsider, the odd man out. It could freely harbor ideas of its uniqueness or democratic superiority. It could handle foreign affairs as an external branch of its domestic policies.

However, decision making and action in foreign politics is a function of the relationships between different governments, relationships over which the United States, no matter how powerful, may or may not have influence. In any case, the procedures and style to be observed must, to some extent at least, conform to those practiced by most other nations of the world. Otherwise, frictions arise, and foreign policy becomes less effective or even ineffective.

The stupendous achievements of the United States on the international scene were due more to its gigantic economic power, its military technology and prowess, and its organizational skills than to its diplomacy. Having become a superpower, it could expect that the rest of the world should accept and conform to its peculiarities. But only to some degree. For the rest, the United States would have to act as other states do, that is, like any other "ordinary" country.

Never before in history has a great democracy wielded world power. None of the world empires were democracies—not Alexander's, not Rome's, not Napoleon's. Even the British, at the stage of their empire building, were more an oligarchy than a democracy.

Alexis de Tocqueville warned that, in the conduct of foreign relations, democratic governments are decidedly inferior to governments based on other principles. What would he have said if he had known that this country, with its democratic ideals and processes as they existed in his time, was to play the role of a world power?

De Tocqueville referred to the question of secrecy as an important element of successful diplomacy, an element in which a democracy is deficient by its very nature. Openness was one of the early principles of American policy, both in domestic and foreign affairs. When carrying out research on the Turkish Straits, I came across a draft treaty signed in 1799 between the United States and the Ottoman Empire. This treaty was to provide for an exchange of diplomatic ministers between the two countries, thereby establishing diplomatic relations. As was customary for the Sublime Porte at that time, a secret clause (of no significance whatsoever) was included in the treaty. Because of this secret article the Senate declined to approve the treaty, and, consequently, no diplomatic relations existed between Washington and Constantinople until 1830. During that period American citizens in the empire remained deprived of the benefits of consular protection as well as consular jurisdiction, and American shipping and commerce were denied equal treatment with other Western powers. It was loyalty to a principle (of doubtful value) but bad politics.

I have often heard that secrecy in government, including in foreign affairs, is un-American. Indeed, in one of his Fourteen Points, President Wilson demanded that "there shall be no private international undertakings of any kind. . . . Diplomacy shall proceed always frankly and in public view." Furthermore, he advocated "open covenants openly arrived at."

Any practitioner of foreign affairs would agree that such propositions or principles are impractical and illusory. In any bargaining situation — and much of diplomacy consists of bargaining with other countries, both friends or adversaries — the disclosure of instructions to negotiators, of offers made, and even of the content of negotiations themselves should be avoided if the best results are sought. Of course, the end result of negotiations, the agreement, should generally be made accessible to the public, and under the Constitution a formal treaty requires the consent of the Senate. But any premature exposure of negotiations should be avoided for the sake of success and for the sake of the confidentiality to which one is by duty bound with one's negotiating partner.

After the allegedly realistic years of the Nixon-Kissinger foreign policy the Carter administration initiated another series of crusades in favor of an ideological or idealist foreign policy by placing principles before political expediency. It reminded me of the stratagem recommended to college students when entering a public debate: "If you don't know the facts, assert principles!"

For Rose and myself, both victims of an arbitrary totalitarian regime and of a disregard for human rights, the dramatization of the human rights issue in the Carter program offered an unusual attraction. We discussed endlessly the significance and possible import of such policy. Its emotional appeal electrified Rose more intensely than it did me. I remained highly skeptical about the highfalutin campaign rhetoric applied to this issue and about the possibility of translating it into a feasible foreign policy plan. My inclinations were to avoid extreme categorizations; my distrust of abstract differentiations revolted against what I considered principled ignorance. A pragmatist should be able to distinguish on practical grounds not only between right and wrong but also between right and right and between wrong and wrong.

"If you are unwilling to approve Carter's human rights campaign," Rose reproached me, "you have become unfaithful to your convictions. There are violations of human rights all over the world, but to your and my personal knowledge the governments behind the Iron Curtain are the worst offenders in this respect. These governments recently promised to respect these principles in the Helsinki agreements but, of course, they failed to abide by their promises."

"The principle of human rights Carter propounds is, of course, admirable," I replied. "I would be the last man in the world who would hesitate to support the respect for human rights. Unfortunately, the question is more complex in practice than it is in theory. There are really two kinds of difficulties in the implementation of a human rights program in foreign politics. First, you must have a sense of proportion and a sense of history. Some governments are clearly violating human rights as we understand them; others do it only to a relatively milder extent, and others again solely under exceptional circumstances. We have to realize that many countries, even in peacetime, live in a state of siege; they are pressured by hostile neighbors or subverted from within, or both. In order to survive, they feel they have to resort to measures that oppose our standards. For them, it is a life-and-death struggle; they believe that they could not survive otherwise. We should not forget that even in our democracy American citizens of Japanese extraction were deported from the West Coast after Pearl Harbor in disregard for their human and constitutional rights.

"Secondly," I continued, "it is questionable whether overt interference in favor of those who suffer from an infringement of their human rights is always expeditious. But it should also be asked whether it is in the best interest of the United States to antagonize so many governments on this account, including friends and allies. In other words, is it profitable for our country and for those whom we wish to help to be the world drumbeater of human rights? In my view, it would generally be more promising to carry out a quiet, persuasive, and selective diplomatic action instead of publicly sermonizing and protesting."

"What do you mean by selective diplomacy? Shall we make exceptions or pick out only certain countries?"

"Using human rights as the measure, you cannot condemn and oppose all the countries in the world that disregard these rights. Out of about one hundred fifty independent states on our globe perhaps only thirty or fewer are governed by democratic principles. All the others are prone, in one or another respect, to commit serious or even outrageous violations of what we conceive of as human rights. If human rights are the sole or largest measure, what will become of our relations with the other hundred-odd nations? And of the other matters that comprise our relationships with them—matters such as trade, war, and peace? Even President Carter has already abandoned useless generalizations; he has toned down his campaign against Soviet breaches of human rights. He is, for example, concentrating heavily on South Africa."

"It is good that you mention South Africa," Rose responded. "Well, we have been to that country and observed with our own eyes what it meant to be a nonwhite there. Don't you think that in this case pressures are not only justified but also expedient?"

"Yes, disapproval of apartheid is certainly justified. But in politics—and we are speaking of politics, not of ethics—one should not only be right; one should, first of all, be wise."

"You are telling me that morality should be ignored in foreign policy?"

"By no means! But the options between good and evil in international politics are never simple. You have to choose also between lesser and greater evils. You have to avoid using a remedy that will result in a greater evil than the one that it attempts to cure. Furthermore, what we may regard as morally objectionable our opponents may not. Take South Africa. The Boers, or as they are officially called, the Afrikaners (and they control South Africa), believe in their God-given civilizational mission. They consider their country to be their promised land, their opponents to be stooges of godless Communists, and apartheid to be an equitable method of assuring separate development. They assert—and in this they are right—that 'one man—one vote' would destroy their national and even physical existence as of today. At the same time, they realize that the present situation cannot last forever, and they are trying to bring about change with the establishment of the so-called homelands for blacks, a policy we do not find acceptable or, in principle, right. But they do. In such a way, one moral thesis opposes another moral thesis. We believe we are right. And so do they. I think, in such a case, pragmatic arguments are of greater value and help than principles."

"So in your view," Rose asked, "what can be done?"

"Moral condemnations have little real impact. Given South Africa's position astride the gold, diamond, and uranium trade and her growing autarky (especially in arms), economics pressures can be only slightly stronger. Such exhortations will only incite the black Africans both within and outside South Africa and thus compete with the Russians. If we recognize the mutually exclusive stubborn and absolute natures of the white and black African nationalisms, surely we will wish to avoid the cataclysm their clash could bring. The white South Africans should be persuaded to make larger and more valuable land available to the black nations. The black movement is like others in the world that seek land, a state, to correspond to the nation. Such black nations, if genuine enough, would be congruent with the heterogeneous and diverse nature of the black majority. Such a movement could gradually lead to a partition that would separate whites from blacks, for any analogy with the racial question in the United States is erroneous.

"The proportions," I continued, "are in reverse: in the United States, one nonwhite against ten whites; in South Africa, six nonwhites against one white. 'One man–one vote' would inevitably lead to an exclusively black government and to the destruction of the white population. If one wishes to be really moral, then one has to consider the ultimate results of one's policy, not only the immediate goal. The expulsion or extermination of the whites from or in South Africa, where the Boers had been before some African peoples, cannot be seen as an ethical achievement."

"You are very pessimistic, aren't you?"

"I am pragmatic, I believe. I decline to think that the course of history is always inevitable. But I do believe that there are forces that are destructive as well as forces that could prevent regional or global destruction. There are also forces of 'good will,' which in their blindness or ignorance prove to be more dangerous in the long run than the forces of destruction. I don't deny the influence of these impersonal forces but think that the power of individual leaders is often more decisive—for better or worse. I feel convinced that in our times of tensions and crises primacy should be accorded to considerations of foreign policy over domestic issues. We have excellent, talented, experienced, and dedicated persons in our foreign service and also outside the foreign service. But their influence on the conduct of foreign policy is intermittent, whereas those without such qualifications often prevail."

"Are you referring to presidents or the Congress?"

"To both. Do you remember, for instance, when we watched the debates on television between the two presidential candidates in 1976? The performance of both when it came to international politics was pretty poor. And do you remember how frustrated we were when President Ford insisted that the East European countries are 'fully independent'?"

"Yes, I do. At that time I suddenly felt convinced that millions of voters of Polish, Hungarian, Czech, Slovak, or other East European descent would fail to cast their votes for Ford. It could be that he lost the election because of this slip of the tongue."

"I don't remember having read any study on this point. But I remember that subsequently it was explained that Ford meant to say that the United States does *not* regard these countries as fully independent."

"If so, why didn't he say so in the first place? I utterly dislike it when leaders always have to 'explain' what they meant to say. When Andrew Young had to explain what he meant by racism, I was left with the impression at the end that the real racists were not the racists but nonracists — presidents Kennedy and Johnson, for example, and others were the racists."

"I could give you another example of unconsidered pronouncements, even by a foreign policy specialist," I said, "the so-called Sonnenfeldt Doctrine. This State Department counselor told American ambassadors assembled in London that the United States wished to promote an 'organic' relationship between the Soviet Union and the states of East Europe. In my vocabulary *organic* means vital, constitutional, that is, a close and dependent relationship. But subsequently it was explained that *organic* meant a relationship 'that is not based on sheer military force,' that is, one that does not create an organic connection with the Soviet state and military structure. If I had to 'explain' in each of my classes what I meant to say in my previous class, I would be a rotten teacher."

"The world," Rose retorted, "is nowadays such a complicated place that top leaders do not know or understand what appears to knowledgeable persons as something elementary."

"Leaders can see to it that they are well briefed. And when they speak up or participate in talks they can be prepared themselves. It is no excuse to say something which they later must 'retract' or 'clarify.' In this respect the poorest spectacle was offered, as far as I can remember, by British prime minister Chamberlain prior to Munich, when he exclaimed, 'How horrible, fantastic, incredible it is that we should be digging trenches and trying on gasmasks here because of a quarrel in a faraway country between people of whom we know nothing.' Well, if Chamberlain knew nothing of Czechoslovakia or of the meaning of Nazi aggression, he should have given up his premiership. Instead, he sacrificed that country in Munich without saving the world from the horrors of another world war. Amateurs or ad hoc operators of foreign policy are as dangerous as children playing with fire."

"If you think," Rose said, "that the Sonnenfeldt Doctrine is incorrect or misleading, what would your advice be in regard to United States policy toward the East European countries?"

"It is impossible to generalize because these countries are individually different. It is a mistake to lump together, as is often done, these so-called East European nations, some of which are in fact located in Central Europe rather than in Eastern Europe. I could only repeat to you the essence of what I told Ambassador Richard Pedersen in August 1973 before he traveled to Budapest to take up his post there. I emphasized to him that Hungarians (as most other Soviet dominated nations) are generally solid patriots, even if they are Communist Party members. They resent the fact, even if they don't admit it, that their country is not genuinely independent. In Hungary, where relaxation and a relatively liberal policy is now practiced, this lack of independence remains the Achilles' heel of the regime. I therefore suggested to Pedersen that in his conversations with Hungarian leaders and officials he should subtly play on this point whenever an opportunity offered itself. It seems desirable to raise and exploit this issue of Soviet control. The Hungarians, thus approached, cannot come up with a satisfactory answer. Marx or Lenin is no help. This is the best the United States can do at present in order to wean Hungary away from Soviet tutelage or, at least, to remind the Hungarians of their dependence."

"Is there no more efficacious way to end this dependence, a dependence Hungary vainly tried to eliminate in 1956?"

"I am afraid there is none, at least none at this juncture."

I felt genuinely sorry for having been unable to hold out to Rose anything more positive or optimistic. As our conversation shows, we have not lost our interest in our country of birth, despite having safely and finally settled in America and having come to consider ourselves Americans. Some immigrants may yearn, openly or subconsciously, for a return to their country of origin. But I feel no such nostalgia. I cherish too much the diversity of the American environment, with the intellectual freedom this side of the Atlantic offers. I cherish too well the respected and beloved friends who surround me to even think of a return to the "old country," which despite its improvements since 1956 still smarts under an authoritarian regime. But perhaps it is the success of my American career that prevents me from succumbing to the slightest spell of homesickness.

However, I feel no hatred, no desire for revenge for the iniquities or sufferings I had to endure in Hungary, nor for the years during which my abilities were wasted away. Even in the unexpected event that the Communist regime should collapse, we would not — as we have both agreed — think of returning to Hungary for good. Yes, we would wish to go back in order to see our old friends, to visit the places where we had lived. But only for temporary sojourns.

I am often asked by friends and acquaintances why I do not return to Hungary for a visit; I am constantly being reminded that thousands of Hungarians who left Hungary "illegally" in 1956 have since returned without adverse incident. It is not always easy to explain my special situation to persons unfamiliar with my past story and with the circumstances until now prevailing in Hungary. All those who have not been released from Hungarian citizenship, even though they have become naturalized Americans, are dual nationals. The State Department has warned that it cannot always extend consular protection to American citizens who are also considered Hungarian citizens by the Hungarian authorities. These warnings should specifically apply to those who were charged with "criminal" acts prior to their departure from Hungary, or to those who could be charged under Hungarian law with "acts against the state" after their immigration to the United States. Such advice has special significance for me.

In 1963, in the aftermath of the Revolution, after consolidation had been achieved and the waves of unrest appeared to have calmed down, the Hungarian government issued an amnesty decree, which extended pardon to all political offenders with, however, certain important exceptions. Those who had been condemned for high treason or conspiracy were excluded. Accordingly, my sentence of fifteen years has not been commuted, and — legally at least — I may still be wanted by the Hungarian authorities to spend another ten years in their jail. It should be mentioned that under the amnesty decree those who had been condemned for violating "socialist legality," that is, those who had caused death, torture, or illegal imprisonment were allowed to get off scot-free in the event (one that I doubt) that any charges were leveled against them. Thus, those who had been responsible for my unjustified imprisonment and for the illegalities and abuses I suffered during my term of imprisonment were amnestied without any reservation whatsoever. Under such circumstances I have no inclination to risk my freedom once again. In any case it seems doubtful whether a visa for entry into Hungary would be issued to me.

I am thus fully resigned to the fact that, barring yet unforeseen developments, I shall never return to Hungary again. But the vagaries of history may eventuate all kinds of changes. History—in the contemporary setting, politics—is not static but a flow of events and developments. Great transformations have occurred during my lifetime. As I write these lines, I am seventy-three years old, and the average life expectancy at this age is about ten years. If I look back upon the seven decades of my life, I cannot fail to realize that within each of these decades egregious transformations have taken place.

I was born in 1905, under the Austro-Hungarian monarchy. As far as Hungary was concerned, the last violent convulsion prior to my birth occurred in the years 1848–49, and people spoke about these events as we speak of the American Civil War. Austria's last war, the one with Prussia in 1866, had lasted only six weeks, and for the next forty-five years there was peace, a stable currency, and a single ruler, Francis Joseph, who appeared as if he had ruled since time began and was going to rule indefinitely. But within the first ten years of my life World War I broke out, not just a peacetime war of six weeks, but a protracted life-and-death struggle. It affected practically all mankind and, with particular vehemence, the area in which I lived.

The events of the next ten years, from 1915 to 1925, were even more unanticipated and catastrophic. In the summer of 1918 I spent the vacation with my parents in the Tatra Mountains, in what was then known as Upper Hungary (now Slovakia). A peaceful atmosphere prevailed despite the ravaging war, and nobody would have imagined that a mere six months later the Austro-Hungarian Empire was to disintegrate, that the very place where we vacationed would become detached from Hungary and become part of a new country that nobody had heard of before, namely, Czechoslovakia.

In the decade from 1925 to 1935 I experienced further dramatic changes. When I came to London to study in 1929, that city seemed to be the hub of the international political and economic world. I saw participants in the Second Naval Disarmament Conference in 1930 and Mahatma Gandhi attending the Round Table Conference on India. But when the British pound sterling was forced off the gold standard in 1931 and began to slump, and when Hitler started to rearm Germany, the glory and centrality of Great Britain began to fade.

During the ten years between 1935 and 1945 the world ran amok, and my life also went off its track. World War II descended on our globe, and I was sent to Turkey. At the end of this period mighty Germany had collapsed and millions had died.

Between 1945 and 1955 dramatic and tragic transformations again occurred: Soviet Communist rule was established in wide areas of East and Central Europe; my own homeland, Hungary, became part of the Soviet empire; and Rose and I became prisoners of the Communist regime.

The following decade, from 1955 to 1965, was also marked by a major tragedy: the rise and downfall of the Hungarian Revolution in 1956. These ten years brought Rose and me luck. We emerged from prison healthy and active, and we managed to escape from behind the Iron Curtain and settle down in the United States, where by 1963 we had become citizens. The next ten years, from 1965 to 1975, were filled with activity and a successful career as a teacher and writer, and they ended with the conferral on me of the status of professor emeritus.

In retrospect I can only say that I have been extremely fortunate. I escaped death. I did not serve in the armed forces, neither in World War I nor in World War II; I was too young to serve in the first, and of a more mature age during the second. But I could still have been killed on different occasions. Had I not been in Turkey in 1944, the Germans would have taken me into one of their concentration camps (they were looking for me). I could have been thrown into the Danube by Soviet soldiers when crossing it between Bulgaria and Rumania in 1946. I could have been sentenced to death and executed, or died in prison, between 1951 and 1956. I could have been killed during the Hungarian Revolution in 1956 or during our escape to the West.

I consider myself very fortunate for having been given such wonderful opportunities upon reaching the shores of America, for having been helped by so many good people, and for having obtained good jobs and generous grants. And I was more than favored by Providence for having had my wife Rose at my side.

I have completed my agenda; I have come to the end of my major research programs and published their results. Whatever happens, the Grim Reaper cannot snatch that away from me. But I do not propose to rest on my laurels. I shall continue doing creative work. And to do creative things, one has to live as if one would never die.

Two biblical quotations, one from the Old Testament and the other from the New Testament, both deal with the transitoriness of life. We read in the tenth verse of the Ninetieth Psalm: "The years of our life are threescore and ten, or even by reason of strength fourscore; yet their span is but toil and trouble; they are soon gone, and we fly away"; and in the Second Letter of Paul to the Corinthians: "For the things that are seen are transient, but the things that are unseen are eternal" (4:18). While the first of these two passages appears to presage an eschatology of fatalism, the second is optimistic, for it distinguishes between what is transitory and what is perennial. The ups and downs of a turbulent life suggest that behind the transitoriness of one's good and bad fortune, which pass away as they come, there is, unseen, the element of permanency. Though I agree with Blaise Pascal that the "last act will be unmerciful, however charming the rest of the play may have been," even the Last Enemy cannot destroy the unseen.

MONOGRAPHS by Ferenc A. Váli

Die deutsch-österreichische Zollunion vor dem ständigen internationalen Gerichtshof. Vienna: Manz, 1932.

Servitudes of International Law: A Study of Rights in Foreign Territory. London: P. S. King, 1933.

Servitudes of International Law: A Study of Rights in Foreign Territory. 2d ed., rev. and enl. New York: Praeger, 1958; London; Stevens, 1958.

The Hungarian Revolution and International Law. New York: Hungarian Freedom Fighters, 1959. Reprinted from *Fletcher Review* 2, no. 1 (Summer 1959), pp. 9–25.

Rift and Revolt in Hungary: Nationalism Versus Communism. Cambridge: Harvard University Press, 1961.

The Quest for a United Germany. Baltimore: Johns Hopkins University Press, 1967.

Bridge Across the Bosporus: The Foreign Policy of Turkey. Baltimore: Johns Hopkins University Press, 1971.

The Turkish Straits and NATO. Stanford, Calif.: Hoover Institution Press, 1972.

The Unstable Balance in and Around the Horn of Africa. Ebenhausen bei München: H. Eggerberg, 1975.

Politics of the Indian Ocean Region: The Balances of Power. New York: Free Press, 1976; London: Collier Macmillan, 1976.

INDEX

Ferenc Albert Váli was emeritus professor of political science at the University of Massachusetts at Amherst, when he died on November 19, 1984, after a long illness. He was 79.

Born in Hungary in 1905, Váli was educated both there and abroad. He received the Doctor Juris degree from the Faculty of Law and Political Science at the University of Budapest in 1927, the Ph.D. from the London School of Economics and Political Science of the University of London in 1932, and the Diploma of the Academy of International Law, The Hague, Netherlands, in 1932. He held an honorary Doctor of Laws degree from Wayne State University.

During World War II Váli participated in a secret diplomatic mission in Turkey for the Hungarian government. From 1951 to 1956 he was a political prisoner in Hungary. After the Hungarian uprising in 1956 he escaped to Austria and, via England, entered the United States in 1957.

Professor Váli taught international law, international relations, and Soviet and East European politics in the Political Science Department of the University of Massachusetts at Amherst since 1961. He retired in 1975 but continued to teach both at the University of Massachusetts and at Florida International University. He was the first emeritus professor of the university's Political Science Department. From 1958 to 1961 he was a research associate of the Center for International Affairs, Harvard University, and from 1946 to 1949 he was professor of international law at the University of Budapest.

Ferenc Váli was the author of at least eleven books and many articles. His best-known work, the definitive book on the upheaval in Hungary in 1956, is *Rift and Revolt in Hungary: Nationalism Versus Communism.* Other books include *The Quest for a United Germany, The Turkish Straits and NATO,* and the *Politics of the Indian Ocean Region: The Balances of Power.*

Váli was the recipient of several fellowships and grants, including fellowships from Harvard University, the Rockefeller Foundation, the North Atlantic Treaty Organization, and the U.S. Naval War College. He spoke English, Hungarian, French, German, Italian, and Turkish and had a reading knowledge of several other languages. He possessed an extraordinary knowledge of East Central Europe and the Balkans.

KARL W. RYAVEC
University of Massachusetts at Amherst
(adapted from *Slavic Review,* Summer 1985)